D0519266

REFERENCE
FOR USE IN THE LIBRARY
ONLY

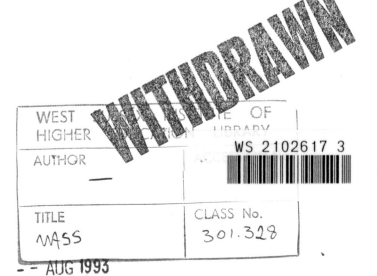

WEST ~~~~~~ ~~~ TE OF
HIGHER ~~~~~~~ LIBRARY

WS 2102617 3

AUTHOR

TITLE   CLASS No.
MASS   301.328

- - AUG 1993

Mass Migrations in Europe

The **European Science Foundation** is an association of its 59 member research councils, academies and institutions devoted to basic scientific research in 21 countries. The ESF brings European scientists together to work on topics of common concern, to co-ordinate the use of expensive facilities, and to discover and define new endeavours that will benefit from a co-operative approach.

The scientific work sponsored by ESF includes basic research in the natural sciences, the medical and biosciences, the humanities and the social sciences.

The ESF links scholarship and research supported by its members and adds value by co-operation across national frontiers. Through its function as a co-ordinator, and also by holding workshops and conferences and by enabling researchers to visit and study in laboratories throughout Europe, the ESF works for the advancement of European science.

This volume arises from the work of the ESF Programme on Regional and Urban Restructuring in Europe (RURE).

Further information on ESF activities can be obtained from:

European Science Foundation
1 quai Lezay-Marnésia
67080 Strasbourg Cedex
France

Tel. 88 76 71 00
Fax 88 38 05 32

MASS MIGRATIONS IN EUROPE
The Legacy and the Future

Edited by
Russell King

Belhaven Press
London

W. SUSSEX INSTITUTE
OF
HIGHER EDUCATION
LIBRARY

Copublished in the Americas with
Halsted Press, an imprint of John Wiley & Sons, Inc., New York

Belhaven Press
(a division of Pinter Publishers)
25 Floral Street, Covent Garden, London, WC2E 9DS, United Kingdom

First published in 1993

© Editor and Contributors 1993

Apart from any fair dealing for the purposes of research or private study, or criticism or review, as permitted under the Copyright, Designs and Patents Act, 1988, this publication may not be reproduced, stored or transmitted in any form or by any means or process without the prior permission in writing of the copyright holders or their agents. Except for reproduction in accordance with the terms of licences issued by the Copyright Licencing Agency, photocopying of whole or part of this publication without the prior permission of the copyright holders or their agents in single or multiple copies whether for gain or not is illegal and expressly forbidden. Please direct all enquiries concerning copyright to the Publishers at the address above.

Co-published in the Americas by Halsted Press, an imprint of
John Wiley & Sons, Inc., 605 Third Avenue, New York, NY 10158–0012

British Library Cataloguing in Publication Data

A CIP catalogue record for this book is available from the British Library

ISBN 185293 224 4

Library of Congress Cataloging-in-Publication Data

Mass migrations in Europe : the legacy and the future / edited by
  Russell King.
      p.   cm.
  Includes bibliographical references and index.
    ISBN 1–85293–224–4. – ISBN 0–470–21927–0 (US)
    1. Europe–Emigration and immigration.   I. King, Russell.
  JV7590.M39   1993
  325.4–dc20   92–36700
                                                                                      CIP

ISBN 0–47021–9270 (in the Americas only)

Typeset by Mayhew Typesetting, Rhayader, Powys
Printed and bound in Great Britain by Biddles Ltd of Guildford and King's Lynn

Contents

List of figures

List of tables

List of Contributors

Gündüz Atalık is Dean of the Faculty of Architecture at the Istanbul Technical University.

Brian Beeley is Staff Tutor in Social Science at the Open University.

Hans-Heinrich Blotevogel is Professor of Geography at the University of Duisburg.

Helena Boubnova is Researcher at the Demographic Institute for Social and Economic Studies of Population, Academy of Sciences, Moscow.

Carminda Cavaco is Professor of Geography at the University of Lisbon.

Antonio Cortese is Director of the National Institute of Statistics, Rome and Lecturer in Demography at the University of Urbino.

Frans Dieleman is Professor of Urban Geography and Applied Demography at the University of Utrecht.

Anthony Fielding is Lecturer in Geography at the University of Sussex.

Reuben Ford is Research Fellow in the Department of Geography, King's College, University of London.

Franz-Josef Kemper is Senior Lecturer in Geography at the University of Bonn.

Russell King is Professor of Geography at Trinity College, University of Dublin.

Armando Montanari is Director of the National Research Council Institute for the Study of the Economics of the Mezzogiorno, Naples and Lecturer in Tourism at the Naval University in Naples.

Ursula Müller-ter Jung is Lecturer in Geography at the University of Duisburg.

Sture Öberg is Professor of Geography at the University of Uppsala and Senior Researcher at the International Institute for Applied Systems Analysis, Laxenburg, Austria.

Philip Ogden is Reader in Geography at Queen Mary and Westfield College, University of London.

John Salt is Senior Lecturer in Geography and Director of the Migration Research Unit at University College, University of London.

Ian Shuttleworth is Research Associate at the Northern Ireland Economic Research Centre, Belfast.

Christian Vandermotten is Professor of Geography at the University of Brussels.

Jean Vanlaer is Researcher in the Institute of Geography at the University of Brussels.

Paul White is Senior Lecturer in Geography at the University of Sheffield.

Gerald Wood is Lecturer in Geography at the University of Duisburg.

Preface and Acknowledgements

The Isle of Capri: two geographers at the foot of a spectacular wooded cliff, sitting on some rocks at the water's edge. The two geographers enjoying the late afternoon sun of a warm October day were a Swede working in Austria and an Englishman living in Dublin, migrants both. In such idyllic surroundings was the idea for this book born. Although the picture projected in this little scene may seem a world away from the problems of Europe's 'mass migrants', perhaps a few moments of quiet hedonism are occasionally necessary to initiate and develop ideas such as those behind this project. Actually Capri is not so very far from the living issues of mass migration — a short boat ride to Naples is sufficient.

The waterside conversation, between Sture Öberg and the editor of this book, came at the end of three days of intense workshop debate about the future population map of Europe. The debate ranged over a large number of highly topical issues — falling birth-rates, ageing, socio-spatial mobility, ethnicity, settlement system change and others. The protagonists were fourteen geographers drawn from many European countries under the umbrella of the European Science Foundation's scientific programme on Regional and Urban Restructuring in Europe — RURE for short. Founded in 1990, RURE is a four-year project examining fundamental changes in the European urban, regional and demographic system. The political changes which took place just as the programme was being planned meant that it could not have been launched at a more propitious, if challenging, time.

RURE is the European Science Foundation's only geography-led programme. Given the breadth of the field of study of RURE, a wide range of themes is being pursued: restructuring of the production system, changes in lifestyle and patterns of consumption, and wider societal and political responses. The entire RURE network comprises some seventy scholars divided into four working groups. The eighteen-strong population group (since Capri it has grown by the addition of four younger scholars who have been awarded ESF fellowships) is one of these. Known affectionately as RURE/POP and acting under the inspired chairmanship of Armando Montanari, this working group investigates current and likely future European population processes, both those which can be interpreted as responses to changes in the production system (notably migration and other forms of socio-spatial mobility), and those which perhaps act independently of economic restructuring or even have a causative influence on it.

Mass migration quickly emerged as one of the main foci of interest of RURE/POP. Following preliminary discussion at the aforementioned Capri workshop meeting in October 1990, the provisional outline for this book was presented by the editor to the RURE General Conference in Lisbon in February 1991. Over the next six months draft chapters were written, pre-circulated and then presented and discussed as papers at the Brussels workshop in October 1991. In the light of these discussions, revisions to chapters were made and final versions were honed at the next RURE meeting in Budapest in February 1992. This sequence of RURE gatherings has provided an excellent Europe-wide framework for comparative research and writing. As editor of this book and as general rapporteur for the RURE/POP group, I should like to pay special tribute to the ESF for its philosophy of encouraging and facilitating European-level geographical research.

Also in my capacity as editor, it is a pleasure to thank my RURE/POP colleagues for producing their chapter drafts on time, and for being so willing to accept editorial suggestions. Welding the various chapters from so many different countries, each with its own distinctive geographical tradition and style of scholarship, into a coherent whole has been a fascinating and thoroughly pleasant task, and it could not have been achieved without the flexibility of individual authors. Most of the chapters have been produced from within the RURE/POP Working Group, but there are a few exceptions. Some RURE/POP members, such as Gündüz Atalık, Hans Blotevogel and Christian Vandermotten, took on co-authors from outside the group, and the editor commissioned three chapters (by Paul White, Philip Ogden, and John Salt and Reuben Ford) from non-RURE colleagues. The collaboration of these migration scholars is warmly acknowledged. Nor should the input of RURE/POP members who are not authors of chapters be overlooked: the discussion contributions of Françoise Cribier, Jan Mønnesland and Tony Champion did much to shape the book at all stages. The encouragement of RURE Steering Committee members Paul Claval, Peter Dicken, Jens Christian Hansen and Arie Schachar is acknowledged, as is the special assistance of Anders Malmberg, RURE co-ordinator at Uppsala, and John Smith, ESF Social Science programme secretary in Strasbourg. Iain Stevenson of Belhaven Press rendered valuable advice and support when it was needed most. In the Geography Department in Dublin, Eileen Russell and Margaret O'Flanagan contributed excellent typing and word-processing against tight deadlines, and Matthew Stout drew many of the maps and diagrams.

Russell King
Trinity College Dublin
June 1992

Introduction: Europe and the future of mass migration

Russell King and Sture Öberg

It is not the purpose of this introduction to give an overview of the book: the contents page and the chapters speak for themselves. However, it is necessary to say something about the changing European context of international mass migration in the late twentieth century. Throughout the continent international migration is once again of great significance. Both within Europe and beyond, millions are on the move, their journeys reshaping the human mosaic whose study lies at the very heart of geography. Albanian boat people on the Adriatic, Pakistanis occupying a disused spaghetti factory in Rome, Filipinos fleeing an erupting volcano, migrants from the East gathering in the grim splendour of Budapest's railway station — these are just some of the images recalled from the past couple of years. Migration has re-emerged as one of the great challenges of the 1990s, important not just in the eyes of economists, administrators and social scientists, but in the minds of ordinary people as well. As the oppressed of the East are lured by the promise of the West, as the impoverished in the South seek a share of the riches of the North, so the political rhetoric takes on a military tone: 'fortress Europe' under siege from the invasion of an army of migrants. Too often, one feels, is mass migration cast in a negative light; too often are European people hypnotized by politicians who make political capital out of the fear of what might occur. Too rarely have attempts been made to learn from the experience of the past, to concentrate on the potential benefits of migration and to recognize its truly historic role.

Questions of polemic often arise out of matters of definition. Guest-workers, immigrants, foreigners and aliens are some of the terms used, and these terms often have meanings which are specific to different countries. The status of immigrants varies enormously, as do the rules and regulations governing citizenship and naturalization. Broadly, countries opt for one of two principles: *ius soli* (birthplace) or *ius sanguinis* (blood ties). In France, for instance, citizenship depends largely on the former, in Germany on the latter. This can affect how fast immigrants become part of their new society. Most French-born children of foreigners become citizens; only a few German-born ones do. Germany now has some of the most liberal immigration and refugee policies in Europe, and yet under laws refined under the Third Reich it is virtually impossible to obtain German citizenship unless 'blood ties' can be proved. This means that even second and third-generation Turks born in Germany are denied citizenship. Yet under *ius sanguinis* anyone of German ancestral origin living in, say, Romania or Russia can become German, even if the link with the 'fatherland' is centuries-old and the people speak not a word of German. Such complications and subtleties — and there are many more between different countries — make any study of contemporary European migration very difficult, especially regarding statistical data.

However this book is also very much concerned with the changing **qualitative** character of migrations in Europe. Mass migrations, as referred to herein, are large-scale migration flows between areas with different cultures or sovereignty. They are flows which change the spatial distribution of the population at the sending or receiving ends, or both. They are of a scale which is clearly recognizable and which often gives a shock to the political or social system. Thus if 40 million Europeans migrate to North America, this is mass migration. If several million Turks move from the countryside and an agrarian life to the cities where they encounter urban culture, this too is mass migration. Smaller numbers can be regarded as mass migration streams if they comprise large proportions of the population. After the Second World War 250,000 Finns mass-migrated from Karelia to Finland, and the same amount (net) moved from Finland to Sweden during the following years. During the 1980s there was a net emigration of 200,000 people from the Republic of Ireland: seen within the context of a country with a population of only 3.5 million, this too is mass migration.

From a West European perspective, there are two main potential source areas for future large-scale international migration flows. The first of these is Eastern Europe. A poll in a Russian newspaper has revealed that one-third of the labour-force would seriously consider a temporary move to the West. With more than 200 million inhabitants in its European parts, the ex-Soviet Union is thus a considerable source of large migration streams. Added to potential labour market movements are ethnic tensions, poverty and ecological problems all over Eastern Europe. Further substantial transfers of population westwards are therefore likely. Already, gateway cities such as Vienna and Trieste are seeing a previously unknown variety of human movement between East and West.

However, the real pressures lie beyond Europe, in the less-developed world. This is the second source area. In a world currently adding 250,000 people to its population every day (or a billion by the end of the century), pressures for migration to richer countries will inevitably mount. Over a slightly longer time-perspective, the population projections are even more dramatic. If current fertility levels are maintained, global population will double by 2025. In the optimistic United Nations (UN) medium projection, based on substantial fertility decline, there will be 'only' 3 billion more people fighting for space and other scarce resources. Practically all population growth takes place in poor countries outside Europe, so of course the temptation to migrate to the rich North must be overwhelming.

Many of these pressures are quite close at hand, just across the Mediterranean. The countries of the southern Mediterranean seaboard will add 50 million people to their populations over the next decade. These populations are youthful, unlike the demographic structures of Europe, which are now permanently old and will, particularly after the turn of the century, suffer a shrinkage in their native labour-forces. Many people therefore believe that Europe's next wave of mass migration will be drawn primarily from countries such as Egypt and Algeria. The beginnings of this future migration wave from the southern Mediterranean and the Third World can already be seen in Italy, itself once an emigration country, which now has an estimated 1 million illegal immigrants from African and Asian countries.

Two scenarios may be suggested as possible outcomes from these processes. One is that European governments, acting in response to internal political pressures from the Right, will continue to control, moderate or stop immigrants. In Europe the Iron Curtain seems to have been converted into a 'welfare curtain' protecting Western Europe from large numbers of Eastern European immigrants. Most European countries are also trying to prevent non-Europeans from migrating into their welfare societies. Ethnic chauvinism has a long tradition in Europe, having caused several wars in the present century alone. However, to close off borders is not possible today and will not be easier in the future. If it did occur, large numbers of illegal immigrants would go into hiding amongst relatives and friends. A general deportation order would be possible only by repressive measures and strict identity controls. The free movement of people within the Common Market would become a thing of the past.

The second scenario, the more probable, is that large migration streams, legal and illegal, into Western Europe will actually take place during the coming decades. Half a million immigrants per year from Eastern Europe into Western Europe and 1 million per year from other parts of the world would result in the same quantity of immigrants as enter the United States. Most of the migrants would go to the large cities where they would be very visible. The new demographic map of Europe would thus be characterized by renewed urbanization, segregation within cities and flows of migrants to and within Europe. A repeat of some of the cultural conflicts of the 1960s and 1970s, although affecting different groups, might take place. Increasingly heterogeneous urban populations would probably be less interested in common infrastructures, and European cities could start to experience some of the problems seen in large American cities.

Of course several of these migratory streams will be directly linked to changes in the production system. The rising demand for immigrants in some regions and sectors of the West European labour market to replace the falling numbers of native new entrants and to rejuvenate an ageing work-force will in turn influence labour and market-oriented economic activities which are locationally sensitive. Large cities with dual labour markets, well educated and less educated, will attract capital. A new spatial division of labour is in the making.

Part 1: Background

Chapter 1

Mass migration and economic restructuring

Anthony Fielding

Introduction

This short chapter attempts to construct a general conceptual framework within which the relationships between economic restructuring and mass migration can be analysed and understood. Its starting-point is Figure 1.1 which traces the main determinants of mass migration, including the role of employment restructuring (arrow 1). The diagram also points to the role of mass migration itself in shaping the course of employment restructuring (arrow 6). This chapter is largely confined to a considera-tion of these two relationships.

Figure 1.1, however, fails to address the conceptual and definitional problems relevant to the task in hand. First, it is not specific about the locations of the causes and the effects. Since our primary interest in this book is with changes in the European urban and regional system, it follows that the causes of mass migration **to** European countries which are located in countries outside Europe (such as poverty or war in Africa or Asia) concern us more than the **effects** of such migrations on these same countries. Similarly, the effects of mass migrations **from** Europe on their non-European destination regions are not considered here in any depth.

Second, if we take the term 'mass migration' to mean 'large net streams crossing cultural and national borders resulting in significant population redistribution', it must presumably refer to both (1) migration flows between countries in Europe and countries outside Europe; and (2) migration flows between the countries of Europe itself. Defined in this way, of course, 'mass migration' excludes most of the migration flows which occur **within** these European countries. However, as will be argued below, such migration flows are sometimes almost indistinguishable in their causes and their consequences from those which cross an inter-national boundary. Furthermore, there are important interdependencies between the two kinds of migration — inter-regional and international. Such similarities and interdependencies need to be specified.

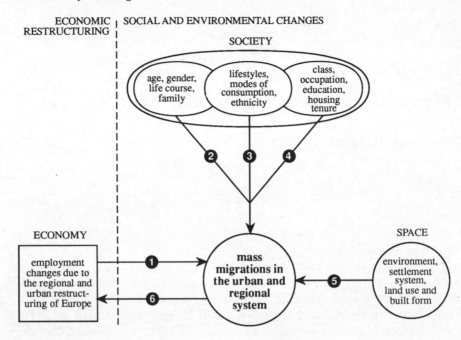

ECONOMIC SOCIAL AND ENVIRONMENTAL CHANGES
RESTRUCTURING

Key to causal connections:

1 economy to migration
1a. 'mass' migrations eg. east-west, south-north (mostly 'speculative')
1b. labour migration eg. inter-regional and international migration of qualified manpower (mostly 'contractual')

2 - **4** society to migration
2. demographic impacts eg. retirement migration
3. role of culture eg. return migration, ethnic minority migration
4. role of class eg. migration and social promotion

5 space to migration
eg. periphery-core migration, ethnic segregation

6 migration to economy
role of migration patterns and processes in shaping the course of employment restructuring

Figure 1.1   Mass migrations in the context of regional and urban restructuring in Europe

The role of economic restructuring in determining the size and nature of mass migrations to, from and within Europe

This section examines those relationships which are grouped along arrow 1 in Figure 1.1. Economic processes can, for the purpose of this exercise, be classified under three headings: the first group relates to the frequent

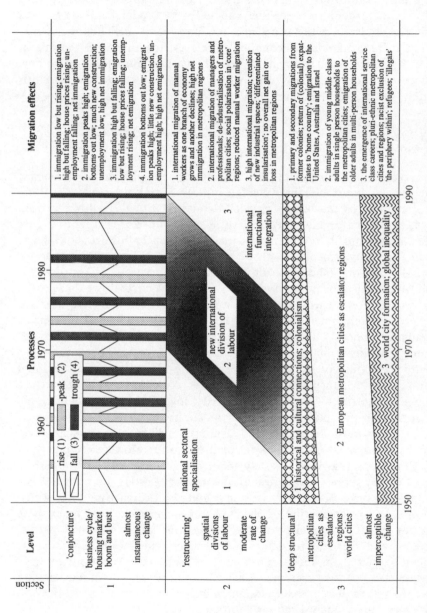

Figure 1.2 The effects of economic restructuring on mass migrations to and from Western Europe's metropolitan cities and regions

The following text appears within the figure:

Section	Level	Processes	Migration effects

Section 1

Level:
- 'conjoncture'
- business cycle/ housing market boom and bust
- almost instantaneous change

Legend:
- rise (1)
- peak (2)
- fall (3)
- trough (4)

Migration effects:
1. immigration low but rising; emigration high but falling; house prices rising; unemployment falling; net immigration
2. immigration peaks high; emigration bottoms out low; much new construction; unemployment low; high net immigration
3. immigration high but falling; emigration low but rising; house prices falling; unemployment rising; net emigration
4. immigration bottoms out low; emigration peaks high; little new construction, unemployment high; high net emigration

Section 2

Level:
- 'restructuring'
- spatial divisions of labour
- moderate rate of change

Processes:
- national sectoral specialisation 1
- new international division of labour 2
- international functional integration 3

Migration effects:
1. international migration of manual workers as one branch of economy grows and another declines; high net immigration in metropolitan regions
2. international migration of managers and professionals; de-industrialisation of metropolitan cities; social polarisation in 'core' regions; reduced manual worker migration
3. high international migration; creation of new industrial spaces; 'differentiated insularisation'; no overall net gain or loss in metropolitan regions

Section 3

Level:
- 'deep structural'
- metropolitan cities as escalator regions
- world cities
- almost imperceptible change

Processes:
1. historical and cultural connections; colonialism
2. European metropolitan cities as escalator regions
3. world city formation; global inequality

Migration effects:
1. primary and secondary migrations from former colonies; return of (colonial) expatriates to 'home country'; emigration to the United States, Australia and Israel
2. immigration of young middle class adults in single person households to the metropolitan cities; emigration of older adults in multi-person households
3. the emergence of international service class careers; pluri-ethnic metropolitan cities and regions; racist exclusion of 'the periphery within'; refugees; 'illegals'

Timeline axis: 1950 1960 1970 1980 1990

and rapid changes which arise from the operation of the business cycle; the second concerns the slower changes which accompany the reorganization of production (economic restructuring in the strict sense of the term); and the third group includes those economic processes which serve to differentiate countries, regions and cities in fundamental ways, and which are, at least in the short and medium term, unchanging.

These different kinds of economic processes, together with the migration flows which result from them, are shown in Figure 1.2. Let us now consider some of the many ideas which have been condensed into this diagram, taking each level in turn.

Level 1: The impact of the business cycle on mass migrations to, from and within Europe

Many economic phenomena (for example, unemployment, vacancies, homelessness, house-building) change rapidly over time, usually in tune with the stages of the business cycle. Economic growth is, for a certain period, a self-reinforcing process, with increases in sales leading to higher profits, higher profits promoting business confidence, business confidence inducing new investment . . . all of which produces higher output and a strong demand for labour, resulting in many job vacancies and low unemployment. At some point, however, the virtuous circle is broken, profits fall, business confidence collapses, output stagnates or falls, workers are made redundant, unemployment rises and job vacancies disappear. A similar cycle occurs in the housing market, with house prices and house-building showing a marked cyclical volatility. Moreover, there are signs that the relationships between the two cycles are increasing; national economic performance and labour market conditions seem in certain European countries — notably the United Kingdom — to be increasingly enmeshed with the 'boom and bust' transitions of the housing market.

One of the most pervasive (and persuasive) lines of argument developed by commentators on international migration flows affecting post-1950 Europe, is that **it is precisely this cyclical variability in the performance of the 'core' economies of north-west Europe (notably (West) Germany, France, Benelux, Switzerland and the United Kingdom) which is central to an explanation of the flows of migrants to and from these countries.** As the economy expands, indigenous labour becomes scarce, expensive and difficult to manage. Employers turn to foreign labour, which is recruited on short-term contracts. When the economy enters a recession these contracts are not renewed, and the immigrant workers are forced to return home. International migrant workers are, therefore, a convenient buffer against labour shortages at the peak of the cycle, and someone else's problem during recession. The sudden reversals in the net flow of migrant workers to West Germany which accompanied the recessions of 1967 and 1974/5 are often used as evidence to support this view of the international migration process (Böhning 1979).

The business cycle can be divided into four stages. The impact of these stages on mass migration might be expected to be as follows:

Stage 1 — the period of growth: immigration would start low and rise rapidly, emigration would start high and fall rapidly; house prices would rise, unemployment would fall; net immigration would replace net emigration.

Stage 2 — the peak of the cycle: immigration would peak high and emigration would bottom out low; house prices would peak high, unemployment would bottom out low; this would be a period of high net immigration.

Stage 3 — the period of decline: immigration would start high and fall rapidly, emigration would start low and rise rapidly; house prices would fall, unemployment would rise; net emigration would replace net immigration.

Stage 4 — the trough in the cycle: immigration would bottom out low and emigration would peak high; house prices would bottom out low, unemployment would peak high; high net emigration would be the result.

Level 2: The effect of changes in the organization of production on mass migrations to, from and within Europe

Some of the early literature on large-scale international migration to Western Europe mistakenly assumed that the changes in international migration flows were brought about entirely by the passage of these Western European economies through the seven (or so) post-1950 business cycles. This is an unsatisfactory view, however, because below the surface of this *conjoncture*, there were other, slower, more 'structural' changes taking place. I refer to transformations in the organization of production now often called simply 'restructuring'.

Three distinct forms of production organization in the post-1950 period can be identified. The first was characterized by the location within each region or nation of the full range of jobs required for the production of particular goods or services. In the early post-1950 period, the propensity to migrate across international boundaries to the large metropolitan cities and regions of Western European countries often reflected nothing more than an **international extension** of the rural depopulation and urbanization which were transforming the **internal** space economies of those same countries. At the intra-national level we use the term 'regional sectoral specialization' to refer to the spatial division of labour which was dominant during this period.

Regional sectoral specialization describes a situation in which each region specialized in the production of those commodities in which it had, as a result of its location, skills or resource endowment, a comparative advantage. These commodities were then sold to customers outside the region and the income so generated was used to purchase other regions' goods and services. The countries of Europe were thus at this time predominantly integrated space economies, an integration achieved through the market. This meant that as the demand for certain goods increased (for example, cars and consumer durables in the 1950s and 1960s) and demand for others stagnated or decreased (for example, coal and steel, ships, textiles, basic foodstuffs), so employment growth in regions specializing in the production of goods in high demand would attract migrants (including manual workers) from regions specializing in the production of those for which demand was stagnant or declining. **It is argued here that this sectoral specialization was also a feature of economic differences at an international level and that we might properly speak of a 'national sectoral specialization' in which some countries, for example, specialized in the production of agricultural goods while others specialized in 'modern' manufactured goods.** This helps to explain the early post-war migrations to the urban-industrial countries of north-western Europe (United Kingdom, West Germany, France) from the rural-agricultural countries of the European 'periphery' (Ireland, Italy and Spain), since the income elasticity of demand for the new consumer goods was far higher than that for food and other agricultural products produced in the periphery.

National sectoral specialization has not disappeared, of course, although it has become overlain by later spatial divisions of labour related to newer forms of production organization (Massey 1984). Specifically, in the 1960s and 1970s it became increasingly common for the different tasks within the firm to become geographically separated from one another, with these separate parts distributed around the countries of the world. Headquarters functions gravitated towards the 'global cities' of certain Western European countries (for example, London and Paris), research and development towards the high amenity and environmentally privileged regions of these same high income industrial countries, and routine production towards low-cost sites in labour surplus regions within these countries, or to 'offshore' production sites located in the European periphery or in Third World countries.

The general term that we use to describe this new geography of production is the 'new' or 'hierarchical' spatial division of labour, although at the international level it is known as the **new international division of labour** (Fröbel *et al*. 1980). This NIDL also implied a fully integrated space economy, except that this time the integration was not brought about through the market exchange of traded goods and services, but through the planned intra-organizational spatial separation of tasks. Whereas regions and nations had previously been multi-tasked and sectorally specialized, they were now increasingly single-tasked and sectorally unspecialized. This multisectoral nature of national economies reduced the need for the international migration of manual workers, since the decline in one sector was often counteracted by the growth of another sector already represented in the country (for example, job losses in agriculture in Ireland, Italy and Spain were counteracted by employment growth in manufacturing industry, tourism and other services). At the same time, however, the new international division of labour, associated as it was with the development of large internal labour markets in transnational companies and international organizations, led to the intra-organizational transfer of managers and professionals from one country to another as these people climbed their individual career ladders (Salt 1984).

The change-over from national sectoral specialization to the new international division of labour was double-edged in its effects on international migration to and from the metropolitan cities and regions in the countries of north-western Europe. As these metropolitan cities lost many of their more routine manufacturing jobs, a sharp deindustrialization often set in and the employment opportunities for manual worker immigrants to these cities and regions were much reduced. However, as the metropolitan cities' and regions' headquarters and research and development functions increased, so they became more than ever the target regions for highly qualified labour and the location of employment growth in financial, business and information-handling services.

On balance, many of the largest metropolitan city regions showed net migration losses during the late 1960s and early to mid-1970s (Fielding 1982). In contrast, the regions and countries of origin of the mass migration streams of the 1950s and early 1960s now often became areas of net migration gain. So the effect of the change-over from national sectoral specialization to the new international division of labour was to reverse migration trends. The extreme cases, perhaps, were western Ireland and southern Italy, both of which saw reversals in their long histories of net emigration (see, e.g., Strachan and King 1982; Horner *et al*. 1987).

Both regional/national sectoral specialization and the new spatial/international division of labour promoted mass migrations — the former from the European periphery to the core cities and regions of the countries of north-west Europe, the latter from these same cities and regions towards the periphery as deindustrialization came to characterize the core, and as manufacturing branch plant investment in many parts of the periphery heightened the prospects for migrants wishing to return (King 1986). Both of these phases of economic and demographic development were **Fordist** in the sense that they involved the mass production of standardized goods for mass markets. They both entailed the migration of 'mass collective workers', though the earlier migration **towards** the core was on a larger scale than the later one **away** from the core, and the later migration was characterized as much by the migration of professional, technical and managerial workers as by that of manual workers.

The period since the mid-1970s has seen Fordist forms of production organization in Western Europe partly superseded, partly overlain, by what some have called 'flexible specialization' (or 'flexible accumulation'). The implications of this change for international migration are not at all clear at present, except that post-Fordist production systems seem to be as inimical to 'mass' migration as they are to 'mass' production and 'mass' consumption.

There continues to be considerable debate about how we can best characterize the changes in production organization which occurred in Western Europe after the mid-1970s (see Sayer and Walker 1992). Clearly, although both Fordist spatial divisions of labour (national sectoral specialization and the new international division of labour) continued beyond the mid-1970s, certain important changes did take place. First, lower rates of growth and higher levels of unemployment implied that the need for mass immigration into the core countries of north-west Europe was much reduced. Second, the trend towards smaller internal labour markets, associated with the 'marketization' of relationships (for example, through the use of subcontractors and franchise systems), reduced the need for the spatial mobility of professional, technical and managerial employees. Finally, the decline of decentralized branch plant investment and the emergence of 'new industrial districts' (the former indicating the spatial mobility of capital, the latter its embeddedness in local social relations) brought about a decline in the possibilities for return migration. **Thus the most important feature of mass migration under post-Fordist forms of production organization is its absence!** Mass migration, from this perspective, can be seen as a corollary to mass production, mass consumption, mass culture and mass society. In so far as flexible specialization moves away from these, it takes spatial mobility along with it, and leaves behind only small-scale and more individualistic forms of inter-regional and international migration.

The events of the 1989–92 period, however, do not allow us to leave the story at this point. Clearly, while changes in the organization of production in Western Europe might be resulting in lower levels of mass migration, those in Central and Eastern Europe point in a very different direction. The economic and political restructuring of the former 'second' world is leading to a degree of impoverishment which is creating an East–West gradient of income differences and life chances which threatens to become comparable to that of the South–North gradient between Central America and the United States. Thus, while the trends in the production system within Western Europe may be reducing the likelihood of mass in-migration, those in the east seem to be making mass migration more likely (King 1991).

Level 3: The role of 'deep structural' processes on mass migration to, from, and within Europe

This last point leads us into a consideration of economic and employment processes which, unlike those discussed above, are so deep-rooted that for all intents and purposes they are unchanging from one decade to another. What is being referred to here are migrations which reflect the basic economic inequalities of the wider world in which we live, especially the massive differences in life chances between Western European countries and those of the Third World.

Given a world in which the economic opportunities facing individuals are extremely divergent, it is inevitable that sizeable numbers of people (especially young adults) will aspire to leave those places where life chances are poor to move to where they are good. In this respect, the countries of Western Europe can usefully be visualized as upward 'escalator regions', that is, as places where the **context** of one's life makes it much more likely that one will obtain social promotion, a secure and rising income, basic life-supporting services and a good education for one's children (while at the same time, of course, being more likely to be unemployed, badly-housed and poorly-paid compared with the members of the host population). Upward social mobility is achieved (or becomes possible) through horizontal spatial mobility.[1]

Three conditions must be met before a region can properly be described as an 'escalator region'. The first is that the region or nation must show net migration gains of young, ambitious, potentially upwardly-mobile adults (stage 1 — stepping onto the escalator). The second condition is that these in-migrants, along with many of the members of the host population, must on average achieve rates of upward social mobility which are higher than those experienced elsewhere (stage 2 — being taken up by the escalator). The third condition is that a certain proportion of those who migrated to the region will, at a later stage in their lives, 'cash in' their accumulated material, social and cultural assets by migrating away from the escalator region, typically of course, back to regions from which they came (stage 3 — stepping off the escalator). Do the countries of Western Europe have migration and social mobility regimes which meet these conditions? Yes, they do, although in two rather different ways. Certain core metropolitan areas of Western Europe have continued to act as escalator regions for those living in the European periphery. Thus educated and ambitious young people migrate from Italy and Greece to Germany, from Portugal and Spain to France, and from Ireland to Britain, many of them to return at later stages of their working lives or at retirement. At the same time others migrate from outside Western Europe into both the core countries of north-west Europe, and into the countries of the southern periphery (notably Italy and Spain), which have now become major immigration countries. Given the extreme contrasts in living standards and opportunities for social advancement between the countries of Western Europe and those of the Third World, one should not be surprised that despite increasingly strict immigration controls, such migrations continue to figure prominently in Western Europe's demographic, cultural and political development.

The role of mass migration in determining the nature and scale of economic restructuring

Until now this chapter has concentrated exclusively on the way in which economic processes have determined in the recent past, and continue to determine today, the content and character of the mass migration flows affecting Western Europe. However, a backward glance at Figure 1.1 (arrow 6) will remind us that mass migrations also themselves affect the scale and nature of economic restructuring. They do so in two major ways. First, they alter the supply of labour in Western Europe's urban and regional labour markets. Second, they alter the social and cultural composition of the populations of Western Europe's cities and regions, which in turn affects the selection of these places for new rounds of manufacturing and service investment and the likelihood that they will witness small firm growth and industrial innovation.

By increasing labour supply in metropolitan and industrial areas mass migrations change the pace and nature of economic restructuring in the following ways:

1. This extra supply of labour may resolve recruitment bottle-necks, thus permitting profitable production and growth, leading to investment in new product development, new methods of production and new production locations (i.e., restructuring).
2. On the other hand, the extra supply of labour may imply that the reorganization of production using labour-saving technology can be postponed. The immigrant workers could then be used in traditional ways in existing locations to produce unaltered goods and services (i.e., no restructuring).

This second possibility is an important consideration. Marxist economists and neo-liberal economists agree, in opposition to a popular consensus on the subject, that net immigration countries enjoy considerable economic benefits from mass immigration. Nevertheless, perhaps surprisingly, **this economic growth does not necessarily result in economic restructuring**. Whether it does so or not will depend on the characteristics and contexts of specific cities and regions. Once again, it seems that 'geography matters!'

The converse arguments apply to regions of mass emigration. The reduction in labour supply may well trigger economic restructuring through investments in capital-intensive forms of production. It may also, however, do exactly the opposite. Bolstered by remittances, the local economy may survive through retrenchment, unaltered.

By altering the socio-cultural and skill compositions of the work-force, mass migrations change the pace and nature of economic restructuring in the following ways:

1. This change in social composition of the work-force may open up opportunities for the production of new products and services in new ways and in new locations — the revitalization of depressed areas by the development of ethnic minority businesses is a case in point.
2. On the other hand, it may alter the attractiveness of areas for new investment by indigenous and foreign capital. This could go either way in its effects on economic restructuring. In the case of the in-migration of highly-qualified manpower it could attract new high-tech investment to these locations; in other cases it could deter such investments.

Conclusion

In the first and larger part of this chapter it was argued that many of the most important aspects of mass migration could be understood as the responses of people, particularly those living in the European periphery and in the Third World, to economic restructuring in Western Europe (which is, in certain instances, linked to restructuring under way in the sending countries). In the second part of the chapter it was argued that the mass migrations themselves can influence the nature of economic restructuring, although whether and how this happens depends on local and regional circumstances.

Note

1. For further discussion of the concept of 'escalator region' and the link between social and spatial mobility, see Fielding 1990 and 1992.

References

Böhning, W.R., 1979, 'International migration in Western Europe: reflections on the past five years', *International Labour Review*, 118(4): 401–14.

Fielding, A.J., 1982, 'Counterurbanization in Western Europe', *Progress in Planning*, 17(1): 1–52.

Fielding, A.J., 1990, 'A search for the "missing link" between social and geographical mobility', *Revue de Géographie de Lyon*, 65(3): 165–70.

Fielding, A.J., 1992, 'Migration and social mobility: South East England as an "escalator" region', *Regional Studies*, 26(1): 1–15.

Fröbel, F., Heinrichs, J. and Kreye, O., 1980, *The new international division of labour*, Cambridge University Press, Cambridge.

Horner, A.A., Walsh, J.A. and Harrington, V.P., 1987, *Population in Ireland: a census atlas*, Department of Geography, University College Dublin, Dublin.

King, R.L. (ed.), 1986, *Return migration and regional economic problems*, Croom Helm, London.

King, R.L., 1991, 'Europe's metamorphic demographic map', *Town and Country Planning*, 60(4): 111–13.

Massey, D., 1984, *Spatial divisions of labour*, Macmillan, London.

Salt, J., 1984, 'High-level manpower movement in North-West Europe and the role of careers', *International Migration Review*, 17(4): 633–51.

Sayer, A. and Walker, R., 1992, *The new social economy: reworking the division of labor*, Basil Blackwell, Cambridge, Mass. and Oxford.

Strachan, A.J. and King, R.L., 1982, 'Emigration and return migration in southern Italy: a multivariate, cluster and map analysis', Leicester University Geography Department, Occasional Paper 9.

Chapter 2

European international migration 1945–90: a statistical and geographical overview

Russell King

Introduction and data sources

The purpose of this chapter is to offer a numerical and spatial overview of the development of international migration in Europe since 1945. In order to limit the scope of the discussion to manageable proportions, certain limitations should be specified at the outset. First, the discussion is restricted to those Western European countries which were the main targets for international migration during the period in question. Eastern Europe is largely left out; migration trends in and from this part of the continent will be analysed in other contributions to this book. Second, the data used are largely those issued by the migrant-receiving countries. This restriction reflects the fact that migrants tend to have a more dramatic geographical impact at the destination end of the migration chain, and the more pragmatic consideration that host country statistics tend to be more detailed and reliable than those of the sending country. Third, the majority of the data presented in this chapter will refer to the period since the 1970s. The earlier period of mass migration and bulk recruitment of labour by the industrialized countries of Western Europe has been comprehensively documented by other writers, notably in the volume of essays edited by Salt and Clout (1976). Although the earlier period will be briefly reviewed as a necessary prologue to what follows — both in this chapter and in others in this book — the migration trends of the past fifteen years will be the main focus, since these data have yet to be comprehensively assembled and analysed. Finally, this chapter will concern itself mainly with the presentation of data rather than with detailed discussion or interpretation of the figures. This is necessary for reasons of space, since the data available are voluminous. Even then only a selection of national-level statistics are dealt with here.

The main reference source of data used is the SOPEMI series of annual migration compilations issued by the Organization for Economic Co-operation and Development (OECD).[1] Here we shall concentrate on total migrant stocks and flows, whilst recognizing that migrant labour has constituted the main driving-force behind European international migration since the Second World War. It should be stressed that the

SOPEMI data are only as good as the figures supplied by the member countries of the organization. The figures are of varying reliability and each country has its own way of defining and measuring migration. Therefore strict comparability between data for different countries cannot, indeed must not, be assumed.

The plan of this chapter is as follows. First the early origins of European mass migration will be briefly touched upon, identifying some common and contrasting historical parallels. Second, the main features of the post-war boom period of mass labour migration will be outlined: for most countries this comprises the period between the 1950s and the mid-1970s. Here, stress will be laid on global figures and on broad geographical patterns, given that this period has already been thoroughly researched. The third and largest part of the chapter will deal with the period since the mid-1970s. This again will look for elements of continuity with the past as well as new trends emerging during the 1970s and 1980s. This section will be built around a number of comparative tables drawn from the aforementioned SOPEMI reports. Finally, possible future trends in European mass migration will be speculated upon for the period leading up to and beyond the turn of the century.

The origins of European mass migration

The mass migrations of the 1950s and 1960s and of decades to come are not without precedent in Europe. Indeed the continent has a long history of human migration, enacting many themes: flight from war, refuge from political persecution, dispossession of land, attraction of urban centres, allure of lands of opportunity (Salt 1976, p. 80). In the nineteenth and early twentieth centuries the predominant movement was out of rather than into Europe as millions crossed the ocean to settle in the New World: an estimated 55–60 million during 1820–1940 of whom 38 million went to the United States. This transatlantic stream reached an annual peak of over 1 million in the years immediately preceding the First World War, with Italy alone sending about 400,000 per year.

Intra-European mass migrations were also under way before 1940, stimulated by both political and economic factors. Industrializing nations drew workers in from neighbouring countries: Irish to Britain, Italians to France, Central Europeans to the German Empire. By 1931 France had 900,000 Italians, and Britain 311,000 Irish-born, a high figure considering the size of the Irish population, less than 3 million. Some of these early labour migration patterns were to reappear and gather strength after 1945, as we shall see.

The geopolitical upheavals accompanying the two world wars caused further massive human dislodgements. Kosiński (1970) estimated that 7.7 million people took part in cross-border movements in Europe as a consequence of the First World War, and perhaps 25 million were

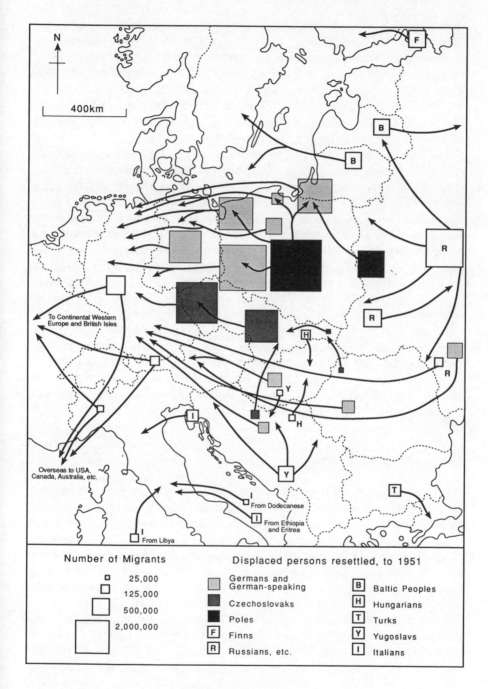

N

400km

R

B

B

F

R

R

R

To Continental Western
Europe and British Isles

H

Y

H

I

Overseas to USA,
Canada, Australia, etc.

Y

I

From Dodecanese

I

From Ethiopia
and Eritrea

I

From Libya

T

Number of Migrants

□ 25,000

□ 125,000

□ 500,000

□ 2,000,000

Displaced persons resettled, to 1951

Germans and
German-speaking

Czechoslovaks

Poles

F Finns

R Russians, etc.

B Baltic Peoples

H Hungarians

T Turks

Y Yugoslavs

I Italians

Figure 2.1 European migrations, 1944–51
Source: After Broek and Webb (1978, pp. 432–3).

shifted, mainly in East-Central Europe, during and immediately after the Second World War. Figure 2.1 shows the predominant East-to-West movement and the importance of Germany and of German-speaking people in this re-sorting of Europe's ethnic and linguistic map. By 1950 West Germany contained 7.8 million refugees and East Germany 3.5 million. The movement continued in the 1950s: between 1950 and the erection of the Berlin Wall in 1961 an estimated 3 million East Germans crossed to the West, mainly through Berlin.

The above distinction between political and economic factors causing migration is only partly helpful. Although in many cases political events created the opportunity or the necessity to migrate, people also took the opportunity to move to enhance their chances of a better material standard of life — as in the movement between former East and West Germany. In the post-war period 'economic migrants' became more and more the norm. Typically these movements began to take place from countries of over-population, rural poverty and high unemployment (southern Italy was the classic migrant source region in the immediate post-war years), to those of slower population growth and greater economic opportunity. It is, perhaps, an interesting historical parallel to note that just as I and others (e.g. Lutz 1991), forecast a new era of mass migration into Europe in the decades ahead, so Kirk (1946), after reviewing the population trends of inter-war Europe, forecast that a boom in international migration in Europe would ensue in the post-war period, with Southern and Eastern Europe as the source areas and Western Europe the destination.

The mass migration boom

Post-war international migration in Western Europe gathered momentum in the 1950s and reached a peak during the 1960s, fading away after the early 1970s. It occurred on a massive scale and has transformed the economic and social geography of the region as a whole. The recruitment of foreign workers has become a central plank for the prosperity of the richer countries of Europe, whilst the social and demographic legacies of the migrants, who have increasingly tended to become settlers, will remain for decades to come. With the emergence of labour shortages in the countries of Northern Europe (i.e., from France northwards), the European labour market became internationalized and capital started to recruit labour from the less-developed periphery of Europe. With the exception of Ireland to the north-west and Finland to the north-east (suppliers of labour migrants respectively to the British and Swedish economies in the 1950s and 1960s), this periphery lay predominantly to the south and extended outwards in an ever-widening trawl for cheap and malleable workers (Sassen-Koob 1980). Initially, in the 1950s Italy was the main Mediterranean supplier, although it was soon succeeded by

Spain and later Greece and Portugal, then Yugoslavia and Turkey, and finally North Africa and the Third World. The principal countries of origin of the migrants thus fell into two groups: first, the Southern European countries mentioned above, and second, the non-European countries — Algeria, Morocco, Tunisia, and the various Third World countries sending migrants to their former colonial masters (West Indians, Indians and Pakistanis to Britain, Francophone West Africans to France, etc.).

The established model of mass Mediterranean migration to North European cities was that migrants were required for the lowest-status and most poorly-paid jobs which, in a tight labour market characterized by rising standards of education and thus employment aspirations, were shunned by the local work-force. Construction, factory employment and low-grade service occupations were typical employment sectors into which migrants were channelled. It was frequently argued that these were the jobs for which migrant workers were well suited because of their poor educational backgrounds and the limited opportunities for skill acquisition in their countries. This argument was far from always the case: many migrants experienced deskilling on moving abroad, as Baučić (1973) demonstrated for Yugoslav migrant workers.

Some key characteristics of migrants and mechanisms of European migration during the boom period are described by Salt and Clout (1976) and by Wils (1991). The ever-widening migrant periphery tended to mean that migrants moved in waves. West Germany, for instance, experienced consecutive waves of East German refugees in the 1950s, Italians from about 1957 to 1965, Yugoslavs in the late 1960s, Turks in the early 1970s and again in the early 1980s, and most recently ethnic Germans from Eastern Europe and the former German Democratic Republic (GDR). On a more micro scale, family members have come in two waves. Workers tended to migrate first, to find work and set up a home. Later they were joined by dependants. Since the 1970s many programmes of family reunion in West European countries have facilitated the joining up of families split by emigration. The family-based mechanism of migration also tended to be linked to the phenomenon of chain migration, whereby individual communities such as villages or small rural districts channelled virtually all of their migrants to a single destination town. Kolodny's (1982) study of Samothrace Islanders in Stuttgart is a case in point. In the literature on European migration, chain migration has been under-estimated as a phenomenon conditioning the micro-scale pattern of spatial links between origins and destinations.

A further distinctive characteristic of migrants during the migration boom period was their age structure. Most moved as young adults. The age structure of the migrant flow determined the age structure of the settled migrant population that developed, having considerable influence over its growth. Because the primary migrants in the 1950s and 1960s were concentrated in the child-bearing ages, their crude birth-rate has

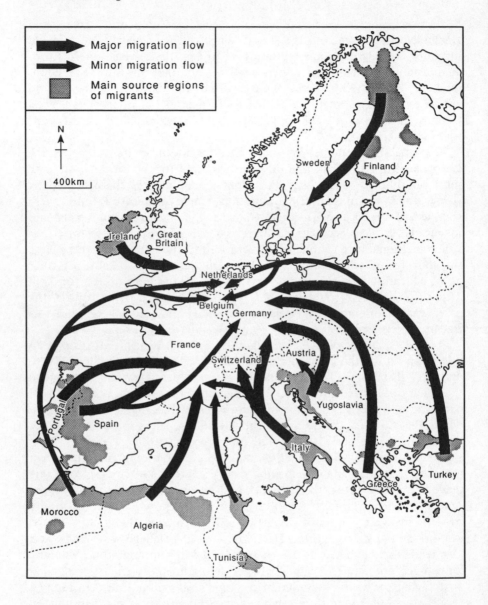

Figure 2.2   European migration flows, *circa* 1973
Source: After Hammar 1985, p. 3; King 1976, p. 71; King 1989, p. 44.

been (and remains) higher than that of the indigenous population, and their crude death-rate lower. Thus the settled migrant population has a tendency to grow faster than the indigenous population. This has parti-cular significance where migrants have been attracted to demographic 'sink-holes': cities, regions or even countries with negative natural

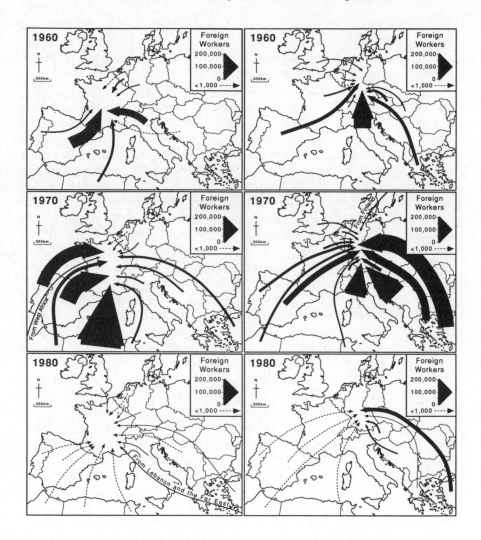

Figure 2.3 Immigration of workers into France and West Germany, 1960, 1970, 1980

Source: Partly after Salt 1976, pp. 89, 92–3.

growth. Since 1972 the indigenous natural growth rate of the West German population has been negative, compensated in part by immigrants' positive natural growth. In France too population increase since 1950 has been largely due to immigration and immigrants' positive natural growth (Wils 1991, pp. 282–3).

Attempts to map the overall pattern of international migrant flows in Europe during the 'mass' period have been made by Hammar (1985, p. 3) and King (1989, p. 44). Figure 2.2 represents a compilation of these flows. Inevitably such patterns are crude approximations of the real detail of what is not only a complex pattern in itself but also one which was constantly changing through time. Certain key features are simple enough, however, notably the orientation from periphery to core, from poor to rich regions of Europe, and from rural to urban districts. Any attempt to map the full variety of significant migration links in Europe is prone to end up looking like a plate of spaghetti. Probably more useful in understanding the evolution of the patterns are single-country maps. The examples of France and West Germany show the broadening range of supply countries from 1960 to 1970 and the sudden shrinkage after the oil shocks of the 1970s (Figure 2.3).

The pattern of the spatial variation in the intensity of out-migration from Southern European countries in the 1960s and 1970s shows a clear tendency in all countries except Turkey for the migrants to come mainly from rural, mountainous, poor and (in relation to resources) over-populated environments (Figure 2.2): northern Portugal, western Spain, southern Italy and northern Greece. The exceptional case of Turkey is probably to be explained by the mechanism of step-migration, whereby most Turkish external migrants moved first to Istanbul or Ankara before going abroad; they were therefore recorded as departing from the cities rather than from their rural homelands (King 1976). Destination patterns were overwhelmingly urban, reflecting the nature of employment of the immigrant workers. Further details are ably synthesized by White (1984, pp. 97–133; and see also Chapter 4 in this volume). Among cities with at least a tenth of their populations made up by foreign immigrants in the early 1970s were Geneva (34 per cent), Brussels (16 per cent), Grenoble (13 per cent), Paris (12 per cent), Lyons (12 per cent), Nuremburg (12 per cent) and Stuttgart (11.5 per cent). In France 40 per cent of the foreign population was (and still is) to be found in the Paris urban region. Figure 2.4 shows the marked concentration of the immigrant population in eastern, urban France and the interesting variations in the national composition of various cities' foreign populations: Algerians and Portuguese dominate overall, but Italians and Spaniards are prominent in south-eastern and south-western French cities respectively.

The migration boom lasted about twenty years until 1974. It was brought to an end by the general recession which had serious effects on many European economies. As we shall see in more detail in the next section, the long-term effects of the recruitment stop were felt differently in the various sending and receiving countries. The immediate effect was quite sharp in countries like Yugoslavia and Turkey: external emigration to Europe virtually stopped for a time. The impact was less severe in Italy, at that time the only Southern European sending-country enjoying the status of full EEC membership. In fact the outflow of emigrants leaving Italy had already peaked early in the 1960s, and by the mid-1970s returning migrants to Italy outnumbered emigrants, on the basis of annual totals, by about 30 per cent.

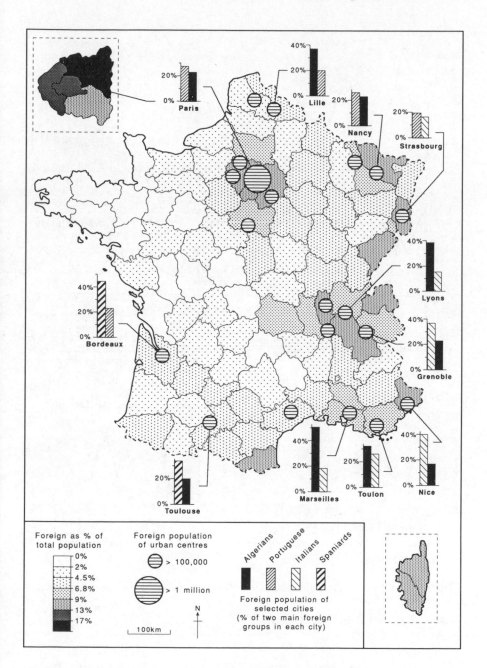

Figure 2.4 The geography of foreign immigration in France, 1975
Source: After George 1986, pp. 281–2; White 1984, pp. 104, 109.

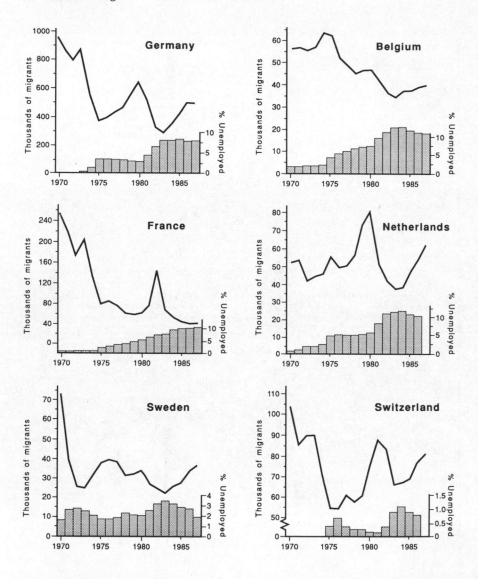

Figure 2.5 Gross immigration and unemployment, selected European countries, 1970–87

Source: SOPEMI Report 1988, p. 12.

Estimates of the situation around 1975, just after the recession 'froze' the European international migration scene, show that there were around 2 million foreign workers in West Germany, about 1.5 million in France, about 750,000 in the United Kingdom and 500,000 in Switzerland (Kirk 1981, p. 61). These figures should be doubled to arrive at approximate estimates of the total immigrant populations. Further details on migrant numbers and their evolution from the mid-1970s to the late 1980s will be given in the next section.

International migration in Europe since the first oil crisis

Various parameters can be used to measure the trend of international migration in Europe across and since the recession years of the 1970s: total migration or worker migration; stocks or flows; gross or net migration; absolute figures or indexed data (measured against resident population for instance). All have their pros and their cons and each contributes a somewhat different facet of the overall picture. In the account which follows, we shall examine mainly stocks and gross migration flows of total migrants, with some reference to numbers of workers and indexed data where appropriate.

The underlying economic rationale of the behaviour of the European international migration system in the early and mid-1970s cannot be ignored. After the oil crisis of late 1973, when energy prices went up by a factor of three or four, the industrial economies of Western Europe were subject to varying degrees of stagnation or decline with increasing levels of unemployment everywhere. The relationship between unemployment and gross immigration is demonstrated for several European countries over the period 1970–87 in Figure 2.5. This shows not only the effects of 1973–5 but also the further falls in immigration which occurred in the early 1980s when renewed recession boosted unemployment rates again.

These crude economic relationships were mediated by political decisions reflecting rising social tension (King 1989, p. 48). The restrictions on worker immigration imposed in France in July 1974 denied entry to Algerians and other North Africans who had been coming to France for jobs and a better economic future since the early 1960s. This policy was modified one year later to allow the entry of families of foreign workers already resident in France. In 1975 West Germany accepted 366,000 immigrants but bade farewell to 655,000, who left to return to Turkey, Yugoslavia, Greece and Italy. Also in 1975 the Federal Republic of Germany (FRG) closed its labour recruitment offices in Greece, Morocco, Portugal, Spain, Tunisia, Turkey and Yugoslavia. The combination of over 1 million unemployed and 2 million foreign workers in the country explains this policy decision (Kirk 1981, pp. 66–7).

Table 2.1 builds on the picture provided in Figure 2.5 by tabulating inflow, outflow (return) and stock data for selected European countries for the period 1973–89. Since these annual figures are mostly for 31 December of each year, the series brings us to the threshold of 1990. Whilst the data are probably valid for time-series comparison along the rows of the table, international comparisons of migrant numbers should not be made on the basis of these figures, since each country has its own

Table 2.1 Annual migration trends 1973–89 for four European countries (all data '000)

	1973	1974	1975	1976	1977	1978	1979	1980	1981	1982	1983	1984	1985	1986	1987	1988	1989
NETHERLANDS																	
Total inflow	93.7	95.1	55.2	48.9	49.9	55.6	72.2	79.8	50.4	40.9	36.4	37.3	46.2	52.8	60.9	58.3	65.4
Total outflow			22.1	25.7	24.7	24.1	24.4	23.6	25.0	28.1	28.0	27.0	24.2	23.6	20.9	21.4	21.5
Stock total	315	345	351	376	400	435	473	521	538	547	555	559	553	568	592	624	642
Stock workers	160	163	176	181	187	196	182	188	193	185	174	169	166	169	176	176	192
GERMANY																	
Total inflow	869.1	538.6	366.1	387.3	422.8	456.1	545.2	631.4	501.1	321.7	273.2	331.1	398.2	478.3	427.3	648.5	770.8
Total outflow	526.8	580.4	600.1	515.4	452.1	405.8	366.7	385.8	415.5	433.3	424.9	545.7	366.7	347.3	334.0	359.1	438.3
Stock total	3966	4127	4090	3948	3948	3981	4144	4453	4630	4667	4535	4364	4379	4513	4630	4489	4846
Stock workers	2595	2360	2227	2000	1950	1948	2025	2116	2096	2029	1984	1855	1823	1834	1866	1911	1941
SWITZERLAND																	
Total inflow	73.0	81.0	46.3	44.9	55.4	53.3	56.8	70.5	80.3	74.7	58.3	58.6	59.4	66.8	71.5	76.1	80.9
Total outflow			121.1	110.3	84.3	63.8	55.8	63.7	64.0	62.6	61.7	55.6	54.3	52.8	53.8	55.8	57.5
Stock total	1030	1065	1013	957	933	898	884	893	910	926	926	932	940	956	979	1007	1040
Stock workers	596	593	553	516	493	489	491	501	515	526	530	539	549	567	588	608	632
SWEDEN																	
Total inflow	24.9	31.9	38.0	39.8	38.7	31.7	32.4	34.4	27.4	26.1	22.3	26.1	27.9	34.0	37.1	44.5	58.9
Total outflow	30.2	20.1	21.4	18.7	14.9	15.6	16.3	20.8	20.8	19.9	17.4	14.6	14.0	15.4	11.6	11.8	13.1
Stock total	397	401	410	418	424	424	424	422	414	406	397	391	389	391	401	421	456
Stock workers	190	200	204	236	225	228	229	234	234	228	222	219	216	215	215	220	237

Source: SOPEMI Reports 1974–90.

Notes: The data are collected on different criteria and with different methods in the four countries.
Netherlands: Flows and stocks of total migrants based on aliens' files kept at communal registry offices; includes asylum-seekers. Outflows are acknowledged as underestimates owing to failure to de-register. Stocks of total foreign population refer to 31 December each year. Stocks of workers are Central Bureau of Statistics estimates of employed foreigners at 31 December each year; includes frontier workers but excludes self-employed and unemployed.
Germany: Flows and stocks of total migrants based on central register of foreigners; includes asylum-seekers. Stocks are for 30 September each year. Stock of workers includes unemployed and frontier workers but excludes self-employed. Data refer to former FRG only.
Switzerland: All figures are for annual and permanent ('establishment') permit-holders; seasonal and frontier migrants are excluded, as are asylum-seekers. Stocks of workers are for 31 December each year.
Sweden: Flows and stocks of total migrants based on parish authorities' records of foreigners. Outflows are probably underestimates owing to failure to de-register. Stocks of workers are based on Labour Force Survey estimates, including unemployed foreigners.

way of measuring migrants (see the notes to the table). The post-1973 patterns revealed by the table are quite complex with considerable variations between the countries. For The Netherlands and West Germany, the inflows of immigrants more than halved during 1973–6, whilst the outflows of returning migrants increased, though not to such a dramatic extent, in both Germany and Switzerland. In Sweden the whole migration situation remained much more stable, reflecting both the greater resistance of the Swedish economy to the recession and the different patterns and history of immigration into that country (Finland being the main supplier of migrants). In fact the Swedish flow data for 1973–6 show the opposite trend to that observed in the other three countries, the inflows increasing and the outflows decreasing. For the other countries, the sharp decline in annual immigration and the increasing rate of return of migrants to their home countries did not markedly diminish the cumulative total of foreign residents. The stocks of total foreign populations tended to be more resistant to erosion by return migration than the stocks of foreign workers. The main reason for this — the substitution of worker recruitment by family reunion — will be explored in more detail shortly. For now it is enough to note how the total foreign population in Holland grew quite rapidly through the 1970s and 1980s whilst the worker totals stagnated, and how Germany's foreign total grew slightly, especially after 1978, whilst worker numbers fell from 2.6 million in 1973 to below 2 million for most of the period covered by the table. The German foreign worker data are particularly interesting when set against the doubling of foreign worker numbers which had occurred in the space of three years between 1968 (1 million foreign workers, 5.2 per cent of the total employed population of Germany) and 1971 (2.2 million and 10.3 per cent). The final feature of interest to note from Table 2.1 is the sudden spurt of inflows (although not of outflows) during the late 1980s. Hence all countries saw their stocks of migrants increase during the last few years.

Table 2.2 elaborates some of the foreign population stock data in Table 2.1 by comparing the evolution of the various migrant groups in six host countries between 1978 and 1989. The four countries represented in Table 2.1 are included, plus Belgium and France. The data in Table 2.2 has the form of a simple matrix which can be read either by comparing the host countries (columns) or the sending countries (rows). The empty cells signify the non-recording of that national group in the destination country; they are not zero entries. The data show how each national group has evolved over the most recent decade for which figures are available, for each destination country where that group is recorded. The most obvious pattern to emerge from the table is the contrasting behaviour of European and non-European migrant groups (counting Turkey as a non-European country for the purposes of this classification). In virtually all destination countries, the stock of migrants from Austria, Finland, Greece, Italy, Portugal, Spain and Yugoslavia

Table 2.2 Stocks of foreign population in selected European countries by nationality, 1978 and 1989 (all data '000)

Receiving country Sending country	Germany 1978	Germany 1989	Netherlands 1978	Netherlands 1989	Sweden 1978	Sweden 1989	Switzerland 1978	Switzerland 1989	Belgium 1977	Belgium 1989	France 1976	France 1985
Austria	159	171			4	3	35	29				
Finland	9	10			188	123						
Greece	306	294	4	5	18	7	9	8	24	21		
Italy	572	520	21	17	6	4	443	379	287	241	466	277
Portugal	110	75	9	8	2	2	8	69	10	15	823	751
Spain	189	127	25	17	4	3	96	115	65	52	507	268
Turkey	1165	1613	107	192	15	24	30	59	59	82	58	146
Yugoslavia	610	611	14	13	40	40	38	117	5	6		
Algeria									10	11	790	821
Morocco	29	62	64	148					81	138	300	516
Tunisia	19	24	2	2					5	6	147	203
Other	813	1342	185	241	149	250	241	265	305	309	607	770
Total	3981	4846	435	642	424	456	898	1040	851	881	3700	3752

Source: SOPEMI 1979, p. 5; SOPEMI 1990, p. 119.

Notes: For Germany, Netherlands, Sweden and Belgium (1989) the figures are based on 'foreigners files' kept at local registry offices (for more details see notes for Table 2.1). For Belgium (1977) the figures are from the sample census of that year and are not strictly comparable with the 1989 Belgium figures. For Switzerland the figures are for annual and 'establishment' permit-holders, not seasonal or frontier migrants. For France the 1976 figure is based on an estimate of an International Working Party; the 1985 figure is based on the census and estimates by the Institut National d'Etudes Démographiques; these two figures are therefore not strictly comparable. In all cases, figures may not tally owing to rounding.

decreased over the period 1978–89. The main exceptions were the increases recorded by Portuguese and Yugoslavs in Switzerland. In certain cases the declines were very marked — e.g., Spanish and Italians in France — although a proportion of these decreases are artificially induced by naturalization. On the other hand the Turkish and North African migrant groups increased their presence in all countries where they were recorded, in some cases — Moroccans in The Netherlands, Turks in France — more than doubling their numbers. The general result is that, of a stable or increasing total foreign population over the period in question, an increasing proportion is from non-European (usually less-developed) countries. The final point worth mentioning in reference to Table 2.2 is the sharply-increasing numbers of migrants recorded in the 'others' category, especially in Germany, The Netherlands, Sweden and France. These 'other' migrants comprise a range of different groups. Some are traditional migrant supply-groups left off the table for reasons of space, e.g., the 97,000 Poles and 93,000 non-Maghreb Africans recorded in France in 1978. Others are migrants from adjacent countries of similar economic standing who move as part of the tendency to inter-change higher-level manpower, e.g., the French and Dutch in Belgium or the Norwegians and Danes in Sweden. Finally, political refugees and asylum-seekers grew in numbers sharply in many countries in the 1980s. For instance in Sweden Chileans increased from 8,400 in 1982 to 19,100 in 1989, Iranians from 3,600 to 35,100 over the same period.

The discussion about the data in Table 2.1 made brief reference to the substitution, from about 1975 on, of family reunion migration for worker migration. This pattern is explored in more depth in Table 2.3, which has a similar matrix form to Table 2.2. The data show that for virtually all migrant groups listed under the four countries, the propor-tion of the total population made up of workers fell markedly between 1974 and 1989. The cases where such a fall was not registered, or where such a fall was minor, were old-established migrant groups (such as Italians and Portuguese in France) where family migration was already in train by 1974. The overall low percentages recorded for Turks and Moroccans in The Netherlands are out of context with the other data in Table 2.3, although they are presumably explained by the particular age structures of these communities in The Netherlands, with many young children and non-working wives.

Further contrasts in the evolution of different national migrant groups in destination countries can be highlighted by examining the gender balance. A low proportion of females indicates a migrant population still at an early stage of settlement; as the ethnic presence matures with more family migration, so the female ratio will rise. Table 2.4 shows this parameter for a selection of donor groups and receiver countries. Most groups have around 42–47 per cent of their total populations female, indicating a situation of approximate balance. The figure drops below 35 per cent only for recently-arrived and therefore small migrant

Table 2.3   Foreign workers as proportion of total foreign population in selected European countries by nationality, 1974 and 1989 (all data %)

Receiving country Sending country	France 1976	France 1989	Germany 1974	Germany 1989	Netherlands 1974	Netherlands 1989	Switzerland 1974	Switzerland 1989
Greece			73.5	39.6				
Italy	45.1	37.5	64.7	39.8			75.6	61.3
Portugal	52.2	55.0	77.3	56.7				
Spain	49.3	37.9	87.3	53.0	76.0	46.0	83.3	64.6
Turkey	60.3	44.5	50.6	40.4	31.8	18.8		
Yugoslavia			77.0	53.9			68.4	61.6
Algeria	53.2	31.5						
Morocco	55.0	36.2			39.1	16.9		
Tunisia	61.2	37.6						

Source: SOPEMI 1975, p. 14; SOPEMI 1979, p. 5; SOPEMI 1990, pp. 118–19.

Notes: The 1974 data for foreign workers are expressed as a percentage of the 1978 figures for total foreign population, these being the closest SOPEMI figures available.

For France the 1989 figure is expressed as a percentage of the 1985 figure for total foreign population.

communities (e.g., Algerians in Germany, Tunisians in The Netherlands). The rather low figures for some other migrant groups (e.g., Italians in The Netherlands, Spaniards in Sweden) seem to be a function of the very small numbers of migrants (e.g., 2,800 Spaniards in Sweden). The labour-force figures (indicating the proportion of the migrant work-force made up of females) show a lower female participation rate, as might be expected, and these rates drop to below 20 per cent in the seasonal and frontier migrants working in Switzerland.

To conclude this section, a number of important features of the post-1974 European migration system may be signalled. As White (1986) has pointed out, it is too simplistic to regard what happened in the 1970s as a simple process of blocked economic growth after 1973 coupled with a massive rise in unemployment leading to the halting of all new in-movement and increased and forced return migration. Many migration flows were maintained across the threshold of 1973–5. What changed was the character of the flows. The migration of family members replaced the migration of single workers, and migration tended to be more buoyant (if more capricious) from the non-European countries. This switch to less-developed countries in the 1970s and 1980s may well be a portent of much larger movements in the future, as we shall see in the next, concluding section of this chapter. Meanwhile, the traditional European supply countries have themselves started to become the target of migrant inflows from North Africa and the Third World. The contradictory place of Southern European countries as a 'proletarian region' with respect to the North, but as a receiving region with respect to

Table 2.4 Proportion of foreign female population 1988 (labour-force proportions in brackets); all data %

Receiving country Sending country	Belgium	Sweden	France (1985)	Germany	Netherlands	Switzerland (a)	(b)
Finland	46.1	53.9					
Greece	44.7	40.8		45.6 (38.8)			
Italy	47.4	30.8	44.4 (28.4)	39.9 (25.1)	32.5 (25.0)	43.2 (31.7)	(7.1)
Portugal	47.3		47.9 (39.5)	48.1 (35.8)	43.7 (33.3)	46.5 (40.5)	(20.0)
Spain	48.3	35.7	47.7 (39.6)	44.1 (32.6)	42.5 (37.5)	45.2 (37.5)	(10.1)
Turkey	46.3	49.6	46.7 (15.6)	45.9 (29.4)	45.6 (18.2)	45.4 (35.8)	
Yugoslavia	42.4	50.4		46.1 (39.1)	46.2 (40.0)	44.4 (36.4)	(13.5)
Algeria			41.2 (22.9)				
Morocco	46.6		43.1 (20.5)		44.0 (17.4)		
Tunisia	35.5		41.7 (19.6)				
Total	46.0	49.4	44.9 (31.5)	45.0 (32.3)	44.4 (27.3)	44.2 (34.0)	(16.5)

Source: SOPEMI 1989, pp. 136–49.

Notes: For Switzerland (a) refers to 'established' workers (holders of permanent or annual permits); (b) refers to seasonal and frontier workers.

immigration from Africa, has yet to be properly investigated (King 1984).

Mass migration in the future

The main purpose of this chapter has been to present retrospective data for the evolution of the European international migration system over the past forty years or so. Other chapters in this book will consider in some detail the prospects for future migration flows. Nevertheless it is perhaps useful at this point to conclude on a forward-looking note.

Several important contextual circumstances can be called into play to provide a setting for future migration development in Europe. The first is the economic context. As we saw in Figure 2.5, international migrant flows seem to respond to economic indicators like employment. Partly this is a natural product of the functioning of the international labour market; partly too it is a relationship manipulated by governments wishing to protect their native work-force from unemployment by hiring and laying off flexible reserves of migrant labour. Second, there is the institutional context of the Single Market and the possibilities of a boost in mobility through the lifting of remaining restrictions on movement within the EC12. The general view amongst informed observers (see, for instance, Molle and van Mourik 1988; Penninx and Muus 1989) is that compared with the all-important economic trends (which cannot easily be forecast, of course), the '1992 effect' will be rather insignificant. The institution of the Treaty of Rome's free movement of labour provisions between 1961 and 1968 did not have a noticeable effect on intra-EEC labour mobility at a time when labour migration was booming (Böhning 1972). If anything, the amount of intra-EEC migration went down as Italians stayed at home (or more correctly migrated from South to North within their own country) and France and Germany encouraged by bilateral agreements the immigration of vast numbers of workers from non-EEC countries like Algeria and Turkey. Although arguing by historical analogy is always dangerous, it does seem that if one round of EEC policy designed to 'free' labour mobility did not have the hypothesized effect, then '1992' will similarly not release the floodgates.

The third key context, also political, results from the remarkable events in Eastern Europe in the past three years. Previously the Western and Eastern European migration systems were virtually separate entities, the former of course many times larger than the latter. The dismantling of the Iron Curtain will undoubtedly lead to enhanced possibilities for migration between the two 'halves' of Europe which were previously almost hermetically sealed off from each other. Those who flocked from East to West Germany both before and after the collapse of the Berlin Wall may therefore be the harbingers of a large-scale East–West movement of people within Europe (King 1991). This potential future movement is also discussed in more detail in other chapters in this book.

The final context is the demographic one, and in many senses this is the most convincing. Discussion on future migration needs increasingly to be linked to the low fertility levels and consequent ageing which are becoming more widespread amongst European nations and regions. Some countries, such as France, Germany and the Scandinavian states, have had their low fertility levels established for some time. Other countries such as Italy, Spain and Ireland are seeing a spectacular collapse of fertility levels which were, until quite recently, high by European standards. Some of the lowest fertility levels in Europe are now recorded in northern Italy and northern Spain. Thus, over the next twenty years or so, there will be a continued decrease in the number of young workers in Europe, and of those who fill entry-level positions into the labour market. By contrast, there is a large surplus of young labour in other regions of the world. Decreasing mortality rates together with continuing high fertility has led to very large 'growth cohorts' in many less-developed countries; although these young adults have received high aspirations through their improving education systems, they have very little chance of finding appropriate jobs in their home countries. According to Lutz *et al.* (1991) these demographic push and pull factors are likely to build up an increasing pressure for massive South–North migration in coming decades: their estimate is for an annual immigration into Europe of 1.5 million by 2010, a flow in excess of anything experienced during the 1950s and 1960s. This 'immigration scenario' may be attenuated by automation, retarded retirement and, in the longer term, by some fertility increase (Swedish fertility has, for instance, begun to rise in very recent years). Ultimately the social and political climate could become so frosty as to deter non-European immigrants, who have already been the subject of substantial racial harassment in Britain, France and Germany. If this happens, the large emigration potential of Eastern Europe with newly opened borders could crowd out non-Europeans, except those managing to enter illegally or as legitimate asylum-seekers. Either way, international migration will almost certainly play a significant role in the demographic and socio-economic future of Europe at the start of the twenty-first century, if not before.

Note

1. SOPEMI stands for Système d'Observation Permanente sur les Migrations and is a statistical monitoring body for the evolving patterns and trends of international migration in most OECD member countries. The SOPEMI annual reports are not formally published but sent in mimeograph form to interested parties since 1973 when the first bulletin was issued. In spite of changes in length and format, the reports are the best source of comparative data on migrant stocks and flows within the West European migration system. For most countries data on both migrant workers and the total

migrant population are presented. These data are tabulated for stocks and for flows of migrants in both directions. Further details on the background and functioning of SOPEMI are given by Salt (1987).

References

Baučić, I., 1973, 'Yugoslavia as a country of emigration', *Options Méditerranéennes*, 5(22): 55–66.

Böhning, W.R., 1972, *The migration of workers in the United Kingdom and the European Community*, Oxford University Press, London.

Broek, J.O.M. and Webb, J.W., 1978, *A geography of mankind*, McGraw-Hill, New York, 3rd edition.

George, P., 1986, 'Les étrangers en France: étude géographique', *Annales de Géographie*, 95(529): 273–300.

Hammer, T. (ed.), 1985, *European immigration policy: a comparative study*, Cambridge University Press, Cambridge.

King, R., 1976, 'The evolution of international labour migration movements concerning the EEC', *Tijdschrift voor Economische en Social Geografie*, 67(2): 66–82.

King, R., 1984, 'Population mobility: emigration, return migration and internal migration', in Williams, A.M. (ed.), *Southern Europe transformed*, Harper and Row, London, 145–78.

King, R., 1989, 'Migration', in Clout, H., Blacksell, M., King, R. and Pinder, D., *Western Europe: geographical perspectives*, Longman, London, 2nd edition, 40–60.

King, R., 1991, 'Europe's metamorphic demographic map', *Town and Country Planning*, 60(4): 111–13.

Kirk, D., 1946, *Europe's population in the inter-war years*, Gordon and Breach, New York.

Kirk, M., 1981, *Demographic and social change in Europe 1975–2000*, Liverpool University Press, Liverpool.

Kolodny, E., 1982, *Samothrace sur Nekar: des migrants grecs dans l'agglomeration de Stuttgart*, Institut de Recherches Méditerranéennes, Aix-en-Provence.

Kosiński, L., 1970, *The population of Europe*, Longman, London.

Lutz, W. (ed.), 1991, *Future demographic trends in Europe and North America*, Academic Press, London.

Lutz, W., Prinz, C., Wils, A.B., Buttner, T. and Heilig, G., 1991, 'Alternative demographic scenarios for Europe and North America', in Lutz, W. (ed.), *Future demographic trends in Europe and North America*, Academic Press, London, 523–60.

Molle, K.W. and van Mourik, A., 1988, 'International movements of labour under conditions of economic integration: the case of Western Europe', *Journal of Common Market Studies*, 26(3): 317–42.

Penninx, R. and Muus, P., 1989, 'No limits to migration after 1992? The lessons of the past and a reconnaissance of the future', *International Migration*, 27(3): 373–88.

Salt, J., 1976, 'International labour migration: the geographical pattern of demand', in Salt, J. and Clout, H. (eds), *Migration in post-war Europe: geographical essays*, Oxford University Press, London, 80–125.

Salt, J., 1987, 'The SOPEMI experience: genesis, aims and achievements', *International Migration Review*, 21(4): 1067–73.

Salt, J. and Clout, H. (eds), 1976, *Migration in post-war Europe: geographical essays*, Oxford University Press, London.

Sasson-Koob, S., 1980, 'The internationalisation of the labour force', *Studies in Comparative International Development*, 15(1): 3–25.

White, P.E., 1984, *The west European city: a social geography*, Longman, London.

White, P.E., 1986, 'International migration in the 1970s: evolution or revolution?' in Findlay, A.M. and White, P.E. (eds), *West European population change*, Croom Helm, London, 50–80.

Wils, A.B., 1991, 'Survey of immigration trends and assumptions about future migration', in Lutz, W. (ed.), *Future demographic trends in Europe and North America*, Academic Press, London, 281–99.

Chapter 3

Migrations, institutions and politics: the evolution of European migration policies

Anthony Fielding

The first two chapters in this volume showed that European mass migrations have both a distinctive history and a very specific geography. They also suggest that strong forces connect mass migration flows to economic developments such as those associated with (1) the business cycle; (2) the restructuring of the production system; and (3) the contrasts in living standards and lifetime opportunities between Western Europe and the Third World. However, mass migration is also a political phenomenon. It is often political in its causes, is almost always politically contested in its occurrence, and typically has significant political outcomes (through its effects, for example, on international relations, and by 'bringing the outside in'). In this chapter we explore some of the important relationships between migrations, institutions and politics through an analysis of the development of both national and European Community migration policies over the last forty years.

The structure of the chapter is as simple as the reality being described is complex. It begins with a short section which sets out the main issues and provides some of the empirical context for what is to come. The second section is very largely descriptive. It examines the different migration policy developments in each of the main receiving countries of Western Europe. The third section draws the threads together by discussing some of the common themes which emerge from the different migration policy experiences. This leaves the final section to confront the political issues surrounding the mass migration aspects of European integration.

Issues and contexts

One might begin by asking the question: Why do states have migration policies? Why not let people choose where they want to live? This is not quite such a stupid question as it might seem at first glance. After all, although migration 'policies' are as old as history, as recently as the period just before the First World War there was little effective intervention in the international migration decisions of individuals. This situation was supported by classical political economists who argued as forcefully for free international movement of people as they did for the free movement of goods and capital. Even today there are those who argue strenuously against state intervention in migration. Some are neo-liberal economists (e.g. Simon 1990) who emphasize the advantages of immigration to high-income countries such as the United States. Others argue that the absence of permission to emigrate from a country or to immigrate to another constitutes a major limitation to an individual's human rights (Nett 1971). From this perspective constraints on mobility condemn people to suffer poverty and political oppression; leaving is therefore a form of free speech, it limits the exercise of tyrannical power, and encourages peaceful social change rather than revolution. Building walls to keep people in is an admission of the inadequacy of the system. To allow free movement would be to do away with the 'situational inopportunity' that millions of people suffer as a result of their place of birth. As Zolberg puts it, 'in a world characterised by widely varying conditions, international borders serve to maintain global inequality' (Zolberg 1989, p. 406).

It is not just the libertarian or neo-liberal positions, however, which might be invoked to question the wisdom of policy restrictions on international migration. One could point out that there is something rather strange about a world in which

1. the flow of information, capital, goods and people is vastly cheaper and faster than ever before;
2. this is accompanied by a growing de-localization of people's lives as they form more and more connections with people and places located in other countries; and yet
3. they are increasingly restricted by immigration rules to work and live in their country of present residence.

This is unjust since those who own capital can make a living by using that capital almost anywhere in the world; however, those who do not own capital and must make a living by selling their labour power can usually only do so in 'their' own country.

The reasons for having migration policies are also, of course, very powerful. Commentators on international relations, for example, point out that in the absence of state controls over immigration, one country could peacefully invade another by colonization. Their conclusion is that 'uncontrolled mass migration would threaten social cohesion, international solidarity and peace' (Widgren 1990, p. 749). Similarly, political theorists often defend national boundaries on the grounds that 'nation states constitute the most comprehensive level at which human beings have been able to develop liberal and democratic forms of political organisation . . . it is necessary to limit membership in some fashion so as to preserve a functioning political community'. Problems are compounded by newcomers who are culturally very different. Liberal democracies have a right to be prudent and hence to restrict their intake to a manageable level (Waltzer 1983).

The problem for the would-be international migrant lies not so much in obtaining permission to **leave** his/her country of origin, as in gaining permission to **enter** the country of destination. This is particularly so since 1989 when changes in the Soviet bloc resulted in a sharp reduction in the number of countries prohibiting or seriously restricting emigration. Nation-states have come to assume the right to determine who may and who may not enter 'their' territories; indeed, the degree of control over such movements is almost a measure of the sovereignty of the nation-state. Although there are international agreements and conventions (notably those relating to political refugees and to the treatment of migrant workers) which marginally limit the discretion of governments with respect to international migration, for the most part governments are free to decide how many people and what kinds of people may enter for purposes of temporary or permanent residence, and under what conditions they will live (Plender 1988).

So the situation is curiously fraught. Because there are so many movements of people for purposes other than migration, the cost in money, time and effort of that part of migration which consists of the physical movement of people from one country to another has been much reduced (in comparison, for example, with the mass migrations of the nineteenth century). Also because of the globalization of economic relationships, 'world cities' have seen their populations become highly cosmopolitan and culturally plural, thus providing a social base for the reception and insertion of new immigrants. Furthermore, employers in the high-income countries benefit greatly from 'unlimited supply of labour', and because of the growing international inequalities in wealth and well-being, the logic for mass migration is stronger than ever before. However, since the governments of nation-states are validated by their defence of 'national' interests, and since nations are defined by the differences in culture and history between 'their' populations and those of 'other' nations, it is necessary for governments to act, and to be seen to act, against uncontrolled immigration. This conflict of interest and of policy in industrialized societies — between maximizing labour supply (and flexibility) on the one hand and protecting a nation's cultural integrity on the other — is a dilemma which admits few easy solutions.

It follows that while international migrants connect with many institutions during their migration and settlement (airlines, firms, trade unions, banks, housing authorities, schools, health and welfare services, immigrant associations, religious institutions and the media), it is their contact with the apparatuses of the nation-state which are crucial in determining the nature of the immigration experience (central and local governments, immigration authorities, and the institutions of law and order — the police, law courts, and prisons).

While these policies and practices of the immigrant country's government are central in determining entry, the composition of the migration streams will be greatly affected by the relationships between people and their governments in other parts of the world. Suffering economic exploitation or political oppression (often both), individuals have the 'choice' between **voicing** their discontent (often impossible in practice) or **exiting** the system (that is, leaving the country). Many of the recent mass migrations to Western Europe have consisted of people who have suffered because their group does not conform with the cultural or political identity of the nation-state where they were previously resident. The tragedy is, of course, that they are also typically non-conforming to the norms and behaviours of the majority of the inhabitants of the country of destination, so that however accommodating the state policies of the immigration country, these people remain 'outside society', and as a result they become the target for racial abuse and for other forms of stigmatization and exclusion (Husbands 1988).

So much for some of the broad issues surrounding migration policy. What about the context of the migration policies of Western European countries over the last forty years? In the early post-war period, the buoyancy of the economies of the major industrial countries of Northern Europe led to labour shortages and the efforts of many governments in the planned recruitment and deployment of around 10 million immigrant workers (Salt and Clout 1976). By the mid-1970s, and precipitated by the 'oil crisis' of 1973/4, the conditions for a pursuit of pro-immigration policies had disappeared. Economic growth was far slower and such growth as existed was 'jobless' in nature, reflecting increases in productivity associated with technological and organizational improvements. By then there were large racial and ethnic minority populations in many cities in Western Europe, and with rising levels of unemployment, government immigration policies began to reflect the racist and xenophobic attitudes of their indigenous populations. Measures to block further primary migration led to a change in the nature of mass migrations to Western Europe. Most of the (far fewer) new entries were members of the families of the previous (mostly male) migrants. This altered the social character of immigrant communities in Western European countries, and at the same time enhanced the value of the permissions possessed by immigrants to reside and work in these countries. As a result, although return migration was considerable (at about 2 million), it never reached the levels required to reduce markedly the ethnic minority populations of these cities and regions (for a useful collection of papers on return migration policies, see Kubat 1984). As the inequalities in living standards between Western European countries and those in the Third World increased during the 1980s, the controls on immigration became ever more restrictive. This resulted in heightened levels of illegal immigration and a large increase in claims for refugee status, which for many people in the Third World became the only 'legitimate' path of entry left open to them. It also resulted in a change in the immigration status of Southern European countries which now became the destinations for migrants from Third World countries, although previously they had been the origins for 'guestworker' migrations to Northern Europe.

As if to add a final twist to the saga, the Soviet Union and its satellite states in Eastern Europe experienced a sudden 'implosion' of their state communist, command-economy systems in 1989–91. This has come to pose a double problem for the immigration policies of the countries of Western Europe. At the level of discourse, Western governments had been fierce in their attacks on the Soviet Union for its civil rights record, and in particular, its refusal to allow its citizens to emigrate. Now that restrictions on emigration were lifted, how could these same governments refuse entry to those who wanted to leave? However, at the level of material interests and practical politics, the political changes in Eastern Europe and the Soviet Union were followed by economic collapse and by violent inter-ethnic conflict (it is calculated, for example, that 1.2 million migrants crossed into Western Europe from the East in 1989, and that the wars in the former Yugoslavia in 1991–2 have created 3 million refugees). This added an extra challenge to the restrictive immigration policies of Western European governments. Given the economic recession of the early 1990s and the rising popularity of anti-immigrant political movements within their countries, how could these governments do other than refuse entry to migrants from the East?

This much-condensed account of the changing economic and political context of European migration policy lacks specificity. The fact is that each country in Western Europe has its own immigration laws, policies and practices reflecting the uniqueness of the country's geographical location, social and political history, economy and culture(s). Thus, although these countries share a single changing world context, their migration policy responses have been interestingly different one from another. These differences are examined in the next section.

The immigration policies of specific Western European countries

The immigration policies of specific countries can be thought of as combinations, changing from one period to the next, of five possible types of entry. These are:

1. unrestricted entry (for example, intra-EC flows);
2. promotional entry ('guestworkers' to Germany pre-1973);
3. permissive entry (managers and professionals of multinational companies);
4. selective entry (family reunion); and
5. prohibited entry (illegals).

Actual immigration experience is also a product of the five types of exit adopted by non-Western European countries. These are:

1. prohibited exit (for example, Eastern Europe and the Soviet Union pre-1989);
2. selective exit (the ban on the emigration of 'brain-drain' professionals);
3. permissive exit (most Western and Third World countries);
4. promotional exit (Turkey and Algeria in the 1960s); and
5. expulsion exit (Ugandan Asians in 1975).

Germany

The special position of Germany (West Germany for virtually the entire period covered here) regarding international mass migration arises from the importance of promotional entry: it was the country which received by far the largest number of guestworkers, whose stock stood at 2.6 million in 1973. This large number of guestworkers reflects not only the links made between the Federal government and those countries promoting exit, but also the size of its economy and the impressiveness of its economic growth. Historically, Germany had used imported temporary labour in this way, although the different conditions of the post-war period resulted in a contradiction between its stated migration policy ('Germany is not a country of immigration') and the facts of its post-war migration history, spelt out in more detail in Chapter 5. Rotation was the basic principle of the guestworker migration system. That is to say, the migrants were encouraged to come and work in (West) Germany as long as their labour was needed in the factories and on the building sites, although only on the basis of short-term contracts. At the termination of the contract, or perhaps after one or two renewals, the guestworkers would return to the Mediterranean countries from which they had migrated to be replaced by new primary migrants (Böhning 1984). This may have been the theory of German immigration policy. In practice, however, migration policy was far more complex than this.

First, the complexity arises from the fact that West Germany had different policies for different groups of migrants. For example, it had an 'open-door' policy towards 'ethnic' Germans — those from East Germany, and the descendants of German populations located to the east of the Oder–Neisse line (mostly in the territory of the former Soviet Union). In the early post-war period the movement of ethnic Germans westward supplied much of the labour required for the reconstruction of the West German economy. It was only after the Berlin Wall had been built in 1961 that such migrations ceased to a trickle and the use of foreign labour from the Mediterranean countries began in earnest. Initially, Italians had formed the bulk of the migrants; however, as the economic 'miracle' proceeded, new sources of manual labour were called for. Inter-governmental agreements were negotiated with Greece and Spain (1960), Turkey (1961 and 1964), Morocco (1963), Portugal (1964), Tunisia (1965) and Yugoslavia (1968), under which, in strictly controlled circumstances, large numbers of young, healthy male temporary workers were recruited to meet the labour needs of major German employers, mostly in manufacturing industry. The workers were housed in hostels, and their physical separation from the host population matched their economic and political status within the country. They had minimal rights, could not vote, and could be deported.

The second complexity derives from the fact that despite the short-term nature of the contracts and the low social and civil status attached to the guestworkers, a certain number of them settled down and inserted themselves into German society. So much so that when the boom came to an end in the early to mid-1970s, and facing the risk of not being able to return, owing to the ban on further primary migration, the vast majority of the guestworkers, now increasingly accompanied by members of their families who had joined them in Germany, stayed on. Of course, one reason for this was that the economic crisis was hitting the economies of the countries they had left, making return migration a risky and unattractive option. Also, other policies such as the family allowance system helped to bring about this change from guestworker to immigrant. However, probably most important of all was the development of social ties in Germany itself, especially those with other members of the immigrant community. Immigrants learnt German and became accustomed to the way things were done in Germany (shopping, schools, hospitals, leisure and entertainment). This 'embedding' process had gone so far that by 1982, 47.5 per cent of all foreigners had been in the country for more than ten years and the policy then enacted to provide subsidies for return had little effect.

The third complexity arises from Germany's geographical location and the events of the most recent period, considered in more detail in Chapter 14. The out-migration from the former Warsaw Pact countries of Eastern Europe towards West Germany was both a symptom of the collapse of the Soviet-dominated state communist system and also a trigger which hastened and completed that collapse. Now the 'open-door' policy towards ethnic Germans resulted in sizeable migrations (71 per cent of the 1.2 million immigrants in 1989 were ethnic Germans). Partly as a result of these changes in the East, and partly owing to events in the Third World as well, the number of migrants claiming political asylum increased dramatically in the late 1980s and early 1990s, and legislation was brought in to speed up the processing of applications for refugee status. The rise of the new Right in the now reunited Germany, shown by the growth in popular support for the Republican Party, has pushed the German government into a much more restrictive stance on immigration, and the signs are that this policy position will continue well into the 1990s.

France

The distinctive features of French immigration policy derive from the fact that France engaged in both unrestricted entry (for many migrants from former colonies) and promoted entry (from the Mediterranean region). France's relative location has meant that its links have tended to be with south-west Europe and North Africa. The historical basis of French establishment attitudes towards immigration can be found in two widely-shared views about France and French culture. The first is that the country is demographically flawed in that its fertility rates have historically been so low that the population was barely succeeding in reproducing itself. Out of this came a strong pro-natalism, reflected in generous social welfare support for child-rearing, and an acceptance of the necessity for immigration. The second view is that racial or ethnic background mattered far less than the quality of being francophile, that is **culturally** French. This partly explains the fact that certain French overseas territories, populated by black people (notably the French Caribbean islands and Réunion) became administratively part of France, with all that this implies in terms of social, economic and political rights, including that of unrestricted entry to France.

In practice, French migration policy in the post-war period has not been as liberal or as enlightened as this picture would lead one to expect, for several reasons. First, the French Immigration Office processed only a part of the immigration stream and a sizeable illegal migrant population came into being. While many migrants from North Africa had citizenship rights in France, those from other countries (notably Portugal) did not. The government went in for 'amnesties' which allowed a regularization of the residence status of illegal migrants after the fact of their migration and settlement. Second, the decolonization was an extremely painful process, particularly in Algeria and also in Indo-China. This led to the return to France of a sizeable embittered colonial settler population (especially the *pieds noirs* from Algeria in 1962). However, the struggles of former colonial peoples for independence also represented a complete rejection of 'Frenchness' as a force uniting black and white, rich and poor, Christian and Muslim. Indeed, one of the main political forces shaping migration policy in the recent period has been the rise of anti-immigrant feeling. Le Pen, the leader of the right-wing National Front Party, won 14.4 per cent of the vote in the first round of the presidential elections in 1988. Third, the rather generous image of French immigration policy was tarnished after the mid-1970s when the French government fell into line with the Germans in adopting strong anti-immigration policies. However, family reunion proceeded apace and there was a growth of clandestine migration. The Mitterrand government took steps to legalize the status of many of these migrants in 1981, although subsequent measures have further restricted the legitimate entry of Third World migrants into France (Hollifield and Ross 1991).

United Kingdom

The United Kingdom is unusual among the main immigration countries in north-west Europe partly because throughout the post-war period it was almost as much a country of emigration as of immigration, and more particularly because its immigrants were for the most part British citizens. This contrasts with those in other countries who were pre-dominantly permanent residents with economic and social rights although without political rights — what Hammar (1985) calls 'denizens'. The United Kingdom's post-war immigration policies cannot, of course, be divorced from its colonial history. In the early part of the period the right of Commonwealth citizens to enter the United Kingdom was firmly established. Yet from 1962 onwards this policy of providing privileged access to Commonwealth citizens was reversed and a quota system established which strictly controlled and reduced to a low level the numbers of Afro-Caribbean and Asian primary migrants permitted to settle in the country.

Thus a predisposition against immigration was established early. It was tested by events in East Africa during the 1970s when post-independence 'Africanization' policies implied the expulsion of large numbers of East African Asians holding British passports. Many of these expellees were accommodated in the United Kingdom, although not without political controversy and racist agitation. South Asian family reunion then became the principal form of Third World migration to the United Kingdom during the 1980s, even if the obstacles placed in the way of such migrations were formidable, mainly owing to the influence on policy of the anti-immigration feeling shared by large sections of the population. Governments could not afford to ignore this feeling and justified severe limitations on 'coloured immigration' on the grounds that these were necessary to ensure good race relations in the country.

However, it is not only its particular colonial ties with the Caribbean and South Asia that places UK migration policies in a different category from those of other West European countries. First, mass migration to Britain has for generations been dominated not by Third World migrants but by the Irish, and despite the sometimes stormy political relationship between the two states since Irish independence in 1923, free movement provisions for Irish migrants to Britain have prevailed and they have been accorded virtually all the rights of UK citizens. Second, British governments have been especially inventive in formulating immigration legislation which, while not racially discriminatory in the letter, is fully discriminatory in its application. This point applies in particular to the concept of 'patriality'. By being able to demonstrate a historical family link, a white-skinned migrant from India or Africa can obtain entry to the United Kingdom whereas a fellow black or brown-skinned migrant could not. Third, as an island, Britain has controlled immigration largely through the 'ports' of entry (such as London's Heathrow and Gatwick

Airports) and illegal entry is thought to be rare (Dummett and Nicol 1990). This has implications for the monitoring and control of the movement of non-nationals within the country, because (unlike the situation in other European countries where forms of registration, sometimes connected to personal identity numbers are the norm) it is difficult in the United Kingdom to reduce the numbers of 'overstayers', that is, those who entered legally, and have exceeded their permitted duration of stay.

Benelux countries

Both The Netherlands and Belgium had colonial pasts which have affected their immigration regimes in the post-war period. This is especially true in The Netherlands which experienced considerable immigration as a result of the early post-war decolonization of Indonesia, and an influx of Surinamese around the time of independence in 1975. However, in both The Netherlands and Belgium immigration policy has been largely addressed to the migration of 'guestworkers' from Southern Europe, Morocco and Turkey. Dutch social legislation affecting immigrant groups is far more liberal and progressive than that in most other European countries (housing policy — described in Chapter 7 — is particularly noteworthy in this respect). Nevertheless, difficult issues of principle and practical policy remain, for example the question of whether or not state agencies should engage in the 'forced' desegregation of schools. In Belgium the problem of cultural identity assumes special importance. Not only is the country bi-cultural (Flemish and Walloon), with large immigrant minorities from Mediterranean and Third World backgrounds, but it is also uniquely pluralistic in its European cultural presence owing to the location of very many European institutions and agencies in Brussels. The location of similar and related institutions in Luxemburg poses similar problems for that small country.

Nordic countries

Perhaps partly because of their northern location, mass migrations have not, except in Sweden, been a major feature of post-war Scandinavian societies. However, two qualifications need to be made to this generalization. The first is that Sweden, Norway and Denmark belong to the Nordic Area in which there is free movement of labour, and in one case — that of the migration of Finns to Sweden — the international migration is of sufficient size and cultural significance to warrant the description 'mass migration'. The second qualification is that, partly owing to their 'internationalism' and to their well-deserved reputations for fair and sensitive treatments of foreign nationals (including encouragement of naturalization), Scandinavian countries, notably Sweden, have been the destination for many asylum-seekers. As a result, refugee communities of people from countries such as Chile and 'Kurdistan' have come into being in cities like Stockholm and Uppsala, producing a considerable cultural diversity.

Switzerland and Austria

Switzerland and Austria reflect immigration policy situations which are almost the exact opposite to those of the Scandinavian countries. First, although of a commensurate population size, the volume of immigration (and therefore the perceived threat to national identity) is far greater (for Switzerland in particular) than it is for countries like Sweden. This is partly, perhaps, because of relative location, since both Switzerland and Austria lie astride the guestworker travel routes from south-eastern Europe and Turkey to the industrial cities in West Germany and the Low Countries. Thus they were the first high-income countries that the migrants reached in their travels northwards from the depressed rural regions of Europe's eastern Mediterranean periphery. Second, however, Switzerland and Austria have had long traditions of anti-immigrant and anti-ethnic minority politics. In Switzerland this was reflected in the attempts (through the Schwarzenbach referenda) to keep Switzerland 'for the Swiss'. As a result, not only have policies been highly restrictive over most of the post-war period, but the manner in which these policies have been executed has also been inquisitorially and unyieldingly firm. Naturalizations, for example, have been at a low level despite the dependence of certain key sectors of the Alpine economy (for example, tourism) on the use of foreign (often seasonal) labour.

The countries of Southern Europe

Consideration of the policy aspects of mass migrations in these countries would tend historically to regard them as countries of emigration. However, recently Italy, Spain, Portugal and Greece have become countries of immigration, and in particular, it is thought, of illegal immigration (Munoz-Perez and Izquierdo Escribano 1989). This is explained partly by their location, linking as they do the continents of Europe and Africa, partly by the residual effects of African colonial influences, and partly by inadequate methods of surveillance and control. It is this last feature which accounts for Italy's current reputation as the 'soft underbelly of Europe' (see Chapter 15).

All of these countries were partners to either France or Germany during the build-up of the guestworker migrant labour system in the 1960s. Promoted exit was seen as a means of reducing unemployment and social and political unrest at home, while also providing both foreign exchange in the form of remittances sent home by the migrants and industrial experience likely to lead to the technological modernization of the sending countries. As we now know, some of these expectations remain unrealized, although the individual improvement of living conditions in many Southern European villages (housing modernization and the purchase of domestic appliances, televisions and cars) has greatly altered the quality of life in such areas.

Migration laws, policies and practices in Western Europe: common themes and tendencies

Despite the national differences discussed above, a number of common themes and tendencies in the evolution of Western European migration policies can be detected. For useful overviews of West European immigration policies, see Hammar 1985, Rogers 1985, Brubaker 1989 and Bovenkerk *et al.* 1990.

The colonial legacy

About half of the major countries of Western Europe have had their post-war migration policies shaped by the fact that they had been, or were still, colonial powers with Third World colonial 'possessions' (United Kingdom, France, Netherlands, Belgium, Italy, Spain and Portugal). What effects did these colonial pasts have? First, and most obviously, they resulted in commercial, linguistic, informational and affinity channels along which the migrants passed. A stereotypical picture would be of a Caribbean living-room with a coronation portrait of Queen Elizabeth II on the wall, in which a young man is reading an English language newspaper containing advertisements for jobs as conductors on London Transport buses. Second, and less obviously perhaps, is the way that these colonial pasts have influenced the nature of racial attitudes among Western European populations. The outcome of this migration from former colonial territories is what some have called 'the Third World within' or 'internal colonialism', implying that the result is nothing less than a geographical displacement of the social conditions of the Third World (and of the exploitative relations between colonizer and colonized) from the former colonial territories to the major industrial and commercial cities of Western Europe.

Institutionalized labour migration: the guestworker system

All of the governments of the advanced capitalist countries of north-west Europe (West Germany, France, United Kingdom, Netherlands, Belgium and Sweden) participated, though to different degrees, in the sponsored migration of manual workers at some time during the thirty years of rapid economic growth following the end of the Second World War. Rising incomes were both the product of economic growth and a major stimulus to that growth since they were spent on new houses, cars, furnishings, 'white goods', and leisure and entertainment. However, with rising incomes came rising expectations, and a shortage of labour in these countries (and especially in the large industrial cities) meant that it was difficult to recruit indigenous workers for the lowest-paid, most-routine, dirtiest, most hazardous, or lowest status jobs. Arrangements were established through inter-governmental agreements whereby national immigration offices in the destination countries would orchestrate the 'guestworker' migration system, matching employers and workers, setting conditions for the issuing of work permits, and overseeing the vetting of prospective migrants. Mass labour migration in early post-war Europe was a product of planned state intervention to a degree probably unmatched either before or since (Castles *et al.* 1984).

The 'crisis'

Before the oil crisis of 1973/4 the variations in migration policy between the countries of Western Europe had (despite the two common themes discussed above) reflected those countries' individual histories and divergent interests. This all changed as a result of the crisis. Suddenly the countries of Western Europe seemed to step into line on the question of immigration. Whatever the previous position had been, governments now passed legislation to ban or very seriously restrict further primary migration. The migrants from former colonies were turned back, the guestworker system dismantled. Several countries went so far as to set up funds for the purpose of encouraging or facilitating return migration. The intention was to halt completely mass migration to Western Europe. That these measures did not do so was, first, because of the strength of the momentum behind the international migration (which meant that much of the migration became clandestine), and second, because of the continuity of many of the key relationships (for example, the responsibilities of former colonial powers for oppressed or threatened minorities in former colonial territories). Above all, the primary migration of young men gave way to various forms of family reunion (migration of spouses, children and elderly parents). So a common theme of the period after 1974 was that while the official policy was for no further immigration, the reality was more complex and included 'secondary' migration (which of course implies the immigration of many people who will eventually enter the labour market in the destination countries) and illegal immigration.

Migration of women

Only a small proportion of the first wave of guestworker migrants were women, and it was only subsequently that women came to form the larger part of the migration streams. The migration from former colonial territories was rather different. In many cases this was **family** migration from the outset, though in certain instances the bias was towards the migration of women (as in the recruitment of medical and domestic staffs). The main policy issues on the migration of women and children concern the manner in which existing practices in service provision (housing, health, education and social welfare) served to exclude migrant families. Slowly, changes in law and practice were made which recognized the **social embeddedness** of the migrants' families and the equality of their needs with those of the poorer sections of the indigenous population.

The social and political status of immigrants

Mass migrations to the countries of Western Europe have brought into being new ethnic minority communities in many cities and regions, their populations economically and socially inserted (although not, for the most part, integrated) into the host society. The political status of these populations, however, does not match, in general, the contribution they make to the economy and society. While they generally have rights to permanent residence, levels of naturalization are extremely low. For this reason, most of Western Europe's immigrants are denied political rights such as voting in general elections, and participation in formal politics is minimal (Layton-Henry 1990). This is not to say, however, that there is a total lack of political and cultural mobilization of ethnic minority populations. Immigrant associations abound, and organization around issues such as discrimination in the job and housing markets, racial harassment, defence of religious observance, and the content of school curricula has become a common occurrence (Rex *et al.* 1987). The big issue, of course, is that of citizenship. The countries of Western Europe are slowly facing up to the fact that the migrants and their families are 'here to stay' and that it is difficult to withhold permanently the rights of citizenship from those who are required to fulfil the responsibilities of citizenship such as payment of taxes (Wihtol de Wenden 1991).

The 'second generation'

The post-1945 mass migrations to Western Europe peaked initially in the immediate post-war years, then reached a second, higher peak in the early 1970s, and seem now to be building up to a third peak in the early

1990s. Already by the end of the 1970s there was a sizeable 'second generation' of immigrants — young people born, socialized and acculturated in the countries of Western Europe. State institutions in these countries were forced to reconsider policies and practices in the light of the fact that large proportions of young people were 'between two cultures' — or, to be more accurate, were engaged in the creation of new cultural identities which differed from those of both their parents and the host society (Liebkind 1989). Inevitably, it was the state education services which were the initial sites for these adjustments; schools in large industrial cities came to have first a large minority of children from immigrant backgrounds, then in many cases a majority of children from such backgrounds. These children grew up to become adults with different expectations and aspirations from their parents; the expectations of the second generation were rooted in the experiences of the host population as these were communicated through television and the popular press. Such expectations were often dashed as these young people entered the labour market (Wilpert 1988). Unemployment rates for ethnic minorities became far higher than those for the host population, and discrimination against 'immigrants' often took forms which were too well hidden to be combated by anti-racist or equal opportunities legislation.

Socio-spatial segregation of ethnic minorities

Although Western European central and local governments did not plan the spatial segregation of ethnic minorities, they condoned processes which helped to produce and sustain such segregation. A good example of this is the way that the rules of access to 'social' housing tended initially to exclude members of ethnic minorities, and subsequently to ensure a concentration of ethnic minority households in particular (usually low quality and low status) parts of the housing stock. However, the main force shaping the segregation of ethnic minority populations was their poverty — they tended to find themselves in those parts of the city which contained the cheapest accommodation (see Chapter 4). Sometimes this was located on the periphery of the city where, in the early period, and even latterly in Southern Europe, shanty towns of 'informal' housing were to be found. More usually, however, it was the older housing of the poorer inner suburbs which became the main focus for such minorities. As such populations grew, the bases for settled community life also developed. Places of religious observance tailored to the needs of the ethnic minority became available (mosques, churches, temples), as did specialist shops, restaurants, clubs, and even banks and schools (for example, Qur'anic schools). This, and the fear of racist or nationalist hostility in other parts of the city, encouraged the spatial grouping of the members of these ethnic minorities (Glebe and O'Loughlin 1987).

Anti-immigrant politics

In addition to the day-by-day harassment of members of ethnic minority groups, Western Europe witnessed the uneven development of racist political movements and 'anti-immigrant' political parties. The basic unit of social organization at the aggregate level in Western Europe is the nation-state, and nation-states call forth a distinction between 'us' (the members of our nation-state) and 'them' (the non-members). It has proved difficult in the extreme for governments and intellectuals to persuade 'ordinary' people that collective effort for 'us' (working in the 'national interest') is a good thing, while at the same time contending that the category 'us' includes people who are different from most of us in skin colour, and/or language, and/or religious affiliation. For one group of people (extending beyond those who are particularly ignorant or inadequate), such efforts are to no avail. They see their own problems (low pay, unemployment, low quality housing, poor schooling, etc.) as arising from the presence of 'them', that is, the socially and culturally non-conforming members of their own society. As Chapter 8 shows, the political movements which draw support from such people are primarily of the authoritarian right (the National Front in France and Britain, the Republican Party in Germany), although institutions of the left have also flirted with such values, notably some labour unions. Even the parties of the social and liberal democratic centre have differed in their stances on 'immigrants': some seek integration and assimilation, others accept the compromises with national identity implied by the notion of a 'multi-cultural society'. As for the 'immigrants' themselves, there is a strong tendency (where they have the right to do so) for their members to support existing parties of the Centre-left, although as social class divisions develop within the ethnic minority communities, successful owners of small or medium-sized businesses have often come to support the parties of the neo-liberal Right.

Illegal immigration

The prejudices against non-conforming minorities discussed above are also expressed in the mental association that many members of the host population make between ethnic minorities and illegal activities such as 'street crime', drug-dealing, theft and crimes of violence. Not all 'immigrants' are law-abiding of course, but then nor are the equally poor (although less stigmatized) members of the host population. The problem is that the law is not always equal in its effects on communities possessing different cultural traits. For example, while the abuse of alcohol is widespread among the indigenous population of Britain, it is rare among the members of the Afro-Caribbean community and is not illegal, whereas the smoking of marijuana is widespread among the Afro-

Caribbean population, rare among British whites, and is illegal. The relationships between the agents of law and order — the police — and the members of ethnic minorities (especially young adult males) sometimes deteriorate to such an extent that general lawlessness (arson and looting) can erupt in outbursts of 'popular violence'. The main problem, however, facing many immigrants and their family members is the legality of their status within the West European city. As immigration rules have become increasingly restrictive, a growing proportion of immigrants have found the legitimacy of their residence undermined. With no rights and no means of achieving redress, they become prey to extreme forms of exploitation. Many European governments have adopted measures to discover the presence of illegal immigrants (notably by the inspection of workplaces); however, in countries where it is not a requirement that one carries identity papers or residence documentation, monitoring illegal immigrants is more difficult.

The refugee 'crisis'

One group of migrants to the countries of Western Europe — political refugees — should in theory be free from these problems of harassment by the authorities over their status as immigrants. Under international agreements the countries of Western Europe are required to welcome those whose lives and fundamental freedoms are threatened by the governments of their own countries. Most large European cities have small refugee communities as a result of the political oppressions of the post-war period (Chileans, Kurds, Hungarians, South Africans and Tibetans). However, the oppressions of the Third World are so many, the wars so frequent, and the treatment of ethnic minorities and political dissidents so unjust, that the number of asylum-seekers has increased enormously over the period, and especially so in the last few years (Loescher and Monaghan 1989). The problem for the governments in the destination countries is that there is no valid mechanism for distinguishing between true 'political' refugees and the many migrants who are attempting to escape poverty. This is hardly surprising since political corruption and state-sponsored violence tend to correlate closely with economic exploitation. The effect of a clampdown on 'spurious' refugee applications is that 80 per cent of the 1.6 million requests to EC and European Free Trade Association (EFTA) countries for asylum made between 1983 and 1990 were turned down. However, it is thought that a majority of these unsuccessful applicants stayed on, thus boosting the ranks of illegals.

Migration of highly qualified manpower

Most of the common themes in European migration policy and practice discussed above relate only to the migration of manual workers. However, highly qualified people also migrate to Western Europe — from Third World countries (for example, Indian doctors), from non-European advanced capitalist countries (for example, Japanese bankers), and from other European countries (for example, the professional and managerial staffs of multinational companies and organizations). These migrations take place under dispensations which allow governments to issue work and residence permits for qualified workers in important posts in the host economy. Thus there is some substance to the argument that the immigration laws and practices of the destination countries are class as well as colour-biased. In general, it is not difficult for a wealthy businessman or high status professional to obtain entry first and citizenship later, whereas someone who is poor or unqualified will be excluded (notice, for example, the class bias in the arrangements for the migration to Britain of the Chinese who wish to leave Hong Kong before 1997). These migrations of the highly qualified, although individually contracted, have reached such a level that they might well qualify for the description of 'mass migration' (see Chapter 16). The large net migration streams of foreign professionals and managers to cities such as Brussels, Amsterdam, Dusseldorf, Paris and London have contributed considerably to the population growth of these cities and have greatly altered their cultural and social compositions. The international migration of students (including many from the Third World) is having a similar effect on some of the main university cities of Western Europe (for example, Florence, Utrecht, Heidelberg and Montpellier).

International retirement migration

Finally, one 'mass' migration which is often ignored is that which produces a permanent Northern European presence in Southern Europe — the migration of the 'young' old and the footloose, and of those who provide services for them, towards the sunnier and more scenically attractive areas of the Mediterranean littoral and countryside. This migration has occurred despite the marked national differences in land and property systems, and in health care provisions, so that sizeable cultural enclaves in parts of south-eastern Spain, southern Portugal and central Italy already exist.

Summary

To summarize, a picture of diverse national immigration regimes and policies for the period up to 1973/4 containing both ex-colonial and guestworker elements, was thereafter replaced by regimes that stressed just one thing: immigration control. Heightened restrictions, however, have not stopped mass migrations to Western Europe. Some of these migrations were sanctioned, albeit reluctantly (notably refugee flows and family reunions); others were not. In any event, by now there has come into being a very large ethnic minority population in Western Europe, heavily concentrated in the largest industrial cities (Gerholm and Lithman 1989). This presence has brought about changes in perspective and practice on the part of many institutions. Central and local governments, firms and trade unions, health, housing, education and social welfare service providers, and the media, have all had to adjust to the fact that the societies of Western Europe today are, as a result of the mass migrations of the post-Second World War period, truly **multicultural** in character.

The European Community and migration

Until now the emphasis has been entirely on the national migration policies of the fifteen or so main Western European countries. However, for a subset of these countries, initially six, then nine, then ten and now twelve, the free movement clauses of the Rome Treaty setting up the European Common Market apply. This final section of the chapter discusses this European dimension of the mass migration issues already discussed above.

The free movement of labour

Under the Rome Treaty a citizen of one member country can migrate to another EC country for work purposes or to seek work. This is seen as an essential prerequisite for the establishment of a European Common Market because such a market requires free trade and the unfettered mobility of the factors of production, notably capital and labour. In practice, of course, the right to work in another country of the EC is fairly useless unless qualifications gained in one country are regarded as valid in the other. An important part of the process of completing the Single European Market (SEM) in 1992 is concerned precisely with this issue and with the lifting of the remaining restrictions on the migration of labour from Spain and Portugal. Migration considerations are sure to play an important role in discussions about the enlargement of the European Community in the post-Soviet Union period that we are now entering (Baldwin-Edwards 1991).

The historical record: migration, trade and the mobility of capital

How these discussions about future enlargement will progress will depend in part on our understanding of the role that European integration has played in promoting international migration in the past. At the time of the signing of the Rome Treaty in 1957 it was thought likely that the free movement of labour stipulations would produce heightened flows from the rural low-income regions of southern Italy and western France to the urban industrial high-income regions of north-western Europe. For the most part this did not happen. Instead of people moving, goods and capital moved (Molle and van Mourik 1988). The mass migrations of the 1960s and early 1970s were almost entirely from countries **outside** the European Community. Similar predictions of mass migrations between member states accompanied the later enlargements when the United Kingdom, Ireland and Denmark entered, when Greece became a member, and now that Spain and Portugal have joined. It is not that migrations between the member countries do not occur, it is that such migrations tend to form parts of middle-class work histories rather than assuming the form of mass migrations of manual workers. In part, of course, the explanation for the lack of these mass migrations within the European Community lies in the high rates of economic growth experienced by the countries of the Southern European periphery in the 1970s and 1980s. Also important is that the opening up of EC markets for the goods and services provided by peripheral regions has sometimes helped to stabilize employment and reduce emigration. However, perhaps most important of all has been the movement of new investment into the emigration regions. Capital mobility has to some extent substituted for labour mobility (see Chapter 1 above); the rapidly expanding firms of the core regions of Western Europe have seen profitable opportunities arising through the decentralization of parts of their production to the European periphery. This stems emigration and provides the basis for labour-intensive service employment growth in the periphery.

The present situation: SEM, Trevi and Schengen

Does this mean that '1992' — the completion of the Single European Market — has little significance for our discussion of mass migration policy? Not necessarily. The argument runs like this. Previous stages of European integration occurred at times when manual worker mobility remained important and when the 'globalization' of economic relations was only in its early stages. In 1992 both of these contexts have changed. Now it is the mobility of the members of the 'service class' of professional, technical and managerial employees which is dominant. Service-class mobility is not only higher than working-class mobility, it is also more spatially extensive. And it is the service class which is most implicated in the globalization of economic relations which has proceeded so rapidly in the recent past. This means that international migrations to and between European 'global' cities might be expected to increase very considerably during the 1990s. There are signs that this is already happening in the migration of Irish graduates to continental European cities such as Paris and Munich, and in the increasing role of international service-class migrations in the population changes of cities such as London. Chapters 16 and 17 towards the end of this book pick up on some of these issues.

European economic integration, however, implying as it does the unhindered movement of people and goods across the international boundaries of the EC member states, has raised problems of a political and social nature. It is now far easier for political undesirables (such as terrorists) or for undesirable substances (such as hard drugs and weapons) to pass across these boundaries. The Trevi Group was established in 1986 to consider ways of monitoring and controlling such movements. It sets up the mechanisms for cross-border co-operation on matters relating to serious crime and national security, and because this implies the international exchange of information on individuals it has attracted the attention of those defending civil rights. The Schengen Agreement, signed in 1985, was a forerunner of the post-1992 situation in which it is intended that all internal frontier controls within the European Community will be abolished. It applied to the Benelux countries, France and West Germany, and consisted of steps necessary to abolish the controls and to prevent any abuse which might arise as a result of their disappearance. In these ways during the 1980s the European Community was moving towards the goal of a truly integrated social and economic space.

European Monetary and Political Union

Further steps towards European Union were taken at the signing of the Maastricht Treaty in 1991. At the time of writing it is not clear to what extent Maastricht will be put into effect — the political momentum towards unification, and specifically towards the creation of a federal European state has largely disappeared (though perhaps only temporarily so). The significance of these further steps towards unification for migration policy lies in the possible outcomes from European Monetary Union (EMU). Until now it has been possible for national governments within the European Community to protect the incomes and levels of employment of those who live in their most backward regions by adjustments to the exchange rate. A devaluation of the currency should mean an increase in exports and a decrease in imports, which ought to lead to higher levels of growth, the creation of new job opportunities, and the spatial decentralization of investment towards peripheral and backward regions as firms seek out cheaper sites and reserves of labour. EMU takes away this possibility and might be expected, therefore, to lead to sharp increases in regional inequalities. These widening differences in living standards and employment opportunities would be likely, it is argued, to give rise to new patterns of inter-regional and international migration. The resources of the European Community's structural funds would need to be far greater than is presently envisaged for EC intervention to be capable of counteracting such inequalities.

Present EC policy on immigration

As a way of bringing this chapter to a close, we can examine the latest EC Commission policy statement on immigration to see what the current priorities are and how it is envisaged that the problems arising from immigration will be tackled (Commission of the EC 1992). There are three elements in the present EC policy position. The first is that while meeting international obligations with respect to refugee migrations to the EC, the general posture of the Community towards immigration is a negative one, that is, that further immigration into Western Europe from the South and East is to be firmly discouraged. The second element is concerned with the ethnic minority populations already present in the countries of Western Europe. The Commission proposes that every step necessary for a progressive integration of these populations within their host societies should be taken. The third and final element is in some ways the most interesting (and the most unrealistic). It is that the European Community should foster such relations with the countries from which the migrants to Europe would come in order to ensure, through development aid, that the need for such migrations would cease. It is difficult to take this proposal seriously. The degree of political and economic commitment to Third World and former Soviet bloc development which would be needed to produce this outcome is surely not at present, or in the foreseeable future, in the realms of the politically possible.

References

Baldwin-Edwards, M., 1991, 'Immigration after 1992', *Policy and Politics*, 19(3): 199–211.
Böhning, W.R., 1984, *Studies in international labour migration*, Macmillan, London.
Bovenkerk, F., Miles, R. and Verbunt, G., 1990, 'Racism, migration and the state in Western Europe', *International Sociology*, 5(4): 475–90.
Brubaker, W.R. (ed.) 1989, *Immigration and the politics of citizenship in Europe and North America*, University Press of America, Lanham, Maryland.
Castles, S., Booth, H. and Wallace, T., 1984, *Here for good: Western Europe's new ethnic minorities*, Pluto Press, London.

Commission of the EC, 1992, *Immigration and Asylum (Background Report)*, ISEC/B6/92, London.

Dummett, A. and Nicol, A., 1990, *Subjects, citizens, aliens and others: nationality and immigration law*, Weidenfeld and Nicolson, London.

Gerholm, T. and Lithman, Y.G. (eds), 1989, *The new Islamic presence in Western Europe*, Mansell, London.

Glebe, G. and O'Loughlin, J. (eds), 1987, *Foreign minorities in continental European cities*, Steiner, Wiesbaden.

Hammar, T. (ed.), 1985, *European immigration policy: a comparative study*, Cambridge University Press, Cambridge.

Hollifield, J.F. and Ross, G. (eds), 1991, *Searching for the new France*, Routledge, London.

Husbands, C.T., 1988, The dynamics of racial exclusion and expulsion: racist politics in Western Europe, *European Journal of Political Research*, 16(6): 701–20.

Kubat, D. (ed.), 1984, *The politics of return: international return migration in Europe*, Center for Migration Studies, New York.

Layton-Henry, Z. (ed.), 1990, *The political rights of migrant workers in Western Europe*, Sage, London.

Liebkind, K. (ed.) 1989, *New identities in Europe: immigrant ancestry and the ethnic identity of youth*, Gower, Aldershot.

Loescher, G. and Monaghan, L. (eds), 1989, *Refugees and international relations*, Oxford University Press, Oxford.

Molle, W. and van Mourik, A., 1988, 'International movements of labour under conditions of economic integration: the case of Western Europe', *Journal of Common Market Studies*, 26(3): 317–42.

Munoz-Perez, F. and Izquierdo Escribano, A., 1989, 'L'Espagne, pays d'immigration', *Population*, 44(2): 257–89.

Nett, R., 1971, 'The civil right we are not ready for: the right of free movement of people on the face of the earth', *Ethics*, 81(3): 212–27.

Plender, R., 1988, *International migration law*, Nijhoff, Dordrecht.

Rex, J., Joly, D. and Wilpert, C. (eds), 1987, *Immigrant associations in Europe*, Gower, Aldershot.

Rogers, R.M. (ed.), 1985, *Guests come to stay: the effects of European labour migration on sending and receiving countries*, Westview Press, Colorado.

Salt, J. and Clout, H. (eds), 1976, *Migration in post-war Europe: geographical essays*, Oxford University Press, London.

Simon, J.L., 1990, *The economic consequences of immigration*, Blackwell, London.

Waltzer, M., 1983, *Spheres of justice: a defence of pluralism and equality*, Basic Books, New York.

Widgren, J., 1990, 'International migration and regional stability', *International Affairs*, 66(4): 749–66.

Wihtol de Wenden, C., 1991, 'Immigration policy and the issue of nationality', *Ethnic and Racial Studies*, 14(3): 319–32.

Wilpert, C. (ed.), 1988, *Entering the working world: following the descendants of Europe's immigrant labour force*, Gower, Aldershot.

Zolberg, A. R., 1989, 'The next waves: migration theory for a changing world', *International Migration Review*, 23(3): 403–30.

Part 2: Legacies

Chapter 4

Immigrants and the social geography of European cities

Paul White

The salience of the issues

The presence of ethnic minority populations in Western European cities is part of the everyday experience of all urban residents. The Pakistani corner shop in Britain and the local 'Arab' grocer in France; market stalls and specialist shops offering foodstuffs from other cultures, and the particular clientele attracted; the presence of exotic restaurants — Italian, Greek, Indian, North African, Chinese: these and many other features form part of the 'taken-for-granted' world of city-dwellers throughout the greater part of Western Europe.

To these observational phenomena are added the consciousness of media and political discussion of ethnic minority presences, misleading though some of this discussion may be — of demonstrations concerning the Rushdie affair in the United Kingdom, of the media association of second-generation youth with violence and delinquency in suburban housing estates in France, of policies of voluntary repatriation in various countries, and discussion of the creation of ghettos with the resultant 'labelling' of certain districts such as Brixton in London, la Goutte d'Or in Paris, or Kreuzberg in Berlin.

These levels of experience and consciousness are the paths by which the mass migrations of the post-war years have impinged upon the lives of non-migrant urban residents. The influxes of labour which started during the years of economic reconstruction, and which later developed into family movement, have created whole communities of ethnic minorities in most large European cities. The purpose of this chapter is to examine how these developments have been accommodated within the social geographical structure of Western European cities, and to identify the evolutionary contemporary processes at work. Particular attention will be paid to the partly interrelated issues of housing and of neighbourhood change.

There are dangers in attempting too facile a series of generalizations about these issues. A distinctive feature of the West European scene in immigration and ethnic minority formation, as in so many other social and economic dimensions, is diversity. Ethnic minorities in Western

Europe today have been drawn from very varied cultural and geographical origins, and have arrived in response to different economic and political circumstances. We should not expect the evolutionary scenarios affecting the original guestworker groups in Germany and Austria, the post-colonial movement of the Surinamese to The Netherlands, the Chinese refugee arrivals from South-East Asia in France, or the post-industrial (and often clandestine) migration from Third World countries into Italy and Spain to parallel one another. Whilst a certain set of controlling factors have been present in each case, the actual outcomes have been contingent upon local conditions within receiving countries, upon specific features of the migration groups, and on the timing of developments within the economic and political cycles of the post-war years.

This chapter deals only with post-war international flows, although it is clear that certain emergent effects on the social geography of destination cities mirror the impacts of international movements in earlier decades, and of recent internal rural–urban migration within certain Southern European countries.

It is very difficult to produce accurate comparative information on the ethnic minority populations of Western European cities. Whilst data in certain countries (such as Germany) are available from continuous population registers, elsewhere (as in France) the only real source is the periodic census (with the results of the 1990–1 census round not being fully available at the time of writing). There are also important issues arising from known under-enumeration (partly resulting from clandestine migration) as well as more complex questions of definition, particularly regarding second generations and those who, whilst of migrant background, hold the citizenship of the country of destination (as with New Commonwealth migrants in the United Kingdom and most Surinamese in The Netherlands). Definitional issues also raise the spectre of external 'labelling' of groups who may not wish to be identified in this manner (see also Ogden's Chapter 6 of this book).

In total the different terms used in different countries — immigrants, ethnic minorities, foreigners and so on — reflect a series of historical and political processes, differing from country to country. While the data shown in Table 4.1 are therefore to be regarded with caution, taken together they produce a statistical statement about the recent significance of ethnic minority populations of migrant origin.

Table 4.1 shows data for the 1980s for the largest cities of several West European countries, although without any indication of rates of change. In most cities the evidence suggests a steady increase in the proportionate importance of ethnic minorities, partly through the internal dynamics of these groups (with above-replacement fertility and further net in-movement in many cases) and partly through the reduction of the indigenous population as a result of migration to the suburbs. The co-existence of these processes is particularly well documented in the Dutch

Table 4.1 Foreign populations of major Western European cities

Country and city	Date	Foreign population as percentage of total population	Notes
Austria			
Vienna	1981	7.4	
Belgium			
Antwerp	1981	7.7	
Brussels	1981	23.8	
Liège	1981	19.4	
France			
Lyons	1982	12.2	
Marseille	1982	10.4	
Greater Paris	1982	13.9	
Strasbourg	1982	10.9	
Germany			
West Berlin	1987	13.9	*Source: Statistiches*
Hamburg	1987	10.2	*Jahrbuch der Deutschen*
Munich	1987	16.6	*Gemeinden 1988*
Cologne	1987	15.6	
Essen	1987	6.4	
Frankfurt	1987	24.4	
Luxemburg			
Luxemburg City	1988	42.6	*Source:* Gengler 1990
Netherlands			
Amsterdam	1988	21.4	Foreigners plus Dutch of
The Hague	1988	17.3	Surinamese or Netherlands
Rotterdam	1988	17.2	Antilles origin (children in
Utrecht	1988	13.2	households where head born in Surinam or Netherlands Antilles). *Source:* van Amersfoort 1990.
Switzerland			
Geneva	1980	29.0	
United Kingdom			
London	1986–8	16.6	Non-white ethnicity, by
W. Midlands	1986–8	12.5	self-assessment in the Labour Force Survey. *Source:* Haskey 1991.

Note: Where no source is shown, it is the population census of the relevant year.

and German cities (van Amersfoort 1990; Friedrichs and Alpheis 1991). Increasing proportions of the foreigner and ethnic minority populations of most West European countries are generally to be found in the biggest cities so that there is little sign of any dispersion tendency on the inter-regional scale. In France, for example, the proportion of foreigners living in agglomerations of over 100,000 inhabitants rose from 48 per cent in 1962 to 65 per cent at the time of the 1982 census during a period when counter-urbanization trends were starting for the population at large.

In short, ethnic minority populations of migrant origin now form a very visible and growing element in the population and social geography of the bigger urban centres, yet with considerable diversity both between groups and between cities and countries in the contextual circumstances in which evolution and growth have occurred.

Housing

In considering the impact of the creation of ethnic minority communities in West European cities, geographers have been most interested in patterns of residential distributions and the extent to which these show evidence of segregation. Where such segregation exists, there is then an attempt made to uncover the processes by which this has occurred. In analysing residential distributions, the role of housing is obviously of prime importance, and residential location also controls the possibilities of access to urban facilities — employment, education and leisure amenities — as well as to other groups of similar background.

Housing circumstances reflect a series of immigrant attributes. The most important of these include immigrants' economic status, their family composition and demography, their cultural identity and in-group orientation; important 'external' factors include the actions of housing managers and gatekeepers within the hegemonic forces of the host society (Huttman *et al.* 1991).

Ethnic minority housing has often been analysed in terms of housing classes, following the concepts advanced by Rex and Moore (1967) in their study of the Sparkbrook district of Birmingham. However, the characteristics of housing classes are not universal, differing markedly from city to city. Table 4.2 shows conceptualizations of housing classes with particular reference to immigrant and ethnic minority populations in four West European cities. The classifications for both Birmingham and Paris are to a large extent based on types of tenure and on the right to occupy, whilst those for Vienna and Amsterdam depend more on housing age, quality and cost. These differences reflect local circumstances. Thus the absence of the classification of owner-occupation in Vienna and Amsterdam results from the very small size of that housing sector in both cities (less than 7 per cent of housing stock and of no relevance as housing for immigrants). In Britain and France, by contrast, important groups of immigrant-origin populations (Indians and Pakistanis in the former; Portuguese and Italians in the latter) have moved into the large urban property-ownership sectors of those countries.

Housing sectors normally have some form of status labelling attached

Table 4.2 Housing classes identified in selected Western European cities

Birmingham (Rex 1968)	Vienna (Lichtenberger 1984)	Paris (White 1987)	Amsterdam (van Amersfoort 1990)
Outright owners of large houses in desirable areas	Tenants of post-war property (public or private landlord)	Owner-occupiers	Tenants in post-1965 expensive social housing
Mortgage payers who are becoming owners of houses in desirable areas	Tenants of inter-war social housing	Tenants of normal social housing	Tenants of early post-war social housing of good quality and moderate cost
Local authority tenants in houses built by the local authority	Tenants in pre-1919 rental property with rent control	Tenants in private property	Tenants of pre-war social housing: good quality and moderate cost
Local authority tenants in slum houses awaiting demolition		Living-in domestic servants	Tenants of low rent pre-1920 housing of poor quality
Tenants of private house-owners		Housed by industrial employers	Tenants of inner-city property of varied types including furnished rooms
House-owners who must take lodgers to meet repayments		Tenants of institutional housing specifically for immigrants	
Lodgers in rooms		Residents of *bidonvilles*	

to them. In Table 4.2 the ordering of classes within each city roughly follows the local status hierarchy, although there are obvious possible reinterpretations of the ordering from the perspective of specific subgroups of the population. This, indeed, is the conclusion from recent work on ethnic minority housing, emphasizing that specific housing submarkets within individual classes have sometimes been created by individual minority groups (Sarre 1986).

The crucial general conclusion from housing class studies of ethnic minority housing is that minority groups are not randomly spread between classes, and their inter-class distribution does not mirror that of the rest of the population. Instead they are particularly concentrated in certain housing classes and largely absent from others. Whatever the local housing structure, four particular influences are present within the allocational mechanisms: economic and income controls; demographic controls; the aspirations and in-group orientations of the minority community; and the actions of housing managers.

Socio-economic or class-based explanations of ethnic minority housing segregation emphasize the weak financial position of immigrant groups and their inability to afford high rents or expensive house purchase. Issues of rent affordability loom large in German cities where a very high proportion of the total dwelling stock is rented on the open market and where housing classes therefore tend to be bounded by rent and quality criteria rather than by tenure. The equation linking ethnic minority employment in low-paid jobs with poor quality and cheap housing appears to be generally strong everywhere. The reverse is also true, in that where international migration has created communities of high status, high-earning minorities, the housing occupied by such groups, in both type and location, has been a clear reflection of their higher income position. Examples include the Japanese in Düsseldorf (Glebe 1986) and the various employees of international organizations in Brussels (Kesteloot 1987).

Nevertheless, cheap housing is not necessarily found in the same housing class throughout Europe, nor are ethnic minorities always to be found in it. Whilst the lowest costs may generally be in the privately rented sector, such property is sometimes of very great age with historic rent control legislation leading to the retention of immobile elderly non-migrant residents: examples include the cities of Vienna and Paris (White and Winchester 1991, p. 43). Also slum property is not necessarily cheaply rented, particularly where immigrant residents are exploited by landlords who may be of the same ethnic origin — a situation that achieved notoriety in West London in the 1960s.

There are also many examples of poor immigrants pooling resources and buying into higher levels of the housing hierarchy than would be expected from individual incomes. Such has been the case with house purchase (albeit at the cheapest end of the owner-occupier sector) by Pakistani families in the United Kingdom (Cater and Jones 1987), and is becoming commoner amongst North Africans in France (Ailloud and Labrosse 1986, p. 151), whilst the Chinese refugee presence in a high-rent high-rise district of Paris is explicable through the system of communal sharing of financial resources practised by the community (White *et al.* 1987).

Thus, although socio-economic factors provide a basis for the understanding of the exclusion of ethnic minority populations from the higher status and higher-cost housing sectors in many cities, they cannot be regarded as full explanations of the distribution of immigrant populations throughout the housing structure.

A second factor of importance is demographic structure. Over the decades of mass migration into Western Europe, the demographic composition of immigrant populations has changed from a male-dominated group of workers to a balanced family structure. These demographic changes have brought new housing demands, and in particular, the desire for the raising of housing quality as an environment for family life.

The most obvious reflection of demographic influences lies in the distinctive housing patterns of initial migrant streams of males — the commonest receiving housing sectors in many cities being dormitories and hostels provided by employers or by agencies connected with industrial interests, or inner-city furnished rooms and lodgings of the sort identified as separate housing classes in both Birmingham and Amsterdam (Table 4.2). With family reunification the importance of employer housing and migrant worker hostels has diminished. The presence of families has helped to generate movement into housing sectors where ethnic minorities and other populations come into contact and possible competition, namely into tenancies from private landlords and into social housing. Family reunification has generally been associated, therefore, with an increase in the proportion of the migrant worker's pay-packet which goes into housing, with a reduction in the savings element (Lichtenberger 1984).

A third major influence on housing market segregation is what some commentators have called 'cultural' factors, or in-group orientation. One of the most important aspects of this is the exceptionally limited housing search methods used by many minority groups, by which information is gathered only through personal contacts and relates solely to a very narrow sector of the housing market, often with equally narrow geographic limits. The extent to which the resultant high degree of housing segregation is desired by the minority community is actually debatable: some surveys have shown the wishes of minorities to have closer contact with the majority population (Gans 1990), whereas others have identified high proportions of (often more culturally distinct groups) who wish to retain or enhance their degree of segregation (Phillips and Karn 1991). In general, however, both the actual housing search behaviour of the migrants and the operation of the housing market are such as to restrict dispersion and greater contact, even where it is desired. Indeed, in the competitive housing market of European cities, with inter-community competition being a possible element in racist feeling, the 'taking over' of a particular housing submarket by a minority group may in part be a defence mechanism, also enabling a retention of cultural norms in the face of external threats (O'Loughlin 1987; Phillips and Karn 1991).

The self-segregation of minorities even where other factors might allow their dispersion is very common, as Glebe (1986) has shown in Düssel-dorf where the high-status Japanese are actually the most segregated foreigner group in the city, confined to one segment of the overall hous-ing market and found only in two small neighbourhoods. For all minority groups, most especially for those with the most distinctive infrastructural demands (such as religious facilities, educational provi-sion, or specialist retailing), residential concentration in certain districts which offer other minority-related facilities is frequently observed. Expectations of early return migration have also been identified as leading to self-segregation by minority groups, often separating different groups within the city (Robinson 1979).

Useful though these economic, demographic and cultural explanations of housing market segregation may be, a key role, indeed arguably the dominant role in many cities, is played by housing 'managers' with the power to grant or restrict access to accommodation for particular groups. Control of social housing has been of particular importance, since it has been the lack of access to this housing class in many cities in the past that has played the greatest role in perpetuating the segregation of immigrants from non-migrant groups of similar socio-economic and demographic status. The application of maximum percentages and quotas for estates has been common (Flett 1982; O'Loughlin 1987). Some of the results can be seen in the coexistence of large numbers of vacant dwell-ings at the same time as long housing waiting-lists for foreigners, common in many French cities (Ailloud and Labrosse 1986). Elsewhere individual cities (for example in The Netherlands) kept foreigners inelig-ible for social housing as long as possible, often by insisting on extended residence criteria, and then applied ceilings to minority tenancies.

Even where specific quota policies for social housing do not exist, concepts of thresholds of tolerance (effectively thresholds for interven-tion) have been commonly used, for example in Belgium (Kesteloot 1986), Germany (Holzner 1982), The Netherlands (Mik 1991) and France (Grillo 1985), where the concept was publicly revived in 1991 by Presi-dent Mitterrand. Where housing demand threatens these thresholds, a common response has been the use of certain estates as 'dumping grounds' for foreign families, creating extreme levels of ethnic minority allocations and population concentrations (Sporton and White 1989).

Finally we should also note that prejudicial allocation policies are not exclusive to the public sector: the allocation processes of private landlords have been far more discriminatory and also far less susceptible to identification.

Neighbourhoods and concentrations

One of the notable features of the European experience of ethnic minority concentration (certainly in comparison with North America) is that residential segregation in Western European cities is rarely on the district scale, so that few 'ghettos' (itself a very emotive term in many European countries) are identifiable. Several commentators have noted that at most segregation tends to be on a house-by-house basis, rather than on the street or neighbourhood level (White 1984; Peach 1987), and overall city-wide segregation levels are much lower than in the United States. Districts such as the Goutte d'Or in Paris (Vuddamalay *et al*. 1991) or the Bangladeshi-dominated Spitalfields in London (Curtis and Ogden 1986) are exceptional.

Within individual houses, particularly in the poorest privately rented property, groups of migrants of similar origins are often found, although from house to house the nationalities may change. Thus even in districts where there are high proportions of ethnic minority residents in total, there may be high levels of segregation, both on the micro scale of residences and in behaviour patterns, between different migrant groups. Wherever immigrants are present in European cities, they are almost invariably living close to indigenous populations, even if not within the same building. The proximate groups of the majority population tend to be subsectors of the total, with the result that researchers have uncovered low levels of spatial segregation between ethnic minorities and groups such as single people or young one-parent families from the majority society (van Amersfoort 1990). On the other hand, if the minorities are considered by age group, a common finding is of higher levels of segregation and isolation of children, because of the confining of these ages to family housing in limited locations (Glebe 1990).

It should, however, be noted that segregation indices appear to have been falling over recent years in several cities (for example, Amsterdam, Bradford, Brussels and Zürich), often in the wake of family reunification and its accompanying housing adjustments (Arend 1982; Kesteloot 1986; Rees and Ram 1987; van Amersfoort 1990). Evidence from both the United Kingdom and Sweden has shown that an evolutionary process of residential dispersion has in fact been operative amongst certain of the earliest and least distinctive migrant groups (King and King 1977; Lindén and Lindberg 1991). Whether this will also happen for the more visible and more recently-arrived populations is debatable: Gans (1990), for example, has found that in Kiel in Germany Turks were actually becoming more concentrated in location during the 1980s. We might also observe that the economic restructuring of major urban centres in Europe currently under way may restrict the opportunities for further apparent assimilation. Instead it is possible that with inner-city gentrification and area-upgrading pressures, the reconquest of city centres by the wealthy will engender ethnic minority dispersion (as is happening in Paris) to new segregated locations around the city edge.

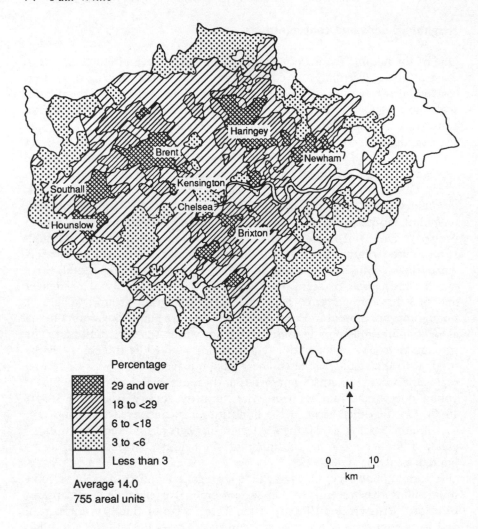

Figure 4.1   London, 1981: residents in private households with head born in
New Commonwealth or Pakistan

Source: Congdon 1983.

Figures 4.1, 4.2 and 4.3 show the residential distributions of ethnic
minority populations in three major West European cities in the early
1980s, using local definitions for the identification of the groups
concerned. For Greater London the definition deals with the New
Commonwealth and Pakistan (therefore excluding ethnic minorities of
other origins) and includes all those living in households of which the
head was born in those countries. Here it is clear that most peripheral
areas have low percentages of ethnic minorities, although the maximum
values do not occur at the city centre. Instead the neighbourhoods where

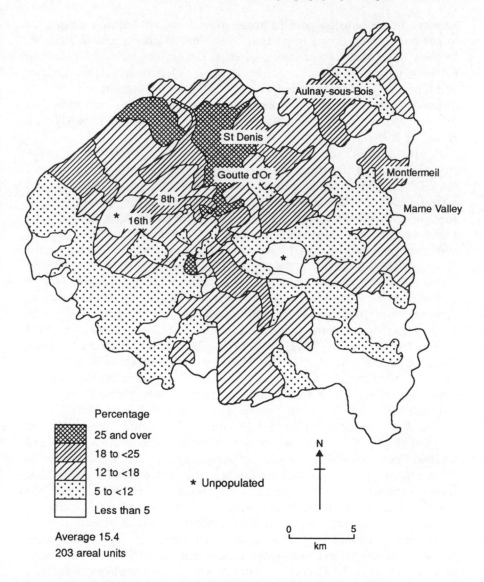

Figure 4.2 Foreigners in Paris and surrounding *départements*, 1982
Data source: Recensement Général de la Population, 1982.

ethnic minority populations are of greatest significance lie in an arc around the inner suburbs (generally of Victorian property) north of the Thames, with fewer areas of concentration south of the river.

The effects of housing market controls are clearly visible in London. Thus the great areas of single-family council housing on the north bank of the Thames in the east of the city have few minority presences. However, concentrations occur in areas of both high owner-occupancy in

Southall and Hounslow and in areas of very mixed housing classes, as in the borough of Brent, in parts of Newham, Haringey and in Brixton. In these latter cases the accession of ethnic minorities into social housing (often high-rise flats) has occurred through selective allocation policies (Phillips 1987). More detailed analysis of the 1981 census results also displays that there are different distributions of the minorities of different origins, both through different housing classes and, partly as a result, spatially.

Figure 4.2 shows the distribution of those of foreign nationality in the city of Paris and the three inner suburban *départements* at the time of the 1982 census. The overall pattern shows both similarities to and differences from that of London. Similar are the low proportions of foreigners in certain outer areas, once again particularly in the east. However, in the Paris area the zone of greatest concentration of foreigner presences is clearly sectoral in nature and stretches into the inner city from St Denis in the north. This sector accords with the traditional industrial areas of the city. Indeed sectors are a distinctive feature of the Paris map, with three slices of territory displaying particularly low concentrations of foreigners: to the south-west of the city — the suburban higher-status zone; to the south-east; and along the Marne valley where few foreigners have yet purchased the small owner-occupied houses characteristic of this area. However, concentrations of foreigners in outer suburban *communes* such as Aulnay-sous-Bois or Montfermeil occur where particular social housing estates have been the scene of ethnically-selective allocation policies (Sporton and White 1989).

One final interesting difference between London and Paris is that in London (Figure 4.1) the high-status residential areas of Kensington and Chelsea have lower-than-average ethnic minority presences, whilst in Paris prestigious districts such as the 8th and 16th *arrondissements* have high proportions of foreigners, an association resulting from the continued use of domestic labour and *concierge* systems in this area. It is notable, however, that such employment affects a specific set of ethnicities (predominantly Portuguese) so that, as in London, the distributions of different foreigner groups are quite distinct, and evolve in different ways as a result of both housing and employment factors.

The final map of foreigner distributions concerns guestworkers in Düsseldorf (Figure 4.3), although here the map shows only four classes of foreigner proportions. Looking solely at the areas of highest concentration, however, it is clear that these are quite widely distributed throughout the city, occurring both in the inner-city area, particularly the Oberbilk district, and also in a number of industrial suburbs such as Rath and Benrath. Indeed a distinctive feature in Düsseldorf, as in other German cities, is the coincidence of high guestworker presences with industrial areas through the eligibility of guestworkers for company housing owned by the firms for which they work (see also Chapter 5, especially Figure 5.2 and its associated discussion).

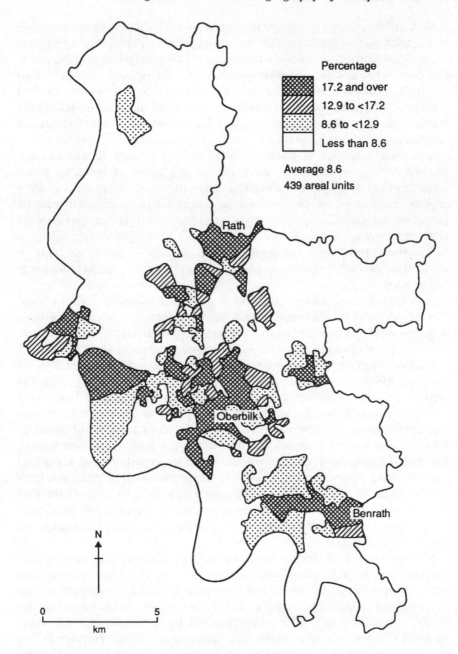

Figure 4.3 Guestworker nationalities (Turks, Greeks, Yugoslavs, Italians and Moroccans) in Düsseldorf, 1982

Source: Redrawn from Glebe 1984.

In Düsseldorf, as to some extent in Paris, the demographic composition of the minorities differs between inner-city and suburban concentrations, with inner-city residents more often being single males, as in the Parisian Goutte d'Or (Vuddamalay *et al.* 1990), and the suburban residents consisting of families. In Germany this distribution in fact represents a transformation from the early years of guestworker movement when the suburban *Wohnheime* for industrial workers created a dispersed pattern of locations of single foreigners.

The three examples of London, Paris and Düsseldorf all demonstrate the significance of housing sectors in creating areas of minority group concentration, and it is also clear that the particular determining housing market conditions are locally specific. Thus the high accession rate of foreigners to social housing in Paris contrasts with their general absence from this sector in Düsseldorf (Glebe 1984). The relationship between employment and housing (operating both for the domestic servants in Paris and for industrial employees in Düsseldorf) is a further factor of importance.

However, residential concentrations do not necessarily lead to identifiable ethnic minority neighbourhoods. For example, while single male workers predominated in cities of Germany, Switzerland and Austria, they often constituted a semi-invisible presence, even in their districts of habitation: instead railway stations and other central meeting-points took on a behavioural and symbolic significance for the migrants. With the growth of whole ethnic minority communities, certain neighbourhoods have taken on visible characteristics demonstrating the presence of new activities and norms. The presence of women and children, the development of commercial activities (particularly small businesses) catering for minority groups, and the growth of specific recreational and cultural facilities have effectively converted residential distribution maps into new mental maps of cities, although given the generally micro-scale nature of segregation patterns, the establishment of real ethnic minority hegemony is by no means always a straightforward process, being contingent on local circumstances.

The emergence of ethnic minority neighbourhoods has been highly controversial in many cities, and has met a series of official policies and informal responses. At one time European countries had no legal restrictions barring immigrants from residence in certain areas. With the rise in the proportions of ethnic minority residents in certain districts, fears of ghetto formation have arisen and action has ensued. Holzner (1982) has described the ban on foreigner movement into three city districts by the West Berlin authorities in 1975 as being similar to South African legislation, although the measure was later overturned as a result of a court judgment on the violation of human rights. The Gol law of 1984 in Belgium enabled the Ministry of Justice to give municipalities similar powers of refusal to register foreigners (Kesteloot 1986). These, and the general discussion of segregated neighbourhoods in media and political forums, have created a climate of mistrust between indigenous and immigrant (and even between immigrant) groups. As Huttman (1991, p. 37) has pointed out, establishment views in Western Europe follow 'from the idea that a concentration of minorities is wrong'. The results have been both direct and indirect policies favouring dispersal. Added to the elements of such policies that manipulate ethnic minorities for specific socio-spatial goals have been the everyday incidents of racial tension and harassment, often at their worst on housing estates where dispersal policies have resulted in a thin scatter of minority residents, sometimes escalating into more major outbreaks of violence in which ethnicity has played a part alongside various aspects of deprivation.

All these forces tend to marginalize the actual desires of individuals and groups within the ethnic minority communities, making their aspirations (whether for employment, housing, community solidarity, or cultural preservation) both less 'acceptable' and less possible for fulfilment, except through strong community action and a reassertion of identity. Although there are signs in certain countries that some policy-makers are prepared now to think in terms of limited multicultural models of society, elsewhere the lesson of the early 1990s has been that assimilationist (and even exclusionist) ideas are still of considerable, and even growing, importance. The reasons for this lie, at least in part, in the growing visibility of certain ethnic minority communities.

However, not all groups are so visible. As with the demographically-restricted guestworker males of the past in Germany, so the female domestic servants of Paris and other cities (including now those of Southern Europe) have evolved a non-place community, with little neighbourhood visibility (White 1989), and in many cities the Italian, Spanish and other European immigrant populations (including the Finns in Swedish cities and the Irish in Britain) are less and less 'visible', either in the landscape or in public consciousness (Walter 1986).

Conclusion

This chapter has demonstrated that the legacy of large-scale migration to West European cities over the post-war period can be explained only by a clear understanding of the evolutionary processes at work, a recognition of the distinctive features of West European cities and of their diversity, and a realization of the distinctions that must be made between ethnic minority communities of different origins.

The ethnic minority communities of Western European cities are not immutable. Changes in the composition, location, self-identification and organization of such communities are today taking place alongside, and partly because of, other macro-scale changes in Western society in a period of economic restructuring, associated also with changing attitudes to the city. Vulnerable ethnic minority groups are being squeezed from both sides — by the reduction in many of the economic opportunities to which they were initially attracted to fill, and by inner-city gentrification which reduces the availability of cheap housing. At the same time the general halting of social housing construction in most West European countries over the past decade has terminated the growth of what was starting to become an important alternative. Political reactions to the presence and continued growth of minority communities are also becoming more strongly negative in several countries than they were ten years ago, as indicated by the rise of right-wing political movements campaigning on 'anti-immigrant' platforms in countries such as Austria, Belgium, France and Germany (see also Chapter 8 of this book).

With signs of economic and social polarization now visible throughout Western Europe, the outlook for many ethnic minorities looks bleak — a future offering possibly three alternatives: apparent assimilation and dilution of identity through the acceptance of majority-group norms (as with the Italians in many countries); polarization as the opposite of the dominant majority (in other words, unemployed, under-educated and housed in peripheral ghetto-like estates, as increasingly appears the lot of large segments of the population of North African origin in France); or developing a pluralist society largely separated from the majority except through commercial transactions from a position of relative strength (as with the Chinese of Paris or the Indian community in certain British cities). Even were the first of these scenarios desired by the minorities themselves, this is still a route blocked for most by prejudice and racist labelling by the majority society, as well as by the starting-point of economic, social and political disadvantage which the minorities currently hold.

Mass migration in Western Europe has therefore created an urban legacy which will be of long duration, and which will not remain static. New elements have been added to the already complex structures of European urbanism, the landscape of individual cities has been changed, and the life chances and everyday experiences of millions of ordinary people have been transformed. In many respects the forces set in train have been as significant in European urban history as were the forces of nineteenth-century urban-industrial growth itself.

References

Ailloud, D. and Labrosse, J-M., 1986, 'L'accessibilité au logement de la population étrangère dans l'agglomération lyonnaise', *Hérodote*, 43: 140–52.

Arend, M., 1982, 'Sozialökologische Analyse der kleinräumigen Ausländer-verteilung in Zürich', in Hoffmann-Nowotny, H.J. and Hondrich, K.O. (eds), *Ausländer in der BRD und der Schweiz*, Campus, Frankfurt, 294–374.

Cater, J. and Jones, T., 1987, 'Asian ethnicity, home-ownership and social reproduction', in Jackson, P. (ed.), *Race and racism: essays in social geography*, Unwin Hyman, London, 191–211.

Congdon, P., 1983, *A map profile of Greater London in 1981*, GLC Statistical Series No. 23, London.

Curtis, S.E. and Ogden, P.E., 1986, 'Bangladeshis in London: a challenge to welfare', *Revue Européenne des Migrations Internationales*, 2(3): 135–50.

Flett, H., 1982, 'Dimensions of inequality: Birmingham council housing allocations', *New Community*, 10(1): 46–56.

Friedrichs, J. and Alpheis, H., 1991, 'Housing segregation of immigrants in West Germany', in Huttman, E. *et al.* (eds), *Urban housing segregation of minorities in Western Europe and the United States*, Duke University Press, London, 116–144.

Gans, P., 1990, 'Changes in the structure of the foreign population of West Germany since 1980', *Migration*, 7: 25–49.

Gengler, C., 1990, 'Les étrangers au Grand-Duché du Luxembourg: aspects démographiques et socio-économiques', *Espace, Populations, Sociétés*, 1990–2: 291–303.

Glebe, G., 1984, 'Tendenzen ethnischer Segregation und Konzentration von Gastarbeiterminoritäten in Düsseldorf 1974–1982', *Zeitschrift für Wirtschaftsgeographie*, 28(2): 91–111.

Glebe, G., 1986, 'Segregation and intra-urban mobility of a high-status ethnic group: the case of the Japanese in Düsseldorf', *Ethnic and Racial Studies*, 9(4): 461–83.

Glebe, G., 1990, 'Segregation and migration of the second generation of guestworker minorities in Düsseldorf', *Espace, Populations, Sociétés*, 1990–2: 257–78.

Grillo, R.D., 1985, *Ideologies and institutions in urban France: the representation of immigrants*, Cambridge University Press, Cambridge.

Haskey, J., 1991, 'Ethnic minority populations resident in private households — estimates by county and metropolitan district of England and Wales', *Population Trends*, Spring: 22–35.

Holzner, L., 1982, 'The myth of Turkish ghettos: a geographic case study of West German responses towards a foreign minority', *Journal of Ethnic Studies*, 9(4): 65–85.

Huttman, E.D., 1991, 'Housing segregation in Western Europe: an introduction', in Huttman, E. *et al.* (eds), *Urban housing segregation of minorities in Western Europe and the United States*, Duke University Press, London, 21–42.

Huttman, E.D., Blauw, W., Saltman, J. (eds), 1991, *Urban housing segregation of minorities in Western Europe and the United States*, Duke University Press, London.

Kesteloot, C., 1986, 'Concentration d'étrangers et politique urbaine à Bruxelles', *Revue Européenne des Migrations Internationales*, 2(3): 151–68.

Kesteloot, C., 1987, 'The residential location of immigrant workers in Belgian cities: an ethnic or a socio-economic phenomenon?', in Glebe, G. and O'Loughlin, J. (eds), *Foreign minorities in continental European cities*, Steiner, Wiesbaden, 223–39.

King, R.L. and King, P.D., 1977, 'The spatial evolution of the Italian community in Bedford', *East Midland Geographer*, 6(47): 337–45.

Lichtenberger, E., 1984, *Gastarbeiter: Leben in zwei Gesellschaften*, Hermann Böhlau, Vienna.

Lindén, A-L. and Lindberg, G., 1991, 'Immigrant housing patterns in Sweden', in Huttman, E. *et al.* (eds), *Urban housing segregation of minorities in Western Europe and the United States*, Duke University Press, London, 92–115.

Mik, G., 1991 'Housing segregation and policy in the Dutch metropolitan environment', in Huttman, E. *et al.* (eds), *Urban housing segregation of minorities in Western Europe and the United States*, Duke University Press, London, 179–98.

O'Loughlin, J., 1987, 'Chicago an der Ruhr or what? Explaining the location of immigrants in European cities', in Glebe, G. and O'Loughlin, J. (eds), *Foreign minorities in continental European cities*, Steiner, Wiesbaden, 52–69.

Peach, C., 1987, 'Immigration and segregation in Western Europe since 1945', in Glebe, G. and O'Loughlin, J. (eds), *Foreign minorities in continental European cities*, Steiner, Wiesbaden, 30–51.

Phillips, D., 1987, 'The rhetoric of anti-racism in public housing allocation', in Jackson, P. (ed.), *Race and racism: essays in social geography*, Unwin Hyman, London, 212–37.

Phillips, D. and Karn, V., 1991, 'Racial segregation in Britain: patterns, processes and policy approaches', in Huttman, E. *et al.* (eds), *Urban housing segregation of minorities in Western Europe and the United States*, Duke University Press, London, 63–91.

Rees, P.H. and Ram, S., 1987, 'Projections of the residential distribution of an ethnic group: Indians in Bradford', *Environment and Planning A*, 19(10): 1323–58.

Rex, J., 1968, 'The sociology of the zone in transition', in Pahl, R. (ed.), *Readings in urban sociology*, Pergamon, Oxford, 211–31.

Rex, J. and Moore, R., 1967, *Race, community and conflict*, Oxford University Press, Oxford.

Robinson, V., 1979, 'The segregation of Asians within a British city: theory and practice', Research Paper 22, School of Geography, University of Oxford.

Sarre, P., 1986, 'Choice and constraint in ethnic minority housing: a structurationist view', *Housing Studies*, 1(2): 71–86.

Sporton, D. and White, P.E., 1989, 'Immigrants in social housing: integration or segregation in France?', *The Planner*, 75(4): 28–31.

Van Amersfoort, H., 1990, 'La répartition spatiale des minorités ethniques dans un Etat-providence: les leçons des Pays-Bas 1970–1990', *Espace, Populations, Sociétés*, 1990–2: 241–55.

Vuddamalay, V., White, P.E. and Sporton, D., 1991, 'The evolution of the Goutte d'Or as an ethnic minority district of Paris', *New Community*, 17(2): 245–58.

Walter, B., 1986, 'Ethnicity and Irish residential distribution', *Transactions, Institute of British Geographers*, 11(2): 131–46.

White, P.E., 1984, *The West European city: a social geography*, Longman, London.

White, P.E., 1987, 'The migrant experience in Paris', in Glebe, G. and O'Loughlin, J. (eds), *Foreign minorities in continental European cities*, Steiner, Wiesbaden, 184–98.

White, P.E., 1989, 'Immigrants, immigrant areas and immigrant communities in postwar Paris', in Ogden, P.E. and White P.E. (eds), *Migrants in modern France*, Unwin Hyman, London, 195–211.

White, P.E. and Winchester, H., 1991, 'The poor in the inner city: stability and change in two Parisian neighbourhoods', *Urban Geography*, 12(1): 35–54.

White, P.E., Winchester, H. and Guillon, M., 1987, 'South-East Asian refugees in Paris: the evolution of a minority community', *Ethnic and Racial Studies*, 10(1): 48–61.

Chapter 5

From itinerant worker to immigrant?
The geography of guestworkers in Germany

Hans Heinrich Blotevogel, Ursula Müller-ter Jung and
Gerald Wood

Historical background

Germany can look back upon a long tradition of employing foreign
workers.[1] In the nineteenth century there were waves of emigration
from Germany to countries abroad when mass poverty spread in the
wake of the erosion of traditional social structures during the first half
of the nineteenth century. By the end of the 1880s, however, industrialization was well under way and a lack of workers started to emerge, so
that between 1890 and 1914 Germany became a country to which rather
than from which people migrated.

Those who came were drawn mainly from Poland and Austria (the
Hapsburg Monarchy) and generally worked in agriculture, particularly in
the eastern part of Prussia (Bade 1983, p. 29). The political consensus
at the time was not to allow any immigration to take place, but rather
to tolerate the foreign workers for one season only. This explains why,
at the beginning of the 1890s, a restrictive control system was devised
(which was completed by 1907), whereby a return home during the winter
was imposed upon the foreign workers. Additionally, the foreigners were
tied by a bond (*Legitimationszwang*) to their employer during their stay.
When enforcing the compulsory return of the foreigners, the authorities
not only discriminated on the grounds of nationality but also according
to the different social and professional standings. Generally, a
compulsory return was imposed upon those people with the lowest levels
of qualification. Because of these measures Germany did not become an
immigration country but rather the second largest importer of workers
after the United States.

Right from the start discrepancies existed between the unions, whose
interest it was to protect the indigenous workers, and the employers who
preferred foreign workers because of the lower wages they were willing
to accept.[2] On the other hand, however, it was admitted that the hard
nature of some of the jobs made them unsuitable for indigenous
workers. This explains why, for instance, Italian labourers were by
preference employed in the building industry.

The employers began to regard the foreign worker as a buffer who, according to the economic situation, could be dismissed more easily than their German counterparts. This dismissal, however, could be exercised only upon the workers from the East because only they were included in the restrictive control system. Other foreigners to whom these regulations did not apply competed directly with the indigenous work-force. From the early 1890s until after the First World War there was a clash of interests in the public discussion regarding the question of limiting the number of migrant workers. Such a discussion of migration policy was common practice only in 'real' immigration countries.

When at the beginning of the First World War a sufficient provision of food for the population became uncertain, compulsory repatriation was abolished, or rather, returning home was prohibited initially because the foreigners were needed for farm work. This quite clearly demonstrates the migrant workers' role as a 'reserve army'. The control over the admission of foreigners into Germany and the limitation of the foreigners' role to that of a buffer or replacement function now unfolded in a qualitatively new fashion. Whereas during the time of the Empire the anti-Polish security policy was decisive, now economic interests prevailed. The overriding aim was to restrict foreigners to those jobs which could not be filled by German workers. For instance, visas were granted only if indigenous workers were not available. By 1927 the state had created a complex and flexible instrument for balancing market tensions through the institution of a public labour administration which was firmly rooted in the law. However, an abrupt change occurred in the 1930s as a result of the Depression and its mass unemployment.

When in 1933 the National Socialists came to power the period of 'migrant workers' was brought to an end — a period which had been so important for the Empire and the Weimar Republic. Now the so-called *Fremdarbeiterfrage* came to the fore.[3]

The large-scale employment of foreign workers only emerged when, after the beginning of the war, the Germans had access to the labour-force of the occupied territories. Initially, these were people working on farms in Poland. Then another 1.8 to 2.0 million Poles were deported as *Zwangsarbeiter* to work in the German war economy. As the war intensified, the demand for workers to replace those who had been drafted rose steadily. This demand was met by further compulsory recruitments in the occupied territories. In complete contrast to the policy of compulsory repatriation which had been practised during the time of the Empire and the Weimar Republic, the 'regulations for foreigners' of 1939 decreed a general ban on leaving the country. Furthermore, there was a remarkably discriminatory treatment of the 'imported' workers. Differences were highlighted between those who belonged to the 'master races' (*Herrenvölker*) such as the French, Belgians and Dutch, and those from the East, notably the Poles and the workers from the Soviet Union who were regarded as racially inferior subhuman creatures (*Untermenschen*). The extent to which the war economy was reliant upon foreign workers is demonstrated by the fact that in 1944 one-fifth of the civilian work-force consisted of foreign workers and prisoners of war.

Stages of labour immigration

Early recruitment: 1955–61

The time between 1945 and 1949 was characterized by a large influx of expellees and refugees into the areas controlled by the Western allies. It was only after 1955 that owing to an expanding market economy with its associated growing demand for workers, a shift in the motivation and in the composition of those who migrated to Germany occurred. This new situation was reflected by the fact that foreign workers were employed on an organized basis, such as the hiring of Italian labour from 1955 onwards through the recruitment agreement of that year. Further agreements with other Mediterranean countries were to follow (see Table 5.1). Typical of all these agreements was the fact that the recruitment of foreign workers took place only on the basis of orders that had been placed by the employers and examined by the relevant authority. Thus the impetus given to migration began in Germany rather than in the countries of origin. It is remarkable that at the time of the first recruitment agreement (1955) the unemployment rate was around 7 per cent, despite the expanding economy. It follows from this that migration to Germany took place not under the conditions of full employment (with a corresponding political climate), but rather because of certain bottle-necks which existed in individual companies in some industries and regions.

From the very beginning, the employment of foreigners was fundamentally influenced by the principle of 'rotation' — very similar to the concept of seasonal work at the end of the nineteenth century. The employers believed that the foreign workers would only stay a limited length of time in Germany, long enough to save a sufficient amount of money which would allow them an independent existence in their home countries to which they were expected to return. In the case of renewed labour demand, foreign workers would be recruited once again.

A further analogy can be drawn by looking at the function of the foreign workers. They were primarily used as a stopgap, carrying out work that Germans would no longer do. Historically speaking, the employment of foreign workers once again led to an increase in the vertical mobility of the German work-force. Germany now possessed a new lower class. Moreover, foreign workers were again being regarded as buffers. Extensive legal requirements (laws and special employment

Table 5.1   Public policies regarding foreigners in the Federal Republic of
Germany

(a) Recruitment agreements	
1955	Italy
1960	Spain, Greece
1961	Turkey
1963	Morocco
1965	Tunisia
1968	Yugoslavia
(b) Other policies	
1965	'Foreigner Act': equal status for employees from EEC countries (Italy) and indigenous employees. For others: principle of temporary residence.
1973	Stop of recruitment from non-EC member states.
1975	Child allowance regulation: substantial increase for children living in the FRG; start of family reunions.
1975–1977	Limitation of migration in certain agglomerations.
1978	Changes in the general regulations for the execution of the Foreigners Act (permanent residence permit after five years, right of abode after eight years).
1980	Resolution by the federal government to develop policies regarding foreigners (particularly in view of the second generation).
1983	Act to promote the willingness of the foreigners to repatriate.
1990	Act for the revision of the regulations regarding foreigners.

Source: Treibel 1990, p. 43.

contracts for foreigners) were to assign the foreign workers the role of a readily available pool of labour which could be adapted to the demands of the labour market far more easily than could the German work-force.

Expansion: 1961–74

In the early 1960s the situation of the German labour market tightened. First, when the Berlin Wall was built in August 1961 the former GDR as a constant supplier of labour was cut off from the FRG's labour market. Second, the attainment of full employment meant that there were no labour reserves available amongst the population of the FRG. This situation led to a sharp increase in migration from abroad (Table 5.2).

A break occurred in 1966–7 when the economic recession, with its rise in unemployment, forced down the numbers of foreign workers. This downward trend rather graphically illustrates the function held by the so-called guestworkers (Kayser 1972). Soon after, however, there was a renewed demand for labour which resulted in the recruitment of workers mainly from Turkey and Yugoslavia. This trend culminated in 1973 when

Table 5.2 Employment of foreigners in the Federal Republic of Germany 1954–87 ('000)

Year	Foreign employees Total	As % of total work-force	Italy	Greece	Spain	Turkey	Portugal	Yugoslavia
1954	72.9	0.4	6.5	0.5	0.4	–	–	1.8
1955	79.6	0.4	7.5	0.6	0.5	–	–	2.1
1956	98.8	0.5	18.6	1.0	0.7	–	–	2.3
1957	108.2	0.6	19.1	1.8	1.0	–	–	2.8
1958	127.1	0.6	25.6	2.8	1.5	–	–	4.8
1959	166.8	0.8	48.8	4.1	2.2	–	–	7.3
1960	279.4	1.3	121.7	13.0	9.5	2.5	0.3	8.8
1961	507.4	2.5	218.0	43.9	51.0	–	–	–
1962	629.0	3.1	239.0	70.4	83.9	–	–	–
1963	773.2	3.7	264.9	106.3	112.2	–	–	–
1964	902.5	4.3	267.9	143.2	138.4	67.8	–	–
1965	1,118.6	5.3	328.6	179.2	171.5	118.8	10.8	–
1966	1,244.0	5.8	362.1	191.5	175.2	149.9	18.9	–
1967	1,013.9	4.7	266.8	150.1	127.0	133.1	18.4	94.3
1968	1,018.9	4.9	275.9	139.8	112.6	141.2	18.9	106.4
1969	1,365.6	6.5	327.0	177.9	135.0	215.8	26.9	222.7
1970	1,806.8	8.5	363.7	229.8	162.9	323.1	40.2	373.6
1971	2,128.4	9.8	393.6	260.9	179.7	418.5	54.3	452.2
1972	2,284.5	10.5	411.8	268.1	181.1	488.7	63.1	462.9
1973	2,595.0	11.9	450.0	250.0	190.0	605.5	85.0	535.0
1974	2,286.6	10.9	331.5	229.2	149.7	606.8	78.5	466.7
1975	2,060.5	10.2	292.9	203.0	129.1	550.5	70.2	416.6
1976	1,924.8	9.6	274.0	178.4	110.8	523.5	63.5	387.7
1977	1,872.2	9.3	277.3	160.6	99.6	512.9	60.0	374.4
1978	1,857.4	9.3	284.3	146.3	92.4	510.8	58.7	366.8
1979	1,924.4	9.3	297.0	139.1	89.6	535.8	58.9	364.4
1980	2,018.3	9.6	304.5	132.2	86.1	578.2	58.5	353.7
1981	1,911.9	9.2	286.5	123.3	81.5	577.9	54.8	336.7
1982	1,783.9	8.8	258.6	115.5	76.6	553.9	50.8	312.6
1983	1,713.6	8.5	238.9	108.8	72.3	540.5	46.4	305.9
1984	1,592.6	7.9	214.0	98.0	67.3	499.9	39.6	288.7
1985	1,584.0	7.8	202.0	103.0	67.0	499.0	35.0	294.0
1986	1,591.5	7.7	193.3	101.5	65.9	513.0	35.1	294.8
1987	1,557.1	7.5	177.1	101.1	64.2	511.6	35.4	284.2

Source: Treibel 1990, p. 46.

11.9 per cent of the entire work-force were foreigners (see Table 5.2). Most of the foreign workers were employed either in expanding industries, such as the automobile or the metal-processing factories, or in unattractive trades, such as foundries or steel mills. In both cases a very low level of qualification was required.

Consolidation and reunion of families: 1974–88

Between 1967 and 1974 the foreign population increased from 1,806,700 to 4,127,400. After this stage of expansion recruitment was stopped on 23 November 1973. According to government announcements, this was owing to the oil crisis of the same year. Never before had there been a more dramatic measure affecting the employment of the foreigners. Further measures were subsequently introduced (Table 5.1). At the same time steps were taken to safeguard the right of the indigenous population to work. Germans who were seeking employment were given priority over foreign workers whose work permits were to be extended only if no German had applied for the same job. However, because of the above-mentioned increase in the vertical mobility of the Germans, native workers were in fact not competing with the foreigners for the same jobs. Hence this measure did little to change the situation of the foreign workers.

The halt to recruitment in 1973 put a formal end to the principle of rotation, which in any case had become obsolete by the end of the 1960s. In 1983 a policy of selective displacement prevailed, which was to reduce the number of foreigners by granting them financial incentives if they were prepared to return home. This policy, however, achieved little success because it offered a solution only to the ideological rather than the factual problems of mass unemployment. The official argument to justify the measure was the belief that the home countries of the foreign workers would benefit from the qualifications the returning migrants had obtained whilst working in Germany.

However, because of the poor working and living conditions in their home countries and the policy of family reunion (*Familienzusammenführung*) introduced by the German authorities, the expected large-scale return did not take place. On the contrary, the duration of the foreigners' stay increased during the period in question. By 1988, 46.8 per cent of all foreigners had been living in Germany for fifteen years or longer (see Table 5.3), a process which Körner (1990) describes as a 'working life long residence'.

Because of the halt in recruitment a structural change in the composition of the foreign population took place. Instead of young, single men looking for work, members of families were migrating to Germany, which now became an immigration country, not *de jure* but *de facto*. This was so because a decrease in the number of employed foreigners was not matched by a reduction in the number of the foreign population. On the contrary, the foreign population rose from 4,127,400 to 4,489,100 between 1974 and 1988. However, this was not a smooth process; rather the changes occurred in waves. Particularly striking is the rise in the number of the Turkish population, from just over 1 million in 1974 to over 1.5 million in the 1980s (1974 — 1,027,800; 1980 — 1,462,400; 1982 — 1,568,700; 1985 — 1,401,900; 1988 — 1,523,700).

Table 5.3 Duration of stay in the Federal Republic of Germany, 1981 and 1988

Nationality	Absolute fig. ('000)	Duration of stay (years): % distribution						
		<1	1–<4	4–<6	6–<8	8–<10	10–<15	15+
1981								
Turkey	1,580.7	3.3	21.7	10.9	10.4	17.4	30.0	6.3
Yugoslavia	631.7	2.0	9.8	6.3	6.3	14.2	51.8	9.6
Italy	601.6	3.5	15.8	9.9	6.0	9.0	31.2	24.7
Greece	300.8	2.3	8.2	5.1	6.3	9.5	42.1	26.5
Spain	173.5	1.4	5.5	3.8	4.9	10.8	38.3	35.3
Total	4,666.9	4.5	18.9	8.8	7.8	12.7	31.1	16.4
1988								
Turkey	1,523.7	4.4	10.2	4.2	6.9	13.2	23.6	37.6
Yugoslavia	579.2	5.5	5.8	2.6	4.0	5.3	14.6	62.1
Italy	508.7	4.3	9.8	4.5	5.4	7.3	15.1	53.5
Greece	274.8	6.9	7.0	3.1	4.1	4.0	12.8	62.2
Spain	126.4	1.8	4.3	2.1	2.6	3.1	10.8	75.2
Poland	171.6	37.4	27.0	7.5	10.3	3.8	3.2	10.8
Total	3,184.4	6.5	9.7	3.6	5.9	9.1	18.1	46.8

Source: Statistisches Bundesamt 1982 and 1990.

Recent tendencies since 1988

The more restrictive the manner in which individual countries use regulations to control immigration, the more people will migrate illegally. This is the case in Germany at the moment. In addition, over the past two to three years there has been a growing number of people who wish to resettle (in the main people of German descent living in Eastern European countries) and of those who seek political asylum (cf. Kemper's Chapter 14 in this volume). These tendencies can be seen as a direct result of the liberalization in Eastern Europe, the opening of the Berlin Wall and other recent political events, particularly the war in the former Yugoslavia.

The macro scale: regional distribution of foreigners

The foregoing brief overview of the development of migration after the Second World War has shown that the period of reconstruction strongly stimulated the demand for labour. This explains why prosperous regions such as the agglomerations around Munich and Stuttgart or the Rhein–Main area were the first to generate such a demand. So did those industries for which indigenous workers were not available in sufficient numbers.

The spatial distribution of foreign migration in Germany has always been heavily dependent upon the location of the recruiting companies. Right from the start migration concentrated strongly upon industrial agglomerations, reflecting the key role of economic geography in the macro-regional distribution of foreigners. Ritschard (1982) argues that migration patterns are the result of the requirements of regional labour markets and the spatial distribution of economic sectors and branches of industry. For instance, by 1961 the cities of Essen and Düsseldorf — both located in western Germany — were among the areas with the highest levels of foreign population. In Essen 8.7 per cent and in Düsseldorf 7.6 per cent of the population were foreigners. In Munich the rate was 8.0 per cent and in Neckar-Franken it stood at 12.1 per cent.[4]

The diffusion of foreigners was an inter-regional process starting in the south and spreading northwards. At the same time an intra-regional pattern developed, in which a preference for conurbations was typical (Giese 1978; Mühlgassner 1984). Both these authors share the view that the concentration of foreign workers in the western and northern parts of Germany is not only an outcome of direct immigration but also the result of internal migration, since immigration itself is controlled by a spatial process of diffusion. In this context it is important to note that the spatial patterns which evolve are contingent upon the readiness of employers to hire foreign labour and that this willingness is not a given condition. The necessary change in the attitude of the management does not take place simultaneously throughout the country, being itself a process of spatial diffusion on which other patterns of diffusion depend.

The heavy concentration of foreigners in the urban-industrial agglomerations (see Figure 5.1) has led to the limitation of further migration to these areas. The Secretary of State for 'Work and Social Order' (*Arbeit und Sozialordnung*) initiated this measure which was jointly introduced by the federal state and the individual states (*Länder*) in April 1975. Migration could be stopped in areas where the level of the foreign population exceeded 12 per cent. In certain cases local authorities could be included whose level was over 6 per cent only. According to the official explanation, this measure was necessary in view of the heavy demand that was made on the local infrastructure. On the whole this course of action was aimed primarily at the newcomers.

In January 1977 the cities of Cologne (with a foreign population of 11.3 per cent), Frankfurt (17.1 per cent), Hanover (8.5 per cent), Munich (15.4 per cent) and Berlin (9.4 per cent) declared themselves 'overstrained' areas. Rist (1978) argues that these cities were not so much under social pressure but rather under economic strain, and that the primary aim was to reserve labour for the Germans rather than to ease the burden on the social infrastructure. He substantiates his claim by pointing out that the level of the foreign population in Cologne, Hanover and Berlin was well below 12 per cent while at the same time the unemployment rates amongst the German work-force were extremely high. The whole measure was charged with ideological dispute and

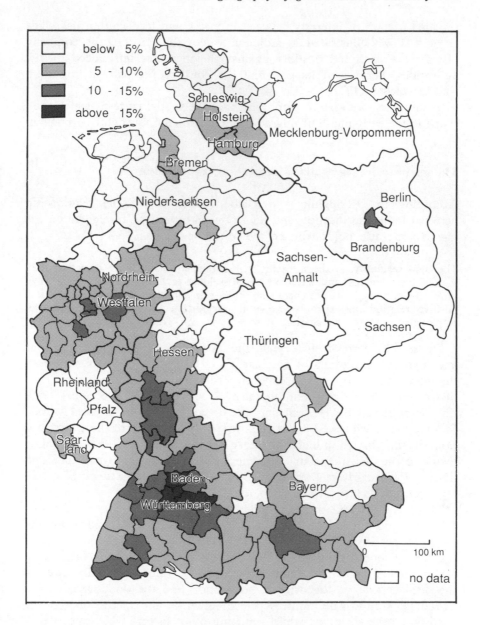

Figure 5.1 Foreign employees as percentage of all employees in West Germany, 1991

revealed a clash of interests between industry and local authorities. This clash was well illustrated in Cologne where the Ford motor company displayed a profound hostility against the measures introduced by the authorities. Because of its potential for conflict, the ban on migration was repealed in 1977.

In summary, we wish to emphasize that the spatial patterns which took shape in the early phase of migration have altered only slightly over time.

The micro scale: segregation, integration, assimilation

According to O'Loughlin and Glebe (1984, p. 9), the relationship between industrial location and high concentrations of foreigners on the macro scale also holds true on the micro scale:

The dual regularity — the movement of foreigners being more dispersed than that of the Germans, and the maps of Düsseldorf revealing more dispersal than those of Duisburg — is not surprising when one considers the hypothesis that a positive relationship exists between the proportion of workers in industrial employment and the segregation of socio-economic groups in a city.

Figure 5.2 impressively reveals the proximity of industrial locations and high concentrations of foreigners in Duisburg. The district next to the integrated steel works of Thyssen, Bruckhausen, has the highest level of foreigners in the city, standing at 52.7 per cent on 31 December 1990. This is followed by Hüttenheim, the location of another steel works, Mannesmann, with a 33.7 per cent share of foreigners.[5] The concentration of the foreign population close to industrial locations is mainly owing to the fact that many foreigners live in company-owned flats and houses. Particularly in Duisburg, companies have a large stock of dwellings, most of which are close to the factories.

There are different theories which try to explain the concentration of foreigners on the micro scale. No consensus, however, exists on the theory of succession-invasion. Bürkner (1987) points out the problems of this theory which assumes that after segregation has started to take place, a continual influx of an ethnic group sets in which eventually leads to the displacement of the original population and the dominance of the 'invading' group.[6] The implied cycle of invasion and succession assumes ideal-type generalizations whilst omitting other factors which also determine the decision of the 'displaced' group to move away, such as the age and the condition of the housing stock. Therefore, the spatial distribution is not so much an expression of an ethnic as of a social segregation, and of discriminating distribution mechanisms of the housing market (Bürkner 1989). A correlation between high concentrations of foreigners and old and poor housing stock has been proved in Frankfurt (Helmert 1982), Göttingen (Bürkner 1987; 1989), Augsburg (Ruile 1984) and Berlin (Brocke 1983).

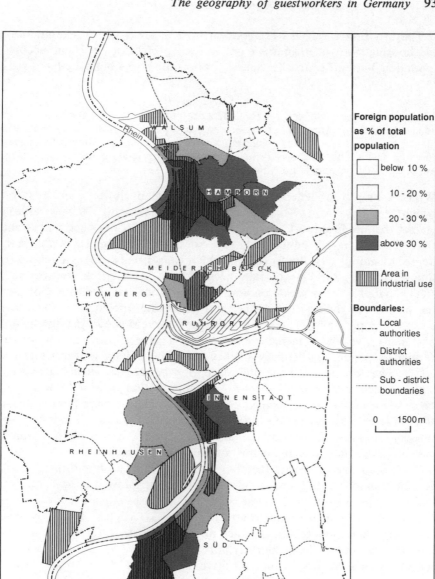

Figure 5.2 Foreigners in Duisburg, 1991

The fact that foreigners are concentrated in areas with predominantly old housing stock is attributable not to their preference for cheap accommodation but rather to the lack of opportunity to obtain better dwellings.

The poor housing conditions for foreigners are not caused by the inability to pay adequate rents but the lack of opportunity to do so. In this respect, the role played by real estate agents, public housing officials, housing cooperative agencies and factory housing owners in opening up their facilities to immigrants is important. (Glebe and O'Loughlin 1987, p. 67)

What is more, foreigners usually live in flats of lower standards for which they have to pay higher rents than Germans do. Helmert (1982) claims that in Frankfurt foreigners have to pay 20 per cent more rent than the indigenous population. One of the reasons given is the high degree of mobility of the foreigners which causes rents to rise much more quickly than in the case of flats accessible to the German population.

The patterns of segregation and concentration are indicative of the mechanisms of the housing market and not of the foreigners' wish to live close to people from their home countries. Surveys show that foreigners prefer to live in a mixed neighbourhood where only a few other foreigners reside, particularly if they plan on staying longer (Bürkner 1987). The Japanese are the only exception because of their high social status which makes high-standard accommodation accessible and also because they consciously segregate themselves in view of the limited duration of their stay (Glebe 1984; 1986; Zielke 1982). Japanese schools and nursery schools are elements of an ethnic-specific infrastructure which can be taken as viable indicators of this process of segregation.

The importance of social factors governing segregation and integration is emphasized by the fact that unemployment rates amongst foreign employees are substantially higher and that their net income is lower than that of their German counterparts (Figure 5.3). Higher unemployment rates can be explained by the fact noted earlier that foreigners act as labour market buffers. Furthermore, foreigners generally work in industries which are highly sensitive to market fluctuations. This, together with the policy of reuniting families, has aggravated the situation of foreigners in the recent past.

According to Hoffmann-Nowotny and Hondrich (1982), integration can be measured according to the degree of participation in social values (i.e., professional position and income) and in organizations (trade unions, clubs, etc). Assimilation, on the other hand, is an active participation in the mainstream culture. It is plausible to conclude that assimilation and foreigners' willingness to be assimilated are heavily contingent upon the readiness of the indigenous population to integrate the foreigners. As long as the model of rotation was at the heart of public policy, integration (and assimilation even less) would be of no importance.

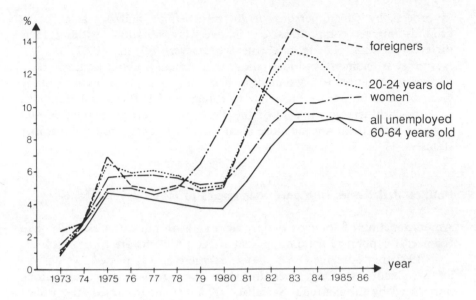

Figure 5.3 Unemployment rates of 'problem groups' in West Germany, 1973–86

Source: Statistisches Bundesamt, Datenreport 1987, Bonn, p. 95.

A fundamental difference between Germany and traditional immigration countries such as the United States, Canada and Australia is that most of the people who migrated to Germany never abandoned the idea of returning home. This can be seen as a strategy which helped the individual immigrant to cope psychologically with the new situation and the associated fundamental insecurities.

However, it had a delaying effect upon the processes of integration and assimilation. On the other hand, politicians themselves envisaged only a temporary integration initially, because at the back of their minds they regarded foreigners primarily as economic stopgaps. The outcome of such a concept could be only an extreme uncertainty, which made it difficult for the foreigners to plan ahead.

Politicians have by now acknowledged the flawed and indefensible nature of these notions, and as a consequence they have enacted administrative regulations such as the 'measures for professional and social integration'. In the official nomenclature, integration is defined as the realization of equal rights in housing, schooling and at work. However, this is made conditional upon the foreigners' decision in favour of remaining in Germany. Only on this condition can they be fully integrated, i.e. naturalized, a strategy which is being attacked by critics as compulsory Germanization. Typical of this approach is the complete assimilation of the foreigners, a conformity to German cultural traditions, 'a process by which persons of different ethnic and/or racial back-grounds interact comprehensively in everyday situations without their different descent playing any role whatsoever' (Goetze 1987, p. 71). Nevertheless, numerous studies show that bringing about contacts as a necessary condition for assimilation does not take place because many Germans are not prepared to relate to foreigners (cf. Bürkner 1987). This is particularly true in the case of the Turks whose different religion and customs make them appear more alien than foreigners from EC member states.

Political deficiencies with particular regard to recent developments

An examination of some of the problem areas in our overview will make the need for political action apparent if the problems are to be resolved.

In 1965 the 'Foreigners Act' (*Ausländergesetz*) was passed, which was an even more stringent measure than the *Fremdenrecht* regulations introduced by the National Socialists. The Act incorporated the 'Police regulations for foreigners' dating back to 1938. However, whilst the latter made the admission and expulsion of foreigners conditional upon their behaviour, the former made the interests of the Federal Republic the yardstick of the state's policies. This has put foreigners in a most precarious and unpredictable position.

Zander (1982) criticizes the fact that despite the rise in the number of foreigners and despite the difficult labour market, the federal government has so far not devised a comprehensive policy to deal with the situation.

Although there has been a drop in the number of employed foreigners, the foreign population on the whole has increased. Despite this, the government still refuses to acknowledge that Germany has *de facto* become an immigration country. 'The Federal Republic is not an immigration country. Germany is a place of residence for foreigners who will eventually return home voluntarily' (Basic principle I in the report of the 'Bund-Länder-Kommission' of 1977, quoted in Franz 1984, p. 120).

This position, however, cannot be maintained if the stay of the foreigners is regularly extended by the authorities, because doing so establishes the right of abode in Germany. This is why some critics demand to end the so-called guestworker policy (*Gastarbeiterpolitik*), since the guests have long since become citizens who need to be integrated into the German society on the basis of equal rights (cf. Franz 1984). The Federal Republic is in need of a comprehensive and consistent policy which comprises not only economic considerations but also the realization that the foreigners of the past have become part of the political, social and cultural system of Germany.

A particular problem area in this context is the situation of the second generation which is aggravated by the German schooling system. The fact that foreign children lack cultural experience and a primary school education prevents them from obtaining a better secondary education and thus relegates them to the lower social ranks. This matter is a clear expression of the political and economic thinking governing public policies regarding foreigners. Rist (1978) draws a parallel between the different stages in the development of the school regulations for foreign children and the stages of migration to Germany after the Second World War outlined earlier. During the first stage ('expansion'), compulsory schooling was introduced for all foreign children. In line with the model of rotation, the children were to be taught in their native languages in order not to threaten the ties that existed between the children and their home country. During the following stage ('consolidation'), the idea of integration into the German schooling system received highest priority because now the integration of the foreign workers and their families as functional members of society was pivotal to contemporary political thinking. During the third state ('securing a structural marginal position'), linguistic assimilation was intended. Simultaneously the linguistic, cultural and historical ties with the home countries were to be fostered.

Both of the opposing notions of rotation and integration are incorporated in the schooling policies of individual states. Bavaria, for instance favours rotation whilst Berlin supports the second notion. Both extremes are untenable, as the discussion centring on a multicultural society reveals. At the heart of this notion lies the acceptance of different, even opposing, cultural identities and the rejection of models such as the ones of rotation and integration. However, the idea of a multicultural society has no tradition in Germany, nor in any of the other European nation-states, except possibly in Holland (see Dieleman's Chapter 7 in this volume). Therefore no lobby exists which endeavours to translate the idea of a multicultural society into action and only slowly does it gain acceptance.

In the meantime the entire issue of how to integrate foreigners has developed into a highly charged matter which needs urgent political action, not least because of recent events such as the attacks by right-wing radicals on people seeking asylum. The inability of the political parties to come to grips with the problems has given rise to the criticism that the whole debate has gone wrong and that this will only lend support to nationalist tendencies. Others criticize the failure to acknowledge the fact that Germany has become an immigration country and that it therefore needs an immigration policy. This is why Geissler (1991) quite logically concludes that the solution to the problems caused by the asylum-seekers is the necessary condition for a more sophisticated policy aimed at the integration of foreigners which would help to address the major problem, namely world-wide mass migration. Geissler emphatically calls for a life **with** foreigners and rejects any renaissance of German nationalist sentiments.

The notion of the multicultural society he supports would make demands on Germans and foreigners alike. The Germans must be prepared to live with people with diverse cultural backgrounds by accepting cultural heterogeneity. The foreigners on the other hand need to accept the universal human rights of the Federal Republic (e.g., equal rights for women, freedom of worship and of conscience, religious freedom), and they must have a good command of the German language.

On the political level a programme is required which tackles the hostility towards foreigners. Furthermore, the image that foreigners are responsible for unemployment amongst the Germans and that the situation would improve if they returned to their home countries needs to be corrected. It must be emphasized in public debate that not only is the German economy heavily dependent on foreign workers but also that the foreigners stimulate demand, pay fees into the pension funds, add to the gross domestic product and pay taxes. In view of the fact that the German population is persistently decreasing, the foreigners also play a crucial part in stabilizing society in Germany. Unfortunately the Federal Republic is presently lacking a theoretical approach which takes up the challenges posed by foreign migration and which transcends national boundaries in order to deal with the complex patterns of internationally linked mass migration.

Notes

1. The problem of definition is extensively discussed in Mühlgassner 1984, p. 70; Schrettenbrunner 1982, p. 20.
2. cf. Max Weber's *Verdrängungstheorie* which suggests that the extension of the initially limited employment of foreigners led to the displacement of the indigenous workers.
3. The policies of the National Socialists regarding foreigners opened up a new and particularly tragic chapter in the history of foreign employment in Germany, which was more than an enforcement of the policies that had been practised until then.
4. Data from *Raumordnungspolitische Steuerung der Ausländerbeschäftigung*, 1976, p. 50.
5. Data from Amt für Statistik und Wahlforschung, Duisburg.
6. Hoffmann-Nowotny and Hondrich (1982) claim that this is true in Frankfurt where the indigenous population moved away upon the arrival of the foreigners.

References

Bade, K., 1983, *Vom Auswanderungsland zum Einwanderungsland? Deutschland 1880–1980*, Colloquium-Verlag, Berlin.
Brocke, H., 1983, 'Das Wohnen von Ausländern in Berlin', in Arin, C. (ed.), *Ausländer im Wohnbereich. Dokumentation eines Seminars der Internationalen Bauausstellung Berlin*, Express Edition, Berlin, 159–66.

Bürkner, H.-J., 1987, *Die soziale und sozialräumliche Situation türkischer Migranten in Göttingen*, Breitenbach, Saarbrücken.

Bürkner, H.-J., 1989, 'Binnenintegration — Probleme der Entwicklung türkischer Immigranten-Kolonien in der Bundesrepublik Deutschland, dargestellt am Beispiel türkischer Migranten in Göttingen', in Schaffer, F. and Heller, W. (eds), *Türkische Arbeiterwanderung und Stadtentwicklung. Tendenzen in der Bundesrepublik Deutschland und in der Türkei*, Selbstverlag, Augsburg (Beiträge zur Angewandten Sozialgeographie, 21), 53–75.

Franz, F., 1984, 'Die Bundesrepublik Deutschland: Zufluchtsort politisch Verfolgter und Einwanderungsland zugleich — Sammellager die notwendige Konsequenz?', in Sievering, U.O. (ed.), *Politisches Asyl und Einwanderung, Arnoldshainer Texte, Vol. 22*, Haag und Herchen, Frankfurt, 120–37.

Geissler, H., 1991, 'Wir brauchen die Ausländer. Ein Plädoyer gegen die völkische Renaissance der Deutschen', *Die Zeit*, 11 October: 83.

Giese, E., 1978, 'Räumliche Diffusion ausländischer Arbeitnehmer in der Bundesrepublik Deutschland 1960–1976', *Die Erde*, 109(1): 92–110.

Glebe, G., 1984, 'Tendenzen ethnischer Segregation und Konzentration von Gastarbeiterminoritäten in Düsseldorf 1974–1982', *Zeitschrift für Wirtschaftsgeographie*, 28(1): 91–111.

Glebe, G., 1986, 'Segregation and intra-urban mobility of a high-status ethnic group: the case of the Japanese in Düsseldorf', *Ethnic and Racial Studies*, 9(4): 461–83.

Glebe, G. and O'Loughlin, J. (eds), 1987, *Foreign minorities in continental European cities*, Steiner-Verlag, Stuttgart.

Goetze, D., 1987, 'Probleme der Akkulturation und Assimilation', in Reimann, H. and Reimann, H. (eds), *Gastarbeiter. Analyse und Perspektiven eines sozialen Problems*, Westdeutscher Verlag, Opladen, 67–94.

Helmert, U., 1982, 'Konzentrations- und Segregationsprozesse der ausländischen Bevölkerung in Frankfurt a. M.', in Hoffmann-Nowotny, H.-J. and Hondrich K.-O. (eds), *Ausländer in der Bundesrepublik Deutschland und in der Schweiz*, Campus-Verlag, Frankfurt on Main, 256–93.

Hoffmann-Nowotny, H.-J. and Hondrich, K.-O. (eds), 1982, *Ausländer in der Bundesrepublik Deutschland und in der Schweiz*, Campus-Verlag, Frankfurt on Main.

Kayser, B., 1972, *Cyclically-determined homeward flows of migrant workers*, OECD, Paris.

Körner, H., 1990, *Internationale Mobilität der Arbeit. Eine empirische und theoretische Analyse der internationalen Wirtschaftsmigration im 19. und 20. Jahrhundert*, Wissenschaftliche Buchgesellschaft, Darmstadt.

Mühlgassner, D., 1984, 'Die Gastarbeiterwanderung in Europa', in Lichtenberger, E., *Gastarbeiter — Leben in zwei Gesellschaften*, Verlag Böhlau, Vienna, 69–81.

O'Loughlin, J., 1987, 'Chicago an der Ruhr or what? Explaining the location of immigrants in European cities', in Glebe, G. and O'Loughlin, J. (eds), *Foreign minorities in continental European cities*, Steiner-Verlag, Stuttgart, 52–69.

O'Loughlin, J. and Glebe, G., 1984, 'Intraurban migration in West German cities', *Geographical Review*, 74(1): 1–23.

Rist, R.C., 1978, *Guestworkers in Germany: the prospects for pluralism*, Praeger, New York.

Ritschard, R., 1982, 'Die makroregionale Verteilung ausländischer Arbeitskräfte in der Schweiz und in der Bundesrepublik Deutschland', in Hoffmann-Nowotny, H.-J. and Hondrich, K.-O. (eds), *Ausländer in der Bundesrepublik Deutschland und in der Schweiz*, Campus-Verlag, Frankfurt on Main, 195–254.

Ruile, A., 1984, *Ausländer in der Großstadt. Zum Problem der kommunalen Integration der türkischen Bevölkerung*, Selbstverlag, Augsburg (Beiträge zur Angewandten Sozialgeographie, 7).

Schrettenbrunner, H., 1982, *Gastarbeiter: Ein europäisches Problem*, Diesterweg, Frankfurt on Main.

Treibel, A., 1990, *Migration in modernen Gesellschaften. Soziale Folgen von Einwanderung und Gastarbeit*, Juventa-Verlag, Weinheim.

Zander, J., 1982, 'Ausländer in Deutschland — Einführung in die Probleme', in Geißler, H. (ed.), *Ausländer in Deutschland — für eine gemeinsame Zukunft, Vol. 1: Entwicklungen und Prognosen*, Olzog, Munich, 14–35.

Zielke, E., 1982, *Die Japaner in Düsseldorf. Manager-Mobilität — Voraussetzungen und Folgen eines Typs internationaler geographischer Mobilität*, Selbstverlag des Geographischen Instituts der Universität Düsseldorf (Düsseldorfer Geographische Schriften, 19).

Chapter 6

The legacy of migration: some evidence from France

Philip Ogden

Introduction

Immigration to France and the controversies that surround it are not new. Tribalat (1991a and 1991b), for example, suggests that about 14 million of the current population resident in France are of foreign nationality or have foreign ancestry no more than two generations back. Certainly, from the late nineteenth century, the economic and demographic fortunes of the country have been intimately related to immigration, which has at various periods provided an eagerly grasped solution to labour shortage (Noiriel 1986). The origins of migrant flows have been complex, and any stereotype of 'immigrants' which seeks to portray simple characteristics is bound to be mistaken. Migrants and their descendants are present in every walk of French life. In order to understand their role we need to look very carefully at the nature of the French state and its attitude towards nationality, citizenship and colonialism; at the state's role in defining and implementing migration policy; and at the changing nature of the French economy.[1] Immigration has frequently proved uncontroversial, with large numbers of migrants arriving, forming families and pursuing successful careers in France without undue comment. Yet, the current preoccupation with immigration in French politics,[2] with renewed discussion about all aspects of migration and its consequences, has clear historical precedents. The frenzied tone of much of the present comment, successfully fermented by the Front National over the last decade, suggests the need for a more reflective and long-term view. Concern has manifested itself in previous periods during the twentieth century: Schor (1985), for example, in his study of the press has documented the rise of racism and anti-semitism during the 1930s. Nevertheless, in a recent collection of essays on 'Race, nation, classe', Balibar and Wallerstein (1990, p. 303) have suggested that whilst in a broader context there may be nothing that distinguishes the present from the rest of the post-war years, there is some difference between contemporary racism and previous phases of xenophobia.

Who are the 'immigrants'?

We need to be clear at the outset about who qualifies for the term 'immigrant' in France and the mechanisms by which status may change. It is important to be clear about definitions, for there is much misunderstanding of the wider issues as the result of an over-simplified view of who the 'immigrants' are. It is also important to understand the mechanisms by which French nationality may be obtained and the reasons which underlie the political control of these mechanisms. As we shall see later, rights to acquire French nationality are crucial to the future of the descendants of first-generation immigrants and have provoked heated debate in the later 1980s and 1990s.

In France the possession or acquisition of nationality is the key determinant of many political and civil rights. For example, only those with French nationality may vote. Thus 'immigrants' and 'foreigners' are frequently taken to be synonymous or, worse still, immigration has been increasingly 'racialized', whereby 'immigration has become constructed as a "problem" of North African Muslims and their children in a traditionally homogeneous, white and Christian society' (Silverman 1991, p. 337). Much political debate concentrates on the population of foreign nationality, who numbered some 3.58 million at the time of the 1990 census. The breakdown by major national groupings at recent censuses is given in Table 6.1, and the long-term evolution of the foreign population is presented in Figure 6.1. The latter shows the peaks and troughs in the size of the foreign population. There were already a million foreigners by the 1880s, and there was much recruitment during the inter-war period and again during the post-war years. There have been quite marked changes in the balance of nationalities, too, reflecting as in other European countries colonial links and competition for labour with other countries. Thus, while Europeans still account for a high proportion of France's foreign resident population in 1990, their relative importance has declined in favour of groups from outside the European Community. Detailed breakdown by nationalities[3] is given in Table 6.2, which emphasizes the importance not only of North African groups, but also of other groups such as the Portuguese: the former account for about 40 per cent of the total. The 1990 census shows that while the total foreign population born abroad fell by 10,000 between 1982 and 1990, this was made up of a decline of 180,000 for those from the European Community and an increase of 170,000 for non-EC citizens (Labat 1991). Figure 6.2 shows the geographical distribution of foreign nationals in 1990, highlighting the concentration in cities, especially in the Paris basin and in north-eastern, eastern and southern France.

Yet there are two points which must lead us to beware of using these figures without careful qualification and of conflating the notions of 'immigrant' and 'foreigner' too readily. First, people's own national status changes by the processes of acquisition and naturalisation (see

Table 6.1 Evolution of the foreign population in France 1975–90, by major national groups (in thousands)

	1975	1982	1990	change 1982–90
All foreigners	3,440	3,680	3,580	− 100
Born in France	670	830	740	− 90
Born outside France	2,770	2,850	2,840	− 10
Ratio of women to men	62	71	79	
EC foreigners	1,870	1,580	1,300	− 280
Born in France	340	310	210	− 100
Born outside France	1,530	1,270	1,090	− 180
Ratio of women to men	82	84	88	
Non-EC foreigners	1,570	2,100	2,280	+ 180
Born in France	330	520	530	+ 10
Born outside France	1,240	1,580	1,750	+ 170
Ratio of women to men	43	61	73	

Source: Labat 1991, p. 2.

Table 6.2 France: naturalized population and foreign population, 1982

Nationality (present or former)	French by acquisition	Foreigners
Italian	412,028	340,308
Spanish	269,000	327,156
Portuguese	67,700	767,304
Yugoslav	21,110	62,472
Polish	160,208	68,804
Algerian	74,792	805,116
Moroccan	31,468	441,308
Tunisian	45,480	190,800
Other African	25,760	157,548
Cambodian Vietnamese	31,692	104,188
Turkish	11,756	122,260
Other	270,574	357,936
Total	1,421,568	3,745,200

Source: Guillon (1988, p. 139) from the Census of Population, 1982.

line c in Figure 6.1). Table 6.2 shows the previous nationality of those who had acquired French nationality at the time of the 1982 census: a heavy bias towards those of European origin. Italy, Spain and Poland provide between them some 60 per cent of this naturalized population, reflecting both the longer history of immigration and also, as we shall see, the encouragement given to some groups of migrants rather than others to assimilate by this means. Naturalization of non-European

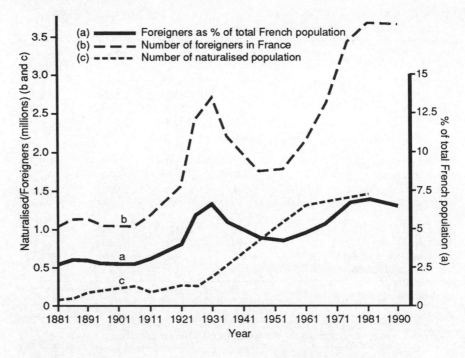

Figure 6.1   Evolution of numbers of foreign and naturalized population in France and foreigners as a proportion of the total resident population, 1881–1990

Note: Figures for the naturalized population in 1990 are not yet available.

Source: INSEE 1985, pp. 15, 18; Labat 1991, p. 2.

groups has, though, been increasing rapidly of late. Guillon (1988) suggests that there is evidence of different strategies by different national groups: the Yugoslavs and those from the states of the former Indo-China seem to opt more readily for French nationality than, for example, the Portuguese who cling to the notion of return and keep their nationality.

By 1990, of the French population of 53.05 million, some 1.29 million were those born outside France who had subsequently obtained French nationality. Thus, Figure 6.3 suggests that when the latter figure is added to the foreign population born outside France, a better figure for the population of what the French census office calls *immigrés* is around 4.13 million. We should also note that some three-quarters of a million of those with foreign nationality in 1990 are children born in France to foreign parents, most of whom will have automatic rights to acquire French nationality when they reach the age of majority. Details by nationality show the shift away from European origins, although we need to bear in mind the operation of two factors: the life cycle effect, that

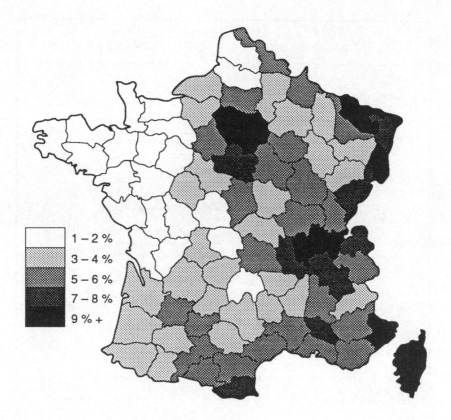

1 – 2 %
3 – 4 %
5 – 6 %
7 – 8 %
9 % +

Figure 6.2 Proportion of foreigners in the total population of French departments, 1990

Source: Labat 1991, p. 1.

is, migrants from some areas are still in the middle stages of family formation whereas others from Europe have already reached a degree of demographic 'maturity'; and second, that there is already strong evidence of declining fertility amongst immigrants from the Third World (Tribalat 1988).

Yet, this too is only part of the story if we are really interested in the process of migration. The French population also includes large numbers of migrants with French nationality from colonies and ex-colonies: the two best examples are migrants from the overseas departments of the French Caribbean (Condon and Ogden 1991) and Réunion, and the *pieds noirs* who arrived in metropolitan France in large numbers in the early 1960s consequent upon the political upheaval in North Africa. In the case of the Caribbean migrants, for example, there was no difference in status between those going to France and those migrating from the British colonies to the United Kingdom at roughly the same time. What

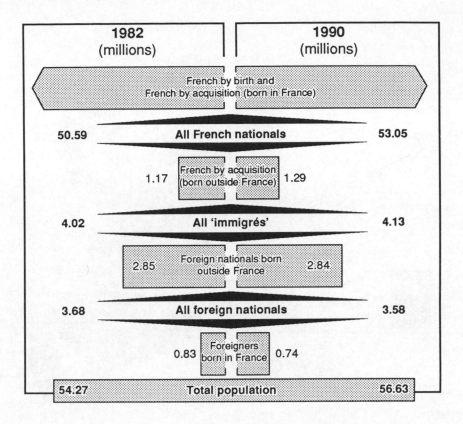

Figure 6.3   Elements in the make-up of the resident population in France in 1982 and 1990

Source: Lévy 1991.

has differed is the interpretation placed by the state at different times on their status. This is equally true of the Algerians whose status was redefined from French to foreign after the end of French colonial rule. Finally, we should note that quite outside any of these categories come the illegal migrants or *clandestins* whose numbers were estimated at around 300,000 in the early 1980s (Marie 1983; 1988). Here again, the attitude of the state towards these migrants has varied: sometimes the state has allowed almost free entry and 'regularization' afterwards; at other times, not least at the present, the status of 'illegal' has carried with it a particular ignominy.

We may thus make two points from a consideration of the complexity of the above data. The first is that the state defines and uses categories of nationality and resident status in different ways at different times. Second, the very complexity of both the migration itself and the ways in which nationality is defined and may be acquired mean that at the very

least we should beware of making too simple generalizations about the
'immigrant' population and its impact on French society. The integration
of people from outside metropolitan France into the population is an
ancient process, and as proved by the figures quoted above from
Tribalat, has been particularly intense over the last century or so. Even
for the period between the censuses of 1982 and 1990, when the foreign
population total remained stable, Lebon (1991) has shown that some
500,000 people who were counted as foreign at the first date had become
French by the second, and that there were a large number of arrivals and
departures of migrants every year. In sum, the 'foreign' contribution to
French society is central and cannot logically be stigmatized as recent and
exceptional, with current 'immigrants' treated as a marginalized group.

Questions of nationality and citizenship

It follows from the discussion above that the process by which French
nationality is acquired by the children of first-generation immigrants is
of central importance to their role in French society. Legislative
arrangements are complex, details change frequently and cannot be fully
discussed here (although see, e.g., Laacher 1987). However, among the
most important aspects are that any child born in France to at least one
parent who was French is automatically French; and that any child born
in France to foreign parents may either claim French nationality or be
awarded it automatically on reaching the age of majority, given certain
residence requirements. In addition, anyone marrying a French person
may take French nationality as may children of foreign nationality whose
parents become French by naturalization. By these processes of mixed
marriage and birth in France, as well as by naturalization, the gradual
transformation of one generation of foreigners to the next generation of
French nationals may take place, with its associated advantages of full
rights of citizenship. Nevertheless, recent political developments have
called into question the way in which nationality is granted, and it is
worth reflecting on what these recent moves indicate and also upon the
historical origins of the current legislation.

As the debate on 'immigration' in France intensified in the 1980s and
as the whole debate shifted to the Right under pressure from the Front
National (Ogden 1987; Husbands 1991), there has been increasing
pressure not only for tighter border controls on new arrivals but also for
stricter regulation of the ways in which French nationality may be
obtained. The recent call by ex-President Valéry Giscard d'Estaing not
only for what he termed the 'invasion' of immigrants to be halted but
also for the French nationality granted to children born in France to
foreign parents to be no longer automatic is a clear reflection of these
political pressures. The various Socialist governments under President
Mitterrand held the line against extreme measures on immigration within

an overall policy of quite strict control on new entries. In the early 1980s, for example, measures were introduced to 'regularize' the presence of many illegal workers and their families who had arrived in France during the period of rapid economic growth and high labour demand of the 1960s and 1970s. However, the brief right-wing government of 1986–8, led by Jacques Chirac, proposed fundamental changes in the nationality laws (see Wihtol de Wenden 1991). The automatic acquisition of nationality for children born in France to foreign parents at the age of majority was to be limited: a request must be made at some point between the ages of 16 and 23 and could be refused on various grounds including any form of criminal offence. The proposals were referred to a commission of inquiry which subsequently moderated the proposals, and in the event the government of Chirac lost power before any legislative changes could be made. The issue remains, however, a live focus of discussion both within and between the major political parties, as the recent remarks from Giscard d'Estaing indicate, and the Front National has identified the 'liberal' laws on nationality as a brake on possible 'repatriation' and in need of reform. The basic proposal to modify the *ius soli* (nationality through place of birth) was of significance: as Amar and Milza (1990, p. 224) remark, 'the whole concept of a national identity founded upon a culture shared from childhood was brought into question in favour of some sort of superior identity that one ought to deserve' rather than acquire by right.

This recent debate mirrors discussion at several previous periods in French history. The idea that *ius sanguinis* (the transmission of nationality solely through parents) needed to be supplemented by a broader concept of nationality related to birth and/or residence on French soil has its roots in the mid-nineteenth century. Its development has been intimately connected with France's labour needs and with its perceived demographic shortfall. Thus, as Massot (1985, p. 9) has reminded us:

for more than a century, the republican legislator, for reasons of national interest, at first essentially military in 1851 and 1889, then demographic in 1927 and 1945, has wanted to confer French nationality on people of foreign 'blood' without their having either the obligation to take positive steps or even sometimes the possibility to refuse. By the automatic effect of the law, innumerable children of foreigners have been considered French from their birth or have become French before or at the age of majority.

Certainly in 1945 this approach was fundamental to the use that the government planned to make of immigration to fill labour shortfall, not only temporarily but also on a permanent basis by turning 'foreigners into French men and women'. It was recognized then that some nationals were to be favoured over others and the recent opposition to granting nationality to those of North African origin has clear historical roots. Indeed, as Amar and Milza (1990, p. 221) point out, xenophobia against other, European, groups has previously carried the day: for example, the attempts by the government to speed up naturalization of young men in the later 1930s to bolster France's military forces were met by charges from the far Right that France was being 'sold off, like a jumble sale, to the dregs of Europe'. The Vichy regime followed this up with anti-semitic legislation, withdrawing nationality retrospectively from some sections of the population.

This attitude to nationality also has roots in the attitude of the French to their colonial territories, and the problems generated by decolonization bear directly on the prospects of integration for the descendants of France's post-war immigration. A central plank of French colonial rule was the imposition of French culture on the colonized areas, including the French language, educational and political systems, and the granting of nationality was seen as a way of ensuring the triumph of French values (Ageron 1991). We may draw a useful distinction between the Afro-Caribbean population currently resident in France on the one hand, and the population of Algerian origin on the other. In the first case, the Caribbean islands of Guadeloupe and Martinique were given the status of Overseas Departments after the Second World War, with French citizenship for the people and full political integration with the *métropole*, including free movement of citizens from the islands. A considerable migration began in the early 1960s and the Afro-Caribbean population in France numbered around 200,000 by 1990. The status of the islands has not changed and the migrants are not, of course, counted with the foreign population. They attract little comment in discussions about immigration and are indeed quoted approvingly by the Front National as examples of people who assimilate into French society. That does not mean, though, that they escape discrimination or racism of a less overt kind. Algerian immigrants who arrived at roughly the same time — from the early 1960s to the late 1970s — have fared less well. Critics seek justification in the differing cultural origins of the migrants — they are Muslim rather than Catholic, for example — although just as important is the changing status of Algeria. French before 1962, Algerians subsequently became nationals of their own country after a bitter war of independence which resulted *inter alia* in the arrival of well over 1 million *pieds noirs*, as mentioned above. It has proved easy for politicians of the far Right to exploit the idea of Algerians as a threat, given the lasting effects of the political upheaval (see Lloyd and Waters 1991). It is interesting, though, that the French state has remained equivocal in its attitude to the Algerians' status. For example, those children born to Algerian parents (who had been French before 1962) living in France are considered Algerian by the Algerians but French by the French. Thus, the 1982 census recorded a large number of children as Algerian because that is how their parents recorded them, though they are in fact fully fledged French nationals (see Labat 1991). The implications for military service had been resolved in 1983, although for Amar and Milza (1990, p. 223) this 'question of nationality in the case of Algeria retains all its symbolic importance, well beyond administrative practice. It indicates in fact France's reticence to break with the past, to recognize that Algeria was not France'. This confused background has not assisted their integration (see Khellil 1991) and it is interesting to compare the Front National leader Jean-Marie Le Pen's comment in 1958 that the Algerians would 'in due course form . . . the new blood of a French nation into which we shall have integrated them' (quoted in Milza 1988, p. 78), with his more recent pronouncements on the supposed 'Islamization' of France (Lloyd and Waters 1991, p. 62).

The debate on nationality has also broadened into a discussion of the nature of French citizenship, leading, as Silverman (1991) has recently argued, to a reassessment of the traditional links between the state, the nation and civil rights. As Hargreaves (1991) and Wihtol de Wenden (1991) have indicated, this is linked in part to the growth of a politically conscious 'second generation' of North African origin, not least in the suburbs of Paris, Lyons and Marseilles. As Wihtol de Wenden emphasizes, this is a heterogeneous group: some are French, some are nationals of the three North African countries, some are born to mixed marriages, some are the children of *harkis*.[4] The relaxation of rights of association for non-French nationals by the Socialist government in 1981 has also aided this process. In addition, the increasingly racist attacks from the far Right have simulated an anti-racist movement, represented for example by SOS Racisme, which has asked challenging questions about the rights of long-standing residents as well as of those with French nationality. Thus,

the debate around the reform of the Nationality Code has contributed to a discussion of the possibility of dissociating nationality and citizenship. The second generation is claiming a more participative citizenship, founded more on residence than on nationality and affiliation, within a multicultural society. Local social movements are promoting a citizenship for all those who live together with the same problems. They have also introduced the idea that a new process of politicisation might develop, founded on concrete aims and practices (such as employment, local life, housing, education, defence of rights), with the rights to democracy consisting less in having citizenship than in being citizens. (Wihtol de Wenden, 1991, p. 330)

Mitterrand himself has occasionally referred to the idea of allowing foreigners the right to vote in local elections, though the degree of hostility towards the notion has made it politically impossible for the moment.

Some historical perspectives on the evolution of state policy

The questions of nationality and rights, and their changing definitions, are intimately connected to the general evolution of state policy on immigrant recruitment: frontier controls, selectivity, attitudes to family reunification, illegal migration and so forth. The role and status of migrants and their descendants in France has indeed long been determined by the attitude of the French state. As Bovenkerk *et al.* (1990, p. 480) have recently emphasized, the influence of the state on the social, economic and political position of migrants has been rather underestimated in research on most European countries. The perception of immigration as being linked above all to the expansion of capitalism in the post-war years has rather camouflaged the central role of the state, in its various forms, as a key influence. Thus, in the French case, while there is no doubt that the need of the economy for labour was at the centre of the recruitment of immigrants, the state had a role in determining overall policy and the definition of the type of immigrants who were to be allowed entry. This definition varied over time.

Therefore, if we look back to the later decades of the nineteenth century and the early years of the twentieth century, we see that the state was already conscious of the fact that slowing population growth promised to create difficulties both for the labour market and for military strength. Whilst pre-1914 immigration was largely spontaneous, Noiriel (1986) has drawn attention to the recruitment of labour for the mines and steel works in northern France by the Comité des Forges de l'Est. During the inter-war period, attempts at organization by both the state and private sector interests, sometimes working in tandem, increased (see Ogden 1989, pp. 44–5), and the total number of foreigners more than doubled in twenty years to reach 2.7 million in 1931. The first North Africans arrived at this time, forming a subproletariat among foreign workers. Cross (1983, p. 12) goes on to argue, indeed, that France experienced in the decade after the First World War what the rest of north-west Europe was not to experience until the 1950s:

economic growth became possible in a society in which the native population was unwilling to participate fully in its cost . . . . Employers were thus able to obtain prosperity without fully accepting the responsibility for the modern social costs of labour — citizenship and improved labour standards . . . . French workers sought to avoid . . . arduous labour, French capital the economic consequences of competition.

Most important, perhaps, and with telling parallels in the post-1945 years, was that foreign labour became a 'radically distinctive class in France. Not merely were immigrants predominantly propertyless and unskilled, but they were non-citizens' (Cross 1983, p. 16).

The recourse to immigration was renewed after the Second World War. Although the detailed history of this period is covered elsewhere (Ogden 1989; 1991), we may profitably draw out a number of themes of relevance to the present status of immigrants and their descendants and their prospects for the future. One of the key themes must be the confusion and inconsistency in, and sometimes the straightforward lack of,

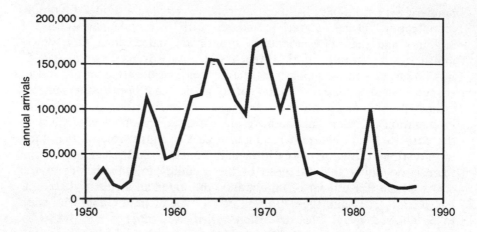

Figure 6.4   Annual arrivals of permanent foreign workers in France, 1951–87
Source: Based on data from Costa-Lascoux 1989, p. 42.

governmental policies. Nevertheless, the state in its various incarnations has played a leading role for much of the post-war period. At the end of the war, immigration was identified as a cornerstone of economic recovery. Yet, from the outset, immigration was to be selective and indeed was to form the basis of permanent additions to the population rather than temporary labour. Thus, Le Bras (1991, pp. 180–3) in his recent controversial book on France's 'demographic obsession', traces the links between 'populationism', implicit racism, and the selection of immigrants among the post-war policy-makers (see e.g., Debré and Sauvy 1946). Clear preference was expressed for the Italians and for others from neighbouring European states. As Figure 6.4 shows, though, immigration was at first slow, and preferred sources proved incapable of satisfying the demand.

The great boom in immigration from the mid-1960s to the mid-1970s had three principal features. First, for some nationalities men predominated, with the assumption that some would return home. Second, migrants were drawn increasingly from new sources in Southern Europe and North Africa (and there was also an important immigration of French citizens from the overseas departments, which are not included in Figure 6.4). Third, and perhaps most important, immigration escaped governmental control. Despite the fact that in theory the National Immigration Office had a monopoly over recruitment, in practice immigrants arrived both spontaneously and in direct response to the needs of private capital. Many, therefore, escaped any form of governmental regulation and the practice developed of 'regularization' of status after arrival (Freeman 1989, p. 164). This is a good example of the state bending the rules — at this period turning a blind eye to 'illegals' in a way that would be unthinkable in the early 1990s (see Weil 1991). Thus, perhaps as many as 80 per cent of migrants during the 1960s were given legal status only after their arrival (Tapinos 1975, pp. 66, 87). As I have pointed out elsewhere (Ogden 1991, p. 299), questions of secret and illegal entry, exploitative work for low salaries, work in the black market and life in the *bidonville* or shanty town became the chief characteristics of immigrant labour. Or, as Tapinos (1975, p. 66) has put it:

just as immigration developed and as those countries that had been absent from traditional migrant flows played an increasing part, nothing was done to prepare public opinion for the integration of these new arrivals into French society. In addition, the deplorable conditions in which the entry and installation in France . . . took place had the effect of giving a very biased image to the supposed life-styles of this new population . . . and to create the illusion of a foreign population much greater than it in fact was.

From the early 1970s, however, things began to change. The last two decades have been marked not only by an increasing politicization of the immigration issue, but also by a series of twists and turns in government policy, whose ultimate failure is perhaps best illustrated by the extraordinary hold which immigration has established on the French political consciousness in the early 1990s. It seems to be fair comment that governments of neither Right nor Left have succeeded in developing a coherent policy on the regulation of new arrivals and on the thorny questions of economic and social integration. The main force underlying restrictions placed on entry from the early 1970s, well illustrated in Figure 6.4, was not so much political necessity as the changing needs of the economy. Immigration of men to traditional unskilled jobs was less in demand and migration has become increasingly feminized, for example as employment shifted from manufacturing to services. Thus, Lebon (1988, p. 93) points out that between 1973 and 1985 there was a decline of 43 per cent in the number of foreigners in industry, 47 per cent in building and public works and a matching growth of almost 30 per cent in the service sector. In addition, the greatest increase in the foreign population has come from family reunion and family formation in France rather than primary immigration of workers. Figure 6.5 shows the evolution of arrivals of family members which peaked during the early 1970s, and has continued at a lower level during the last two decades. Overall, as Table 6.1 indicates, the ratio of women to men in the foreign population rose from 62 to 79 between 1975 and 1990. We should also note that the diversification of sources of migrants has continued through France's more liberal policies on refugees, who have come from South-East Asia, Africa and Central Europe (Tribalat 1988).

The last two decades may be divided into two discrete periods: the first from 1974 to 1981, under the presidency of Giscard d'Estaing, and the second following François Mitterrand's election in 1981. As well as the restrictions on entry for new workers during the 1970s, some limits were

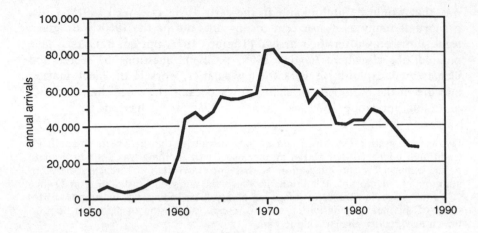

Figure 6.5   Annual arrivals of family members of foreign nationals in France, 1951–87

Source: Based on data from Costa-Lascoux 1989, p. 38.

placed on the arrivals of family members. Equally important, though, and a major contributor to the increasing politicization of the immigration issue, were two factors: first, the continued arrivals of 'illegals', for whom the regularization of the 1960s was less and less possible and whose status was thereby redefined as a problem and a threat to social peace; and second, an experiment with the encouragement of return migration with repatriation payments (Poinard 1979) and with the use of expulsion for certain categories of illegals. This proved an effective way of souring the political atmosphere. Thus, Verbunt (1985, p. 146) has drawn attention to the creation of notions of 'good' and 'bad' immigrants, recalling the post-war policy-makers' view on assimilation: the 'good' were the Europeans, the 'bad' the North Africans. Lloyd and Waters (1991) have drawn attention also to the rise of violence against the latter during the 1970s, which has endured. On taking office in 1981, the Socialist government tried to defuse what had become an explosive issue, with only partial success. Nevertheless, the halt placed on expulsions, the regularization of some 150,000 *clandestins* (the effect is clearly visible in Figure 6.4) and the granting of rights of political association did attempt to infuse into French political consciousness the idea of the inevitability of a large permanent ethnic minority population. As Silverman (1991, p. 342) has cogently argued, though, the persistent and misleading confusion between 'illegals' and 'immigrant workers' has never been adequately resolved: not only has 'immigrant' been increasingly reduced to 'Arab' but also immigrants have continued to be identified 'as a problem, outside the law and outside the nation'. The rise of the Front National, though, made anything resembling liberal measures on migration and status increasingly impossible. For too long, indeed, the debate concentrated on 'immigration' as such rather than on questions of effective integration. Nevertheless, as discussed above, the proposals on nationality put forward by the Chirac government of 1986–8 and the worsening political climate surrounding immigration in the late 1980s prompted the succeeding Socialist government to take the issue of integration seriously. As Wihtol de Wenden (1991, p. 328) has indicated, by 1989–90 Prime Minister Rocard was attempting to establish some degree of political consensus across parties (though excluding the Front National, of course). The degree of electoral advantage that lies in exploiting the issue, however, makes any such consensus extremely unlikely.

Conclusion

Balibar and Wallerstein (1990, p. 304) have recently written that 'the many "communities" to which we all belong, from which we take our "values", towards which we express "loyalty" and which define our "social identity", are all historical constructions'. This chapter has tried to show the extent to which constructions of immigrant identity and the prospects for integration have been influenced by a variety of forces in the post-war years and before. Not only has immigration been increasingly politicized — to the point that in the early 1990s it has become a political obsession — but also it has increasingly been constructed as a 'problem' and a problem of the 'Arab' presence in France. This chapter has sought to show the heterogeneity of migration and to point to its long-standing nature. Yet, as Miles and Singer-Kerel (1991, p. 273) have indicated, 'political interests seek to homogenise it, or rather its ideological homogenisation is the outcome of political struggle'. Moreover, the general identification of immigration with foreign nationality is both misleading and inaccurate, and encourages the exclusion of ethnic minorities from the political process. The debate on nationality and the increasing call for rights of citizenship to be redefined is instructive. In addition, no analysis of the current prospects of migrants and their descendants can be divorced from the analysis of the changing role of the state in defining and redefining both migration policy and the supposed acceptability of particular groups.

Notes

1. The material in this chapter builds on my other recently published work (Ogden 1989; 1991).
2. See, for example, the special issue of *Ethnic and Racial Studies*, 14(3), 1991: 265–416, on 'Migrants and migration in France'.

3. Full details on the French census of 1990 were not available at the time of writing.
4. The term *harkis* refers to the Algerian population who backed the French in 1962, were given French nationality after independence and who now live in France. They are particularly disadvantaged socially (Amar and Milza 1990, pp. 163–5). The term *beur* is sometimes applied to second-generation North Africans.

References

Ageron, C.-R., 1991, *La décolonisation française*, Armand Colin, Paris.

Amar, M. and Milza, P., 1990, *L'immigration en France au XXe siècle*, Armand Colin, Paris.

Balibar, E. and Wallerstein, I., 1990, *Race, nation, classe. Les identités ambiguës*, Editions La Découverte, Paris.

Bovenkerk, F., Miles, R. and Verbunt, G., 1990, 'Racism, migration and the state in western Europe: a case for comparative analysis', *International Sociology*, 5(4): 475–90.

Condon, S.A. and Ogden, P.E., 1991, 'Afro-Caribbean migrants in France: employment, state policy and the migration process', *Transactions, Institute of British Geographers*, 16(4): 440–57.

Costa-Lascoux, J., 1989, *De l'immigré au citoyen*, La Documentation Française, Paris.

Cross, G.S., 1983, *Immigrant workers in industrial France: the making of a new laboring class*, Temple University Press, Philadelphia.

Debré R. and Sauvy, A., 1946, *Des Français pour la France*, Gallimard, Paris.

Freeman, G.P., 1989, 'Immigrant labour and racial conflict: the role of the state', in Ogden, P.E. and White, P.E. (eds), *Migrants in modern France. Population mobility in the later nineteenth and twentieth centuries*, Unwin Hyman, London, 160–76.

Guillon, M., 1988, 'Les français par acquisition: dossier documentaire', *Revue Européenne des Migrations Internationales*, 4(3): 125–45.

Hargreaves, A., 1991, 'The political mobilisation of the North African community in France', *Ethnic and Racial Studies*, 14(3): 350–67.

Husbands, C., 1991, 'The support for the Front National: analyses and findings', *Ethnic and Racial Studies*, 14(3): 382–416.

INSEE, 1985, *Recensement général de la population de 1982: les étrangers*, INSEE, Paris.

Khellil, M., 1991, *L'intégration des Maghrébins en France*, Presses Universitaires de France, Paris.

Laacher, S. (ed.), 1987, *Questions de nationalité. Histoire et enjeux d'un code*, L'Harmattan, Paris.

Labat, J.-C., 1991, 'La population étrangère. Recensement de la population de 1990', *INSEE Première*, 150.

Lebon, A., 1988, 'L'emploi étranger à la fin de 1985', *Revue Européenne des Migrations Internationales*, 4(1-2): 85–105.

Lebon, A., 1991, *Immigration et présence étrangère en France 1990–91. Les données, les faits*, La Documentation Française, Paris.

Le Bras, H., 1991, *Marianne et les lapins. L'obsession démographique*, Olivier Orban, no place of publication given.

Lévy, M.L., 1991, 'Etrangers, immigrés, Français d'origine étrangère, renouvellement de la population', *Population et Sociétés*, 262: 4.

Lloyd, C. and Waters, H., 1991, 'France: one culture, one people?', *Race and Class*, 32(1): 49–65.

Marie, C.-V., 1983, 'L'immigration clandestine en France', *Hommes et Migrations Documents*, 1059: 4–21.

Marie, C.-V., 1988, 'L'immigration clandestine et l'emploi des travailleurs étrangers en situation irregulière', in Commissariat Général du Plan, *Immigrations: le devoir d'insertion*, La Documentation Française, Paris, 331–73.

Massot, J., 1985, 'Français par le sang, Français par la loi, Français par le choix', *Revue Européenne des Migrations Internationales*, 1(2): 9–19.

Miles, R. and Singer-Kerel, J., 1991, Introduction, *Ethnic and Racial Studies*, 14(3): 265–78.

Milza, O., 1988, *Les français devant l'immigration*, Editions complexes, Brussels.

Noiriel, G., 1986, 'L'immigration en France: une histoire en friche', *Annales, Economies, Sociétés, Civilisations*, 41(4): 751–69.

Ogden, P., 1987, 'Immigration, cities and the geography of the National Front in France', in Glebe, G. and O'Loughlin, J., (eds) *Foreign minorities in continental European cities*, Steiner-Verlag, Wiesbaden, 163–83.

Ogden, P.E., 1989, 'International migration in the nineteenth and twentieth centuries', in Ogden, P.E. and White, P.E. (eds) *Migrants in modern France. Population mobility in the nineteenth and twentieth centuries*, Unwin Hyman, London, 34–59.

Ogden, P.E., 1991, 'Immigration to France since 1945: myth and reality', *Ethnic and Racial Studies*, 14(3): 294–318.

Poinard, M., 1979, 'Le million des immigrés', *Revue Géographique des Pyrénées et du Sud-Ouest*, 50(4): 511–39.

Schor, R., 1985, *L'opinion française et les étrangers en France, 1919–1939*, Publications de la Sorbonne, Paris.

Silverman, M., 1991, 'Citizenship and the nation-state', *Ethnic and Racial Studies*, 14(3): 33–49.

Tapinos, G., 1975, *L'immigration étrangère en France*, INED/Presses Universitaires de France, Paris.

Tribalat, M., 1988, 'Chronique de l'immigration', *Population*, 43(1): 181–206.

Tribalat, M., 1991a, 'Combien sont les français d'origine étrangère?', *Economie et Statistique*, 242: 17–26.

Tribalat, M., 1991b, *Cent ans d'immigration. Etrangers d'hier, français d'aujourd'hui*, INED/Presses Universitaires de France, Paris.

Verbunt, G., 1985, 'France', in Hammar, T. (ed.) *European immigration policy: a comparative perspective*, Cambridge University Press, Cambridge, 127–64.

Weil, P., 1991, *La France et ses étrangers. L'aventure d'une politique d'immigration 1938–1991*, Calmann-Lévy, Paris.

Wihtol de Wenden, C., 1991, 'Immigration policy and the issue of nationality', *Ethnic and Racial Studies*, 14(3): 319–32.

Chapter 7

Multicultural Holland: myth or reality?

Frans Dieleman

Introduction

From its very beginning, The Netherlands has been a nation with a diversity of cultural traditions and religious beliefs. After the war against Spain, which ended in 1648, the country was divided into a predominantly Protestant north and a mainly Catholic south. To survive this division as one nation, society had to develop a tolerant attitude towards a variety of beliefs and opinions. The Netherlands became a haven for people persecuted for their beliefs elsewhere. Over the years Portuguese and East European Jews, Huguenots, and Germans from Westphalia found refuge in the country and contributed to the cultural diversity of The Netherlands (WRR 1989).[1] The cultural diversity later became institutionalized in a three-pronged system of political, educational, broadcasting, trade union and other organizations. In each of these spheres of society, there would typically be a Protestant, a Catholic and a secular organization. A good example is the school system, in which each local community would have a Protestant, a Catholic and a public elementary school (Clark et al. 1992). All types of schools qualify for funding from the public purse on an equal footing. It seems that the immigrants of the last decades should be able to profit from this tradition of tolerance and equal treatment by the government.

A second condition that seems to be to the advantage of immigrants is the extensive system of provisions by the Dutch welfare state. The proportion of GNP that is redistributed by the government is very large in comparison with other Western European countries. As a consequence, services such as social housing, education and social security are well developed, and access to these provisions is comparatively easy (Nauta and Van der Wusten 1992). For example, the social housing sector comprises 42 per cent of the total stock in The Netherlands and 50 per cent of the stock in the cities of Amsterdam and Rotterdam (Dieleman and Jobse 1991). In France, the United Kingdom, and Germany this percentage is only 27, 24 and 16 respectively. As in other West European countries, the Dutch government cut public spending in the 1980s under the pressure of economic recession and a policy of increased reliance on free market forces. However, most of the basic welfare state provisions are still in place. It seems that immigrants should be able to benefit from these services more readily than in some other countries, where austerity measures have been more severs.

In this chapter I shall look first at immigration flows and the current foreign population in The Netherlands in more detail. Then I shall consider the position of immigrants in Dutch society and discuss the level of tolerance and welfare provisions for immigrants. Both the political debate and the scientific research on immigrants tend to follow a certain pattern over time. First, issues of housing and residential segregation catch the eye of politicians and researchers. Then schooling, (un)employment and ethnic entrepreneurship are discussed. Finally questions of cultural identity and freedom, and of political representation become important. I shall deal with each of these issues in turn.

Patterns of immigration

The Netherlands has a low proportion of residents who are of foreign origin. An estimated 4.3 per cent of the population have a non-Dutch nationality, while 7.8 per cent were born outside The Netherlands (Moors and Beets 1991). At first glance, the small number of people of foreign origin living in The Netherlands (about 950,000 persons) is a little surprising in the light of the tradition of tolerance and the well-developed welfare state. Probably three circumstances have mainly determined the fairly low volume of the immigrant waves to this country over recent decades.

In the first place, The Netherlands lost large parts of its seventeenth-century colonial empire long ago. The decolonization of the most populous country of that empire, Indonesia, occurred soon after the Second World War. Ties with The Netherlands were severed almost completely, and no further waves of immigration took place after the repatriation of the colonial 'Dutch'. Substantial numbers of the people arriving from Indonesia were of mixed descent and had never been to The Netherlands: therefore they may be considered true immigrants. The countries in South America and the Caribbean which retained their colonial ties with the Netherlands had small populations.

In the second place, The Netherlands was no demographic 'sink-hole' in the 1960s (cf. Chapter 2 of this volume). The transition from high to low birth-rates occurred late in The Netherlands, and the rate of natural population growth of the Dutch was much higher than in surrounding countries (Van de Kaa 1987). Therefore labour shortages and a large influx of guestworkers from Southern Europe and North Africa started later, at the end of the 1960s and in the early 1970s. This was just before the economic stagnation of the 1970s halted the recruitment of labour from those regions. The Netherlands is atypical in this respect if compared with other West European countries.

Finally, The Netherlands is located at some distance from the areas in Europe which currently bear the brunt of the overspill of population from North Africa, such as Italy, Spain and France. The Netherlands is also not one of the countries which feel the demographic effects of political change in Eastern Europe, such as Italy, Austria and Germany. Poles and Czechs have appeared in The Netherlands as illegal workers over the last few years, though not yet in massive numbers.

As elsewhere, political and economic factors have given the main impetus to waves of immigration toward The Netherlands. During the Second World War, Japan occupied Indonesia. This set off a rapid process of decolonization, which was completed by the early 1960s. About 250,000 people were repatriated. Since the seventeenth century there had been traffic and interaction between Indonesia and The Netherlands, including the presence of Dutch people in the colony. Many Dutch men cohabited with Indonesian women, and by 1848 mixed marriages were made legal. Not surprisingly, many of the migrants from Indonesia to The Netherlands were of mixed Dutch–Indonesian desent or were Indonesians married to Dutch. They had never been in their 'homeland', to which they now came for the first time. Most of these people knew the Dutch culture and language fairly well, however. Neither the government nor researchers paid much attention to them. This group is now considered to be completely integrated in Dutch society (Blauw 1991). They are not treated as a special group in the statistics, and therefore little is known about their actual position in Dutch society. Only recently were some data collected for this group (Beets and Koesoebjono 1991). By 1990 an estimated 472,000 people born in Indonesia, or with at least one parent born there, were residing in The Netherlands. I shall not try to analyse their position in the housing and labour markets because the data for this is lacking. However, the general impression is that they hardly differ from the Dutch in these respects. Evidently this early group of immigrants had profited from the growth of the welfare state and the expanding economy during the 1950s and 1960s in much the same way as the Dutch population in general.

Inhabitants of the Moluccan islands also came to The Netherlands. They fought alongside the Dutch for independence from Indonesia, and after the war, 4,000 soldiers brought their families to The Netherlands. This group has now grown to 40,000 people, partly with Dutch nationality. The Moluccans have resisted complete integration in Dutch society, instead retaining their own culture and leadership to a larger extent than the colonial 'Dutch' discussed above. They have developed into an identifiable immigrant group.

The second wave of immigration resulting from decolonization took place much later, in the early 1970s, with the transition of Surinam from colonial status into an independent state. In 1975 Surinam became a republic, and in 1980 the Dutch government imposed a visa requirement for Surinamese who wanted to settle in The Netherlands. Even before

1970, upper and middle-class Surinamese migrated to The Netherlands in small numbers. However, in the 1970s the political unrest that accompanied decolonization provoked a massive migration of less-educated population groups, reaching a peak just before Surinam became independent. An estimated quarter of a million people of Surinamese and Caribbean origin are now residents of The Netherlands. Many Surinamese had or now have Dutch nationality, which makes it hard to identify them in statistics. However, more research on their position is available than for the immigrants from Indonesia. Their integration into Dutch society cannot be taken for granted, for many of these immigrants have a low level of education, and they arrived just before the Dutch economy took a downturn. In this chapter some data on this group of immigrants can therefore be presented.

The 'economic' migration from Mediterranean countries to The Netherlands followed the more familiar pattern of labour recruitment to Northern European countries from the South in the period of economic boom. In the 1960s, Dutch industries, mainly in the older and labour-intensive sectors like textiles, mining and shipbuilding, started to invite guestworkers to fill the labour shortages in the rapidly expanding economy. Workers from Spain and Italy were the first to come in large numbers. However, as mentioned earlier, labour recruitment started fairly late in The Netherlands, at a date when the main supply of labour had shifted from European countries to the north of the Mediterranean towards Turkey and countries in North Africa. The Dutch government signed agreements for labour recruitment with Turkey and Morocco, and these countries became the dominant sources. Immigration peaked in the mid-1970s. At that time, guestworkers were no longer given a residence permit.

At first, the guestworkers, as well as the Dutch government and employers, assumed that their stay in Holland was only temporary. They were expected to return to their home countries when the labour shortages were over. Of course, however, the well-known stages of labour migration also occurred in The Netherlands (Van Amersfoort and De Klerk 1987). Family reunification in The Netherlands was the next step in the process. It took place mainly between the mid-1970s and early 1980s, mostly among the Turkish and Moroccan populations. However, the process is not over yet; it is more extensive than anticipated and still makes an important contribution to the immigration flows (Van Amersfoort 1991). In 1989, 25 per cent of the Turkish immigrants and 60 per cent of the Moroccans came to The Netherlands to join their families. Now a third stage in the process is evolving: young adults, both men and women, are bringing over marriage partners from the original home countries (WRR 1989). In 1989, 40 per cent of the Turkish and 30 per cent of the Moroccan arrivals settled in The Netherlands because they married somebody already living there. This trend is likely to continue. The Turkish and Moroccan populations, which include many young

Table 7.1   Major groups of population (of at least 10,000 persons) with non-Dutch nationality and/or of non-Dutch descent, residing in The Netherlands as of 1 January 1989, by country of origin

(Former) colonies	
Surinam	210,000
Antilles	66,000
Moluccas	40,000
Labour recruitment regions	
Turkey	176,500
Morocco	139,500
Spain	17,500
Italy	16,000
Yugoslavia	12,000
EC (other)/US	
Germany	41,000
United Kingdom	37,000
Belgium	23,000
United States	11,000
Refugees	
Various countries	27,000

Source: WRR (1989).

families, have high birth-rates. Accordingly, these groups are expected to grow by 30 to 40 per cent over the next five years (Nusselder 1991).

If we exclude the diverse group of people of Indonesian descent (Table 7.1), we see that Surinamese, Turks and Moroccans were the dominant groups of foreign origin in The Netherlands by the end of the 1980s. The variety of nationalities in The Netherlands is of course much wider than the table shows. At least thirty groups of other nationalities, each comprising 1,000 people or more, live in The Netherlands. Nevertheless no new major immigration waves have changed the legacy of the major patterns of mass migration to The Netherlands described above. Of course, immigration did not stop in the 1980s, and it is increasing again: the migration surplus was 26,000 in 1988 and 46,000 in 1990 (persons aged 15–64). In recent years people seeking political asylum form an increasing proportion of those who want to enter The Netherlands on a permanent basis. Not all of these are refugees in a strict sense, that is, not all have been forced to leave their country because their lives are threatened by political persecution, war, natural disaster, etc. Many are driven by dire poverty from their home countries. They hope to enter The Netherlands by applying for asylum, because this is the only legal way for them to gain residency in the country. The Dutch government takes a very restrictive stance on accepting refugees, however. Therefore, in most cases, these people are not given a residence permit. The way

Table 7.2 Percentage of foreign population in The Netherlands by population size of municipality, 1 January 1990

Size of municipalities	Not born in The Netherlands	No Dutch passport
> 200,000	20.4	12.5
100,000 < 200,000	9.1	5.1
50,000 < 100,000	8.4	4.4
< 50,000	4.5	2.2
The Netherlands	7.8	4.3

Source: DEMOS, 7 (7), 1991: 55.

asylum applicants are treated and housed while awaiting a decision on residency and the way they are deported if their request is denied are rapidly becoming issues of political debate and controversy in The Netherlands.

Residents from neighbouring countries and the United States also contribute to the variety of nationalities in The Netherlands (Table 7.1). It may be assumed that most of these residents are highly skilled employees of Dutch plants of transnational corporations. However, statistics and research on these groups of foreign residents are lacking (see Chapter 16 in this volume). The debates on immigration policy and the position of immigrants in Dutch society do not refer to these people. In this chapter we are mainly concerned with the Surinamese, Turks and Moroccans.

To understand the position of the immigrant population in The Netherlands as well as its influence on Dutch society, one must analyse their patterns of residential location in the country. More than 40 per cent of the total immigrant population live in the four largest cities (Amsterdam, Rotterdam, The Hague and Utrecht), while only 11.5 per cent of the Dutch population reside there. In the cities, they comprise large proportions of the population, whereas elsewhere in the country their presence is hardly important (Table 7.2). Amsterdam has always been a gateway for Surinamese entering The Netherlands: 20 per cent of this group live there. The urban concentration of the Mediterranean immigrants was created by employment opportunities. It was later enhanced by access to housing and to the special services the immigrant groups created for themselves (markets, restaurants, places of worship, schools). With respect to housing, their concentration in the cities was advantageous: the extremely large social rented sector there offered unexpected housing opportunities, as we shall see in the next section. With respect to employment, however, the urban concentration of immigrants was devastating. Soon after they arrived to work in the old urban industries, this sector collapsed with the economic crisis of the late 1970s, leaving many immigrants unemployed (Dieleman and Musterd 1991).

Access to housing and residential segregation

In this section I shall discuss the housing situation of the three largest immigrant groups: the Surinamese, Turks and Moroccans. Their position in the Dutch housing market is primarily determined by four factors: income; stage in the immigration process; institutional arrangements; and general processes of urban change. These will now be described in more detail.

The three immigrant groups comprise on average low-income households. Of course, this influences their housing situation. Whereas 43 per cent of the Dutch households own their homes, only 15 per cent of the Turks, 14 per cent of Surinamese, and 5 per cent of Moroccans are home-owners (Blauw 1991). They are mainly concentrated in the urban housing stock of moderate rent levels (Van Praag 1989). This orientation toward rented housing is determined only partly by their socio-economic position. It also reflects the tenure structure of the urban housing stock, with only 10 to 15 per cent owner occupation (Dieleman *et al.* 1989). The residential patterns of the immigrant groups are fairly similar to those of Dutch households with a comparable income and family structure. In the 1980s they were able to improve their housing situation considerably (Van Praag 1989). Thus, even though the immigrants live in the cheaper parts of the urban housing stock, by no means do they form a marginalized group in the Dutch housing market.

The housing situation of the immigrants shows rapid changes over the last two decades in both tenure and dispersal over neighbourhoods in Dutch cities. Bovenkerk *et al.* (1985) distinguish three stages in the residential careers of former guestworkers (Table 7.3). In the first stage the immigrants were mostly single guestworkers and were concentrated in overcrowded boarding-houses owned by private landlords, mainly in the city centres. Blatant exploitation of the immigrants was widespread. However, after family reunification this pattern changed radically. Because the social rented sector was still closed to the immigrants, they were forced to buy into the low end of the owner-occupied sector. Dutch property-owners (and later on immigrant owners) seeking windfall profits exploited this captive market. Immigrants often paid exorbitant prices for a dwelling. To meet the costs of mortgages, the home-owners often had to sublet rooms; sporadically, shanties started to appear in their backyards (Bovenkerk *et al.* 1985).

The housing situation of immigrants was strongly influenced by the gatekeepers of the large Dutch social housing stock: the municipalities and housing associations. Guestworkers did not qualify for this stock because they did not have Dutch citizenship. The families they wanted to bring over had not lived in Holland long enough to qualify according to the criteria of the mid-1970s. Gradually, these criteria were changed, giving immigrants good access to this housing by the early 1980s (Van Hoorn and Van Ginkel 1986; Van Amersfoort and De Klerk 1987; Mik

Table 7.3 Three stages in the housing career of immigrants in Dutch cities

Period	Neighbourhoods	Stage in immigration	Tenure class
1960–73	Inner city and old neighbourhoods	Single men	Boarding-houses and rented rooms
1970–80	Old lower and middle-class neighbourhoods	Family reunification	Owner-occupied housing
1978–present	Newer lower and middle-class neighbourhoods	Second generation dispersal	Social rented sector

Source: Bovenkerk *et al.* 1985.

1991). This improved their housing situation dramatically. The change is expressed in a completely different pattern of location, with an increasing presence in neighbourhoods with inexpensive social housing. Figure 7.1 illustrates this pattern for the Turkish population in Amsterdam and Rotterdam. In Amsterdam, most Turks live in neighbourhoods built in the period 1906–30. However, between 1983 and 1990 their presence has increased in neighbourhoods built between 1931 and 1945, as well as in areas dating from the 1950s and 1960s with cheap social housing (Van Kempen 1991). In Rotterdam the Turks tend to be more concentrated in the older neighbourhoods and the pattern is more stable than in Amsterdam. The municipality has bought up large parts of the older private rental housing for renovation as social housing. This may partly explain the difference between these cities.

While the social housing stock was opening up, there was a series of inadequate efforts to disperse immigrants over the social stock. The rationale was to minimize resistance by Dutch occupants and to maximize integration of immigrants into Dutch society. Rotterdam, for example, started a '5 per cent rule' (no more than 5 per cent immigrants per complex) and later tried a policy of 'clustered deconcentration' (Mik 1991). In other cities local authorities joined the housing associations in efforts at 'social engineering' by taking geographical measures. By the early 1980s these policies were abandoned, having been ruled unlawful. Moreover, they drew severe criticism from the immigrant groups themselves, from political parties and from researchers. In Amsterdam, for example, several neighbourhoods with social housing were closed to immigrants for a while in response to complaints to the municipal housing associations by Dutch residents. A heated debate between political opposition parties and the city government of Amsterdam raged between 1977 and 1980. Sociologists and geographers organized studies and conferences on the topic. They actively helped to sway the allocation policy of the local government and the housing associations (see

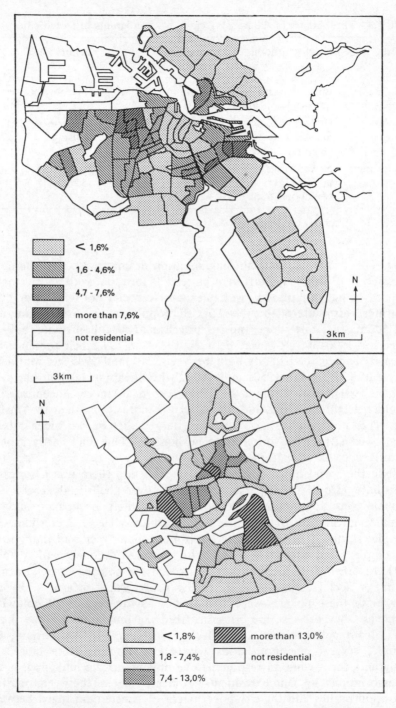

Figure 7.1   Turks as a percentage of the neighbourhood population in
Amsterdam (top), and Rotterdam (bottom) in 1990

Source: Van Kempen 1991.

Overleggroep Pensions 1979). So equal treatment of the Dutch and the immigrants in the social housing sector was not easily accomplished. However, since the early 1980s, immigrants have had good access to social housing and to housing allowances which bridge the gap between income and rent for low-income households. Like other low-income groups, they are also suffering from the austerity measures the Dutch government has been implementing since the mid-1980s: rents were raised above the rate of increase in buying power, and government payments on housing allowances have been tapered off (Dieleman and Jobse 1991).

General urban change has also influenced the housing situation of immigrants. During the 1970s there was massive suburbanization of Dutch families (Atzema 1991), which led to a substantial turnover of tenants in the urban housing stock. At the same time, it created ample opportunities for immigrant families to occupy the vacancies left by Dutch households. Immigrants could also benefit from the lack of interest among Dutch families in the abundant stock of newer high-rise apartments in the big cities. For example, large numbers of Surinamese moved into a high-rise housing estate in Amsterdam, the Bijlmermeer (Van Kempen 1986; De Klerk and Van Amersfoort 1988).

With respect to the housing situation, the immigrants to The Netherlands have indeed reaped the benefits of the tradition of equal treatment for all population groups and the broad range of services provided by the welfare state, including social housing. Equal treatment of immigrants in the allocation of social housing was not automatic, however. Local action and debate were needed to assure immigrants good access to social housing, although this goal was achieved in a fairly short time. Nevertheless, the housing situation of immigrants is still far from ideal, their domain being the cheaper part of the stock available. In general, however, their housing is reasonable in comparison with that of low-income Dutch households. The urban orientation of the immigrants has been beneficial to their housing situation because the cities have a large stock of inexpensive social housing.

Employment, schooling and entrepreneurship

Many immigrants from Southern Europe came to the Dutch cities in the late 1960s and early 1970s to work in the old industries. As elsewhere, they filled the demand for workers at the bottom of the job market (Waldinger *et al.* 1990). Unfortunately, they were very unlucky. The economic crisis hit the Dutch economy soon afterwards, especially the old urban industries that employed immigrants. Of course, the shift from industrial employment to office jobs in the Randstad cities was already in progress before the 1970s. In the 1950s, 40 per cent of the employment in Amsterdam was still industrial; in the mid-1980s, only 14 per cent (Jobse and Needham 1988). However, the economic crisis accelerated this process: industrial employment in the Randstad cities declined twice as quickly as in the rest of the country (De Smidt 1991).

Not surprisingly, immigrants living in the cities were the major victims of plummeting industrial employment. From guestworkers they rapidly became recipients of social welfare benefits. More than 40 per cent of the Turks and Moroccans and 27 per cent of the Surinamese were unemployed in 1988, in contrast with 13 per cent of the Dutch. In the period 1983–8 unemployment among the Dutch decreased to 83 per cent of the 1983 level, whereas among the various immigrant groups it rose by 15 to 38 per cent. This shows that immigrants have poor access to service sector jobs in the Randstad. This is largely because their schooling and language skills do not meet the requirements of the newly developing job market (WRR 1989). The immigrant groups are now in danger of becoming long-term and hard-core populations of unemployed. This has sparked off considerable political debate because the government's efforts to combat chronic unemployment have been largely unsuccessful. The soaring public expenditure on social security, with a built-in guarantee of benefits at a minimum income level, is now a major political concern. The debate is partly concentrated on immigrants. Some politicians argue that because many immigrants belong to the long-term unemployed, this group should be pressured into acquiring the right skills to qualify for the new jobs. Others have proposed measures that would force firms to employ certain quotas of immigrants.

The lack of appropriate schooling seems to be the major obstacle preventing immigrants from finding new jobs. This handicap also seems to have been passed on to their children, who are now enrolled in elementary and secondary schools. Turkish and Moroccan children in particular lag behind in elementary school tests, and few embark on or complete higher education (Penninx 1988). The general consensus of the educational community is that three main factors affect the poor school performance of immigrant children in The Netherlands (Clark *et al.* 1991). First is their poor command of the Dutch language: many Turkish and Moroccan children came to The Netherlands after the age of four and were socialized in their own language until they reached school age. Second, there are cultural differences between school and the home. Immigrant parents often consider good schooling of their children to be important (less so for girls). However, they are often unable or unaccustomed to helping with homework and maintaining contact with schools. Third, there is the problem of poor adaptation of schools to the special problems of minority children.

Fortunately, the Dutch government decided to earmark extra funding for schools with many immigrant children. This would allow them to deal with language problems and to develop teaching materials for children with a non-Dutch background. For a while it seemed as if the debate on schooling of immigrants would concentrate on school segregation, on 'black' and 'white' schools (Clark and Dieleman 1990). Because

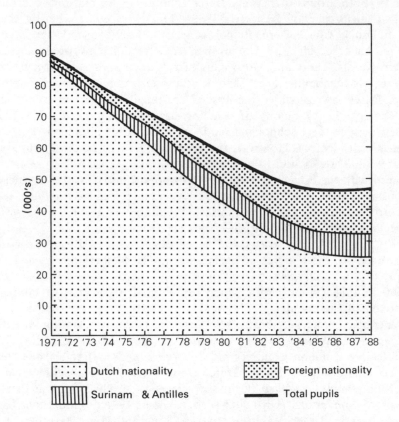

Figure 7.2 Pupils in primary education in Amsterdam, 1971–88

Dutch families moved out of the cities and immigrant families took their place, minority children now account for about half of the pupils in primary education in the big Dutch cities (Figure 7.2). The system of equal funding for public and denominational schools in The Netherlands, along with free school choice, gave rise to substantial school segregation between Dutch and immigrant children. Indeed, schools which are nearly all 'black' and those which are nearly all 'white' exist in close proximity, which indicates that choices for schools are very selective (Clark and Dieleman 1990).

Various municipalities have proposed mandatory integration in schools by measures like those enforced in the United States. Amsterdam attempted to establish school districts with mandatory enrolment zones.[2] Utrecht tried to limit the number of immigrant children per school to 20 per cent or less. Nevertheless, both proposals for 'geographical' measures of integration (reminiscent of measures to promote residential integration) failed because of opposition from both Dutch and immigrant parents. Both groups of parents prefer schools with a majority of Dutch pupils (Van Breenen and Dijkstra 1989). This is, of course, hardly possible in Dutch cities where 50 per cent of school-age children have a foreign background. The Dutch then take recourse to predominantly Dutch schools. Turks and Moroccans turn to their second choice: Islamic schools. As 'denominational' schools, these also qualify for full funding under Dutch law, provided the lessons are taught in the Dutch language and the criteria for quality of teaching are met (Clark *et al.* 1992). At least twenty of these schools currently exist, and this number is expected to grow considerably. However, the great majority of Muslim immigrant children still attend non-Islamic schools.

Faced with the exclusion from new job opportunities in the restructuring urban economy, some immigrants try to make a niche for themselves as entrepreneurs of small businesses (Waldinger *et al.* 1990), a sector which has expanded rapidly over the last twenty years, though not as much as in the United States and some other Western European countries. Even so, the number of businesses in The Netherlands owned and operated by immigrants has risen rapidly: there were approximately 43,500 in 1988 (WRR 1989), which represented 8 per cent of all firms registered in the country.

Generally immigrant businesses first develop by catering for the immigrant community itself: (Turkish) coffee shops, pizzerias and butchers are common examples in The Netherlands. After a while these services may also cater for the Dutch population. However, the extent to which immigrants establish businesses varies widely between the various groups of immigrants (Dijst and Van Kempen 1991). Immigrants from Egypt, Algeria, Israel, Pakistan, India, China and Hong Kong are very active in small trade, retail and restaurants. More than 15 per cent of the population of these immigrant groups are entrepreneurs. The Egyptians rank highest, with 34 per cent of their group in business. Italians and Greeks are also frequently self-employed, particularly in restaurants. Among Turks and Moroccans, however, only 1.3 and 0.8 per cent respectively earn a living this way. Much depends upon traditions brought from the home countries, on social networks built up in The Netherlands and on opportunities that open up to individuals (Waldinger *et al.* 1990; Rekers *et al.* 1991).

For its impact on local society and its visibility within the social geography of the city, the distribution of immigrant enterprises is very important. Because many immigrant businesses start up by catering for the proprietor's own group, they are concentrated in certain neighbourhoods, where they have a strong impact on shops, restaurants, etc. In Rotterdam, for example, there are four neighbourhoods where more than 20 per cent of all businesses are run by immigrants. Of all the restaurants and cafés in some neighbourhoods, 45 per cent are owned by minorities (Bakkers and Tap 1987). This certainly helps to give multicultural Holland a high profile.

Discussion: multicultural Holland?

The repatriation of Dutch citizens from Indonesia and the immigration of a substantial number of Indonesians to The Netherlands in the early 1960s clearly made a mark on Dutch culture. A substantial body of literature, by both Dutch and Indonesian authors, as well as Indonesian words and expressions in the Dutch language, keep the colonial past alive. Indonesian festivals and cuisine have certainly added to the cultural diversity of Dutch society. Yet, despite the relatively large number of people who came from Indonesia to the Netherlands, this wave of immigration did not create a truly multicultural Holland. The immigrants knew the Dutch language well and intermarriage between Indonesians and Dutch was quite common. Moreover, their presence did not lead to the establishment of institutions like churches, schools and political parties especially geared to the needs and traditions of Indonesians. Also, the economy was expanding at that time, so there were ample employment opportunities.

The first waves of guestworkers consisted of Spaniards, Italians and Yugoslavs. Their position in Dutch society developed more or less like that of Indonesians, although of course they retained some of their traditions. Like the Indonesians, intermarriage with the Dutch became quite usual. Similarly, participation in Dutch society occurred through existing institutional frameworks rather than through organizations peculiar to the home culture. Moreover, like their predecessors, the majority of these immigrants were also able to find a place in the job market.

Both the Dutch people and the Dutch government probably expected immigrants from Surinam, Turkey and Morocco to find a niche in Dutch society in much the same way as the immigrant groups of earlier years. However, this turned out to be wishful thinking. The religious and cultural background of many of these newcomers differs fundamentally from that of the Dutch. Furthermore, exposure to Dutch language and customs was non-existent for the Turks and Moroccans before they came to the Netherlands. Most Turks and Moroccans and some Surinamese are Muslims. They established mosques as soon as they were present in sufficient numbers to support their own religious and cultural centres (Doomernik 1991). There are now some 300 mosques in The Netherlands. The establishment of Islamic schools suggests that immigrants of the last two decades will develop their position in Dutch society rather differently from what the authorities may have expected.

Moreover, the lack of employment opportunities for low-skilled people during this decade further entrenches the immigrants' position as separate groups in Dutch society. Authorities tend to identify them as problem groups, and unemployed Dutch people consider them as undesirable competitors in the job market. At present, the immigration groups of the two last decades are the subject of considerable public debate. Islamic religion and culture seem to provide a focus for the discussion. I shall return to this debate later.

In big cities like Amsterdam and Rotterdam, the immigrants from Surinam, the Antilles, Turkey and Morocco form sufficiently large groups and have maintained their cultures to such an extent that they have made a definite mark on city life. In many neighbourhoods, open-air markets, restaurants, coffee shops and street life exude the unmistakable flavour of the immigrants' home countries. Multicultural Holland has become a reality in the cities, though not elsewhere. Immigrant groups living in other areas are generally so small that they have a minor impact on the structure of the local communities. Sometimes the establishment of temporary hostels for foreigners who seek political asylum in these areas provokes dissent and action. Some elements of the local Dutch community distrust these facilities and protest against their existence, although this has seldom led to violence. Yet others object to the restrictive policy of the Dutch government with respect to residence permits. They protest against the way people applying for asylum are discouraged from normal participation in society. There are some widely publicized instances of Dutch people hiding refugees from government procedures and giving them shelter in churches.

In the beginning of this chapter I raised the question of whether immigrants to The Netherlands could benefit from the tradition of equal treatment of various cultural and religious groups by the government, and from the wide range of services provided by the Dutch state. To some degree, this does indeed seem to be the case. I have mentioned the large stock of social housing in the Dutch cities which was made accessible to immigrants, though only after some struggle, and I have pointed out the financial support for Islamic schools. Access of immigrants to social security benefits, the system of medical care and housing allowances are other examples of benefits for immigrants in Dutch society.

In The Netherlands, immigrants with non-Dutch nationality also have the right to participate in local elections for municipal government if they have lived in the country for at least five years. This is quite unusual for a West European country. However, in a recent analysis of elections in Rotterdam, Rath (1990) argues that the real significance of such rights is questionable. Only a small number of immigrants appeared on the slates of major political parties, resulting in only one immigrant member on a municipal board. Just 20 per cent of the enfranchized Surinamese and 26 per cent of the Moroccans actually voted. In general, Turks have a higher degree of organization than other immigrant groups (cf. Doomernik 1991): in the Rotterdam election, 42 per cent of the Turkish electorate cast their vote. Political influence is mainly limited to advisory boards for immigrant issues and the like (Rath 1991). At the same time, the number of votes for small extreme right-wing parties with anti-minority policies increased (refer to Chapter 8 in this book). That support has grown despite the fact that representatives of right-extremist parties are actively ostracized in municipal policies by the other parties, a stance which is applauded by the media.

The tradition of equal treatment of groups of various cultures and beliefs is also visible in the financial support for the Turkish cultural centres (mosques), as reported by Doomernik (1991), although this is officially against the rules. It is manifest in the support for radio and television programmes that are produced for and by immigrants. It was also given a high profile recently by the subsidy from the central government to establish a chair of Islamic studies at the University of Amsterdam.

These examples illustrate that immigrants can still profit from the way in which Dutch society has developed and is now organized. This does not mean that Dutch tolerance for immigrant populations is as great as often stated. Moors and Beets (1991) report that three-quarters of the Dutch support the restrictive policy on immigration enforced by the present government. Nearly 50 per cent of the respondents to this survey stated that immigrants should return to their home countries even if they have worked in The Netherlands for a long period. Whatever value such polls may have, it is clear that Dutch tolerance for people of other cultures and religions has fairly narrow limits at present and is certainly not shared ubiquitously.

This is also reflected in Dutch policy toward immigrants and foreigners seeking political asylum. The government used to take a protective stance on the problems of immigrants in Dutch society. Now the prevailing attitude is 'no nonsense': let the immigrants themselves make more serious efforts to acquire the necessary qualifications for the present Dutch job market (Van Amersfoort 1991). Recently, government officials proposed to limit immigration permits for Turks and Moroccans coming to The Netherlands as marriage partners. The government is also extremely strict with applicants for political asylum. Very few receive residence permits, and the treatment of those who have to leave is often quite harsh.

The present debate in the press about Islamic institutions such as mosques and schools is also indicative of a lessening tolerance in Dutch society. Not everybody seems to take it for granted that the freedom to establish such organizations along religious lines is a basic and undisputed right in Dutch society. The emphasis in the discussion is on whether such organizations will help to integrate immigrants into Dutch society, not on equal rights.

Notes

1. This important source of Dutch immigration policy is cited as WRR (1989) in the text for the sake of brevity; it is listed in the References under Wetenschappelijke Raad voor het Regeringsbeleid (1989).
2. See the policy statement issued by Amsterdam municipality: Nota Minderhedenbeleid in het Amsterdamse Onderwijs 1989, Gemeenteblad, Bijlage N, Gemeente Amsterdam.

References

Atzema, O.A.L.C., 1991, *Stad uit, stad in, residentiele suburbanisatie in Nederland in de jaren zeventig en tachtig*, Faculteit Ruimtelijke Wetenschappen, University of Utrecht, Utrecht.

Bakkers, E.S.J. and Tap, L.J., 1987, *Etnische ondernemers in Rotterdam en Utrecht*, Hoofdbedrijfschap ambachten, The Hague.

Beets, G. and Koesoebjono, S., 1991, 'Indische Nederlanders: een vergeten groep', *DEMOS*, 7(8): 60–4.

Blauw, W., 1991, 'Housing segregation for different population groups in the Netherlands', in Huttman, E.D., Blauw, W. and Saltman, J. (eds), *Urban housing segregation of minorities in Western Europe and the United States*, Duke University Press, London, 43–62.

Bovenkerk, F., Bruin, K., Brunt, L. and Wouters, H., 1985, *Vreemd volk, gemengde gevoelens — etnische verhoudingen in een grote stad*, Uitgeverij Boom, Meppel.

Clark, W.A.V. and Dieleman, F.M., 1990, '"Zwarte" en "witte" scholen in Nederland gezien vanuit de Amerikaanse ervaringen', *Geografisch Tijdschrift*, 24(2): 139–47.

Clark, W.A.V., Dieleman, F.M. and De Klerk, L., 1992, 'School segregation: managed integration or free choice?', *Environment and Planning C, Government and Policy*, 10(1): 91–103.

De Klerk, L. and Van Amersfoort, H., 1988, 'Surinamese settlement in Amsterdam 1973–83', in Cross, M. and Entzinger, H. (eds), *Lost illusions — Caribbean minorities in Britain and The Netherlands*, Routledge, London, 147–63.

De Smidt, M., 1991, 'Bedrijfsprofiel van de Randstad, winnende en verliezende milieus', in Hooimeijer, P., Musterd, S. and Schroder, P. (eds), *De Randstad: balans van winst en verlies 1*, Stedelijke Netwerken, University of Utrecht, Utrecht, 17–34.

Dieleman, F.M., Clark, W.A.V. and Deurloo, M.C., 1989, 'A comparative view of housing choices in controlled and uncontrolled housing markets', *Urban Studies*, 26(5): 457–68.

Dieleman, F.M. and Jobse, R.B., 1991, 'Multi-family housing in the social rental sector and the changing Dutch housing market', *Housing Studies*, 6(3): 193–205.

Dieleman, F.M. and Musterd, S., 1991, 'Maatschappelijke veranderingen en de herstructurering van de Randstad', *Geografisch Tijdschrift*, 25(5): 490–501.

Dijst, M. J. and Van Kempen, R., 1991, 'Minority business and the hidden dimension: the influence of urban contexts on the development of ethnic enterprise', *Tijdschrift voor Economische en Sociale Geografie*, 82(2): 128–38.

Doomernik, J., 1991, *Turkse moskeeën en maatschappelijke participatie*, Instituut voor Sociale Geografie, University of Amsterdam, Amsterdam (Nederlandse Geografische Studies 129).

Jobse, R.B. and Needham, B., 1988, 'The economic future of the Randstad, Holland', *Urban Studies*, 25(4): 282–96.

Mik, G., 1991, 'Housing segregation and policy in the Dutch metropolitan environment', in Huttman, E.D., Blauw, W. and Saltman, J. (eds), *Urban housing segregation of minorities in Western Europe and the United States*, Duke University Press, London, 197–98.

Moors, H. and Beets, G., 1991, 'Opvattingen over buitenlanders sterk bepaald door politieke kleur', *DEMOS*, 7(7): 55–6.

Nauta, A.P.N. and Van der Wusten, H., 1992, 'Provision of services and the welfare state', in Dieleman, F.M. and Musterd, S. (eds), *The Randstad, a research and policy laboratory*, Kluwer, Dordrecht, 219–36.

Nusselder, W., 1991, 'Buitenlanders in Nederland — verdere stijging verwacht', *DEMOS*, 7(1): 1–4.

Overleggroep Pensions, 1979, *Niet hier maar daar*, Overleggroep Pensions, Amsterdam.

Penninx, R., 1988, *Minderheidsvorming en emancipatie — balans van kennisverwerving ten aanzien van immigranten en woonwagenbewoners*, Samson Uitgeverij, Alphen aan den Rijn.

Rath, J., 1990, *Kenterend tij: migranten en de gemeenteraadsverkiezingen van 21 maart 1990 te Rotterdam*, Vakgroep Culturele Antropologie, University of Utrecht, Utrecht.

Rath, J., 1991, *Minorisering: de sociale constructie van 'etnische minderheden'*, Uitgeverij SUA, Amsterdam.

Rekers, A., Dijst, M. and Van Kempen, R., 1991, 'Beleid inzake etnisch ondernemerschap gelokaliseerd', *Rooilijn*, 91(6): 176–81.

Van Amersfoort, H., 1991, 'Internationale migratie en bevolking in Nederland', *Geografisch Tijdschrift*, 25(4): 321–29.

Van Amersfoort, H. and De Klerk, L., 1987, 'Dynamics of immigrant settlement: Surinamese, Turks and Moroccans in Amsterdam 1973–1983', in Glebe, G. and O'Loughlin, J. (eds), *Foreign minorities in continental European cities*, Franz Steiner Verlag, Stuttgart, 199–222.

Van Breenen, K. and Dijkstra, H., 1989, *De Amsterdamse basisschool een buurtschool?*, Instituut voor Sociale Geografie, University of Amsterdam, Amsterdam.

Van Hoorn, F.J.J.H. and Van Ginkel, J.A., 1986, 'Racial leapfrogging in a controlled housing market — the case of the Mediterranean minority in Utrecht, The Netherlands', *Tijdschrift voor Economische en Sociale Geografie*, 77(3): 187–96.

Van de Kaa, D.J., 1987, *Europe's second demographic transition*, Population Bulletin 42(1), Population Reference Bureau Inc., Washington, DC.

Van Kempen, E., 1986, 'High-rise housing estates and the concentration of poverty', *The Netherlands Journal of Housing and Environmental Research*, 1(1): 5–26.

Van Kempen, R., 1991, 'Lage-inkomensgroepen in de grote stad: spreiding en koncentratie in Amsterdam en Rotterdam', Stedelijke Netwerken, University of Utrecht, Utrecht.

Van Praag, C.S., 1989, *De woonsituatie van etnische minderheden; een analyse van het woningbehoefte-onderzoek 1985/1986*, Sociaal en Cultureel Planbureau, Rijswijk.

Waldinger, R., Aldrich, H. and Ward, R., 1990, *Ethnic entrepreneurs: immigrant business in industrial societies*, Sage, London.

Wetenschappelijke Raad voor het Regeringsbeleid, 1989, *Allochtonenbeleid*, Rapporten aan de Regering 36, SDU, The Hague.

Chapter 8

Immigrants and the extreme-right vote in Europe and in Belgium[1]

Christian Vandermotten and Jean Vanlaer

Introduction

The attitude of the West European population towards immigration is becoming increasingly rigid at the moment, and these hardening opinions are reflected in some spectacular electoral successes for the extreme Right. The relationship between the phenomena of immigration and right-wing politics is, however, complex. A geographical analysis, undertaken on different levels, may contribute to an understanding of the interrelationship. Such an analysis is attempted in this chapter, first of Europe, then of Belgium and finally of Brussels.

Attitudes towards foreign immigrants

The *Eurobarometer* opinion polls carried out for the European Community reveal the popular reaction to the presence in the Community of non-EC nationals.[2] The poll carried out in spring 1991 indicated that half of the Europeans interviewed considered that there were too many non-EC immigrants in their particular country; 34 per cent thought that there were many, although not too many; 9 per cent thought that there were not many; and 7 per cent expressed no opinion.

The impression of an excessive presence of foreigners was particularly strong in the countries of north-west Europe where immigrant workers are concentrated: 56 per cent of Belgians and French surveyed expressed this feeling, as did 55 per cent of German and 54 per cent of UK respondents. Interestingly the highest figure was recorded in Italy (63 per cent), where immigration is a recent phenomenon compared with the other countries. The percentages of respondents who thought there were too many immigrants were very much lower in countries which contain few foreigners and which lack an immigrant tradition — thus Ireland recorded 12 per cent, Portugal 18 per cent, Spain 25 per cent and Greece 29 per cent. Denmark (43 per cent) and The Netherlands (44 per cent) occupy an intermediate position, just below the Community average of 50 per cent.

The restrictive attitude towards workers from outside the European Community is directed as much towards East Europeans as towards people originating from the Mediterranean region: only 14 per cent of the interviewees are ready to accept them without restriction. Once again, the Belgians have the most uncompromising attitudes: only 6 per cent of Belgian respondents would accept southern Mediterranean immigrants without restriction, and only 7 per cent would similarly accept East Europeans. Belgians are also the most unwelcoming towards immigrants seeking political asylum. Only 12 per cent of Belgians look favourably on such entries, compared with 24 per cent in Europe as a whole.

These cool, even xenophobic, attitudes towards foreign immigration appear to be increasing. When asked whether the rights of immigrants should be restricted, 33 per cent of Europeans surveyed in 1991 answered affirmatively, compared with only 19 per cent in the 1990 *Eurobarometer* poll.[3] Yet again the Belgians exhibited the most restrictive attitudes, 50 per cent wanting to restrict immigrants' rights in the 1991 survey. The result is rather ironic when it is considered that foreigners, even those originating from other EC countries, do not have any political rights in Belgium, either at national or municipal level. On the other hand, the proposal to extend immigrants' political rights was viewed favourably by 33 per cent of Europeans during the poll of autumn 1990 (25 per cent of Belgians), although by only 19 per cent of Europeans (13 per cent of Belgians) during the spring 1991 poll. On this occasion the Belgians were not the least liberal; the lowest percentages came from countries where an important fraction of the *de facto* foreigners are *de jure* citizens (France, United Kingdom), or where immigrants have some electoral rights (Denmark). Germany scored the same percentages as Belgium.

The electoral geography of the European extreme Right

The political parties grouped here under the label 'extreme Right' are characterized, at least on the level of their political rhetoric, by the following features:

- an exaggerated nationalism reinforced by 'Euronationalism' and sometimes by a tinge of anti-Americanism;
- an affinity to neo-nazism and neo-fascism, though this has become less explicit;
- virulent anti-communism and anti-leftism in general;
- affirmation of white supremacy;
- clear xenophobia, especially directed towards immigrant workers; and
- a strong anti-trade union stance, sometimes compounded with a distrust of the big owners of capital.

Extreme-right parties also support a hierarchical, authoritarian social system with no class struggle, based on small companies in a strong state imposing low taxes (Husbands 1982; Vanlaer 1984; De Schampheleire and Thanassekos 1991).

Such a discourse is, or rather was, mainly articulated by the 'cadres' of these parties, following the tradition of the small restricted groups of the historical extreme Right. Without a doubt, this message is not shared by all the modern voters of the extreme Right, whose parties are now polling several per cent, even more than 10 per cent, of the electorate in some parts of Europe. Instead, people are voting for the extreme Right for other reasons, such as:

- a lack of a sense of security at a time when social polarization is becoming more acute;
- the transition to a more flexible and heterogeneous economic system which has eroded the social framework of the working classes;
- the economic progress of the 1980s which has not solved the unemployment problem;
- the collapse of 'real socialism' in Eastern Europe which has carried away any social projects in which underprivileged classes in the West could find some hope;
- the fact that a vote for the radical left is no longer a realistic expression of opposition to the dominant political forces; and
- because the ecological parties present a message which is too intellectual for the working classes.

Thus the recent successes of the extreme Right are the result of an electoral shift from the traditional, elitist extreme Right towards a much more populist base, which is especially attracted by the role of the extreme Right as guarantor of law and efficiency.

Although we acknowledge that as the new populist extreme Right grows stronger, it is more and more difficult to draw the line between the old and new extreme-right parties, we exclude from our analysis parties expressing an anti-state or *neo-poujadiste*[4] appeal, even if these parties exploit xenophobic feelings, such as the *leghe* or 'leagues' of northern Italy. Finally we have not taken into account (except for a brief mention in our commentary on the Belgian election results) a rather perverse effect of the progress of the extreme Right, and that is the new tendency of the historical or classical Right to fall into line on the immigration issue. Evidence for this can be seen in the racist cartoons taken from an election pamphlet for two Brussels candidates on the PRL list (the Liberal Party, representing the classical Belgian Right) issued at the last legislative election in November 1991 (Figure 8.1). Similar evidence for the convergence of political parties' stance on the immigration issue can be seen in the ideological evolution of the Austrian liberals; and even some leftist parties are taking a stern attitude towards the integration of immigrants.

Figure 8.1 Cartoons from an election pamphlet issued by two Brussels
candidates of the Belgian Liberal Party, 1991. The cartoon on the
right shows 'Folkloric dances of the ancient Belgians'. That on the
left is captioned as follows: 'I'll help you, madam . . . for the full
naturalization you insert 50 francs and push button A . . . Then,
for your children, button C . . . If you want to bring in your aunts
and uncles, button X . . . Finally, button Y to obtain a provisional
allocation.'

The main parties whose electoral geography is studied in this chapter
are therefore as follows: the *Republikaner* and the *Deutsche Volksunion*
in Germany; the *Front National* in France; the National Front in Britain;
the MSI–DN (*Movimento Sociale Italiano/Destra Nazionale*) in Italy, the
Centrumpartij in The Netherlands, the *Vlaams Blok* and the *Front
National* in Belgium, *Ethniki Parataxis* in Greece, *Unión Nacional* in
Spain, and *Action Nationale*, the *Mouvement Républicain* and *Vigilance*
in Switzerland.[5]

A spatial analysis of the electoral penetration of the European extreme
Right can be conducted either on the European scale or within the
various national patterns. Figure 8.2 displays the results for the extreme
Right at the last European elections held in June 1989, in the countries
where it fielded candidates. This map shows the extreme-right vote on a

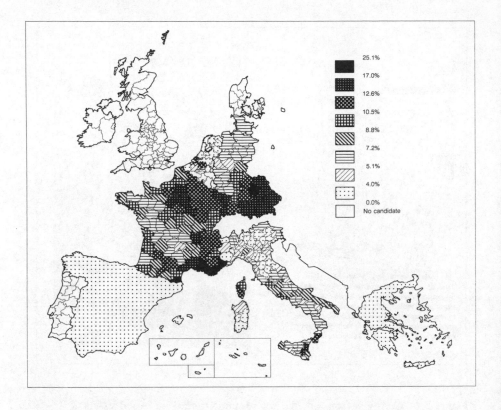

Figure 8.2   Percentage vote recorded by the extreme Right in the European elections, 1989

common scale (Lentzen *et al.* 1989). Figure 8.3, on the other hand, gives the extreme-right vote in different regions compared with its national average performances at the election during the last two decades when the extreme Right achieved its biggest electoral success (Vanlaer 1991).

The exploitation of the immigration theme has undoubtedly led to the success of the extreme Right in the countries of the industrialized 'centre' of Europe. Within these countries, it is the industrialized regions and the main urban areas which record the highest extreme-right vote. In France these regions are Île-de-France, Nord, Alsace-Lorraine and Rhône-Alpes, to which one must also add the Mediterranean coast where not only are there many immigrants, but also *pieds noirs* (repatriated French colonials) who vote for the extreme Right (Jaffre 1984; Rollat and Plenel 1984; Charlot 1985; Perrineau 1985). The far Right's urban bias is also strongly evident in the United Kingdom, where the lack of proportional representation prevents the National Front from having a bigger political impact (see Taylor 1979; Whiteley 1979; Harrop *et al.* 1980), and in Belgium, The Netherlands and Switzerland (Gilg 1972). The geography of

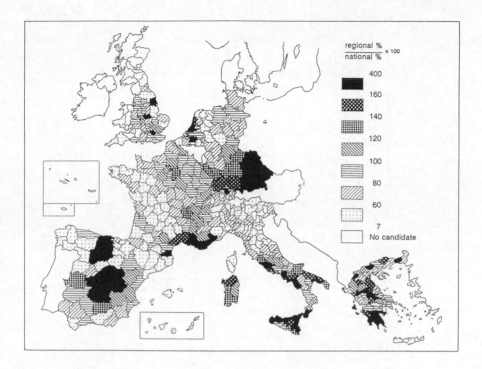

Figure 8.3 Extreme Right vote in Europe compared with respective national average, for the election with the best result for the extreme Right during 1971–91

the Republikaner vote in (West) Germany is neither specifically urban, nor 'central' or 'peripheral' within the country's rather homogeneous space-economy. Instead it is strongest in the south, where there has been a greater influx of immigrants and the highest rates of economic growth, as well as other cultural factors operating.

The interpretation of the maps (Figures 8.2 and 8.3) can be complemented by a 'centre–periphery' tabulation of the data for the election since 1971 at which each national extreme-right party achieved its highest share of the vote (Table 8.1). The table also divides each of the centre and periphery into high and low status urban areas and remaining non-urban areas. It is clear that in the centre the extreme Right finds its most favourable breeding-ground in the urban and industrial areas. Where data are available, they show a higher extreme-right vote in the working-class urban areas. However, in Italy the MSI–DN is more prominent in the bourgeois urban areas; working-class urban populations are still fairly faithful to the Partito Democratico della Sinistra, the modern descendant of the Italian Communist Party.

This urban-industrial breeding-ground may also be fertilized by the

Table 8.1 Impact of extreme-right vote on European countries

	% vote at national level (election year)	% vote in 'centre' urban areas bourgeois	% vote in 'centre' urban areas working-class	% vote in 'centre' non-urban areas	% vote in 'periphery' urban areas bourgeois	% vote in 'periphery' urban areas working-class	% vote in 'periphery' non-urban areas
France	9.8 (1986)	14.1		11.2		7.4	6.0
Great Britain	1.2 (1979)	1.4	2.4	1.0		1.0	1.0
Netherlands	2.6 (1984)	5.9		2.6		2.0	1.6
Flanders	6.6 (1989)	13.8		5.6		4.8	3.1
Switzerland	9.4 (1971)	8.5	15.0	–		–	–
Italy	9.2 (1972)	11.8	6.8	4.5	25.9	17.8	11.7
Greece	6.8 (1977)	5.3	6.8	6.8		6.1	8.1

Notes on definitions of 'centre' and 'periphery' and of urban and non-urban areas.

France: centre = north-eastern half of the country; urban = Paris and the *petite couronne*, and towns of over 100,000 inhabitants.

GB: centre = south-eastern part of the country; urban = Greater London and West Midlands.

Netherlands: centre = Holland and Utrecht province; urban = cities with over 100,000 inhabitants.

Flanders and Brussels: centre = Brabant and Antwerp; urban zones defined by Vandermotten and Vandewattyne (1985).

Italy: centre = northern half of country (excluding Rome); urban = cities with over 100,000 inhabitants.

Greece: centre = eastern coastal fringe and north of the Peloponnese; central urban zones = Greater Athens, Patras, Larissa, Volos, Salonika, Kavala; peripheral urban zones = cities of over 10,000 inhabitants.

In GB, working-class areas are identified by the Labour vote, in Italy by the Communist vote.

existence of regional political subcultures, such as Flemish nationalism in Belgium, or even enlarged to encompass less central semi-rural areas, as with nationalist conservatism in Catholic southern Germany. Extreme-right success may also be fed by political crisis in other parties. The crisis of the Parti Communiste Français and of French big industry has carried with it an ideological disintegration within traditionally 'red' towns and industrial suburbs. On the other hand the breeding-ground may be sterilized by the survival of hegemonic regional political cultures in working-class urban regions such as the northern Italian cities of Turin and Bologna where the communist tradition (PCI, now PDS) is still strong, or in Wallonia or the Ruhr. However, the recent elections in Bremen, a traditional socialist stronghold in northern Germany, show that this 'sterilization' may be only temporary.

Other extreme-right forces were present in European peripheral regions in the 1950s and 1960s. Examples here are the fascist parties of Portugal and Spain, the MSI in the Italian Mezzogiorno, and the case of Greece where the extreme Right was active inside the classical Right. These parties represented the interests of the traditional dominant classes, or they expressed the frustrations of regions and social groups which became marginalized and left out of European economic growth and integration.

Thus, to sum up, in the centre, economic restructuring and the flex-ibilization of the production system have led to the rearrangement (if not demise) of many major industrial companies and the dismemberment of the trade union framework which formerly provided the context for class-based political parties. A parallel collapse — provoked by secularization — can be observed in regions where the church provided an analogous socio-political role to the trade unions. Chronologically, the first enlargement of the extreme Right came during the period which started in the early 1970s and was sustained by people from the tradi-tional Right parties. But, soon after, a second enlargement came from the former leftist voters, from people who had not voted before (either because they were too young or had abstained), and from new voters breaking from the family political tradition; this enlargement of the 'new Right' vote comes at a time when football supporters' clubs are offering a stronger membership framework than the political youth organizations, and it is now more characteristic of countries and regions of the centre than of the periphery.

Immigration in Belgium and the increase in the extreme-right vote

An analysis of the Belgian case is interesting for at least four reasons. First, the number of foreigners in the country is quite high in relation to the Belgian population. Second, recent opinion polls have revealed a particularly unfavourable attitude towards granting political rights to

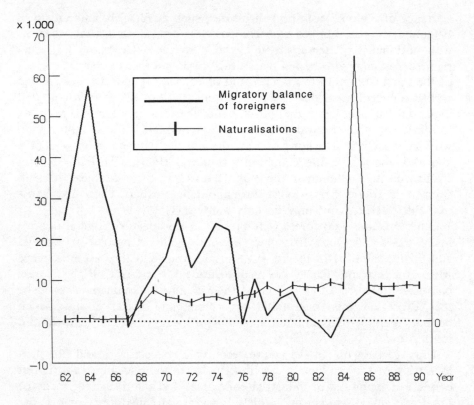

Figure 8.4   Immigration and naturalization of foreigners in Belgium, 1962–90

immigrants. Third, the extreme Right has just recorded a spectacular electoral thrust. And fourth, a cartographic analysis on different scales shows the complex interaction between patterns of immigrant settlement and different political cultures within a federal state.

Throughout the ensuing discussion, the ethno-linguistic division between northern, Flemish-speaking Flanders and southern, French-speaking Wallonia must be borne in mind. This division has also had a complex, and changing, economic expression. Early on, the industrial prosperity of the Haine–Sambre–Meuse coalfield axis, running parallel to and south of the ethno-linguistic boundary, gave Wallonia a measure of prosperity which attracted many migrants, notably to Charleroi, Namur and Liège. Since the 1950s, however, Wallonia's industrial employment has fallen sharply, in contrast to the now more prosperous Flemish region (Thomas 1990).

The growth of the foreign population in Belgium has been very rapid. Large numbers arrived in the 1960s and 1970s; during the 1980s the migration balance for foreigners was close to zero (Figure 8.4). The stock of foreigners grew from 368,000 in 1947 to 453,000 in 1962, and then to

Table 8.2 Structure and evolution of the foreign population in Belgium, 1947–89

% distribution amongst major migrant 'types'	Belgium					Brussels				
	1947	1961	1970	1981	1989	1947	1961	1970	1981	1989
'Invisibles'	54	38	33	29	27	63	61	33	23	20
Poles and European Mediterraneans	41	58	53	44	39	28	30	45	34	31
Non-European Mediterraneans	0	0	10	20	26	1	0	16	32	37
Others	4	3	5	7	8	8	9	6	11	12
Total ('000)	368	453	696	904	879	74	67	174	239	264
% Belgian population	4	5	7	9	9	7	7	16	24	27

Notes: 'Invisibles' include north-west Europeans, North Americans, Australians.
European Mediterraneans include Spanish, Portuguese, Italians, Greeks, Yugoslavs.
Non-European Mediterraneans include Moroccans, Algerians, Tunisians, Turks.
'Others' include Asians (excluding Turks), Africans (excluding Maghrebins), stateless and refugees.

759,000 in 1972 and to 912,000 in 1982, the historical maximum. These figures are set out in Table 8.2, which also records the increasing percentage of the Belgian population who are foreigners: 4.9 per cent in 1962; 9.2 per cent in 1982. In 1991 foreigners totalled 905,000, although one must also take into account the automatic naturalization in 1985 of children aged under 18 who were born in Belgium and who had at least one Belgian parent (see Figure 8.4). Naturalization 'converted' 22,000 individuals during the 1960s, 63,000 during the 1970s, and 140,000 during the 1980s (64,000 in 1985 alone). A recent law, opposed vigorously not only by the extreme Right but also by the liberal Right, now grants Belgian nationality to 'foreigners' of the third generation born in Belgium of parents who were themselves born in Belgium.

Figure 8.4 shows two main waves of immigration, both linked to major periods of economic expansion. The first lasted from 1962 to 1966, with an annual average of 36,000 net in-migrants; the second, with an annual average of 18,000, covered the years 1969–75. The immigration of non-EC workers stopped in 1975, since when the net immigration figure has averaged only 3,500 foreigners. However, clandestine immigration, which developed especially in the second half of the 1980s, means that this figure underestimates the in-movement. The fundamental point, however, is that the Belgian extreme Right has started to make political capital out of the immigration issue at precisely the time when immigration from the Mediterranean region is no longer a mass phenomenon. Now, any change in numbers of foreigners in Belgium is produced mainly by natural increase, partly compensated by the process of naturalization.

From a sociological point of view, one may distinguish a number of 'classes' of foreigner living in Belgium. First, there are those whose presence goes virtually unnoticed — north-west Europeans and North Americans. Second come the Polish immigrants of the immediate post-war years and substantial numbers of European Mediterranean workers, mainly Italians but also some Spaniards and Greeks. Third, and lower down the social scale of 'acceptability' as perceived by Belgians, are the immigrants from the Maghreb (mainly Moroccans) and Turkey. Black Africans are not very numerous in a country which did not grant the right of residence in the metropolis to its colonial subjects; hence this last group is mainly made up of students, diplomats and business people. Table 8.2 summarizes the numerical evolution of these four principal groups, although it should be noted that the predominantly working-class character of the European Mediterraneans, who came in as miners, factory-workers, etc., is modified by a sizeable presence of international civil servants and managers amongst the Italians, Spanish, Greeks and Portuguese.

Figure 8.5 shows the distribution of foreigners in Belgium, by municipality, in 1989. They are concentrated overwhelmingly in the urban areas although they display different characteristics in the various

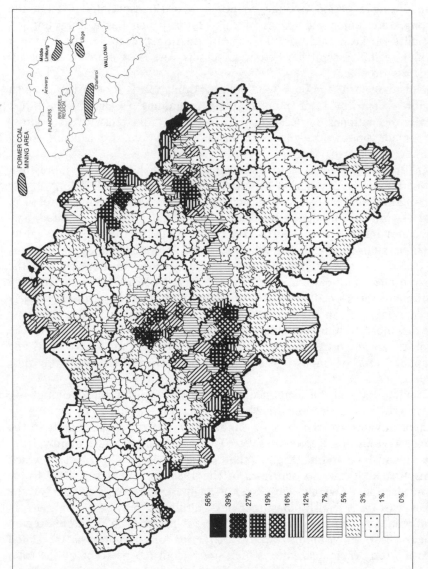

Figure 8.5 Spatial pattern of foreigners in Belgium, by municipality, 1989

urban regions. Along the Walloon industrial axis, where the Italians are dominant, the immigration dates back to the inter-war or immediate post-war periods when Italy and Poland furnished the coalfields and heavy industries with important supplies of much-needed unskilled labour. These immigrants became well integrated with the local population during a period of high economic growth, especially through the strong trade union movement of this region which has a long-standing socialist workers' tradition. The same situation prevails in the Limburg mining region, except that here the socialist vote is of more recent origin and less dominant.

Outside central Limburg the foreign population is low in the Flemish region except for some municipalities containing foreigners from just across the national border. Antwerp has nearly one-tenth of its population made up of foreigners, about half of whom are Muslim, from Turkey and North Africa.

In Brussels the proportion of foreigners is much higher — more than a quarter of the population (Table 8.2). However, not all belong to the 'immigrant worker' category. Low-status immigrants are concentrated in and around the city centre, especially in the older suburbs of the inner-city, and mainly to the north, west and south of the centre. Wealthy foreigners have more or less the same residential distribution as Belgians of the same socio-economic status; they cluster particularly on the eastern and south-eastern radials of the city. In Brussels, as in Antwerp (although not in Wallonia), the presence of immigrant workers is fairly recent, dating from the late 1960s. The migrant influx to Brussels, one of the most 'tertiarized' cities of Europe, has to be seen within the context of the progressive dualization of the labour market and the dramatic loss of industrial employment opportunities over the past twenty years.

Having outlined the social geography of immigration into Belgium, we move now to the elections of 24 November 1991 which recorded a spectacular advance for the extreme Right, moving from 2 to 13 seats in the 212-seat House of Representatives. This achievement came mainly from the Flemish extreme Right, the Vlaams Blok (12 seats), which consolidated further its successes in the 1988 municipal and 1989 European elections. Overall, the extreme Right polled 10.8 per cent of the votes cast in Flemish constituencies, although only 2.9 per cent in Wallonia, in spite of a stronger immigrant presence in the latter region (Figure 8.6). In Wallonia the dissatisfaction of the voters is translated into a strong ecological vote, which grew from 6.5 per cent of the total in 1987 to 13.5 per cent in 1991. In Flanders the 'green vote' was almost stagnant: 7.3 per cent in 1987, 7.9 per cent in 1991. These results seem to express the differential impact of the two political cultures: protest 'to the Left of the socialists' in Wallonia (even if the greens claim a not left, not right, but 'somewhere else' position); and intransigent anti-Belgian, pro-Flemish nationalist protest in Flanders, where there was a tradition

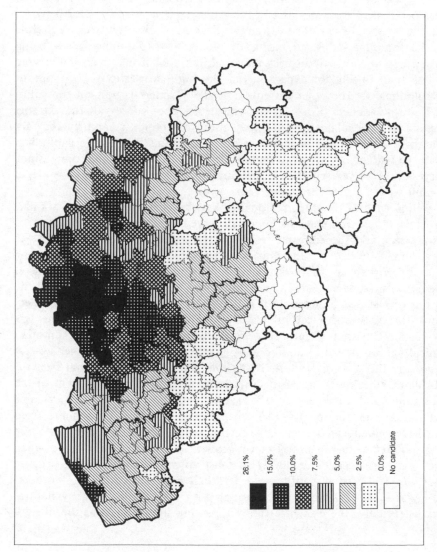

26.1%	■
15.0%	
10.0%	
7.5%	
5.0%	
2.5%	
0.0%	
No candidate	

Figure 8.6 Extreme Right vote in Belgium, 1991

of being pro-German and collaborationist during the Second World War. It is also necessary to note that the francophone extreme Right have failed to take the federalist route, linked in Wallonia to leftist political thought; this could also help to explain the better performance of the extreme Right in Brussels, more 'pan-Belgian' than Wallonia. In Flanders the success of the extreme Right diffuses from its Antwerp stronghold: 26.1 per cent of the votes cast in the Antwerp constituency, 21.2 per cent for the *arrondisement*. The extreme-right vote is also far from negligible in the Limburg industrial basin, dominated by coal-mines (now being closed down), heavy industries and multinational firms, even if the vote is less than one might expect, given the high proportion of immigrant populations. At the other extremity of the Flanders region, in the south of western Flanders (Kortrijk-Roeselare), the poor success of the extreme Right may be explained by the low quota of foreigners and by the fact that here industry has been based on endogenous small-scale capitalism in a Christian Democrat social milieu. In Wallonia, the few minor successes of the extreme Right are limited to the bigger cities — Liège, Namur and, to a lesser extent, Charleroi.

Within each of the three regional political systems (Flanders, Wallonia, Brussels), there is some link to be observed between the distribution of immigrants and the electoral results of the extreme Right, although the level and nature of the link varies. However, there is an equally strong link with urbanism, and with marginalized groups whose social role in the city is no longer clear. Swyngedouw and De Winter (1991) studied the results of the Belgian extreme Right in the 1984 and 1989 European elections for Antwerp. Electoral transfers to the extreme Right came less from the Christian Democratic fold, whose members hold Christian ethical values, or from the liberal Right, and more from younger voters, especially those voting for the first time. Thus, whilst the initial basis of the Vlaams Blok was the Flemish nationalist right-wing component of the Volksunie and members of the semi-clandestine paramilitary Vlaams Militante Orde, the most significant electoral transfers today come from the less well-educated socialist electorate of intermediate age, who are disappointed with the promises of growth and employment made when they were teenagers. The elderly socialist voters are more stable, because they are still strongly influenced by their experiences in the workers' struggles and the Resistance, although they are disappearing by natural deaths. Finally, the extreme Right is picking up votes from the abstentionists.[6]

The extreme Right in Brussels

Having looked at the European and Belgian levels, we turn finally to the case of a single city — Brussels. The capital of Belgium consists of eight electoral constituencies which partly overflow into surrounding Flemish municipalities beyond the limits of the 19 *communes* of the Brussels city-region. The Brussels case illustrates on a more micro scale the differential penetration of the extreme Right amongst the French-speaking and Dutch-speaking populations: 9 per cent of the votes, mainly for the Front National, within the French-speaking electorate; 15.4 per cent, mainly for the Vlaams Blok, amongst the Dutch speakers, even though the latter are more concentrated in the peripheral municipalities where there are fewer immigrants.

The publication of election results only by constituency (each of which usually contains several municipalities) does not really permit a detailed spatial analysis. However, recourse may be made to municipal-level estimates by combining the legislative election results of 1991 with earlier returns from the communal (municipal) elections described by Delruelle-Vosswinkel *et al.* (1989). Figure 8.7 displays the results, together with other relevant data on average income and distribution of foreigners.

The extreme Right achieved its best results in run-down municipalities with a very high immigrant population. Thirty years ago these were socialist strongholds populated by the Brussels labouring class. Actually, it seems that the best results for the extreme Right come from areas on the fringe of immigrant districts rather than from their centre. The scores for the extreme Right are also less favourable in communes where socialist municipal management remains strong and is based on forceful personalities who are pushing through urban renewal projects. Examples are Saint-Gilles, 48 per cent immigrants and 8.5 per cent vote for the extreme Right; and Saint-Josse, 56 per cent immigrants, 9 per cent vote for the far Right. The extreme-right poll tends to be higher in socially mixed municipalities where the socialists' municipal power has been weakened by personality clashes (e.g., Anderlecht, 24 per cent of immigrants, 19 per cent estimated vote for the extreme Right; or Molenbeek, 37 and 25 per cent). In Schaerbeek, where 36 per cent of the population are foreigners, the extreme-right vote was only 12 per cent, although here the former major, who was a Liberal Party candidate, put forward strong anti-immigrant propaganda, so here not all of the anti-foreigner vote went to the extreme Right.

In contrast to the situation in the working-class municipalities, in the wealthy constituencies to the east and south-east of the city centre, and further out in the peri-urban zone of the French-speaking Walloon Brabant, the extreme Right made much less progress amongst the highly educated middle and upper classes resident in these areas. However, it is also true that in certain high-status residential areas, some liberals and others of a similar political persuasion who have strong local electoral bases, have developed a security-oriented anti-immigrant message which differs little from the political discourse of the extreme Right.

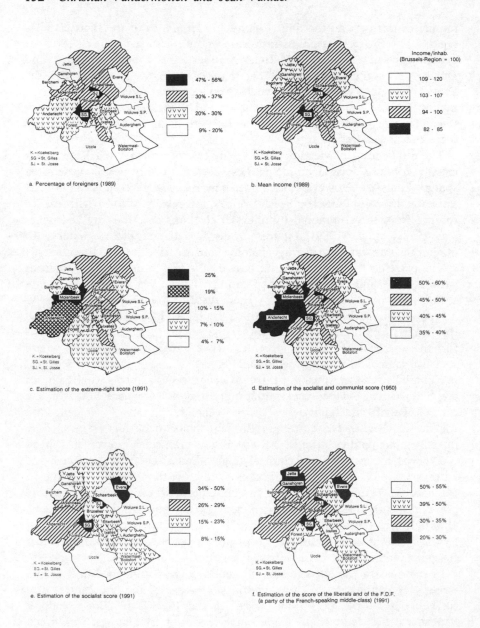

Figure 8.7   Social and electoral structure of the Brussels region, by municipality

Conclusion

Within Western Europe the mass presence of Mediterranean migrant workers, especially those of Islamic culture, and the recent arrivals from Eastern Europe, are feeding the electoral success of the extreme Right. At the same time, the extreme Right is changing its electoral appeal: in geographical terms from the European periphery to the centre; and in sociological terms from the middle and upper-class 'classical' Right towards the *petit-bourgeois* self-employed and towards the working-class suburbs and deprived inner-cities. The traditional Right is also exploiting the electoral potential of the immigration debate, even though their xenophobic statements are aimed at a voting population which is not directly confronted with large numbers of immigrants. The extreme-right vote is becoming politically more important and is extending beyond the run-down working-class urban districts. As we have seen, the diffusion of the extreme Right's success depends on the following conditions being present in some combination:

1. a condition of progressive social polarization, which is particularly evident in tertiary cities;
2. a regional or local industrial crisis, whose social effects are aggravated by the general contraction of public spending and urban renewal programmes;
3. a regional political culture marked by traditions of nationalism and of closed conservatism; or
4. the collapse of left-wing ideological management — as in the PCF's suburban strongholds in France, or the xenophobic demonstrations in the former GDR.

The immigration 'problem' has some explanatory power in accounting for the rise of the 'new' European extreme Right, although the relationship is not simple and direct, and many other factors are also relevant. The cultural context varies, as was revealed by our discussion on Belgium. Also important is the differential manner in which certain political leaders have been able to seize on the exploit the immigrant issue.

Notes

1. Translated from the French by Russell King.
2. See *Eurobarometer*, 34 (1990) and 35 (1991), published by the Commission of the European Communities, Brussels.
3. The 1990 poll concentrated less on the immigration issue than the 1991 survey, so the results may not be strictly comparable.
4. Named after Pierre Poujade, the leader of a right-wing, populist, anti-state, anti-capital movement in rural France in the 1950s.

5. For relevant literature on some of these parties, see Liepelt 1975; Bartolini 1979; Larsen *et al.* 1980; Husbands 1982; Letamendia 1982; Milza 1985; De Schampheleire and Thanassekos 1991.
6. Voting is compulsory in Belgium. Abstentionists are those who opt out because of (perhaps faked) medical reasons, or those who vote but spoil their ballot slips.

References

Bartolini, B., 1979, 'Analisi ecologica del voto del MSI–DN alle elezioni politiche del 20 giugno 1976', *Rivista Italiana di Scienza Politica*, 9(2): 297–316.

Charlot, M., 1985, 'L'emergence du Front National', *Revue Française de Science Politique*, 35(1): 14–29.

Delruelle-Vosswinkel, N., Noel, F., Vanlaer, J. and Vandemotten, C., 1989, 'Les élections communales du 9 octobre 1988: évolution des familles politiques et géographie electorale', *Bulletin du Crédit Communal de Belgique*, 169: 31–49, plus atlas.

De Schampheleire, H. and Thanassekos, Y. (eds), 1991, *L'extrême-droite en Europe de l'Ouest*, VUB Press, Brussels.

Gilg, P., 1972, 'Der Erfolg der neuen Rechtsgruppen in den Nationalratswahlen von 1971', *Revue Suisse d'Economie Politique et de Statistique*, 108(4): 591–622.

Harrop, M., England, J. and Husbands, C.T., 1980, 'The bases of National Front support', *Political Studies*, 28(2): 271–83.

Husbands, C.T., 1982, 'Contemporary right-wing extremism in Western European democracies: a review article', *European Journal of Political Research*, 9(1): 75–99.

Jaffre, J., 1984, 'Les élections européennes en France', *Pouvoirs*, 31: 123–48.

Larsen, S.U., Hagtvet, B. and Myklebust, J.P. (eds), 1980, *Who were the Fascists? Social roots of European fascism*, Universitetsforlaget, Oslo.

Lentzen, E., Mabille, X. and Vanlaer, J., 1989, *Les élections européennes de juin 1989*, Centre de Recherche et d'Information Socio-Politique, Brussels.

Letamendia, P., 1982, *Les partis politiques en Espagne*, Presses Universitaires de France, Paris.

Liepelt, K., 1975, 'Supporters of the New Party of the Right: a report and discussion of the German NPD's sources of support', in Brewer, G. D. and Brunner, R.D. (eds), *Political development and change*, Free Press, New York, 128–58.

Milza, P., 1985, *Les Fascismes*, Imprimerie Nationale, Paris.

Perrineau, P., 1985, 'Le Front National: un électorat autoritaire', *Revue Politique et Parlementaire*, 89(918): 24–31.

Rollat, A. and Plenel, E., 1984, *L'effet Le Pen*, Le Monde/La Découverte, Paris.

Swyngedouw, M. and De Winter, L., 1991, 'Het Vlaams Blok in de Europese verkiezingen', in De Schampheleire, H. and Thanassekos, Y. (eds), *L'extrême-droite en Europe de l'Ouest*, VUB Press, Brussels, 115–27.

Taylor, S., 1979, 'The incidence of coloured populations and support for the National Front', *British Journal of Political Science*, 9(2): 250–5.

Thomas, P., 1990, 'Belgium's north–south divide and the Walloon regional problem', *Geography*, 76(1): 36–50.

Vandermotten, C. and Vandewattyne, P., 1985, 'Les étapes de la croissance et de la formation des armatures urbaines en Belgique', *Bulletin du Crédit Communal de Belgique*, 154: 41–62.

Vanlaer, J., 1984, *200 millions de voix. Une géographie des familles politiques européennes*, Laboratoire de Géographie Humaine de l'Université Libre de Bruxelles et Societé Royale Belge de Géographie, Brussels.

Vanlaer, J., 1991, 'Opposition centre–péripherie et vote d'extrême-droite en Europe', in De Schampheleire, and H., Thanassekos, Y. (eds), *L'extrême-droite en Europe de l'Ouest*, VUB Press, Brussels, 41–55.

Whiteley, P., 1979, 'The National Front vote in the 1977 local government elections: an aggregate data analysis', *British Journal of Political Science*, 9(3): 370–80.

Chapter 9

What mass migration has meant for Turkey

Gündüz Atalık and Brian Beeley

Introduction

Migrations of Turks in recent decades differ from those of earlier times
in their scale, speed and impact. Indeed, since the 1950s, internal and
international migration has probably been the main motor of change in
Turkish society and in the Republic's links with Europe. There has been
a profound change in the distribution of Turks within their country,
whilst in Western Europe a large Turkish community of workers and
their dependants has become established. Because of its size, and because
of its European links and aspirations, Turkey today is a compelling case
study of mass migration and its impact on economic and social change
in general and on urbanization in particular.

The Turkish Republic was proclaimed in Ankara in 1923 for the
Anatolian core of the dismembered Ottoman Empire, together with a
European corner in Thrace. The census four years later showed a largely
rural population of 13.6 million. Even by 1960 more than two-thirds of
the population were still rural. By 1985, however, slightly more than half
were listed as urban with nearly one person in five living in one of the
three major centres, Istanbul, Ankara and Izmir. The 1990 census reports
a total population of 56.5 million — a figure comparable to that for
France, Italy, or the United Kingdom. The same census indicates that the
inhabitants of the 73 provincial (*il*) capitals and 829 district (*ilçe*) centres
account for 59 per cent of the Turkish total. The equivalent figure for
1927 had been only 24 per cent.

While Turkey resembles some countries of Western Europe in population size, its rate of annual population increase looks non-European.
Even though the present Turkish figure of 2.17 per cent per year is lower
than hitherto, it contrasts with 0.7 for Greece and Spain and with rates
of growth near zero in Belgium, Denmark, the United Kingdom and
elsewhere.

This chapter deals with both external (emigration and return) and
internal migration. We shall develop the topics of Turkey's vulnerability
to outside — notably West European — decisions and actions on the
scale and complexion of migrant movement, of the role of funds sent
back to Turkey and of the repercussions for the national economy and

society of the return of long-term migrants. We suggest that though the features of the Turkish experience in migration are not unique, their content and combination leave the Republic arguably more vulnerable to change resulting from migration than other European states. We think that mass migration is about qualitative as well as quantitative change, and argue that movement, even for short periods, necessarily changes people such that return to a place of departure cannot be a return to a *status quo ante*.

Rural–urban migration

In population change as in other aspects of Turkish modernization, it is conventional to make a sweeping distinction between the more developed west and the more backward east of the country. This primary spatial contrast appears to be confirmed when generalized inter-regional net migration flow rates are mapped for provinces or groups of provinces, as in Figure 9.1 which shows net migration for the early 1970s. Such inter-regional net migration can be 'explained' by regression analysis using various independent variables — distance, GDP, industrial employment — to correlate with migration. Such analysis shows that predominantly 'push' factors deriving from regional disparities are important in stimulating Turkish internal migration flows (Munro 1974; Atalık 1990). These flows, in turn, increase inter-regional disparities.

Whilst the inter-regional movement of groups of people can be interpreted as reflecting the structural perspectives of different areas' variable incorporation into the expanding capitalist economy, this approach overlooks two important considerations: individual choice (conditioned by age, gender and social status); and the wide variation within Turkish regions, particularly between urban centres and rural districts. To a certain extent, these two aspects merge, and the rest of this section of the chapter will examine rural–urban migration from a largely behavioural perspective.

Net population increase in Turkey is markedly urban-biased when both natural growth and migration are taken into account. The censuses from 1927 to the 1970s have consistently shown overall increases in both rural and urban populations. Spatial variety in the pattern of gain and loss became more complex in the 1970s when net population loss was evident in a scatter of areas from Thrace in the west to the Soviet border in the east, and from the Black Sea coastal areas to Hatay in the south (Beeley, 1987, p. 61). Such patterns reveal the over-simple nature of the east–west dichotomy noted earlier; in reality there have always been pockets of underdevelopment in the west and favoured areas of relative progress in the east. In some less-favoured districts there was overall loss of both rural and urban population during the 1970s. By 1980, sixteen of the then sixty-seven provinces were reporting a drop in their rural population, and in five of these there was a small overall decline.

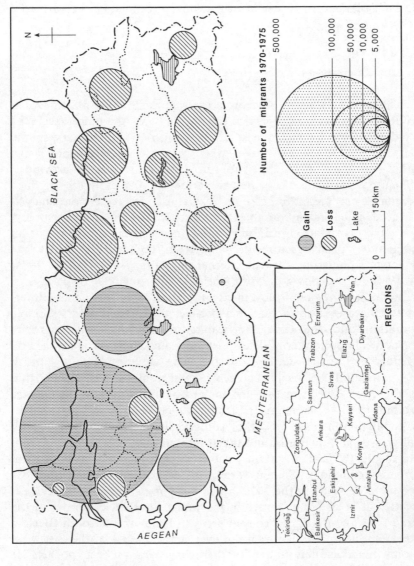

Figure 9.1 Turkey: inter-regional net migration, 1970–5

Source: State Planning Organization, Publication No. 2054 – SPB 396, Ankara, 1986.

The process of population relocation continues, as an analysis of trends for the most recent intercensal period of 1985–90 reveals. During this period thirty-seven provinces (half of the total) recorded a net loss of rural (i.e. subdistrict and village) population. Although most of this was in the less-developed east, eight of the thirty-seven provinces were western, two of them in Thrace. Thirteen more were central provinces close to Istanbul, Ankara and other expanding urban areas. Fifteen of the provinces showing a rural population decrease reveal a drop overall. The extreme case for 1985–90 is the province of Tunceli with annual decline rates of 2.4 per cent overall and 5.2 per cent rural. At the opposite end of the scale of changes stands the province of Istanbul where the population growth averaged almost 4.5 per cent annually over the five-year period, reaching a total of 7.3 million in 1990.

Figure 9.2 indicates that more of Turkey's national territory is now losing population than was the case in the 1970s (Beeley 1987, p. 61). Among the rural communities showing a reverse in the net trend is Şanlıurfa, within the South-Eastern Anatolia Project (GAP) area, where overall growth rates are now generally above the national average. Another example of new rapid growth is provided by the coastal zones in the south-west which are exploiting their potential for tourism. Based on subprovince (*ilçe*) units, Figure 9.2 shows the continuing advance of areas of net population loss across the country. As noted above, maps using the larger province (*il*) units tend to simplify the pattern into a largely west–east division. Indeed 'distance' on Figure 9.2 should be seen as relative levels of development rather than in kilometres.

Most of the areas not reporting net loss during 1985–90 remain below the national growth average (Figure 9.2). This leaves above-average growth in a spatial scatter of differing circumstances. Major urban centres account for most of the growth — as in Adana, Ankara, Bursa and Izmir. Istanbul, Turkey's major concentration of people, includes districts showing recent net yearly growth rates in excess of 10 per cent. However, the central urban core on both sides of Istanbul's Golden Horn reports a net loss of residents, although the daytime population becomes ever more crowded with commuters. Much of the rapid growth in outer areas of Turkey's larger urban areas continues to be unauthorized *gecekondu* ('built-by-night') housing, though current initiatives hold out the promise of the legalization of such districts by municipal authorities. Such acceptance at least facilitates the introduction of basic amenities and some belated measure of planning control.

The principal result of the massive relocation of Turks within their country since the early 1960s has been the ending of the traditionally clear distinction between urban and rural society. This has two main dimensions.

First, many of the inhabitants of Turkey's cities and towns are migrants from villages or from smaller towns. In some cases links with their places of origin have faded as migrants become established in areas

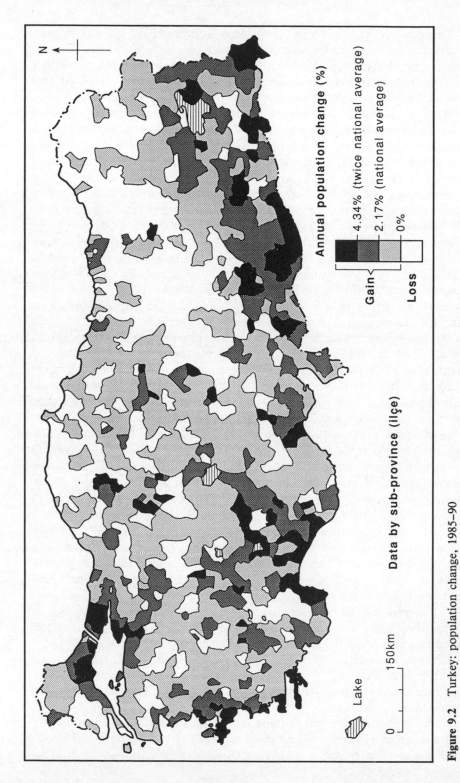

Figure 9.2 Turkey: population change, 1985–90

Source: 1990 Census of Population, State Institute of Statistics, Ankara, 1991, pp. 5–36.

Annual population change (%)

Gain
4.34% (twice national average)
2.17% (national average)
0%
Loss

Data by sub-province (Ilçe)

Lake

0   150km

of new building round older urban cores. In other cases, however, the links with 'home' continue, especially where ties of kinship and property remain strong (Suzuki 1966). Residence in burgeoning urban areas does not necessarily lead to absorption into the urban economy. Most incomers, particularly in the early stages of their relocation, remain without employment in the formal economy and exist at best on the returns from one or more jobs in the informal or casual sector. Neither does establishment bring standard urban housing for new arrivals. Most move into *gecekondu* squatter housing, often without amenities or legal title (Karpat 1976).

Second, rural–urban migration has eroded the traditional contrasts between townspeople and incomers, especially for those born or reared in the new environment, and more rapidly perhaps for men. In the recent past it was still possible to identify people as of the village or of the town by their dress or demeanour. Indeed, informed eyes could distinguish people from one part of the country rather than another. Newcomers in cities adjust to urban norms which are strongly 'European', reflecting the success of reforms in the nineteenth century and after 1923 under Mustafa Kemal Atatürk.

While migrants have been moving largely, although not exclusively, from village to town, modernization on the European model has been going the other way. The inception of co-ordinated national planning soon after 1960 was based on the contention that rural people should become indistinguishable from their urban compatriots as quickly as possible. The removal of disparities between town and country, between regions, and between socio-economic groups became an underpinning rationale for a succession of development plans. What the planners underestimated was the willingness of rural people to participate in the development process by moving to where they saw better material conditions, rather than by simply staying at home and waiting for expected improvements to reach them.

In the urbanization of Turkey's 36,000 villages a big part has been played by the state education system. With the spread of access to schooling, pro-urban curricula increasingly persuade pupils that town ways are modern. With electricity now available in most parts of the country, this message is supported by television. Increasingly villagers find themselves with business in other places. Hitherto such contacts were more limited, possibly confined to mandatory military service, another agent of urban-based modernization. Now, the very smallness and inevitable social intimacy of village life may become claustrophobic to those whose horizons have been broadened.

The incorporation of the village into the wider town-led society and economy can be explained as the structured peripheralization of outer areas within an expanding system of capitalist production. Whether its cause is structural or based on individual choice, or reflects the interlinking of both, the two-way change in the urban–rural balance in Turkey has proceeded differently in different places. Some villages are urban-directed in that they have no separate **rural** identity (Kolars 1967). Examples are 'shadow villages' of immigrants from the countryside who cluster in urban squatter settlements, and 'annexed villages' incorporated into expanding urban areas. Some villages appear to be consciously 'market-seeking', while others apparently ignore their resource potential for change and incorporation into the national economy.

The rural–urban dichotomy thus over-simplifies the nature of recent and contemporary population movement in Turkey. Much of the movement is not from village to major urban centre but between other centres within the settlement hierarchy. Some people move from village to nearby small town and only later go further up the scale to a large centre or to one of the 'big four' — Istanbul, Ankara, Izmir, or Adana. Some population movement is rural-to-rural. In some cases nomadic or semi-nomadic people — the professional migrants — move to settled villages, perhaps as part of an officially encouraged resettlement scheme. Some poor, landless villagers establish themselves in more prosperous villages offering a prospect of work beyond the traditional periods for casual work such as harvest-time. Though welcome for their labour, such incomers, in their village *gecekondu*, may find that full acceptance takes much longer. Finally, another variant, the urban-to-rural migration of Western industrial economies during this century, is making its appearance in Turkey (Figure 9.2), and can be expected to accelerate during the next decades as transportation becomes easier and urban pressures themselves persuade increasing numbers of those who can afford to do so to seek a rural identity — as commuter, retired person, second home-owner or, at least, holiday-maker.

The typical pattern of movement from village to town suggests a loss to the former and a gain to the latter. However, the reality is more complex where the departing villager retains links with 'home'. By the same token, the town gains a person when a migrant moves in together with the connections and associations which that individual brings. Usually such links include families or other groups rather than lone people, sometimes even whole communities. In the town, however, the most usual incoming unit is the nuclear family, larger than the urban average although smaller than that of the village.

The spread and extent of the integration of the migrant family within the urban scene depends on the time of arrival, their employment skills, their social adaptability, their connections in the city, and official policy (Eke 1983). Clearly the basis of integration into urban society, as distinct from living jobless in a squatter *gecekondu* on the edge of town, is employment. Whereas the availability of informal work in the town gives the newcomer at least a limited income, his or her access to the established formal sector of the urban economy may prove much more difficult, and may not happen at all for migrants and only ultimately for their children. Migration and the design and construction of squatter dwellings are processes which cannot be separated from each other. The *gecekondu* can be expanded to accommodate more family members or to reflect some level of success in penetration into the urban economy. Perhaps the rural feature to persist most strongly in the urban setting is the readiness to support relatives and neighbours facing special difficulties.

The flexibility of the Turkish urban *gecekondu* extends to the relationship between squatter housing and the formal housing sector. While some 'built-by-night' houses remain seriously substandard and without basic amenities for many years, others are absorbed more quickly into the conventional housing stock — especially where they are built in well-spaced layouts to facilitate the introduction of roads and amenities by the authorities as part of the change of status from informal (and illegal) to accepted parts of the urban residential landscape. The more successful *gecekondu* builders transform their properties into substantial dwellings, adding first one and then another storey as their integration into the urban system brings a return. For their part, urban authorities in Ankara now seem to be absorbing informal housing into the formal sector as quickly as possible.

Emigration from Turkey

A large number of works in recent decades have examined Turkish external migration.[1] However, work on inferential explanatory models of migration remains at an early stage: Davis (1988) attributes this in part to the unpredictability of human behaviour in the face of *ad hoc* and arbitrary changes of rules and policy. Most investigators do, however, see some form of centre–periphery relationship between labour-attracting countries and those, such as Turkey, which are net suppliers. There is less agreement about the extent to which out-migration exacerbates inequalities and depletes the human resource capital of labour-sending countries. Abadan-Unat (1976) stresses that Turkish external migration should be interpreted within the framework of growing disparities between the developed centre and the developing periphery. She sees it as a dependent variable in the context of cyclical economic interaction between sending and receiving countries, systems of education, currency transfers, approaches to development planning and migratory policies.

October 1991 marked the thirtieth anniversary of the first bilateral agreements to move Turkish workers to West Germany. In fact, Turkish labour migration to Western Europe was already under way in 1961, although it was by individual and small-group responses to the initiatives of German and other business enterprises. In her overview of the historical evolution of Turkish emigration, Abadan-Unat identifies this first phase (1956–61) as that of 'recruitment by nomination', in which the migrants soon showed themselves reluctant to return home after a specified contract period (Abadan-Unat 1986, p. 330).

The same author characterizes the years 1961–72 as the phase of out-migration explosion with both governmental intervention and private initiative promoting the migration of individuals. Ankara saw the export of 'surplus manpower' as a contribution to the reduction of internal unemployment levels, though it was noted that skilled personnel should be encouraged to remain at home.[2] In choosing from lists of would-be migrants, the Turkish Employment Service gave priority to people from less prosperous areas (Abadan-Unat 1976, pp. 88–9). There was also 'nominated recruitment' in which an employer would apply for a named person to the Employment Service. Such nomination depended on the existence of networks of individuals already established abroad.

The pattern of bilateral agreements was extended in 1964 to Austria, Belgium and The Netherlands, and in 1965 and 1967 respectively to France and Sweden. Agreements at government level such as these left migration as the official gift in a way not possible for internal migration within national boundaries. What such government control could much less easily arrange was the return of Turkish *Gastarbeiter* and their dependants. Indeed by 1973 host countries recognized the fixed presence of foreign workers in a series of social security and related agreements. The shifting policies of the German government towards Turkish immigrants (the majority group in that country) are outlined in Chapter 5 of this book.

Increased oil prices and recession in 1973/4 brought in the third phase identified by Abadan-Unat. In (West) Germany, overwhelmingly the main destination for Turks by this time, came a ban on new admission of workers and encouragement for those already there to return home. In 1973 over 100,000 new workers went to Germany from Turkey; in 1975 only 640 received a first-time labour permit (Rist 1978, p. 113). Inevitably unauthorized emigration from Turkey surged. A 1975 survey in one Turkish province (Yozgat) found that more than two migrants in five had left to find work in Western Europe as 'tourists' (Abadan-Unat *et al.* 1976).

Reaction to the European 'closed-door' policies was followed, between 1975 and 1978, by a 'settling abroad' (fourth) phase, during which many Turkish migrants came to see themselves as domiciled in Western Europe despite problems of employment, movement of dependants, etc. Most nevertheless maintained an ambivalent view of themselves as ultimately returning 'home' to Turkey (Abadan-Unat 1986, pp. 337–41). Further restrictions on recruitment in Western Europe in 1978 stimulated would-be entrants to request political asylum as a means of entry. The response was a further tightening of controls and a visa requirement for Turks. Overall, the 1978–85 (fifth) phase was marked not only by restriction and reaction but also by the realization that a substantial Turkish community in Germany, with smaller groups elsewhere in Western Europe, had become a permanent feature, with long-term implications for both Turkey and the host countries. 'Jeder dritte ein Türke' ('Every third one

Table 9.1 Region of origin of Turkish emigrant workers, 1963–85

Region	1963–79		1980–85	
	'000	%	'000	%
Marmara	291	33.3	89	26.0
Aegean	130	14.9	22	6.5
Central Anatolia	202	23.1	88	25.9
Mediterranean	48	5.5	28	8.3
Black Sea	109	12.5	71	20.9
Eastern Anatolia	52	5.9	31	9.0
South-eastern	42	4.8	11	3.4
Total	874	100.0	340	100.0

Source: Barışık *et al.* 1991, p. 317.

Table 9.2 Destinations of Turkish workers emigrating through official channels, 1961–86

Years	Total ('000)	Europe		Arab countries		Australia		Other	
		'000	%	'000	%	'000	%	'000	%
1961–67	204	204	100.0	–	–	–	–	–	–
1967–73	586	569	97.1	1	0.2	5	0.8	11	1.9
1973–86	415	32	7.7	355	85.6	5	1.2	23	5.5
1961–86	1,205	805	66.8	356	29.6	10	0.8	34	2.8

Source: Barışık *et al.* 1991, p. 307.

a Turk') proclaimed *Die Welt* in an article of 6 April 1982, pointing out that West Germany's 1.5 million Turkish residents constituted its largest foreign element. More than a million of the Turks were dependants (Salt 1985). In 1984 there were estimated to be a further 535,000 Turks in the seven other European countries having more than 10,000 each. The total of over 2 million for the eight European countries compared with only 206,000 Turks in Saudi Arabia and Libya, the leading Middle East destinations at the time — and only 10,000 of these were dependants (Beeley 1986, p. 168).

The changing geography of departure and destination is shown in Tables 9.1 and 9.2. Some change in the pattern of origin of emigrant workers was apparent by the mid-1980s, with more of the total accounted for by eastern regions of Turkey than in the 1960s and 1970s (Table 9.1). Over the same years there were also major changes in the foreign destinations of such workers (Table 9.2). With movements of Turks to Europe very severely curtailed by 1985, Arab countries quickly became much more important, with Saudi Arabia accounting for the majority. From that year Abadan-Unat's sixth phase was characterized by rather different patterns of labour migration than those to Europe.

Table 9.3   Turkish emigrants abroad, 1982 and 1990 ('000)

Destination	Workers		Dependants		Total	
	1982	1990	1982	1990	1982	1990
Europe: total	785	993	1,368	1,373	2,153	2,366
(West) Germany	576	661	1,077	982	1,653	1,613
France	50	98	63	116	113	214
Netherlands	62	89	91	102	153	191
Austria	30	59	43	71	73	130
Arab countries: total	155	122	3	6	158	128
Saudi Arabia	60	95	1	5	61	100
Libya	66	18	2	1	68	19
Other: total	18	33	18	14	36	47
of which Australia	16	29	17	12	33	41

Source: State Planning Organization, Ankara; some totals for 1990 partly estimated.

Turkish workers to Saudi Arabia and other Arab destinations went — and continue to go — on fixed residence contracts, usually one year, and the overwhelming majority of them have been men without their dependants. Established Turkish communities have not, therefore, emerged in Arab lands, despite the fact that both workers and hosts have Islam in common. Another difference between the Arab and European experience of Turkish migrant labour has been that much of the contract work in the Middle East has been organized by Turkish companies.

The position of Turkish workers living abroad at the start of the 1990s shows the continuing importance of Germany and other European countries (Table 9.3). Germany accounted for nearly two out of three of the Turkish workers in Europe and for more than seven dependants out of every ten. Including both workers and dependants, the size of the Turkish community in reunited Germany was slightly down in size, compared with 1982. In numbers of Turkish residents, France, The Netherlands and Austria showed substantial relative increases — though from very much lower levels than Germany.

Saudi Arabia remained the leading Arab destination in 1990, accounting for 79 per cent of Turks in Arab countries (at least 95 per cent of them workers). In 1982 the Kingdom accounted for fewer than two in five of Turks working in Arab lands. Overall the total for all such countries dropped by a fifth between the two years, most notably on account of a sharp fall in the Turkish contingent in Libya. Further sharp reductions came in Iraq as a result of the Gulf War in 1991.

Australia, by far the largest recipient of Turkish workers and their dependants outside Europe and the Middle East, increased its total between 1982 and 1990. Here, perhaps more than elsewhere, figures for the Turkish community can be blurred to the extent that some acquire Australian nationality.

Return migration

The return of migrants to Turkey parallels similar repatriations to many peripheral European countries. However, in the Turkish case return has been primarily to the urban rather than to the rural areas from which most of those who sought work abroad originated (Eraydın 1981; Gitmez 1984; Wilpert 1984). Such urban areas are, moreover, mostly in western — more developed — Turkey, a spatial bias also reflected in the pattern of remittances from Turks abroad. An inevitable outcome is increased disparities between regions (Keleş, 1985); this is particularly true of the European dimension of Turkish labour migration, with Turkish workers and their remittances coming from Middle Eastern countries having a rather different impact.

As noted, the dominant pattern of migration for work in Turkey's Arab neighbours had been fixed-term contracts interspersed with home visits. The implications of this have been both financial and social. Saudi riyals imported, often as cash, find their way into the maintenance of family left behind in Turkey or go as investment in equipment, building, or a car, possibly as part of a migrant's attempt to set himself up in a trade or other new enterprise. The link between the family and 'home' is not necessarily broken at all, though there are clearly implications for individuals' perception of their roles. A woman, for example, may be required, during the absence on contract of a breadwinner, to assume a leadership role within the family — and even within the farm or business enterprise — and thus becomes more independent than would have been expected traditionally.

Return migration from European countries has differed markedly from the experience in Arab countries in quantity — much greater numbers have gone back — and in cause and effect. Abadan-Unat (1988) identifies two forms. One of these is the officially encouraged return of both migrants and families, as the logical sequel to earlier policies to stimulate movement to Western Europe when countries in that area were short of labour. The other is the privately arranged return of a migrant when circumstances seem to the individual to warrant it. Both types of return have similar implications for Turkey. Most obvious is the effect on the Turkish labour market. Returning workers add themselves to the ranks of the employment-seekers: they may also return with skills and work experience for which the labour market in Turkey has limited demand. Whether they find jobs or not, returning workers and their dependants bring needs for housing, amenities and social support. Migrants returning to Turkish society may find that readjustment is very difficult because they have become accustomed to the social patterns of urban Germany or elsewhere in Europe. Last, but for the Turkish exchequer far from least, the returnee ceases to be an external source of repatriated remittances, though some returnees might liberate savings accumulated in foreign banks.

Abadan-Unat (1988) also distinguishes early from late returning migrants. The early group were those who went abroad in the 1960s and 1970s and returned on a sporadic and individual basis. Most were men. The later returnees, by contrast, were mainly those who chose to return to Turkey after family reunification abroad. Many of the earlier returnees found difficulty in readjusting at home. Typically they found it hard to fit into industrial employment (Toepfer 1985). Where they had been villagers, to resettle at home at all was a challenge for many (Gitmez 1984). Even among those who went back to a village to purchase land with money saved in Europe, many chose to lease their land to others rather than to farm on their own account. With this disappointment as they faced difficulties of re-entry to Turkish society, large numbers of returnees have aimed to seek work abroad again as soon as possible. The overall outcome for Turkey was frustration on two counts. For the state there has been the realization that skills acquired abroad have often failed to make an impact on Turkey's need for human resources. For the individual the same mismatch engenders personal disillusionment.

The return of long-stay migrants since the 1970s has been larger in numbers of people, and has had different social implications from the earlier and short-term movements (Abadan-Unat, 1988). The unit has been the family rather than the individual, and there has been evidence of both push factors (unemployment and xenophobia in Europe) and pull factors (concern with maintaining the Turkish cultural link). The first of these is a function of the circumstances of the European labour market at a particular juncture. To general recession and growing fears that Turks were taking jobs from Germans have been added new migrations within Western Europe itself — notably that of East Germans into what was, prior to reunification, the Federal Republic. Turks lack the freedom to move and work within the European Community shared by nationals or the constituent countries. Turks' religion and cultural difference provides those who seek a basis for discrimination with convenient ammunition. For the immediate future the prospects of Turkish migrant labour in Western Europe are not good, although the position could change dramatically if Turkey achieves some of the closer links with the European Community to which it aspires.

The cultural impact of Turkish labour migration to Europe may prove to be at least as durable and penetrating as the economic. Ironically, a Turk regarded at best as a *Gastarbeiter* in Germany — or at worst as an unwelcome foreigner — may, when he or she attempts to reintegrate into the home country, as seen as an *Almanyalı* (a Turk who is 'from Germany'). In many cases Turks born in Western Europe may feel settled there to the extent that they speak the local language fluently and have gone through a local schooling system. However, where daughters are thus assimilated, Turkish parents may be anxious to return home. Nevertheless, the individual, once back in Turkey, may feel alien — and may be seen as such — especially where the return does not lead quickly to a job and to the type of housing and amenities accepted as normal in Western Europe. Such circumstances may produce the 'one foot in Germany' type of returnee (Wilpert 1984).

Although as few as 1 per cent of Turks established in Germany have taken (or have been allowed to take) citizenship, there are other indicators of assimilation to set against anti-Turkish reaction. Over 45,000 Turks own their homes in Germany. Twelve thousand are university students in the country: two-thirds of these are children of immigrants. The number of returnees to Turkey drops from 210,000 in 1984 to only 30,000 in 1991, reflecting both the difficulties facing those seeking reabsorption in Turkey and the slump in new movements to Germany in recent years. A not-so-rare case might be that of the one-time Anatolian villager whose son or daughter now feels too much of an urban person in Germany to reintegrate, as an *Almanyalı*, back in Turkey. The longer Turks stay in Germany, the less likely they are to return.

The more recent development of labour migration to Arab countries has not produced the same social outcomes for Turkey because dependants have stayed at home. The returning migrant worker therefore has an established immediate family to return to and his stay abroad has typically been no more than one year on a particular contract. While working in the Arab country, the Turkish worker has not usually achieved the assimilation levels of Western Europe. Even shared Islam has typically proved to be less of a factor for the individual's integration than has his Turkishness remained a differentiator. The nature of the contract work and the brevity of the stay have, moreover, meant that migrants from Turkey have not learned Arabic to the extent that their compatriots in Western Europe have acquired a local language.

Turkish workers return from both Western Europe and the Middle East with changed attitudes to other Turks, from relatives and neighbours to employers and those who represent the state. At the family and local level there are changes in generation and gender relationships. Perhaps most marked is the changed place of women, whose *Almanyalı* status may leave them unwilling to resume traditional roles, particularly in Turkish village society. For the men, new-found income, qualifications and skills, and perhaps knowledge of a Western European language all contribute to status elevation *vis-à-vis* traditional patterns based more directly on age, kinship, devoutness or landownership.

Remittances

In the early 1960s the prospect of transforming unemployed and under-employed Turks in Turkey into senders of hard currency from Western Europe held out great promise. By 1965, with some 160,000 expatriates abroad, Turkey received the equivalent of nearly US$70 million in official remittances plus money taken back without going through official accounts. In 1974, in the wake of new restrictions on Turkish workers going to Germany, the 750,000 Turks abroad sent home the equivalent of $1.4 billion. Such remittances peaked at nearly $2.5 billion at the start of the 1980s, by which time there were nearly 800,000 Turkish workers in Western Europe and another 155,000 in Arab countries (Table 9.4). The latter group were thought to be sending back per head nearly twice the sums remitted from Western Europe. The main reason for this contrast lies in the fact that the Turkish workers in Europe have with them large numbers of dependants while those in Arab countries have very few. A further reason is the tendency for workers returning home from Western Europe to take consumer goods with them, rather than cash.

By 1988, workers' remittances stood at $1.8 billion, near the annual average for the decade. The figure for 1988 equalled the deficit on Turkey's external trade in that year and was not far short of the nearly $2 billion brought in by tourism. The sectoral and spatial impact of remittances within Turkey is difficult to measure, although Toepfer (1985) has made some interesting attempts to chart their use at the village level. Certainly much of the incoming money has gone directly into the family or local community of a migrant worker, often to maintain dependants left in Turkey (this is especially true of remittances from Arab countries). In the many cases where migrants abroad do not return to their point of origin in Turkey, much of the remitted money is spent on consumables for the new home. It seems that remittances do not help to reduce imbalances between regions in Turkey, though there clearly are specific improvements — a school or a local park perhaps — made possible by remittances. Indeed, despite the positive impact of remittances on particular schemes or on the balance of payments in general, the net effect is ultimately to increase inter-regional disparities by encouraging investment in already successful enterprises, most of which are located in more developed, notably western, provinces. As for the distribution of personal income across the country there is no sign of a beneficial effect of remittances on the pattern of inequality which has remained much the same, at least since 1973. All this despite the efforts of the government in Ankara to persuade workers to invest their savings in productive activity. Although schemes have been devised to encourage investment in 'Workers' Companies', 'Village Development Co-operatives', etc., results have been disappointing, for people have preferred to rely, when spending their money, on the individual initiative which helped to move them

Table 9.4 Remittances repatriated to Turkey compared with trade deficit, 1967–88 (figures in millions US dollars)

Years	Remittances	Exports	Imports	Remittances as % deficit
1967	67	522	685	57
1968	107	496	764	40
1969	141	537	747	67
1970	273	589	886	92
1971	471	677	1,088	115
1972	740	885	1,508	119
1973	1,184	1,317	2,049	162
1974	1,426	1,538	3,720	66
1975	1,312	1,401	4,640	41
1976	982	1,960	4,993	32
1977	982	1,753	5,694	25
1978	893	2,288	4,479	45
1979	1,694	2,261	4,946	63
1980	2,071	2,910	7,573	44
1981	2,490	4,702	8,864	60
1982	2,140	5,890	8,794	74
1983	1,513	5,905	9,235	45
1984	1,807	7,389	10,757	54
1985	1,714	8,255	11,515	53
1986	1,634	7,583	11,027	47
1987	2,021	10,322	14,008	55
1988	1,806	11,846	13,646	100

Source: Martin 1991, p. 39; based on World Bank and IMF data.

to foreign employment in the first place (Penninx and Van Renselaar 1978).

Conclusion

Turkey has contributed perhaps more than any other country to the mass relocation of European labour which was at its peak in the 1960s. Like other Mediterranean countries, it now has communities abroad and these show signs of staying put — and of sending home less money. Evidently this migration of Turks has been on a larger scale than anticipated. The debate about why it has developed as it has, both internationally and within the country, continues. Academics have offered explanations and state decision-makers have produced proposals. Most obvious of all has been the inability of the Turkish government to **control** migration, either by limiting relocation or by **using** migrants within a conscious programme of social and economic development. It is clear that people move because they perceive opportunity: they may be unaware that their migration is part of the centralizing tendency of capitalist concentration.

It is also clear that migrant workers respond to push and pull forces beyond their own country, and that their government may have little ability to influence such forces in agreed national priorities.

Analytically, it is important to concentrate on those aspects of population change and movement which link migration with national urban systems and regional disparities. At its present stage of demographic transition — high fertility and declining mortality — Turkey presents a distinctive mix of elements among countries experiencing mass migration.

Within Turkey the relocation of people has left more Turks in urban than in rural areas for the first time. Later than in Spain, Italy and elsewhere, large parts of rural Turkey are now losing population, though a national growth rate of 2.17 per cent annually is maintained. The loss of resident population in central Istanbul and other moves out of cities suggest that counter-urbanization has begun in Turkey. The increasing concentration of people in more developed areas reduces the prospects for any marked reduction in disparities between regions.

Within a few decades from now, Turks will outnumber all European national groups except the Russians. The pattern of movement of Turks internationally will depend on the still uncertain outcomes of the Turkish application to the European Community as well as on the attitudes within individual countries, notably Germany. Such international labour migration will continue to affect regional and class patterns within the country by the transfer of remittances and skills and cultural aspirations as well as by the movement of migrants themselves.

Notes

1. For some examples see the various chapters in Krane 1975; also Abadan-Unat 1976; Rist 1978; Paine 1979; Adler 1981; and Martin 1991.
2. See *First five-year development plan 1963–1967*, State Planning Organisation, Ankara, 1963.

References

Abadan-Unat, N., 1976, *Turkish workers in Europe*, Brill, Leiden.
Abadan-Unat, N., 1986, 'Turkish migration to Europe and the Middle East: its impact on social structure and social legislation', in Michalak, L.D. and Salacuse, J.W. (eds), *Social legislation in the contemporary Middle East*, University of California, Institute of International Studies, Berkeley, 325–69.
Abadan-Unat, N., 1988, 'The socio-economic aspects of return migration in Turkey', *Migration*, 1988(3): 29–59.
Abadan-Unat, N., Keleş, R., Penninx, R., Van Renselaar, H., Van Velzen, L. and Yenisey, L., 1976, *Migration and development: a study of the effects of international labour migration in Boğazliyan District, Ankara*, Ajans-Türk Press, Ankara.
Adler, S., 1981, 'A Turkish conundrum: emigration, politics and development,

1961–1980', International Labour Office (World Employment Programme, Working Paper No. 52), Geneva.

Atalık, G., 1990, 'Some effects of regional differentiation on integration in the European Community', *Papers of the Regional Science Association*, 69: 11–19.

Barışık, A., Eraydın, A. and Gedik, A., 1991, 'Turkey', in Serow, W.J. (ed.), *Handbook on international migration*, New York, Greenwood, 301–23.

Beeley, B.W., 1986, 'Migration and planning: the Turkish case', in Drakakis-Smith, D. (ed.), *Urbanisation in the developing world*, Routledge, London, 159–74.

Beeley, B.W., 1987, 'Migration and modernisation in rural Turkey', in Lawless, R. (ed.), *The Middle Eastern village*, Croom Helm, London, 51–76.

Davis, K., 1988, 'Social science approaches to international migration', *Population and Development Review*, 14(3): 245–61.

Eke, F., 1983, *The absorption of low income groups in Ankara*, Pergamon Press, Oxford.

Eraydın, A., 1981, 'Foreign investment, international labour migration and the Turkish economy', in Hamilton, F.E.I. and Linge, G.J. (eds), *Spatial analysis, industry and the industrial environment*, Vol. 2, Wiley, Chichester, 225–64.

Gitmez, A.S., 1984, 'Geographical and occupational reintegration of returning Turkish workers', in Kubat, D. (ed.) *The politics of return: international return migration in Europe*, Centro Studi Emigrazione, Rome, 113–21.

Karpat, K.H., 1976, *The Gecekondu*, Cambridge University Press, Cambridge.

Keleş, R., 1985, 'The effects of external migration on regional development in Turkey', in Hudson, R. and Lewis, J. (eds), *Uneven development in southern Europe*, Methuen, London, 54–75.

Kolars, J.F., 1967, 'Types of rural development', in Shorter, F.C., Kolars, J.F., Rustow, D.A. and Yenal, O., *Four studies on the economic development of Turkey*, Frank Cass, London, 63–87.

Krane, R.E., (ed.), 1975, *Manpower mobility across cultural boundaries*, Brill, Leiden.

Martin, P.L., 1991, *Turkish emigration: the unfinished story*, International Labour Office, Geneva.

Munro, J.M., 1974, Migration in Turkey, *Economic Development and Cultural Change*, 22(4): 634–53.

Paine, S., 1979, *Exporting workers: the Turkish case*, Cambridge University Press, Cambridge.

Penninx, R. and Van Renselaar, H., 1978, *A fortune in small change*, NUFFIC/IMWOO, The Hague.

Rist, R.C., 1978, *Guestworkers in Germany: the prospects for pluralism*, Praeger, New York.

Salt, J., 1985, 'West German dilemma: little Turks or young Germans?', *Geography*, 70(2): 162–8.

Suzuki, P., 1966, 'Peasants without plows: some Anatolians in Istanbul', *Rural Sociology*, 31(4): 428–38.

Toepfer, H., 1985, 'The economic impact of returned emigrants in Trabzon, Turkey', in Hudson, R. and Lewis, J. (eds), *Uneven development in southern Europe*, Methuen, London, 76–99.

Wilpert, C., 1984, 'Returning and remaining: return among Turkish migrants in Germany', in Kubat, D. (ed.) *The politics of return: international return migration in Europe*, Centro Studi Emigrazione, Rome, 101–12.

Chapter 10

A place in the sun: return migration and rural change in Portugal

Carminda Cavaco

Portuguese emigration and return: an overview

A continual process for centuries, emigration may be considered to be a structural phenomenon of Portuguese society.[1] Early phases of emigration reflected Portugal's imperial status: Mozambique, Angola and Brazil were important destinations. Since 1950, North America and Europe (especially France) have been the main targets. The choice of destination also varies according to the motives of the emigrants: in the post-war phase the main reason for emigrating was economic. The regional pattern of origin of the emigrants has varied over time, although certain northern regions have been consistent major suppliers. The strong intra-European flow which developed since the late 1950s was directed first mainly at France and later expanded to other Western European countries, notably West Germany. This continued until the early 1970s when the effects of the economic crisis in the labour markets of the main host countries began to be felt, especially in those employment sectors where most immigrants were concentrated.

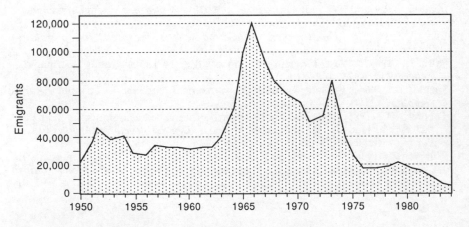

Figure 10.1 Legal emigration from Portugal, 1950–84

Table 10.1 Emigrants by district of origin in mainland Portugal (all data %
except total)

Distritos	1950–9	1960–9	1970–9	1980–4	1950–84	Emigrants per 1,000 inhabitants (1960–75)
Aveiro	13.6	8.0	9.8	15.4	10.0	7.4
Beja	0.2	1.3	2.7	0.7	1.4	2.4
Braga	7.7	11.2	8.4	6.1	9.5	6.5
Bragança	8.1	4.5	2.4	1.4	4.7	9.7
Castelo Branco	1.8	6.2	2.6	1.5	4.1	6.0
Coimbra	6.1	3.4	5.1	4.1	4.5	4.4
Évora	0.1	0.5	1.0	0.4	0.5	1.0
Faro	2.9	4.4	3.3	1.7	3.7	5.1
Guarda	8.6	7.0	3.1	2.6	6.2	10.5
Leiria	5.1	9.2	9.2	5.1	8.1	8.5
Lisbon	2.8	9.7	16.4	24.6	10.4	2.5
Oporto	13.4	10.3	10.4	10.8	11.0	3.6
Portalegre	0.2	0.4	0.4	0.3	0.4	0.9
Santarém	2.5	4.6	4.6	4.0	4.0	3.7
Setúbal	0.4	2.1	4.1	6.7	2.4	1.9
Viana do Castelo	5.9	6.8	4.0	5.2	5.8	9.0
Vila Real	7.1	4.7	5.3	4.9	5.4	7.4
Viseu	13.5	5.7	7.2	4.5	7.9	7.3
Total	286,899	537,760	292,476	46,294	1,145,429	4.9

Source: Secretariado Nacional da Emigração, Lisbon.

According to the official figures on 'legal' emigrants, between 1950
and 1984 1,145,429 people emigrated from mainland Portugal (1,440,723
including those from Madeira and the Azores). Figure 10.1 shows the
temporal profile of this emigration and Table 10.1 its regional expression
at the *distrito* level (for the location of *distritos* refer to Figure 10.5
towards the end of this chapter). In absolute terms, Lisbon, Oporto and
Aveiro accounted for most emigrants: more than 10 per cent of the
national total each. Also important were Braga (9.5 per cent), Leiria (8.1
per cent) and Viseu (7.9 per cent). In relative terms, however, a
somewhat different pattern emerges, with mainly northern *distritos*
predominant: in decreasing order of importance, Guarda, Bragança,
Viana do Castelo, Leiria, Aveiro, Vila Real and Viseu. Table 10.2 shows
the changing pattern of destinations. Brazil dominated during the 1950s,
France in the 1960s, France and West Germany in the 1970s, and the
United States (and to a lesser extent Canada, Australia and France)
during the 1980s. Recently it has been estimated that there are more than
3.8 million Portuguese living abroad: 1.2 million in Brazil; 900,000 in
France; 600,000 in South Africa; 263,000 in the United States; 235,000
in Canada; 220,000 in Venezuela; and 106,000 in Spain.

Table 10.2 Main countries of destination of mainland Portuguese emigrants (all data %)

Country	1950–9	1960–9	1970–9	1980–4	1950–84
Argentina	3.4	0.5	–	0.3	1.1
Australia	–	0.4	0.9	10.4	0.8
Brazil	77.7	12.1	2.9	2.1	24.8
Canada	1.4	3.7	7.6	9.9	4.4
France	5.4	61.2	30.7	11.2	38.3
Germany	–	8.5	29.9	0.4	11.6
Luxemburg	–	0.4	2.6	1.7	0.9
South Africa	0.4	2.3	0.8	1.9	1.4
USA	1.8	4.9	13.9	20.8	7.1
Venezuela	7.5	2.7	5.4	20.7	5.2

Source: Secretariado Nacional da Emigração, Lisbon

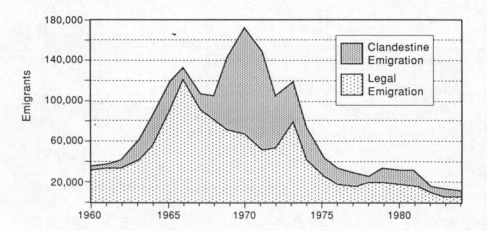

Figure 10.2 Legal and estimated clandestine emigration from Portugal, 1960–84

During the 1960s, the period of maximum efflux, emigration was the main factor accounting for regional patterns of change in demographic structure, in employment and in social organization. It was also seen as the solution to such problems as unemployment, poor living conditions and lack of prospects for development. Emigration continued in spite of the fact that all the migrants could expect abroad were jobs that were low-paid, dangerous, insecure and often seasonal. They emigrated, for whatever time they deemed necessary, to earn and save money in order to improve their way of life on their return to Portugal (Brettell 1979). In contrast to the semi-permanent emigration of whole families to the Americas, the European migration, at least for a time, took away single individuals, predominantly males. Any void left in the manual sectors of the Portuguese labour market — mainly in construction and public works in the big cities and the Algarve — was filled by immigrants from Portugal's ex-colonies, especially Cape Verde.

'Permanent' emigration (as opposed to seasonal or clandestine migration) decreased sharply during the 1970s and was almost non-existent by 1982 (Table 10.1). In the meantime illegal emigration continued to thrive (Figure 10.2), as Portuguese farmers left to do seasonal work such as grape-gathering and fruit-picking in France, Switzerland and Luxemburg. France has generally received the majority of these illegal emigrants: 52.6 per cent during 1970–4 and 43.2 per cent during 1980–4. Thus, seasonal migration has become part of the constantly changing pattern of Portuguese migration to Europe. Proximity and accessibility, allowing the possibility of frequent and extended visits back home, promote this new trend.

In the 1970s, as a result of economic crisis, industrial restructuring and modernization, which led to low-cost automation and unemployment in many industries, the countries of immigration passed measures which limited immigration and gave incentives to those who returned to their country of origin. Such was the case with the Portuguese in France (Poinard 1979). For many migrants, this was the chance to return to Portugal after periods of unemployment or illegal work. Some took the opportunity to re-emigrate to Middle Eastern countries which offered contract work. At the same time, in the European countries of destination, individual immigration gave way to family reunification (cf. Chapter 2 of this volume). Second-generation Portuguese migrants preferred to try to integrate in the country in which they had been brought up and educated.

Although unemployment and the 'return bonus' schemes stimulated many Portuguese to return home during the second half of the 1970s, there were other reasons too. An anticipated return is nearly always part of any emigration decision, and this 'return ideology' constantly directs emigrants' thoughts about future life and work back to the native land (Brettell 1979). Even so, the decision to return is rarely clear-cut, nor is the timing very precisely foreseen. Rocha-Trindade (1973, pp. 141–2) has captured this indecision as follows:

In the beginning, the migrant is in no position to evaluate the time that will have to pass between the two points, departure and return, of the migratory trajectory . . . . The date of return, certain but indefinite, is always left open . . . . In the indecision between staying or leaving is also found the desire of 'continuing just so'.

Emigration and rural change

Before examining the effects of return migration on rural Portugal, it is necessary to explore briefly the impacts of emigration itself on the society

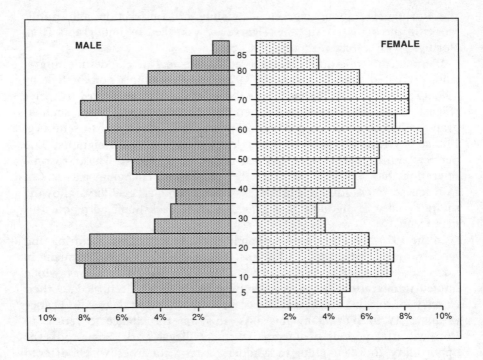

Figure 10.3 Population pyramid for Sabugal, 1981

and landscape left behind. Only long-term changes will be considered; seasonal and short-term migrations whose effects are much harder to discern will be left aside.

The first and most obvious effect of emigration is on the human resource of the regions and communities of departure. Here the main geographical contrast is between the northern and interior regions of Portugal on the one hand, and the coastal region from Braga to Setúbal on the other. The former region, economically depressed, has been the main reservoir of departure, the latter region is economically and demographically much more dynamic (Lewis and Williams 1981). The demographic effects of emigration are particularly evident at local level. In the *concelho* (municipality) of Sabugal, one of the first to be affected by emigration to Europe, the population declined from 43,513 inhabitants in 1950 to 38,062 in 1960, 23,167 in 1970 and 19,174 in 1981. As mainly young adults left, the population pyramid became highly distorted (Figure 10.3), with mainly old people and children left behind. The case of the village of Queiriga, typical of hundreds of others, may also be cited (Rocha-Trindade 1973). This settlement (in Viseu) had 1,621 inhabitants in 1960 and only 759 ten years later. Of a total of 824 emigrants, 758 were in France, 52 in Angola, 8 in Canada, 3 in South

Africa and 3 in West Germany. Asleep for most of the year, such villages awakened only at Christmas and in August when the emigrants returned for family visits and holidays.

Given the overwhelming importance of agriculture in the rural economy of Portugal in the 1950s and 1960s, it was mainly farm-workers who emigrated. All categories left: owner-farmers of holdings which were too small to give them a decent living, family helpers, and day-labourers. These departures brought about a change in the use of the land owing to lack of labour. Land became abandoned and overrun with bush and scrub, which in turn led to an increase in the number of fires. The number of sheep and goats fell, with a concomitant reduction in the production of cheese and other commercialized produce. Thus the rural economy regressed from a partly self-sufficient and partly market-orientated structure to one of reduced output for domestic subsistence. Cottage industries also declined.

Return migration and rural change

As mentioned earlier, the return to their native village, or at least to their native country, was considered by emigrants as the logical conclusion to their migration plan once the economic objectives which had motivated it had been fulfilled. After return, other objectives become important, such as taking care of elderly parents and in-laws, family reunification, looking after their property, and the anticipation of a new and more restful way of life after the years of 'sacrifice' abroad. Thoughts of a definitive return become particularly strong once the emigrants have saved a reasonable nest-egg or perhaps qualified for a pension, once they have built themselves a house equipped with modern conveniences, once they have acquired a car, and once the children are grown up and have their futures guaranteed. Generally Portuguese emigrants are keen to move back to the village where they have their roots and their neighbours whom they have known since birth. Only in such a setting can the full social prestige of their material achievements be reaped (Poinard 1983). However, amongst single returnees there is a greater tendency to resettle in coastal towns and cities.

Figure 10.4 shows the relative impact of returning migrants during the period 1974–81 at the level of *concelho* or municipality. The spatial pattern shows maximum impact in interior northern areas, which were the main areas of departure during the period prior to 1974. However, there is also evidence of a return to coastal districts in central and northern Portugal, and to the Algarve. Central-southern Portugal is hardly affected by return migration (Maranhão and Quintela 1989).

As many studies have shown (see e.g., Brettell 1979; Porto 1984; Silva *et al.* 1984; Lewis and Williams 1986), the return of emigrants to the 'native soil' is generally much more influenced by family reasons than by

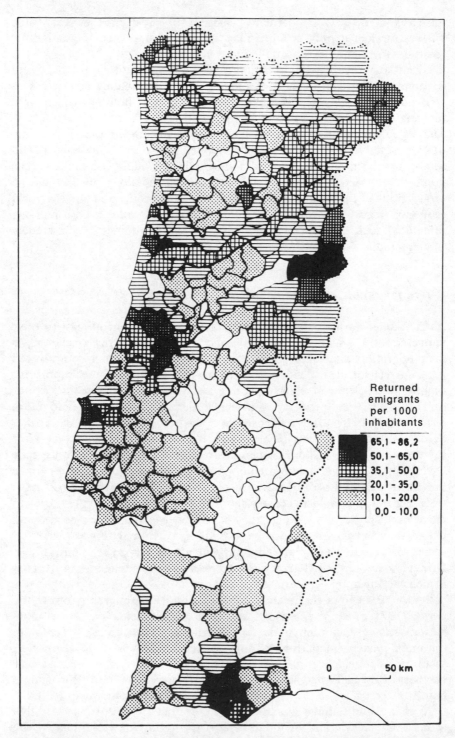

Figure 10.4   Spatial impact of emigrants returning to Portugal, 1974–81

any employment opportunities which may have arisen in their absence abroad. In fact, many returning emigrants find it difficult to integrate economically, while others create their own form of employment as small entrepreneurs, perhaps in partnership with other returnees.

Amongst emigrants, the nature of the 'return project' conditions their behaviour whilst abroad. Many Portuguese migrants (mainly males) initially emigrate alone, leaving their families behind in the villages (Brettell 1987). These migrants regularly remit a portion of their saved income, thereby increasing the spending power of the residual society, assuring its members a better standard of living in food, clothing, domestic comfort and personal services. This, in turn, increases commercial activity at both local and regional levels. Women work the land less and the children spend longer in full-time education. Consequently the domestic economy becomes progressively more dependent on the money sent from abroad by emigrants. To the financial impact of emigration must be added a socio-psychological dimension. Single emigrants return to spend their annual summer holidays (and perhaps Christmas and Easter too) with their families. On these return visits, the migrant's lifestyle becomes ostentatious, for it is a way of making a social statement. When the rural children, studying in nearby villages and towns, come home to spend their weekends and holidays, they too adopt cosmopolitan ways of behaviour. People in Portugal emigrate not only to improve their own standard of living, but also more importantly to ensure that their children have the chance to acquire college diplomas or university degrees. Such a qualification will ensure that the children will find 'respectable' jobs, and this will confer great prestige on their often illiterate parents.

There are remittances when the entire nuclear family emigrates, especially if the intention is always to return, although the scale of remittances may diminish with time abroad. This is because of the high cost of living abroad (especially if foreign-born children are supported), and because the emigrants become progressively attuned to the new standards of living of the host country. Much depends on whether the wife continues to bring in wages.[2]

Emigrants' transfers of foreign currency into Portugal have thus been very considerable. For the district of Guarda, Porto (1984) estimated that emigrants' transfers made up 39 per cent of the gross regional product, a proportion equal to that of the fast-growing industrial and building sector which was itself partly fed by these emigrants' transfers.

Regarding the nature of emigrants' investments in Portugal, the money has been spent on construction and renovation of houses, on acquisition of plots of land, on cars and tractors, and on urban property (Lewis and Williams 1986). Land is often bought speculatively and left uncultivated until the owner returns, or given to family or friends to farm in the interim. Tractors are a form of prestige in rural areas, and they are also a practical investment in that they allow emigrants to cultivate some land during the holiday periods of return. Overall, however, these investments are essentially non-productive and do not induce much dynamic medium-term or long-term economic growth.

In coastal fishing and tourist towns a somewhat different pattern operates. Mendonsa's study of Nazaré, a fishing and resort town 60 km north of Lisbon, found that 44 per cent of returnees had invested in fishing equipment and 33 per cent in commercial establishments (bars, small hotels, etc.) for the growing tourist trade. At the same time, returnees had invested heavily in housing and prestige consumer goods (Mendonsa 1982).

The idea — constantly postponed — of one day returning permanently to Portugal justifies the time and care spent on acquiring housing, including, in some cases, holiday and second homes and units of urban property for renting out to others. Most of the obsession with housing, however, is fixed on the village of origin. In the countries of destination there is social interaction with other Portuguese, especially amongst people from the same village or rural district. Rocha-Trindade has studied the emigrants of Queiriga, who gather every Sunday on the public square in Orsay, an outer suburb of Paris: in this case of chain migration 'where all ages, sexes and family situations are represented, an almost complete transplantation of Portuguese models of behaviour has been possible' (Rocha-Trindade 1973, p. 147). Brettell and Callier-Boisvert (1977) have commented on the general applicability of this model to other Portuguese communities in France and confirm that most social interaction is kin-based. In this way, memories of the migrants' country, village and family are kept alive and they can keep abreast of happenings back home through letters, the comings and goings of other members of the community, local newspapers and local produce. Their strong ties to home and to social relationships of local origin are renewed each year with a visit to Portugal, accompanied by the distribution of gifts and rewarded with invitations to parties and a round of visits to kin and friends. This interest in their home region is frequently demonstrated through the financing of various village improvements which, depending on the amount of the contribution, are a form of prestige. Such improvements also create a more attractive image of their village of which they can feel proud. Contributions may be made for the building of fountains and wash-houses, for the preservation and embellishment of churches, for schools, market-places, roads, bridges, street lighting, pavements, bull-rings, sports stadia, even for vehicles for the local fire service.

The main indication that a return is imminent is, without a doubt, the renovation of the house, either by salvaging the traditional dwelling and modernizing it, or by building a new one on the outskirts of the village. The land for these houses is usually acquired randomly through inheritance or obtained by purchase whenever plots become available. As was the case with previous generations of returnees — the *brasileiros*, the *argentinos*, the *americanos* and the *africanos* — these new homes display the success of the emigration project and are a statement of new social status. The styles, building materials and colours reflect the knowledge gained abroad, where the emigrants often worked in the house-building industry. The character of the houses also reflects the desire to possess something new and unique, so that it will be a contrast to traditional dwelling styles. These new rural houses have been the target of much criticism from that part of the population which is more sensitive to the aesthetic and cultural equilibrium of their surroundings.

Nevertheless the construction of new dwellings has had a marked effect on the regional economy. Small construction businesses and allied trades which market building materials, furniture, domestic appliances, ornaments, etc. have multiplied. Commercial activities have diversified, with a growing number of butchers, boutiques, hairdressers, restaurants, bars, banks and insurance agencies springing up in the towns, principal villages and along the main roads.

Once the fixed return of the emigrant has been accomplished, new influences develop in the markets for consumer goods and personal services, since the demand for them has become permanent and no longer merely seasonal. Migrants' objectives have changed: living and consuming become more important than working, saving and investing. These new objectives are financed mainly by the considerable cash flows which arrive monthly in the form of pensions from abroad, and even include compensation payments for accidents suffered on the job. These pensions exceed the Portuguese farmers' pensions.

Furthermore, population trends register a change of direction. Returns partly compensate for the departures of previous years and slow down demographic changes and distortions; the abandonment of many villages is halted. This, however, happens less frequently in small villages and hamlets with minimal infrastructures, which are probably destined to remain isolated.

The spatial pattern of the new resettlement and the diversity of new economic activities create a new social hierarchy. The prestige of the traditional landowners and farm proprietors is replaced by the owners of construction firms, car repair shops, bank employers and teachers. This new social order is the result of upward mobility made possible by emigration (Poinard 1983). The first to climb socially were the smugglers who organized networks of illegal emigration — with little guarantee, it should be said, of successful emigration or of work. This smuggling of human merchandise was a result of accumulated experience in traditional contraband activities across the border with Spain which became highly lucrative. However, the returnees have been the main agents of retexturing the social structure. Returnees who before emigration were peasants or the sons and daughters of peasants became part of the bourgeoisie upon return. According to Serra-Santana (1984), returnees became a special species of 'eldermen', a part of the local élite although still deprived of political power. That power stays with the traditional élite, the large landowners, established businessmen, the professionals and the public servants.

What of the economic and occupational impact of the migrants who return home to resettle permanently? Besides farming on their own account, returning migrants' reintegration in local economic activities seems to be minimal. Many reasons help to explain this situation, including the returnees' age, low educational levels, lack of experience as entrepreneurs, lack of information about business possibilities, and lack of knowledge of professions outside farming and low-grade manual work. They tend to invest their money and their effort in construction, retail and restaurant businesses, these being the sectors in which they worked abroad. Such businesses are nearly always small scale, run by one person or a family, only occasionally in partnerships with other people, usually returned emigrants.

The return to the land does not really signify a return to their roots. Farming is only a part-time occupation for returnees; it is not their economic mainstay, as it was in the past; and not much effort is expended on it. The purchase of plots of land is a reflection of small-town thinking, an affirmation of a heritage untouched by modern economics, for land confers prestige even when there is no profit to be made from it. For many returnees, farming is not a means of production but rather a healthy pastime to be enjoyed after all the long years of hard work and overtime. Even when abroad, this small peasant mentality survived and found expression. In France, many Portuguese cultivate allotments of land on the urban fringe. They harvest potatoes, cabbages and onions; they keep chickens and rabbits. In this way they reproduce a milieu similar to that of their village. Whilst the internal migratory exodus of rural Portuguese to the towns and cities of the coast is accompanied by the sale of family plots, this supply of land is snapped up by returnees from abroad who use it to create a new 'inheritance' for themselves.

The village as a place for emigrants' summer holidays

The systematic return of the emigrants to their native villages during their annual holidays can be likened to a touristic migration. During these return visits, which may be extended at times of unemployment abroad, returnees bring a mixture of cosmopolitan lifestyle and the desire to recapture something of the village farming tradition. Thus they mix an indolent leisure with occasional help with farming tasks in the vineyards and orchards.

This ritual return to the native village for annual and pluri-annual visits to the extended family is also seen in the internal migrations from the villages of the interior to the cities along the coast. The resemblance, however, stops there. Emigrants come to stay in their houses or supervise construction work; they come with money to spend; and they breathe life into local businesses. Internal migrants, on the other hand, try to spend as little as possible; for them holidays are spent in the country in order to save and because they often lack money to spend on a beach holiday in a vogue resort. For internal migrants the village has lost its emotional personal attraction; their social reference system has transferred to the city.

The departure of emigrants abroad is generally considered a transitory phenomenon (even if many who left will eventually stay for good), whilst migration to other parts of Portugal is always seen as permanent. Those internal migrants who do return once they retired rarely admit they have returned: they say they are still resident in the city. At most they carry out small improvements and introduce minimal extra comforts, almost always with used furniture and other objects from their city home. The rural house becomes a summer home, appreciated by the children although not by the teenagers, who do not care for nature and for villages with no beaches, swimming-pools or discos.

What of the attitude of the emigrants' children towards the land of their parents and grandparents and towards the inheritance that will one day be theirs? In the 1950s, 1960s and early 1970s, emigration led to a socio-economic liberation of many young adults who usually came from big, country families which had barely enough money to live on. At the same time radio and television generated new aspirations for well-being and personal fulfilment. Military service also opened the eyes of many to new realities and lifestyles. However, access to urban jobs in other regions of the country was difficult because of rural people's lack of qualifications and the overall tight job market. If they did manage to find a job away from home in Portugal, their success seemed quite modest in comparison to the wealth of those who went abroad. Consequently, many emigrants left for some time. If they were married, they left their families behind in the village. Sometimes only the children were left, since the wife could also help to earn money and in this way shorten the time spent out of the country.

As the children grew older it was necessary to make a hard choice between leaving them in Portugal in the care of relatives or reuniting the family abroad and enrolling the children in foreign schools. The young people who grew up and studied in other countries often refused to accompany their parents when they came back to Portugal, except if they could not find satisfactory employment abroad. Those who studied in Portugal — and this often entailed a move to a nearby town or city for secondary and further education — were generally able to find jobs and houses there. The attitudes of these two groups towards their parents' and grandparents' homes then becomes similar. The adult children — in Lisbon or in France — visit their parents in the summer, they also invite their parents to spend some time with them in the 'big city', and they look on the inheritance of the ancestral house in the country as an attractive proposition to be used as a second home for holidays and eventual retirement. In contrast to their life in a city apartment, the spaciousness of the rural house, with its yard and garden, is very attractive, especially since rural services (health centres, telephones, shops, etc.) have improved in recent years. In fact, the children of migrants come to feel privileged in comparison to city families who do not have rural roots or a country home. Now these traditional urbanites try to find their own place to buy in the country for their free time and old age.

Although emigration and return have proved to be incapable of generating lasting growth and development in rural areas owing to the failure to modernize agriculture or introduce much viable industry, they have succeeded in conserving (after a fashion) the rural heritage of Portugal and in promoting a rise in the value of these erstwhile marginal regions as recreational resources. This form of embryonic rural tourism has happened spontaneously without any political intervention or subsidies. Moreover, it can lead to other forms of tourism: 'agritourism', hunting, country clubs, etc. Emigrant families, accustomed to dealing with foreigners and speaking other languages, may find an attractive and lucrative vocation in developing these kinds of rural tourism catering mainly for foreigners, following the model set by regions such as the Dordogne or Tuscany. If this happens — and there are already some promising signs — then parts of rural Portugal will become economically revived and less isolated socially and culturally.

Retornados: a special kind of return

The account so far concerns Portuguese returnees from Europe for whom the experience of emigration, life abroad and return has a similar pattern in most southern European countries (King 1979). The story of return migration to Portugal would not be complete, however, without some reference to the special case of the *retornados* — returnees from the Portuguese colonies in Africa who flooded back when Angola and Mozambique achieved independence.

Portuguese emigration to the African colonies — particularly intense during the 1950s — had both similarities to, and differences from, the northward exodus to Europe (de Sousa Ferreira 1976). It was similar in that it was essentially made up of emigrants of humble origin with minimal schooling or professional training. They came mainly from a background of small farms and large families, though some originated from working-class urban districts. When faced with the choice between Africa and Europe, they opted for the opportunity of acquiring an acknowledged and stable social position in the colonial setting, rather than going for low-grade work and quickly-acquired money in Europe. The colonial emigration was always more heterogeneous, however. There had also been an emigration of people with above-average schooling who had gone to Africa as entrepreneurs or to further their careers in the administrative, technical and military sectors. Others had become acquainted with Africa during their military service and chose to remain there after demobilization.

The combined effects of revolution in Portugal and decolonization in Africa were traumatic for the emigrants in Angola, Mozambique and Guinea-Bissau. During 1975–6 an estimated 600,000–800,000 Portuguese were repatriated. A census of these *retornados* held in 1976 recorded 463,000, although this was certainly a huge underestimate, the true figure being perhaps twice as high. Taking the realistic estimate of 800,000, the scale of this refugee movement can be appreciated when it is realised that *retornados* added about 10 per cent to the Portuguese population in the space of a few months. No other West European country has undergone such a dramatic migration experience in recent decades (Lewis and Williams 1985).

The geographical pattern of resettlement of the *retornados* exhibited a dual concentration. Many resettled in their native villages and towns in the rural north: the *distritos* of Bragança, Guarda, Viseu and Castelo Branco. Others were attracted to the more developed coastal and metropolitan areas of Lisbon-Setúbal, Aveiro-Oporto and the Algarve (Faro). Compared with the *regressados* or 'European' returnees, *retornados* were less likely to return to their family roots and more likely to be spatially mobile since return, either within Portugal or re-emigrating to Europe. Many of the better-educated *retornados* were given civil service jobs, which predisposed them to settle in Lisbon and other main administrative centres. For those *retornados* without family connections, such as those born in the colonies, temporary accommodation was found in Lisbon and in hotels in the Algarve, and many eventually stayed in these places. Figure 10.5 shows the regional pattern of resettlement of *retornados* at both absolute and relative levels (note that these maps are based on the 1976 *retornado* census which under-counted by as much as 50 per cent). Although nearly 1 in 3 settled in Lisbon, the relative demographic impact was greater in less densely populated *distritos*. Between 1970 and 1981 many northern regions would have had population losses instead of gains caused by the *retornados*. In others the decline was greatly slowed down: in Guarda, for example, it was a loss of 3.7 per cent instead of 10.5 per cent without the *retornados*. In the more populated districts (Oporto, Lisbon, Setúbal and Faro), the returnees from Africa accounted for about 30 per cent of the 1970–81 population increase (Maranhão and Quintela 1989).

Where the *retornados* had professional qualifications and experience, their resettlement improved the social status and development prospects of certain areas. One example of this is the settlement of those with high-level qualifications in animal husbandry in Trás-os-Montes, Ribatejo and Alentejo. The sectoral employment of *retornados* in 1981 (34.4 per cent

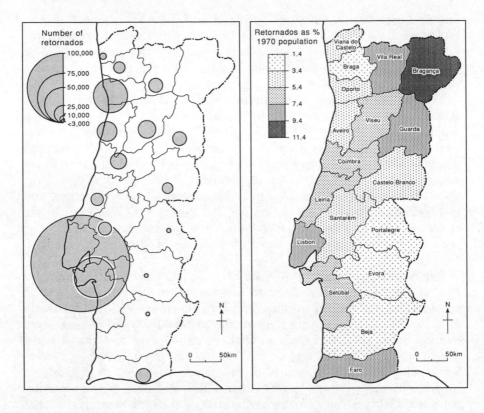

Figure 10.5 Regional impact of *retornados*, 1974–9: absolute and relative distribution, and key-map of *distritos*

Source: Lewis and Williams 1985.

in public and personal services, 18.9 per cent in commerce, restaurants and hotels, 5.8 per cent in banks and insurance, 5.6 per cent in transport, storage and communications, 8.7 per cent in construction and public works, 19 per cent in manufacturing and 5.9 per cent in farming) shows that they were generally employed in higher status post-return jobs than the returnees from Europe discussed earlier (Maranhão and Quintela 1989). There is also a much higher rate of small business owner-ship and self-employment among *retornados*. On the other hand, field interviews carried out with 100 *retornados* in central Portugal by Lewis and Williams (1985) revealed substantial failure to obtain the types of jobs they really wanted on return, with 34 per cent of the sample unemployed, twice as many as intended not to work.

On the whole, the *retornados* coped fairly well with the traumas of uprooting and forced resettlement in Portugal, integrating quite easily into a society which by and large welcomed them. This is not to ignore some stresses, however. Many *retornados* felt betrayed by the post-revolution communist-influenced government which had granted independence to the colonies, and they found the liberal atmosphere in post-coup Portugal very different from the country they remembered. In turn, the *retornados* were resented when it was revealed that some were being housed in luxury hotels at public expense, given credit to start businesses and given preference in public sector jobs (Lewis and Williams 1985). Amongst the returnees there were some individuals who did not adapt so easily and even today have not overcome the problems resulting from reintegration. These are mainly the elderly who have not the means and the strength to try to start again and regain their lost social position. Also included in this problematic category are those born in Africa (some of mixed race) who were unfamiliar with the 'mother country' which they were entering for the first time.

Conclusion

Perhaps no other country in Europe has been so deeply affected by such a variety of migratory phenomena (emigration both to Europe and overseas, voluntary return migration and forced repatriation) as Portugal. This makes the Portuguese experience valuable to study. What has been lacking in Portugal, however, is any real attempt to formulate a migration policy (see de Sousa Ferreira *et al.* 1982; Pereira 1990). This needs to be based on the prospect of new types of emigration within the context of the Single Market; on the careful planning of continued streams of returning migrants; and on the new immigrants from less-developed countries in Africa. For Portugal, like Spain, Italy and Greece, has moved from being a country of emigration to one of immigration in a startlingly short space of time.

Notes

1. As befitting a country with a centuries-long history of emigration, there is a vast literature on Portuguese emigration. For some of the key studies, see Almeida and Baretto 1970; Serrão 1974; de Sousa Ferreira 1976 and 1977; Arroteia 1984; Rocha-Trindade (1979) offers a brief English summary, and Ferreira de Pavia (1983) and Poinard (1988) have provided brief review articles on the topic.
2. The division between the migration of single males and of nuclear families implicit in this account is an over-simplification. Many other patterns may be observed. A common arrangement has been for men to migrate on their own, leaving their wives (and young children if they have any) behind. Sometimes wives follow after a year of two, either with the children, or leaving them in the charge of grandparents. Often the return move is also a staged process: women and children coming back first (perhaps because of the children's education), and the husbands returning later. In this scheme the role of the extended family is crucial: supporting children, working the

land, supervising investment of remittances and house improvements, etc. Nor should the heroic role of the wife be overlooked: either staying at home in Portugal and bringing up the children and working the land single-handed, or following her husband abroad and working at menial jobs in addition to doing all the housework and taking care of any children with them (Serra-Santana 1984).

References

Almeida, C. and Baretto, A., 1970, *Capitalismo e emigração em Portugal*, Prelo, Lisbon.

Aroteia, J.C., 1984, *A emigração portuguesa: suas origens e distribuição*, Instituto de Cultura e Língua Portuguesa, Lisbon.

Brettell, C.B., 1979, '"Emigrar para voltar": a Portuguese idelology of return migration', *Papers in Anthropology*, 20(1): 1–20.

Brettell, C.B., 1987, *Men who migrate, women who wait: population and history in a Portuguese parish*, Princeton University Press, Princeton.

Brettell, C.B. and Callier-Boisvert, C., 1977, 'Portuguese immigrants in France: familial and social networks and the structuring of "community"', *Studi Emigrazione*, 14(46): 149–203.

de Sousa Ferreira, E., 1976, *Origens e formas de emigração*, Iniciativas Editoriais, Lisbon.

de Sousa Ferreira, E. (ed.), 1977, *A emigração portuguesa e o seu contexto internacional*, Iniciativas Editoriais, Lisbon.

de Sousa Ferreira, E., Leite Pereira, J. and Ferro de Pavia, A., 1982, 'Contribuição para o estudo da economia da reintegração dos emigrantes', *Estudos de Economia*, 2(2): 232–40.

Ferreira de Paiva, A., 1983, Portuguese migration studies, *International Migration Review*, 17(3): 138–47.

King, R.L., 1979, 'Return migration: a review of some case studies from southern Europe', *Mediterrenean Studies*, 1(2): 3–30.

Lewis, J.R. and Williams, A.M., 1981, 'Regional uneven development on the European periphery: the case of Portugal 1950–78', *Tijdschrift voor Economische en Sociale Geografie*, 72(2): 81–92.

Lewis, J.R. and Williams, A.M., 1985, 'Portugal's *retornados*: reintegration or rejection?', *Iberian Studies*, 14(1–2): 11–23.

Lewis, J.R. and Williams, A.M., 1986, 'The economic impact of return migration in central Portugal', in King, R.L. (ed.), *Return migration and regional economic problems*, Croom Helm, London, 100–28.

Maranhão, M.J. and Quintela, J.P., 1989, 'Repatriamento e território: impactos regionais', *Sociedade e Território*, 8: 24–35.

Mendonsa, E.L., 1982, 'Benefits of migration as a personal strategy in Nazaré, Portugal', *International Migration Review*, 16(3): 635–45.

Pereira, M.H., 1990, 'Algunas observações complementares sobre a política de emigração portuguesa', *Análise Social*, 25 (108–109): 735–9.

Poinard, M., 1979, '"Le million des immigrés": analyse de l'utilisation de l'aide au retour par les travailleurs portugais en France', *Revue Géographique des Pyrénées et du Sud-Ouest*, 50(4): 511–39.

Poinard, M., 1983, 'Emigrantes retornados de França: a reinserção na sociedade portuguesa', *Análise Social*, 19(76): 261–96.

Poinard, M., 1988, 'Le retour: regresso ou retorno?', *Annales de Géographie*, 97(541): 348–51.

Porto, M. (ed.), 1984, *Emigração e retorno na região centro*, Comissão de

Coordinação da Região Centro, Coimbra.

Rocha-Trindade, M.B., 1973, *Immigrés portugais*, ISCSP, Lisbon.

Rocha-Trindade, M.B., 1979, Portugal, in Krane, R.E. (ed.) *International labour migration in Europe*, Praeger, New York, 164–72.

Serrão, J., 1974, *Emigração portuguesa: sondagem histórica*, Colecção Horizonte, Lisbon.

Serra-Santana, E., 1984, 'Return of Portuguese: economic goals or retention of identity', in Kubat, D. (ed.) *The politics of return: international return migration in Europe*, Centro Studi Emigrazione, Rome, 55–6.

Silva, M., Roque Amaro, R., Clausse, G., Matos, M., Pisco, M. and Seruya, L.M., 1984, *Retorno, emigração e desenvolvimento regional em Portugal*, Instituto de Estudos para o Desenvolvimento, Lisbon, Caderno 8.

Part 3: The Present and the Future

Chapter 11

Europe in the context of world population trends

Sture Öberg

Modern human beings introduced themselves around 35,000 years ago, and soon existed in all continents of the globe. By 1830 their number reached 1 billion. While it took a long time to reach the first billion it took only a hundred years to raise the second. Today, with 5.5 billion inhabitants on the globe, it will only take a decade to add another billion. The global population explosion expected during the next century could be the most serious challenge to the human race so far. This short chapter will describe present global population trends and relate them to European trends. It will draw on statistics from UN agencies[1] and on existing scientific literature including some of my own earlier work (e.g., Tabah 1990; Keyfitz 1991a; Öberg and Springfeldt 1991; Lutz 1992).

Global trends

If the present population were to spread out evenly over all the land area, including deserts and rain forests where conditions for human settlement are bad, the distance between each person would be 170 metres. However, every day there are 250,000 more inhabitants on the globe, so this distance is gradually, but inexorably, shrinking. Most of the population increase takes place in less-developed countries where women on average have 3.8 children, twice as many as in developed countries. Figure 11.1 shows the present population growth rate in different parts of the world. In most southern countries the growth is more than 1 per cent per year; in most northern countries it is less than 1 per cent. The highest rates, more than 3 per cent, are found in Central America, many Arab countries, many African states and Mongolia.

The global population growth according to the best-known projection to the year 2100 is shown in Figure 11.2, and population trends in some major parts of the world until the same year are graphed in Figure 11.3. Note that the population scale varies from graph to graph. The three scenarios in Figures 11.2 and 11.3 (low, medium and high) are based on different assumptions about future fertility. The basic assumption is that fertility rates will stabilize at a low reproduction level in some future

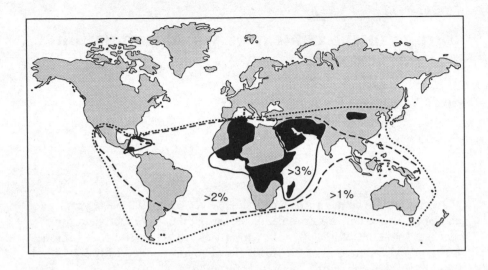

Figure 11.1   Present population growth in different parts of the world

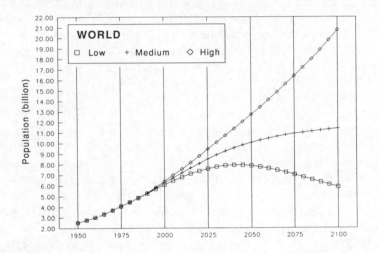

Figure 11.2   Global population growth until 2100 according to the UN and
               IIASA

year, varying for different countries depending on historical trends.[2]
This explains most of the differences in future population size. Further
progress in life expectancy is assumed for each country, the same for all
three scenarios.

Asia (Figure 11.3, top) has four to five times more people than
Europe. The Asian part of the former USSR, with 90 million
inhabitants, is not included in this definition of Asia. Around one-third

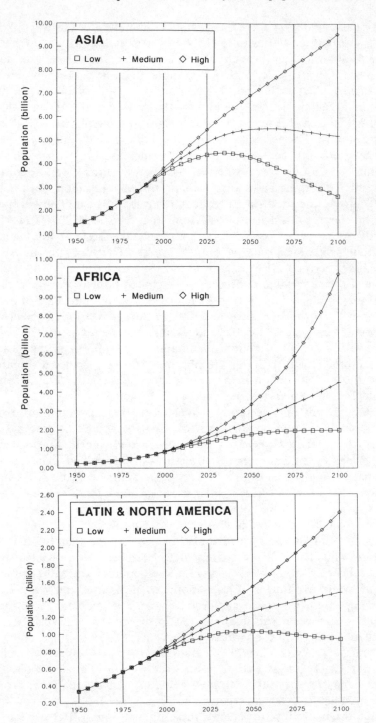

Figure 11.3 Population growth until 2100 in Asia, Africa and America according to the UN and IIASA

of global population increase during the coming decade will take place in the two largest countries in the world in population terms: China with 1,100 million and India with 900 million. Also Indonesia, Pakistan and Bangladesh, with nearly 500 million inhabitants between them, are growing rapidly. Africa (Figure 11.3, middle) will surpass Europe in population in a few years. In predominantly Arab North Africa (Morocco, Algeria, Tunisia, Libya, Egypt and Sudan), the population of 148 million is growing at 2.5 per cent, adding 3.7 million individuals per year. In Africa south of the Sahara the yearly increase is 3.2 per cent or 17 million inhabitants. In America the figures are lower (Figure 11.3 bottom). The ethnic bases were Indian, around 14 million when colonization started; imported slaves from Africa, nearly 10 million before 1850; and immigrants from Europe, 62 million before 1975. The scenarios for North America are quite different from the rest of the continent. Without new waves of immigrants both the United States and Canada will attain zero growth quite soon.

For a social scientist concerned with contemporary processes, the year 2100 may seem a long way off. However, we already have inhabitants whose children will be alive in 2100. In one generation from now, UN demographers believe (and/or hope) that the increase will level off so there will be 'only' 10 billion inhabitants on the globe by the year 2100. On the other hand if present fertility and mortality patterns continue, a population of 40 billion is in prospect for 2100 (Lutz 1992). Then there would be only 60 metres between each person.

Although this may seem an unlikely scenario, an evaluation of earlier prognoses for global population show that the actual increase has nearly always been underestimated. After the Second World War some well-known demographers from the United States predicted that the world's population at the end of the decade, eight years from now, would be 3 billion. It is easy to smile at their expense; however, if we had to make a guess at the global population fifty years from now, we should probably make mistakes of the same magnitude.

The two main ideas on population growth are simply that it is a problem and that it is not. It has often been seen as a problem because of the belief that only very cruel forces could reduce the number of people: Malthus thought of starvation, lethal diseases and wars. Recently the competition for space has become a serious problem. Soon half the people in the world will live in cities; in the developing world the urban population is growing at nearly 5 per cent per year. Other examples of 'pessimistic' views on world population growth are discussed in Ehrlich and Ehrlich (1990), as well as in the next section of this chapter. On the other hand, for healthy, rich and well-educated populations, growth in their numbers is often regarded as an advantage, not a problem. Following the thesis of Boserup (1965), these populations will create the conditions they need and want; these ideas will be dealt with later.

Problems with population growth

For the past two hundred years or so people have been arguing about the problems of feeding an ever-growing population. For the past twenty years there has been concern over the future shortage of resources. In the past few years the environmental debate has taken up the question of whether the whole of the earth may become uninhabitable because of serious disruptions in the global heat balance. Some believe that an increase in population and a more brutal struggle for resources will lead to an increasing number of riots, social and ethnic conflicts and wars, either conventional wars or new warfare. Let us now look at some of these issues connected with population growth in a little more detail.

Is there enough food?

As noted earlier, nearly all population growth now takes place in developing countries. This growth exacerbates their poverty and makes them more dependent on food aid. It is estimated that some seventy countries in the developing world are currently dependent on food imports. Since in many countries the number of mouths to feed is growing more rapidly than domestic food production, dependence on food imports will increase and more countries will join this category (Keyfitz 1991b).

At the same time as perhaps a million people die each year of starvation and perhaps another billion suffer from lack of nourishment, there is on earth a rich potential for growing enough food for all (Heilig and Krebs 1987). Even in Africa, studies of the carrying capacity of land show that the continent could feed sixteen times the expected number of inhabitants in the year 2000 if more land were devoted to farming and if the level of technology were increased (FAO 1986). In the short term the abundance of food in certain countries and the existence of poverty and starvation in others is mainly a problem of distribution — if only mankind were looked upon as one large family. However, international solidarity has its limitations. Even within countries there is often a lack of willingness to help, especially if different social and ethnic groups are affected. In some countries starvation is even used as a weapon to control rebellious groups.

Thus, in the global sense, starvation is not a problem in the sense that the earth's food production resources are theoretically inadequate (FAO 1986). It is, however, regionally and locally a very urgent problem: people are dying of starvation and undernourishment every day. Since there is a lack of determination to allocate existing or potential resources more equally, the gap between rich and poor will continue. The pressure of population will increase. Hostility will remain and the situation is often delicate. As we have seen in various parts of Africa in recent years, food trade and food aid can easily be disturbed by political and military conflicts which then result in large-scale famines.

Will there be enough other resources?

Population pressure creates demands for many resources other than food. Man's insatiable desire to consume can result in unrealistic demands on natural resources, leading in turn to serious conflicts. The battle for oil, for example, is often extremely violent. Many neighbouring countries also fight over the rights to water in shared rivers. Water is a material that is hard to replace and falling groundwater levels are creating serious problems in many areas. More than twenty years ago the Club of Rome calculated that several world resources would soon be exhausted (Forrester 1971; Meadows *et al.* 1972). However, a storm of criticism was raised against these predictions, and a more realistic approach was demanded whereby various mechanisms such as higher prices and new technology would regulate the availability of resources. Higher prices will decrease the use of limited resources although of course they create problems for the poorer sectors of the world's population.

Can Nature cope with so many people?

The mass processing of many materials with different physical and chemical properties creates in every country a variety of environmental problems — at places of work, in the home and in the open environment. Production processes cause a number of poisonous substances and pollutants to leak out into the environment, where they accumulate, creating a frightening future scenario. We do not clean the effluents from our factories and vehicles effectively, which means that heavy metals and other pollutants accumulate in the atmosphere, soil and groundwater until they reach hazardous levels. Sometimes, of course, more dramatic disasters take place, such as that which occurred at the nuclear power station at Chernobyl, when large areas had to be evacuated because they had been polluted by radioactivity.

It is not only production that leads to environmental problems. Apparently harmless consumption is also inextricably bound up with ecological damage. Private households unwittingly contribute to environmental pollution. In Western Europe, for instance, we heat our houses, drive private cars to see our friends and often travel by air on vacation. All this combustion of fossil fuels contributes both to acidification and to an increase of carbon dioxide in the atmosphere. Only in very recent years has there been serious debate on the grave environmental problems that confront us: acidification of water and soils, poisoning of the oceans' continental shelves, damage to the protective ozone layer in the atmosphere, to name but a few.

A future fight between rich and poor?

A never-ending source of international conflict in the coming years will be the division of the world's population into a rich northern minority and a poor southern majority. Only just over 1 billion people live at present in the rich countries of the world. The enormous growth in population on earth is taking place in the developing countries, often the poorest ones. In South Asia one out of three inhabitants is poor, in Africa one out of four (Leonard 1989). Keyfitz (1991b) has documented a group of particularly poverty-stricken countries containing a population of 425 million in 1990 which have great problems feeding their populations, which are in turn growing at a rate of 2.7 per cent per year (and accelerating). With better information flows between rich and poor populations there is the possibility that the poor will become more discontented with their situation. Yet the polarization of countries and socio-ethnic groups is taking place as modern weapon techniques for mass destruction are becoming more widely available. A country does not need to belong to the rich north to have access to these weapons, and with this power it is easier to demand an increased share of global wealth.

Advantages of population growth

Population growth can also been seen as a neutral or positive factor behind economic growth. Some neo-classical economists would argue that the basic problems of starvation, poverty and overconsumption are not caused by the number of inhabitants on the globe. They are caused by the fact that the markets do not work in the sense that they do not self-adjust to take care of the problems. A consequence of these ideas is that more governmental and international control and interference are needed to correct non-market behaviour and to adjust price levels so that they include the external effects of consumption patterns. There is thus no need for family planning programmes. Every newborn child is looked upon as an investment for the future (Simon 1990). Markets would allocate resources in an efficient way. Resource scarcity would be met by technological innovations, shifting consumption patterns and substitution of some scarce resources by others.

By tradition population growth is also often on the political agenda as a goal. Earlier, European governments needed people for colonies, for wars and for domestic production. There are several examples where politicians have tried to influence the fertility level. In former East

Germany young people were encouraged to move in together and have a child in order to obtain an apartment (Heilig *et al.* 1990). In Romania abortions were suddenly forbidden in order to have more children born. In France there is progressive economic support to families with many children in order to stimulate large families. In Sweden, during the low birth-rate period in the early 1930s, radical socialists used the concern among conservatives about the diminishing Swedish 'race' to push through a large number of socio-political reforms. There are also examples where countries try to influence the geographical distribution of their main ethnic population. The tragedies during this century in Europe resulting from the German policy for *Lebensraum*, or the corresponding Russian ideas, are well known.

Can population growth be controlled?

Family planning programmes have made it possible to reduce fertility locally. A majority of countries now support family planning: 128 provide direct support and 17 indirect support.[3] To generalize and simplify, such programmes are efficient if they are supported by the general public; otherwise they tend to fail. There are many who question these programmes, however. The Catholic Church has been criticized for proselitizing ideas that in practice encourage large families and therefore population increase. On the other hand, the present state of knowledge amongst demographers tends to agree that the education of women is one of the critical factors behind a decrease in fertility (see Lappe and Schurman 1989).

It has been estimated by the UNFPA that there would be fewer children born (25 per cent fewer in Africa, 33 per cent in Asia) if women were able to have only the number of children they desired. This gap between wishes and reality is also seen in the tragic figures on women who die from complications after abortions — an estimated 200,000 per year.

Today every second family in developing countries uses modern family planning techniques. Current UN policy is to extend family planning practice to another 200 million families, although the costs entailed would be twice as high as the current \$4.5 billion per year. Outside this UN policy framework, China has made the most energetic large-scale efforts to control population growth, by adopting a number of top–down measures which have resulted in fertility falling to about 2.5 children per woman. The price paid for this is, of course, the limitation of people's traditional right to decide for themselves how many children they want. In most countries the imposition of such restrictions would be unacceptable.

It is not self-evident where restrictions on fertility should start if the goal is to give better opportunities for future generations. One could argue that the lifestyle and per capita consumption in the more developed countries are the main causes of both global inequality and environmental degradation. A citizen of the United States consumes 200 times more fossil fuel than his counterpart in Ethiopia. From this it is not necessarily possible to conclude that two children in the United States in the future will increase the CO_2 pollution of the atmosphere as much as 400 children in Ethiopia, although one can argue that birth control or birth restrictions should first be encouraged in rich countries.

Many people in more developed countries have another view on this problem. They claim that family planning programmes are needed in poor countries to break through the well-known 'poverty trap'. As mentioned earlier, nearly all population increases are now taking place in the less-developed countries. Historically, large families (with many children surviving) are a new social institution. Thus, there could be no old traditions or cultural ties as a rationale for making this new type of family a permanent institution. According to many governments, family planning is a necessity in their countries to overcome poverty and environmental degradation.

Fertility decline and economic growth

When the UN held its first major world conference on population in 1974 in Bucharest, two main, partly conflicting, arguments were put forward. The first, primarily supported by more-developed countries, was that population growth had to be controlled quickly by means of effective contraception methods. The second, supported by many less-developed countries, claimed that a more equal distribution of prosperity, leading to modernization, would solve the population problem. The slogan for the second argument became: 'The best contraception is development'.

Let us address this problem, which is one of the very basic research questions among demographers: Why do women in some countries change their fertility behaviour from many children to few children? It is common to illustrate this process with the **demographic transition**, the well-known model of four typical, historical phases in the development of fertility, mortality and population growth. In Phase 1 the birth and death-rates are high and in Phase 4 they are low. The transition starts in Phase 2, when the death-rate decreases while the birth-rate remains high, which results in a growth of population. Then follows Phase 3 when the death-rate has stabilized at a low level while the birth-rate decreases.

Actual figures from a more-developed country (Sweden) and a less-developed country (Mauritius) show some deviations from the general transition (see Figure 11.4). In Sweden, the transition also included an intermediate stage when both death and birth-rates fell. The transition

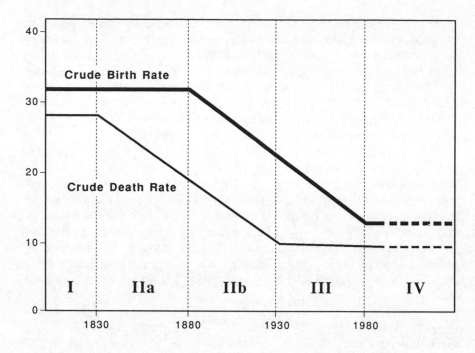

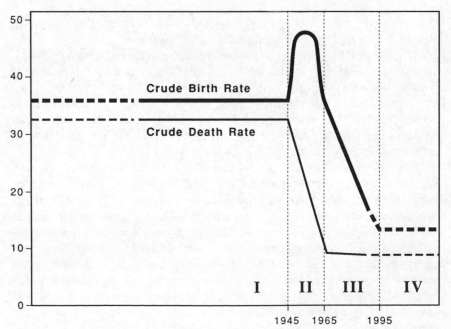

Figure 11.4   The demographic transition in Sweden (top) between 1830 and
1980, and in Mauritius (bottom) between 1945 and 1990, both
based on simplified data

Sources: Lutz and Wils 1991; Öberg and Springfeldt 1991.

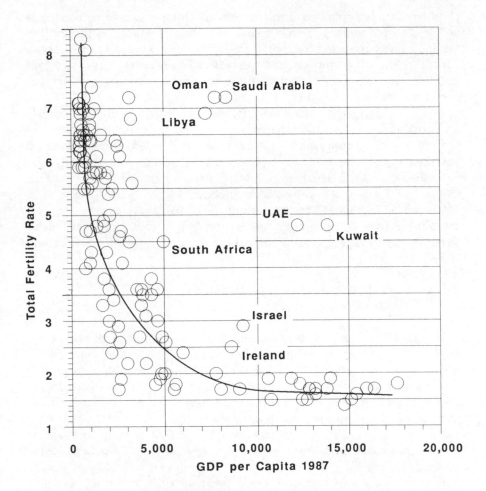

Figure 11.5 Fertility and economic development (GDP) in 140 countries

period, starting with better health conditions and ending with a low fertility, took one and a half centuries. In Mauritius it looks as if the transition will take only one-third of the time. During the second phase of the transition in Mauritius, when death-rates were declining owing to better nutrition and health, there was an increase in the birth-rate. This is said to be common in developing countries because traditional methods of birth control — extended breast-feeding and *post-partum* abstinence — are typically abandoned. Furthermore, some diseases, such as tuberculosis and malaria, lower the fertility of women (McFalls and McFalls 1984).

The classical follow-up question is now: What came first, a decline in fertility or a fall in economic growth? Some argue that some increase in the standard of living is needed before people dare to have fewer children. Others argue that if the number of children can be reduced, this will lead to economic growth. In both Sweden and Mauritius the fertility decline came before the 'take-off' phase in the economy. In most countries it is the other way around (Lutz and Wils 1991). Cross-sectional data on the relation between fertility and gross national product per capita are plotted in Figure 11.5.

Fertility experts know that many factors interacting in unique contexts and combinations influence changes in the number of children born. In the more general approach of global modelling, in which many detailed variables have to be left out, fertility can be treated endogenously. An analysis of this kind (Holm *et al.* 1992), based on available UN statistics, shows that fertility change is a slow process: 94 per cent of the level in 1990 can be 'explained' by the fertility level five years earlier. Furthermore, all efforts to explain changes in fertility by reference to economic variables give less correlation than the following expression of fertility (F) at time (t):

$$(F)_t = 1.9 + 0.5(F)_{t-5} - 0.004 \text{ (Contraception rate)}_{t-5}$$
$$- 0.014 \text{ (Life expectancy)}_{t-5^2}$$

This expression 'explains' 98 per cent of the variation in level and 64 per cent of the change of fertility when tested with five-year data over a period of twenty years for 120 countries (Holm *et al.* 1992). According to this expression, decreased fertility is weakly dependent on the proportion of the population using birth control methods and on increased life expectancy. However, just small changes in the data would make other variables more important. The expression is presented only to illustrate a more pragmatic and less demographic approach to describing global population change.

It is not easy to summarize the present state of knowledge on how global fertility is dependent on economic development or vice versa. Certainly, changes in fertility are contextual and human values and attitudes to life play an important role in deciding the number of children born to each mother. Added to these aspects are the levels of education and health in different countries and among different social groups. In nearly all respects European countries have a favourable situation compared with developing countries. Birth control is normal, women are well educated and health care is well developed. This is also the background to Europe's ever-decreasing share of the global population since the beginning of this century.

The European share

The European share of the world's population is at present 14 per cent (see Figure 11.6). Just over 700 million people live in nearly forty nations

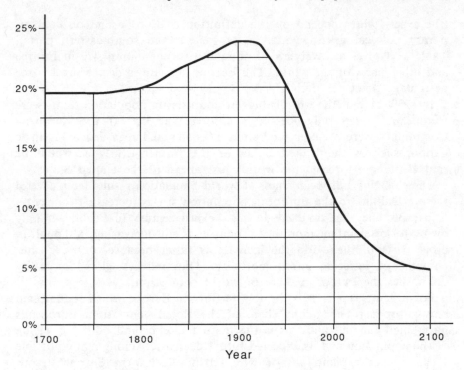

Figure 11.6 European share of global population, 1700–2100

Sources: McEverdy and Jones 1978; UN, *World population prospects 1990*, Population Studies 120, New York, 1991.

Table 11.1 Population and population growth by major world region, 1950–2025

	Population (in millions)				Present annual increase %	Present % of global population
	1950	1975	2000	2025		
North America	166	239	295	332	0.7	5
Latin America	182	350	577	924	1.9	9
North Africa	52	94	179	274	2.5	3
Rest of Africa	170	320	688	1,323	3.2	10
Former USSR	180	255	308	352	0.7	5
Rest of Europe	393	474	510	515	0.2	9
China	555	927	1,299	1,921	1.4	21
India	358	621	1,042	1,442	2.1	16
Rest of Asia	465	806	1,372	1,549	2.1	21
Oceania	13	21	30	38	1.3	1
World	2,534	4,107	6,300	8,670	1.7	100

Notes: North Africa = Morocco, Algeria, Tunisia, Libya, Egypt and Sudan; former USSR is defined as of early 1991; Oceania includes Australia and New Zealand.

Source: UNDP, 1990.

(the exact figures depend on the definition of Europe and on contemporary political developments in its eastern and south-eastern parts). Table 11.1 gives an overview of comparative population size in Europe and other parts of the world. The European share is decreasing by one percentage point per decade.

In 1950 three of the world's biggest countries in population terms were European. Today only Russia is still on the list. If the European Community were a closer federation of states and regarded as a single nation, such as the United States or the former USSR, it would be ranked number three in the world, just ahead of the United States.

The changing European share of world population results from several factors. Adding to the European population size is increasing longevity. Life expectancy has doubled during the last century in Europe, mainly owing to lower infant mortality. Today it is still increasing, although in other parts of the world the increase is faster because of the greater potential of lowering infant mortality. Thus reduced global mortality diminishes the European share of world population.

For a demographer it is the low fertility in Europe which is the main reason for Europe's falling share of the global population. Europeans have small families and this is the main factor behind both the ageing of the population and its expected future decrease. Among many possible social science explanations of why fertility is low in Europe, let us examine some issues with a gender perspective.

This perspective stresses the increased survival among modern women and their stronger social position in industrialized countries. The number of women now living, thanks to decreased mortality, is much higher than the corresponding number of men. Why women have survived longer than men in recent decades is an open question. Some argue that medical progress since the war has been neglecting men and their lethal diseases. Others say that decreased mortality is more a matter of lifestyle differences.

The strong social position of women in Europe today, compared with both yesterday and neighbouring developing countries, has obvious effects on demographic trends: fewer marriages, later marriages and more divorces can be seen in all parts of Europe. Fewer children per mother and children born later in the life cycle result in low reproduction rates. In some countries the average age of women when they have their first child is around 27 years. The result of these changes is that Europe has the lowest population growth in the world (Table 11.1).

Recent history shows that it is difficult to influence fertility or mortality more than marginally in Europe. Neither of these factors is likely to change sufficiently to effect an increase in Europe's share of the world's population.

What about migration, the topic of this book? Europe used to be a region of net out-migration. During the nineteenth century Europeans moved to many other parts of the world, and especially to America.

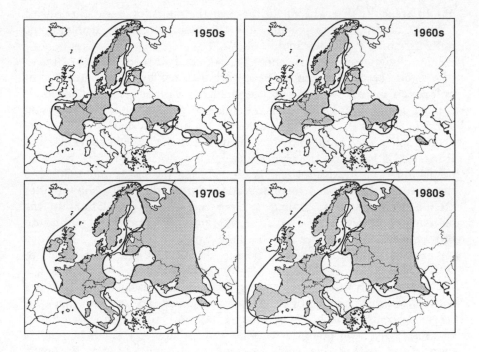

Figure 11.7 Net immigration countries in Europe over the past four decades. Some data are estimated owing to lack of statistics.

Now, and especially since the 1950s, Europe is an area of net immigration. Figure 11.7 shows the changes of the last four decades: the area of net in-migration has progressively enlarged. Since also more countries in the former USSR are now receiving migrants from the Asian parts of the former union, most of Europe today is receiving immigrants. And of course immigrants increase population growth or at least slow down the decline.

Of special interest for future migration into Europe is the development in countries close by, such as Algeria or Turkey, or in countries with pre-existing strong migration links with Europe, like Argentina with Italy, Chile with Sweden or India with Great Britain. South of the Mediterranean, in Morocco, Algeria, Tunisia and Egypt, the relative increase of the work-force is five to ten times as rapid as it is in France, Italy or Greece. As the next chapter in this book shows, demographic differences — such as a young, rapidly increasing population south of the Mediterranean and an ageing population north of it — will, together with differences in living standards (per capita GNP is five times higher in France than in Algeria), create a scenario for potential mass migration. Thus both push and pull factors will contribute to future immigration into Europe, from both neighbouring and more distant countries. The big difference is that whereas in the past the main force was the pull of industry needing cheap labour, now the main forces are demographic push pressures from the South.

Future migration streams cannot be estimated with any degree of scientific rigour because of the way they are affected by a large number of unforeseen factors such as political changes, wars and ethnic tension. It is more common, instead, to make 'educated guesses' and assume certain immigration levels based on expected political scenarios. Then the demographic and economic consequences can be calculated (Lutz and Prinz 1992). Reference to earlier analogous political situations can also be helpful. The Mexican–US migration during the 1970s and 1980s and the European South–North immigration during the 1960s showed that after a decade or two, around 2–3 per cent of the populations of the receiving countries became settled immigrants. If future immigration into Europe were to add 2 per cent to the existing population by 2010, then on average around 1.5 million people should immigrate per year (see Wils 1991).

Thus, the European share of the global population could decrease less with large-scale immigration, although it must be stressed that this scenario seems unlikely to become reality, for socio-political reasons. Present flows from countries outside Europe are very small in relative terms. And the present small streams of around one non-European immigrant per 2,000 Europeans per year in Western Europe already cause ethnic tension and political reactions.

Notes

1. For instance, UNDP, *Human development report 1990*, Oxford University Press, New York, 1991; UNFPA, *Population issues*, UN, New York, 1991; UN, *World population prospects 1990*, Population Studies 120, New York.
2. For example in the medium variant, fertility will be reduced to replacement level in China by 2000 and in Bangladesh after 2025. The global and regional scenarios are identical with UN versions until the year 2025; after this year the calculations are made by T. Buttner at IIASA, although on the same broad methodology as the UN projections to 2025.
3. These figures, and other information in this section, are from UNFPA — see above, Note 1.

References

Boserup, E., 1965, *The conditions of agricultural growth: the economics of agrarian change under political pressure*, Allen and Unwin, London.
Ehrlich, P.R. and Ehrlich, A.H., 1990, *The population explosion*, Simon and Schuster, New York.
FAO, 1986, *Land, food and people*, FAO, Rome.
Forrester, J.W., 1971, *World dynamics*, Wright-Allen, Cambridge, Mass.
Heilig, G. and Krebs, T., 1987, 'Bevölkerungswachtum und Nahrungsversorgung

in Schwarzafrika', *Zeitschrift fur Bevölkerungswissenschaft*, 13(1): 81–119.
Heilig, G., Buttner, T. and Lutz, W., 1990, 'Germany's population: turbulent past, uncertain future', *Population Bulletin*, 45(4).
Holm, E., Öberg, S. and Westlund, A., 1992, 'Global impact analysis', llASA Working Paper, Laxenburg, Austria.
Keyfitz, N., 1991a, *Population and development within the ecosphere: one view of the literature*, llASA, Laxenburg, Austria.
Keyfitz, N., 1991b, 'Population growth can prevent the development that would slow population growth', in Mathews, J.T. (ed.), *Preserving the global environment: the challenge of shared leadership*, W.W. Norton, New York, 39–77.
Lappe, F.M. and Schurman, R., 1989, *Taking population seriously*, Earthscan, London.
Leonard, J., 1989, *Environment and the poor: development strategies for a common agenda*, Transaction Books, Washington, DC.
Lutz, W., 1992, 'World population trends: global and regional interactions between population and environment', llASA Working Paper, Laxenburg, Austria.
Lutz, W., Prinz, C., 1992, 'What difference do alternative immigration and integration levels make to Western Europe?', llASA Working Paper, Laxenburg, Austria.
Lutz, W. and Wils, A.B., 1991, 'The demographic discontinuities of Mauritius', in Lutz, W. and Toth, F.L. (eds), *Population, economy and environment in Mauritius*, llASA, Laxenburg, Austria, 39–65.
McEverdy, C. and Jones, R., 1978, *Atlas of world population history*, Penguin, Harmondsworth.
McFalls, J.A. and McFalls, M.H., 1984, *Disease and fertility*, Academic Press, London and New York.
Meadows, D.H., Meadows, D.L., Randers, J. and Behrens, W.W., 1972, *The limits of growth*, Universe Books, New York.
Öberg, S. and Springfeldt, P., 1991, *The population*, SNA (National Atlas of Sweden), Stockholm.
Simon, J.L., 1990, *Population matters: people, resources, environment and immigration*, Transaction Publishers, New Brunswick, NJ.
Tabah, L., 1990, *World demographic trends and their consequences for Europe*, Council of Europe, Strasburg.
Wils, A.B., 1991, 'Survey of immigration trends and assumptions about future migration', in Lutz, W. (ed.), *Future demographic trends in Europe and North America*, Academic Press, London, 281–99.

Chapter 12

South to North migration in a Mediterranean perspective

Armando Montanari and Antonio Cortese[1]

Introduction

The various events and political and economic crises of the last ten years have placed the Mediterranean very much back in the international arena. The creation of an area of free cultural and technical exchanges is no longer seen as a utopia but as the expression of a strategy responding to a need that has been emerging in several countries in the Mediterranean basin. According to the major national and international organizations the 'Mediterranean' no longer constitutes simply a border or dividing-line but a socio-economic entity in its own right. During the 1980s some important Mediterranean countries joined the European Community. Closer ties were established with Turkey and more extensive commitments were entered into with Yugoslavia and the Middle East. All this has contributed to moving the centre of gravity of the European Community's economic and political interests further south towards the Mediterranean.

What are the dimensions of this new 'Mediterranean' area? To use the term 'Mediterranean' only to define the seventeen countries situated on the rim of the Mediterranean Sea is undoubtedly too narrow. Portugal should be considered a Mediterranean country; likewise Jordan and possibly Iraq. Some experts even include the Gulf states, mainly for strategic reasons. In a new system of international relations, Bulgaria and Romania, and some of the republics of the ex-Soviet Union such as the Ukraine and Georgia, could also justifiably be considered part of the Mediterranean realm.

For the purpose of this chapter we consider eighteen countries, namely all the countries situated around the Mediterranean basin, plus Portugal. Depending on circumstances we shall also include Jordan and Iraq, thus bringing the total up to twenty. Following the events of 1990, it seems likely that in the future Iraq and Jordan will depend more on the Mediterranean area than on the Gulf.

Differentiated population growth in the Mediterranean area

It is no easy job to compare statistics that refer to population censuses conducted at different times using different methodologies (Ciucci 1990). In Europe censuses are held at regular intervals and based on fairly consistent criteria; in Africa and Asia they are usually not homogeneous and are held irregularly. Therefore we shall refer to the data provided by the United Nations rather than to those supplied by the institutes of statistics of each separate country. The scenario on population change has been taken from the UN's *World Population Prospects* (United Nations 1989); we have assumed the projections defined as medium variant to be the most realistic. These represent 'future demographic trends that seem likely to occur, considering observed past demographic trends, expected social and economic progress, ongoing governmental policies and prevailing public attitudes towards population issues' (United Nations 1989).

In 1985, the population of the Mediterranean area was 390 million, i.e., just under one-tenth of the overall world population. This figure refers to the population of the Mediterranean rim countries, plus Portugal, Jordan and Iraq. Figure 12.1 shows that until 1985, more than half of the population of the Mediterranean area resided in European countries; in that year the proportion was 51 per cent. The rest resided in African countries (26 per cent) and Asian countries (23 per cent). Between 1950 and 1985 the population resident in the European Mediterranean countries increased by 31 per cent, as against a 140 per cent increase in the African countries and 160 per cent in the Asian countries.

From the early 1980s a marked division between the pace of demographic growth of the wealthy North and the poorer populations of the rest of the region became increasingly evident. The Mediterranean Sea was no longer simply a geographical division; it was the dividing-line between completely different demographic systems and standards of living. We find nothing similar to this division in any other part of the world, with the exception perhaps of the Rio Grande frontier separating the United States from Mexico. This division could be compared to that separating the southern EC countries (Spain, France and Italy) from the Maghreb countries (Morocco, Algeria and Tunisia). In both of these potential (and actual) migration systems roughly the same proportion lives south of the division line: 33 per cent of the combined US and Mexican population of 317 million live in Mexico, and 34 per cent of the 202 million people living in the six Western Mediterranean countries live in the Maghreb. During the 1980s the migration across the Rio Grande was much greater than that across the Mediterranean. According to the US Immigration and Naturalization Service, an annual average of 1 million Mexicans migrated to the United States during 1978–87, whereas south-to-north migration across the Mediterranean Sea in the 1980s was only a few hundred thousand per year (Cortese 1987; Rettaroli 1990). Yet

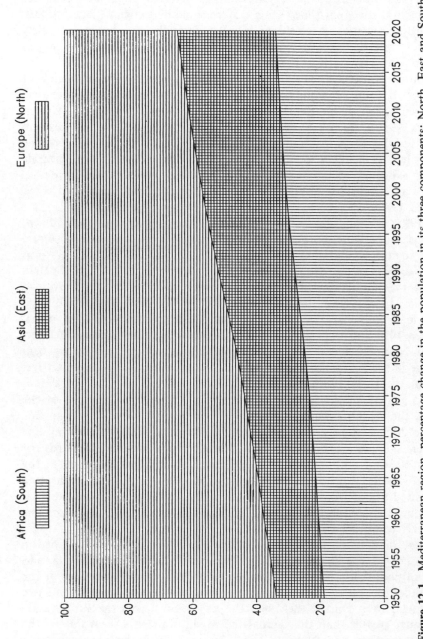

Figure 12.1 Mediterranean region, percentage change in the population in its three components: North, East and South, 1950–2020

Source: Keyfitz and Flieger 1990.

Africa (South)

Asia (East)

Europe (North)

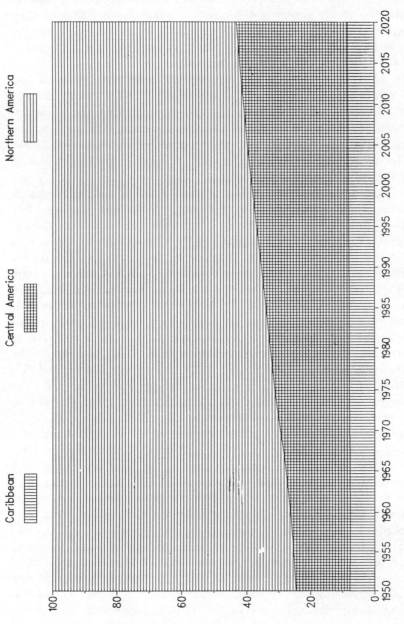

Figure 12.2 American region, percentage change in the population in its three components: Northern America, Central America and Caribbean, 1950–2020

Source: Keyfitz and Flieger 1990.

the rate of population growth in the Maghreb countries exceeds that of Mexico. In the former, the population is expected to double (from the base year of 1985) by the year 2002, in the latter by the year 2028. In the three EC countries (France, Spain and Italy) the growth rate is expected to be much slower: a 4 per cent increase up to 2000 and then a decrease of 1 per cent between 2000 and 2010. In the United States the growth rate is expected to be 12 per cent between 1985 and 2000 and a further 6 per cent in the following ten years.

Figure 12.1, introduced earlier, shows the total population of the twenty Mediterranean countries (Mediterranean basin countries plus Portugal, Jordan and Iraq), graphing the expected changes in demographic composition between the Northern component (Europe) and the Southern component (African and Asian countries) in the period 1950–2020. To recap the countries affected, Europe comprises Albania, France, Greece, Italy, Malta, Portugal, Spain and Yugoslavia; Africa includes Algeria, Egypt, Libya, Morocco and Tunisia; and Asia consists of Cyprus, Iraq, Israel, Jordan, Lebanon, Syria and Turkey. For purposes of comparison in Figure 12.2 we show an 'American region' made up of a Northern zone (Canada and the United States), a Southern zone (Central America: Mexico, Guatemala, El Salvador, Honduras, Nicaragua, Costa Rica, Panama and Belize), and a Caribbean zone (Cuba, Dominican Republic, Haiti, Puerto Rico, Jamaica, Trinidad and Tobago, Guadaloupe, Martinique, Barbados and other small countries). Countries such as Colombia and Venezuela have been excluded though other authors have included them in their studies on South–North migratory flows in America (see Espenshade *et al.* 1991, p. 336). In the Mediterranean region in 1950 there were 227 million inhabitants; in 1985, 338 million; by 2020 there are expected to be 598 million. In the American region there were 220 million inhabitants in 1950; 401 million in 1985; and an expected 574 million in the year 2020. In the Mediterranean region, the Northern component represented 66 per cent of the total population in 1950, 51 per cent in 1985, and is expected to drop to only 35 per cent by 2020. In the American region, the Northern component represented 75 per cent in 1950, 66 per cent in 1985 and is expected to decrease to 57 per cent in 2020. In 1985 there was already a marked difference in the population age structure among the various Mediterranean countries: more than 45 per cent of the population of Algeria, Libya, Jordan, Iraq and Syria were between the age of 0 and 15 years, whereas more than 12 per cent of the population of France, Greece, Italy and Spain were over the age of 65. By the year 2020 more than 35 per cent of the population of Iraq and Jordan and over 25 per cent of the population of Algeria, Egypt, Libya and Syria is expected to be between the age of 0 and 15 years, with more than 19 per cent of the population of France, Greece and Italy over 65 years (Keyfitz and Flieger, 1990).

However, while there is a definite line along the course of the Rio Grande demarcating two demographic regimes and migration situations,

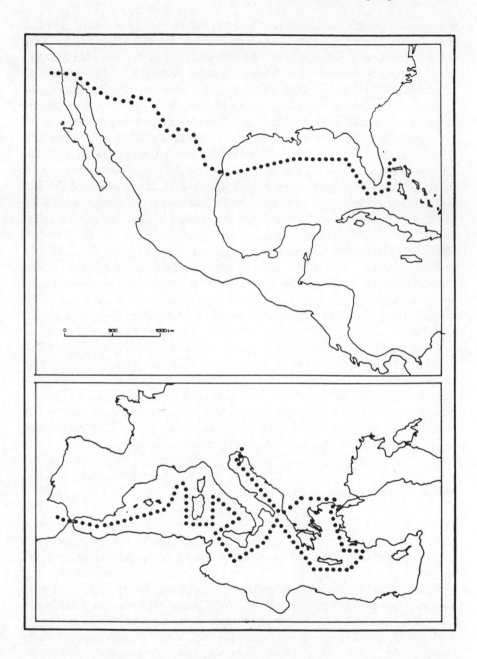

Figure 12.3 Comparison of the Rio Grande border between the United States and Mexico and the North–South border in the Mediterranean (both maps are on the same scale)

it is more difficult to define and bisect (and control) the region around the Mediterranean Sea. The Rio Grande could be likened to the part of the Mediterranean Sea that starts at Trieste, crosses the Adriatic and the Ionian Seas, and then from Malta extends westward to the Straits of Gibraltar. This means that the southern frontier of the European Community extends from Gibraltar to Greece, with tens of thousands of kilometres of coastline, including the European mainland as well as its many islands which give easy access to the entire territory. Hence the frontier is much more extended than that of the United States, and the free movement of foreigners in and out of the EC countries is much more difficult to control effectively (Figure 12.3). If we consider the EC countries as a whole, i.e., the countries constituting the Single Market in 1993, and make them analogous to the United States, we can say that twelve countries form the North of the Mediterranean and thirteen the South. In 1950 these twenty-five countries had a population of 348 million, of whom 75 per cent were resident in the North (the same as the North:South ratio across the Rio Grande in 1950). The growth rate of the population of these two Mediterranean areas is highly differentiated (Figure 12.4). In 1990 the total population of the twenty-five countries was 546 million; the United Nations projection for 2015 is 670 million; and for 2025, 707 million. The population of the countries in the North is expected to decrease from 59 per cent (1990) to 49 per cent (2015), and then to 46 per cent (2025). At the moment Germany is the country with the highest population, followed by Italy, the United Kingdom, France, Turkey and Egypt. In around three decades Egypt will have the largest population, followed by Germany, Turkey, the three other important European countries, Algeria, Morocco, Spain and Syria.

Recent Mediterranean migration

If we want to understand fully the population movements currently under way in the Mediterranean, we need to consider the situation both in various EC countries and in the less wealthy countries of the Mediterranean.

Among the EC countries, those of Southern Europe are currently facing a completely new situation: from being exporters of labour for several decades (Beyer 1976), they have now become the receivers of population movements from other Mediterranean countries, especially those to the South. This is true of Spain, Italy, Greece and, to a lesser extent, Portugal; in all four cases, emigration started to drop in the late 1960s and early 1970s. Earlier, in the 1950 and 1960s, their migratory flows had been directed mainly towards Central and Northern Europe, which then constituted the rich North for the countries of the northern strip of the Mediterranean (see King's Chapter 2 for more details).

In 1972 Italy had a positive migratory balance for the first time; in

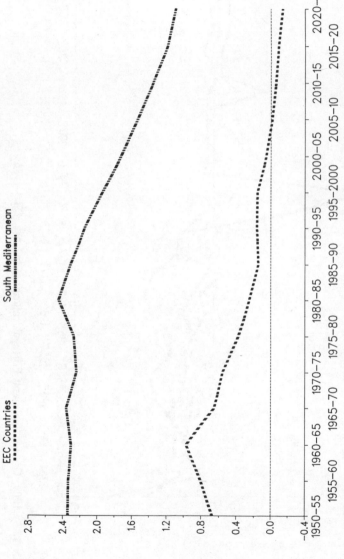

Figure 12.4 The annual population growth rate of EC countries and southern Mediterranean countries, 1950–2025, according to UN medium-variant projection

Source: United Nations 1989.

Note: For the purposes of this graph, the Southern Mediterranean countries comprise Albania, Algeria, Cyprus, Egypt, Israel, Lebanon, Libya, Malta, Morocco, Syria, Tunisia, Turkey.

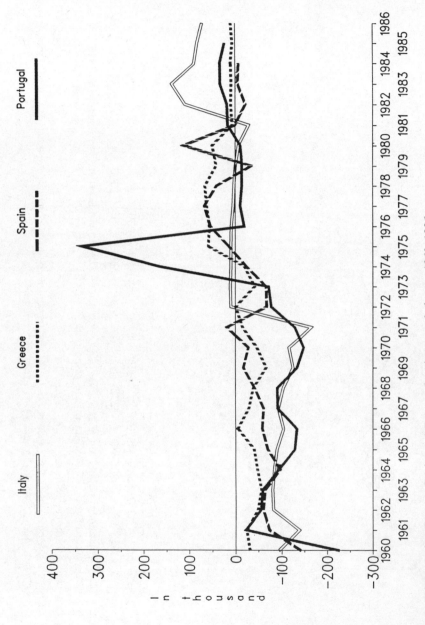

Figure 12.5 Italy, Greece, Spain and Portugal: migratory balance, 1960–1986

Source: Eurostat, various years.

1975 it was the turn of Greece and Spain, and in 1981 Portugal (Figure 12.5). These migration 'turnarounds' were partly due to returning migrants, although there was another important factor: the arrival of increasing numbers of migrants from the economically less-developed countries of Africa, Asia and Latin America (Penninx 1986). This sudden surge of immigrants was unexpected and found the administrative structures and even the cultures of Portugal, Spain, Italy and Greece totally unprepared. Initially they reacted contradictorily, on the basis of the experience and sensitivity typical of countries whose own populations had been accustomed to emigrating. No formal steps were taken to try to control the phenomenon effectively, and increasingly large groups were allowed to settle in the territory illegally: workers without a residence permit, or whose permit had been granted for reasons of study or tourism. For some time, this lax approach and the problems that ensued hindered the formulation of a proper immigration policy which would lay down rules and establish the rights and duties of immigrants. This explains the difficulty of establishing how many foreign citizens actually moved to the four countries. The official data refer only to legal migration; however, the 'hidden' part of the phenomenon is often much greater. Nevertheless, an attempt must be made to assess the size of the illegal foreign population. Recent indications are that Portugal, Spain, Italy and Greece, whose combined populations in 1990 were around 117 million inhabitants, hosted more than 2 million foreign residents. From the mid-1980s these countries (Spain in 1984 and Italy in 1986) began to take legislative and administrative steps to control illegal migration. In part, they were pressurized into doing so by the attitude of the other EC countries, who were willing to implement a policy of economic co-operation with the less-developed countries, although at the same time they were anxious to control immigration flows, and felt the excessive permeability of the southern borders of the Community was having a negative impact. We analyse the specific case of Third World immigrants in Italy in Chapter 15 of this book.

If we now go back a little in time and survey some of the other Mediterranean countries to the east and south of those four just studied, we can observe the following patterns. For the most part, citizens of Turkey and Yugoslavia migrated to Germany; those from the Maghreb countries to France. If we look at the data for the period between 1950 and 1985, we see that France and Germany are the only two European countries belonging to the 'constant large immigration countries' group (Wils 1991, p. 286). Although there were some periods of negative fluctuations such as 1966–7 and 1974–6, in general the migratory flows to these two countries are comparable to those affecting Canada, Australia and the United States on the world level (Wils 1991). At first, those who migrated to France and Germany were other Europeans (Portuguese, Spaniards, Italians and Greeks); during the 1970s, migrants to France and Germany were mainly from Third World countries.

The first South-to-North migrations were initiated by bilateral agreements made at the request of Germany and France respectively. Following the signing of a bilateral agreement between Germany and Turkey (October 1961), the number of Turks working in Germany increased sharply from 7,000 (1961 Population Census) to 185,000 (July 1962). A similar agreement was signed in October 1968 by Germany and Yugoslavia. In 1971, for the first time, the Turks (653,000) outnumbered all the other foreign worker groups in Germany, with the Yugoslavs (594,000) close behind.

Between 1973 and 1976 there was a drastic drop in the number of Turks migrating. After the latter date migration began to increase once more, although directed elsewhere, with Turks moving particularly to Libya (27,000 in 1980) and Saudi Arabia (2,000 in 1980). Some Turks still moved to Germany, however. In 1978 there were 1,775,000 Turks and Yugoslavs in Germany; ten years later they had increased by 19 per cent. As noted in Chapter 2 of this book, family reunion explains much of this recent steady increase.

We find a similar situation for the population movements from the Maghreb countries to France, which started in 1961. According to the 1962 French census, there were 410,000 Algerian, Moroccan and Tunisian nationals in France; according to the 1975 census, 1,100,000; and according to the 1982 census, 1,416,000. By 1985 there were altogether around 5.2 million migrants from Algeria, Tunisia, Morocco, Turkey and the former Yugoslavia resident in Europe.[2]

Citizens from Egypt, Syria, Lebanon and Jordan also emigrated, at first mainly to the countries making up the Gulf Co-operation Council (Bahrain, Kuwait, Oman, Qatar, Saudi Arabia and the United Arab Emirates), and to Iraq and Libya (Birks and Sinclair 1980). Migration to European countries is a more recent phenomenon. As the official figures available for migration from Egypt (the most powerful of these countries in migratory potential) are grossly underestimated, percentage figures are generally more interesting than the absolute values. From 1962 a regular and increasing flow of Egyptians left the country to work elsewhere (Ged 1985). Between 1962 and 1969 more than 20,000 Egyptians migrated, 93 per cent to the United States, Canada and Australia. In 1971 more than 29,000 Egyptians applied for a permit to work abroad. Of these, 78 per cent had a university degree; 81 per cent of the 84 per cent of Egyptians who moved to Arab countries (Kuwait, Saudi Arabia, Libya, etc.) had a university degree.[3] Following the introduction of the *Infitah* policy in 1973, migration from Egypt, again mainly toward Arab countries, increased further.

In 1980, there were over a million foreign workers resident in the countries of the Gulf Co-operation Council, and in Libya and Iraq: 61 per cent from Egypt, 8 per cent from Syria, 6 per cent from Lebanon and 25 per cent from Jordan and Palestine. Falling oil revenues in the 1980s did not, on the whole, dislodge these migrants from the Gulf

(Birks *et al.* 1986); the effects of the Gulf War on migratory patterns have yet to be analysed.

Economic growth and the labour market

Although there has been considerable debate on the United Nations' demographic projections, and on those made by other demographers on the issue, there is greater consensus on the projections for the economic growth and labour market parameters of the countries of the South for the next twenty to thirty years. Whilst it is true that at the end of the 1980s a drop in the fertility rate of some Arab countries, for example Egypt, Algeria and Tunisia, was recorded (Fargues 1987 and 1988), those destined to form the labour market of the next few decades have already been born. This means that there can be no change in the short-term situation of these countries without migration, however much the fertility rates of each country might decrease. Thus it is possible to predict the level of economic growth necessary in each country to maintain constant employment rates, or rather, to define the level of economic growth necessary to absorb the greater labour supply.

The following are the UN medium-variant projections for the population between the age of 15 and 64 (United Nations 1989; Keyfitz and Flieger 1990) to the years 2000 and 2020, compared with 1985 values. In the three European Mediterranean countries that are not EC members (the former Yugoslavia, Albania and Malta) the active population can be expected to increase by 2.2 million between 1985 and the year 2000 and by 800,000 in the succeeding two decades. However, in the initial period, 32 per cent of these increases, and in the second, 96 per cent, will affect Albania whose population constitutes only 11 per cent of the population of the three countries. The situation for the southern republics of the former Yugoslavia is similar, although their high growth rates do not figure in the projections, because they are offset by the lower rates of the more economically advanced republics of the north. In the countries on the African rim of the Mediterranean, the 15–64 age bracket is expected to increase by 31.3 million (43 per cent in Egypt) up to the year 2000 and by 52.4 million people (37 per cent in Egypt and 28 per cent in Algeria) in the period 2000–20. In the countries of the Asian rim the active population will increase by 18.9 million (63 per cent in Turkey) in the first period, and by 28.2 million people (43 per cent in Turkey and 37 per cent in Syria) in the next period. The total increase should therefore be over 52 million for the first period, equivalent to 3.5 million a year, and more than 81 million in the next period, equivalent to 4 million people a year.

Some labour economists have calculated the necessary annual increase in the GDP of the Mediterranean countries to maintain a constant rate of employment, on the assumption that each percentage point increase of the GDP should correspond to a 0.3 to 0.5 increase of the employment rate, depending on which employment/product elasticity scenario is assumed. Thus, depending on the values assumed, to keep the rate of employment constant up to the year 2000, the GDP of the countries of the south-eastern rim of the Mediterranean would have to increase annually at between 5.6 per cent and 9.3 per cent: between 7 and 12 per cent in Libya, Syria and Algeria; and between around 6 per cent and 10 per cent in Morocco, Tunisia and Egypt. There is no way in which any of these countries could ever achieve such values without receiving strong external support and introducing special emergency policies (Venturini 1988). In the 1975–85 period, the GDP increased by just over 4 per cent per year in Egypt, Syria and Turkey; by between 3 and 4 per cent in Algeria; and by just over 2 per cent in Morocco (Summers and Heston 1988). Development reached its peak in the 1970s in Tunisia (7.5 per cent), Egypt (7.4 per cent) and Algeria (7 per cent) and in the early 1980s in Turkey (6.3 per cent). In this situation, emigration will be the only possible solution.

Urban structures and internal migration

In the countries of the south-eastern Mediterranean, absolute numbers in agricultural employment have remained stable or even increased in recent decades, although the percentage weights have decreased because other sectors have grown more. In 1950 more than 70 per cent of the active population of Turkey, Algeria, Albania, Libya, Yugoslavia and Morocco were employed in agriculture. In the mid-1980s, over 50 per cent of the active population in Turkey and Albania was still employed in the agricultural sector, and over 40 per cent in Morocco, 30.5 per cent in Yugoslavia and 26 per cent in Algeria.[4] In Egypt in the same period those employed in agriculture dropped from 60 to 42 per cent. If we analyse regional employment data per economic sector, we see that in most of the countries of the area there is a strong contrast between the rural areas, where agriculture is the only source of employment available, and the large urban areas where the labour supply is concentrated in industry and services. This seems to indicate that the projected marked drop in agricultural employment in the near future will lead to huge movements of population from rural districts to the few existing metropolitan areas. Figure 12.6 shows that this urbanization will be particularly rapid in the Asian sector of the Mediterranean region.

For a comparative examination of the characteristics of the urban structures of the countries of the Mediterranean, it is useful to study the map showing population density per province and region (Figure 12.7). For each country we chose the administrative division best suited to showing up the different usage of territory on the general Mediterranean scale: districts for Portugal (*distritos*), Albania (*rrethet*), Greece (*nomoi*),

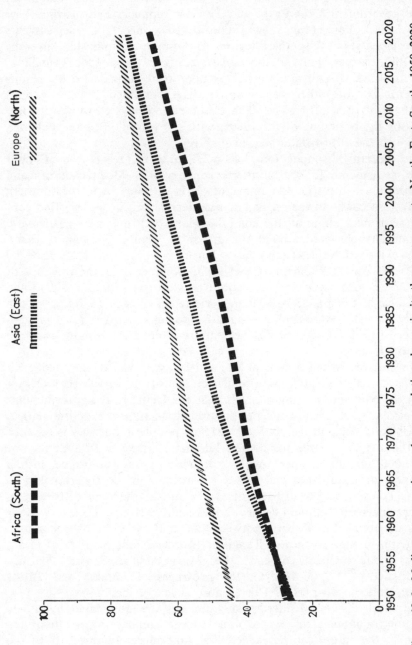

Figure 12.6 Mediterranean region, urban population change in its three components; North, East, South, 1950–2020

Source: Keyfitz and Flieger 1990.

Libya (*muhafeda*), Algeria (*wilajets*), Israel and Jordan; provinces for Spain, Italy, Turkey, Morocco, Syria (*mohafazat*) and Iraq (*muhafadha, liwa*); governorships for Egypt and Tunisia; republics and provinces for Yugoslavia. For France we considered only the departments (*départements*) in the southern regions of Aquitaine, Limousin, Auvergne and Rhône-Alpes, plus all the *départements* in Languedoc-Roussillon, Provence-Côte d'Azur and Corsica. Where available we used the results of censuses and other demographic data published by the various national statistical offices. In all cases the period referred to was the late 1970s or the beginning of the 1980s, with the exception of the Lebanon for which only 1964 data were available.

The pattern of population density (Figure 12.7) shows continuous dense settlements in the northern zone of the Mediterranean, and polarization in a restricted number of areas opening on to the southern and eastern coast. In the regions of Mediterranean Europe, we find constant settlement along all the coastal regions with nodes of particularly high density clustered around the major port-cities (Montanari 1988). The province of Naples (Italy) has a density ranging from 2,000 to 5,000 people per square kilometre. Other areas dominated by the presence of large cities, such as Oporto and Lisbon in Portugal, Madrid, Bilbao and Barcelona in Spain, Genoa, Milan, Trieste and Rome In Italy, have a density of 500–2,000 people per square kilometre. Areas with a population density of 200–500 people per square kilometre are more common and widely spread.

The situation in the regions on the south-eastern rim of the Mediterranean is completely different. Population density is very high in Egypt along the Nile with maximum levels near the Delta, in the governorships of Cairo (25,000 inhabitants per square kilometre), Alexandria (8,000) and Ghiza (2,000). In the district of Algiers population density is between 2,000 and 5,000 people per square kilometre. Areas with a density of 500–2,000 inhabitants per square kilometre are to be found in the provinces of Casablanca and Rabat (Morocco), in the governorship of Tunis (Tunisia), in the districts of Haifa and of the Centre (Israel), in the provinces of Istanbul (Turkey) and Baghdad (Iraq). There are lower levels of population density, between 200 and 500 persons per square kilometre, in the province of Tangiers (Morocco), the districts of Oran, Béchar and Tizi-Ouzou (Algeria), the governorship of Sousse (Tunisia), the district of Tripoli (Libya), the provinces of Latakia and Tartus (Syria), and the districts of Durres and Tirana (Albania).

The south-eastern Mediterranean countries are dominated by a few large metropolitan areas, where most of the population growth of the region in the future can be expected to take place. In this part of the Mediterranean the total population of cities with more than 500,000 inhabitants was around 34 million people. By the year 2000, the population of these cities will have reached around 60 million inhabitants (United Nations 1985 and 1989). The planning problems thrown up by

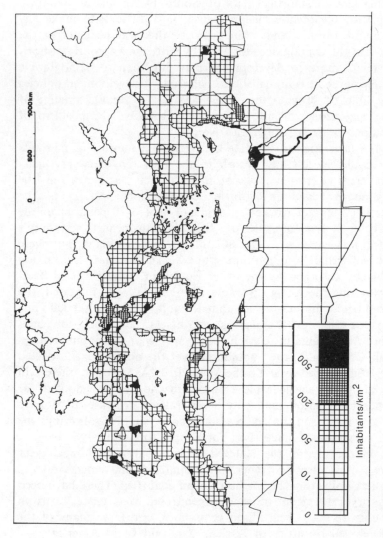

Figure 12.7 Mediterranean region: population density *circa* 1980

Source: National Statistics Offices of the various countries. Demographic data for 1980 or of censuses closest to the year 1980, where available. Africa: Algeria (1980), Egypt (1978), Libya (1978), Morocco (1982), Tunisia (1981). Asia: Cyprus (1979), Israel (1979), Iraq (1977), Jordan (1979), Lebanon (1964), Syria (1980), Turkey (1980). Europe: Albania (1978), France (1982), Greece (1981), Italy (1981), Malta (1980), Portugal (1981), Spain (1981), Yugoslavia (1981).

this massive increase in urban population constitute perhaps the greatest challenge for the future of the Mediterranean (Grenon and Batisse 1989).

South–North migration

Because of the lack of statistical data on South–North migration within the framework of the Mediterranean region, it is difficult to make any predictions about future trends. Since those who will be entering the labour market in the coming decades already exist, the appropriate short-term issues relate more to development planning than to demographic forecasting. However, it is unrealistic to believe that development policies will ever be able to provide the whole answer: a certain amount of South–North migration will still be necessary to solve the problem of excessive manpower (Dell'Aringa and Neri 1987).

Some experts have tried to estimate the maximum number of migrants that Europe could successfully absorb in the next ten to twenty years without too great a trauma. According to their estimates, in the economically more advanced countries of the northern rim of the Mediterranean, immigrant workers should not exceed 10 per cent of the entire work-force in the year 2010. By then the European Community's total work-force is expected to be 80 million, which means that there should be no more than 8 million immigrant workers. A further 5 million could possibly be absorbed by the other European countries (Livi-Bacci 1988). Not counting the foreign workers who have already migrated, the European countries could absorb an annual quota of about 300,000 units according to this criterion. We also have to assess the capacity of countries to absorb immigrants in relation to the ageing of the population. In the European Community, the population over the age of 65 is expected to be 17 per cent of the total by the year 2010. As a result, there will probably need to be considerable changes in the system adopted for calculating pensions, accompanied by a generalized decrease in people's propensity to save, and an increased labour supply following the introduction of various disincentives for people to retire.

However, in considering the 300,000 migrants absorbable each year until 2010, we must also remember that population movements do not concern workers only from the Mediterranean countries. There have been strong migratory flows from other European countries, especially from those with, until recently, centralized economies, and from many of the other less-developed countries of Africa, Asia and Latin America.

Limiting ourselves to the European countries only, we can certainly make a distinction between immigration flows from Third World countries and those from Eastern Europe. Migrations from the ex-communist countries are linked essentially to a negative economic trend which can be expected to improve during the next decade. Migration from Third World countries is, however, a long-term phenomenon. The East

European situation can be considered transitory, with especially the more highly qualified moving to Western Europe for better-paid jobs. This does not mean that migration from Eastern Europe is negligible or to be treated more indulgently. Indeed, migratory pressure is sometimes used as a cunning tool of foreign policy. It can be used to strengthen economic co-operation with the West, as in the case of *perestroika* in the former Soviet Union; or to claim more subsidies and assistance for the transition from a centrally planned economy to a market economy, as has happened in Albania since the summer of 1991. However, while it is possible to predict and control migratory flows of an 'economic' nature, it is much more difficult to limit those which are the result of tragic events. An obvious example is the war in the former Yugoslavia. The Yugoslavs were the most numerous group of migrants to Germany in 1991: between January and September approximately 37,000 people emigrated. Similarly it is hard to stop migratory flows resulting from territorial disputes over the change to self-determination currently under way in many regions of Central and Eastern Europe. It is a vast and complex issue. We cannot rule out the possibility that in the next few decades events will be as sudden and as unpredictable as they have been in the last three years. The problem is so huge that it is hard to imagine any way of solving it, unless something totally sudden and unexpected arises in the meantime. This sometimes does happen, as recent experience has shown.

Conclusions

Migration can now be considered as a global phenomenon which concerns virtually every country and population in the world. In Europe, illegal migration from South to North and from East to West is the main threat to security, having replaced the risk of a military conflict, which was formerly considered the main threat. This recognition of risk came from the Conference of the Ministers of the Interior and of Justice of twenty-eight countries of Europe which met for the first time in Berlin in October 1991 to discuss ways of controlling population movements.

At present in Europe we are witnessing a redefinition of the organization of territory and borders established in the first half of this century. Different political groupings and solidarities, also based on changed population balances, are likely to develop. Europe, West and East, in the next few decades will be a component of the North of the world as the East–West boundary dissolves and North–South becomes the primary global divide. Europe is also currently experiencing a revival of localism. The end of the Cold War and the collapse of the Iron Curtain have sparked ethnic, cultural and religious aspirations that had been squashed for years by harsh repression. The change to self-determination is leading to rebellions, crises and constant upheavals. This means mass migration between one nation and another. Now that communism has (officially) virtually disappeared, we are witnessing in Europe the birth of new concepts of 'nation' (Galtung 1982), giving rise to new forms of diffidence and hostility. Hundreds of new European states could spring up if every cultural and linguistic group were to claim to have its own form of democracy and self-government (Foucher 1991).

In the cities and regions in which the foreign communities settle, maintaining their religion, language, culture, customs and eating-habits, people of different races and religions will live side by side (Matvejević 1987). European cities, especially those in the Catholic South, have never been universal religious or cultural centres; they have only ever had one faith. Rome is a typical example: the city's one synagogue was built only at the end of the last century and its first mosque was completed only in 1992 (Paris already has eight mosques and Buddhist temples). The synagogue or the mosque is where a given community can meet and develop its own culture. For Muslims, the community is global, with Islamic principles governing every aspect of public and private life. The prospect of a clash of values, of non-communication and cultural intolerance, is very real.

At the moment the most difficult problems are being encountered in the housing sector. Most migrants in Mediterranean Europe live in a situation of overcrowding, poverty and degradation. As things stand now, low-cost social housing cannot satisfy the demands of even the poorer native populations. In any event, the special conditions set up for those entitled to this type of low-cost housing are not usually suited to the financial and social situation of Third World migrant workers. The shortage of low-cost housing and the complete lack of facilities to accommodate migrants when they arrive have forced foreign workers — especially those in the EC countries which have only just started to receive immigrant workers — to resort to temporary, precarious solutions, such as occupying abandoned factories inside the large metropolitan areas. The former Pantanella factory in Rome was occupied in 1987, and the Cascina Rossa in Milan offers shelter to thousands of Arabs, Africans and Asians who live together in subhuman conditions in an explosive mix of races and traditions. However, housing for immigrant workers is a problem that is far from being solved even in countries with decades of experience with immigrant workers (Begag 1991). A typical example is Vaulx-en-Velin, the dormitory city for North African migrants on the outskirts of Lyons in France. In October 1990 the city witnessed two whole days of fighting, fires and looting. The rioting brought to the fore the issue of whether to relegate migrants to huge impersonal dormitory blocks on the outskirts of cities, or to try and integrate them in the existing urban network, perhaps readapting housing and structures no longer in use.

It is more than likely that in the next few years some millions of individuals will be abandoning the countries of the south-eastern

Mediterranean to work in EC countries. Shorter and more temporary periods of migration will become increasingly likely with the development of new transport infrastructures and more modern and rapid forms of communication. We need only think of the huge structures near Istanbul linking Asia permanently to Europe and the proposed bridge between Europe and Africa near Gibraltar as well as other plans to link Rion and Antirion in Greece and Sicily and the mainland in Italy. The building of such infrastructures will greatly facilitate communications from the North to the South of the Mediterranean.

In addition national and international tourist movements can also be considered a form of temporary migration. These can be expected to increase mainly in the opposite direction, i.e., North to South. According to the UNEP 'Blue Plan' forecasts, depending on the level of economic development hypothesized, by the year 2000 there will be between 268 and 409 million 'tourists' and by the year 2025 between 379 and 758 million. The vast majority of such movements will affect northern Mediterranean countries (Grenon and Batisse 1989).

In the next thirty years the countries of the Mediterranean basin can expect an increase of around 200 million people. Although some will migrate to Central and Northern Europe, a large majority will remain in the Mediterranean area. As a result of demographic growth, permanent migration, temporary migration and tourism, the population of the Mediterranean countries — at least in certain periods of the year — can be expected to be somewhere between 700 and 800 million by the year 2000 and over one billion by 2020.

Clearly this will have a tremendous impact on the natural and cultural environment of the Mediterranean region. If we consider that the temporary and permanent population of 1980 will have doubled by the year 2020, it is obvious that housing, services and various other facilities will have to be expanded to cope with this increase. For example, we should be planning for double the consumption of water, when even the present supply is insufficient; and for treating at least double the quantity of waste products and waste water. According to an investigation carried out following an EC directive on waste waters, in order to extend the sewerage system of the EC countries enough to cope with twice the number of people, the huge sum of 200 billion ECUs will have to be spent by the early 2000s, of which 17 billion will be needed in Italy and 7 billion in Spain.

It is not easy to quantify exactly what changes will occur and what demands will be placed on the natural environment on the basis of the UN and UNEP data. However, it is more than obvious that the environment, and especially the natural and cultural environment, is decisive in defining additional population movements and singling out areas capable of absorbing additional settlements without too great and damaging an impact on the Mediterranean countries.

Notes

1. Although this chapter is a joint work by the two authors, Cortese wrote the Introduction and the section on economic growth and the labour market, Montanari was responsible for the rest of the text.
2. The figures given in this and the previous two paragraphs are from SOPEMI (Continuous reporting system on migration) *Annual Reports*, various years, OECD, Paris.
3. Data from Capmas, *Population movements across the boundaries of ARE*, Cairo, various years.
4. Data from *Yearbook of labour statistics*, ILO, Geneva, various years; and *Economically active population: estimates and projections*, ILO, Geneva, 1986.

References

Begag, A., 1991, *La ville des autres: la famille immigrée et l'espace urbain*, Presses Universitaires de Lyon, Lyons.

Beyer, G., 1976, 'Migration from the Mediterranean basin to Central, West and North Europe', in Istituto di Demografia (ed.), *Emigration from the Mediterranean basin to industrialised Europe*, Angeli, Milan, 13–29.

Birks, J.S., Seccombe, I.J. and Sinclair, C.A., 1986, 'Migrant workers in the Arab Gulf: the impact of declining oil revenues', *International Migration Review*, 20(4): 799–814.

Birks, J.S. and Sinclair, C.A., 1980, *International migration and development in the Arab Region*, ILO, Geneva.

Ciucci, L., 1990, 'Le migrazioni in Africa: riflessioni su necessità di dati e possibilità di rilevazione', in Società Statistica Italiana, *Atti della XXXV riunione scientifica*, CEDAM, Padua, 273–85.

Cortese, A., 1987, 'Le migrazioni per l'estero, in particolare verso l'Italia, dei paesi dell'Africa mediterranea', in Di Comite, L. (ed.), *La demografia dell'Africa mediterranea*, CNR-IREM, Naples, 89–116.

Dell'Aringa, C. and Negri, F., 1987, 'Illegal immigrants and the informal economy', *Labour*, 1(2): 107–26.

Espenshade, T., White, M. and Bean, F., 1991, 'Patterns of recent illegal migration to the United States', in Lutz, W. (ed.), *Future demographic trends in Europe and North America*, Academic Press, London, 301–36.

Fargues, P., 1987, 'La transition démographique dans les Pays Africains riverains de la Méditerranée', in Di Comite, L. (ed.), *La demografia dell'Africa mediterranea*, CNR-IREM, Naples, 13–34.

Fargues, P., 1988, 'La baisse de la fecondité arabe', *Population*, 43(6): 975–1004.

Foucher, M., 1991, *Fronts et frontières*, Fayard, Paris.

Galtung, J., 1982, 'On the meaning of "nation" as a variable', in Niessen, M. and Peschar J. (eds), *International comparative research: problems of theory, methodology and organisation in Eastern and Western Europe*, Pergamon Press, Oxford, 17–34.

Ged, A., 1985, 'Migrations et transformations économiques et sociales en Egypte', *Revue Tiers-Monde*, 26(103): 493–506.

Grenon, M. and Batisse, M., 1989, *Futures for the Mediterranean: the Blue Plan*, Oxford University Press, Oxford.

Keyfitz, N. and Flieger, W., 1990, *World population growth and aging: demographic trends in the late twentieth century*, University of Chicago Press, Chicago and London.

Livi Bacci, M., 1988, 'Lo sviluppo demografico dei paesi del Mediterraneo: conseguenze economiche e sociali', *Rivista Economica del Mezzogiorno*, 2(2): 323–45.

Matvejević, P., 1987, *Mediteranski Brevijar*, GZH, Zagreb.

Montanari, A., 1988, 'A modern perspective: the recent development of port cities in Southern Europe', *Mediterranean Historical Review*, 3(1): 166–85.

Penninx, R., 1986, 'International migration in Western Europe since 1973: developments, mechanisms and controls', *International Migration Review*, 20(4): 951–72.

Rettaroli, R., 1990, 'Migrazioni e politiche migratorie', in Livi Bacci, M. and Martuzzi Veronesi, F. (eds), *Le risorse umane del Mediterraneo: popolazione e società al crocevia tra Nord e Sud*, Il Mulino, Bologna, 281–314.

Summers, R. and Heston, A., 1988, 'A new set of international comparisons of real product and prices: estimates for 130 countries, 1950–85', *The Review of Income and Wealth*, 34(1): 1–25.

United Nations, 1985, *Estimates and projections of urban, rural, and city population, 1950–2025: the 1982 assessment*, UN, New York.

United Nations, 1989, *World population prospects, 1988*, UN, New York.

US Immigration and Naturalization Service, 1988, *1987 Statistical yearbook of the immigration and naturalization service*, US Government Printing Office, Washington, DC.

Venturini, A., 1988, An interpretation of Mediterranean migration, *Labour*, 2(1): 125–54.

Wils, A.B., 1991, 'Survey of immigration trends and assumption about future migration', in Lutz, W. (ed.), *Future demographic trends in Europe and North America*, Academic Press, London, 282–99.

Chapter 13

Ethnicity, nationality and migration potentials in Eastern Europe

Sture Öberg and Helen Boubnova

Introduction

Geopolitical changes in Europe make it important to use theories from both economic and social geography in order to prepare for understanding the future consequences of a new political order. Here we will apply them first to migration from Eastern Europe (which here means the former USSR or Russian Empire) to other parts of Europe, and second, to migration between nations or republics in Eastern Europe.

A free mobility of production factors like capital and labour would, according to economic theory, lead to capital moving east and people migrating west. To understand the potential strength of these flows and how they are encouraged or opposed by important actors is one aim of this chapter. The other is to understand the ongoing restructuring of the population within Eastern Europe, with special reference to the prospective homogenization of the ethnic and territorial distribution of nationalities. How could increased freedom in the political system affect migration? Both voluntary and forced migration have already increased and future mass migration flows might emerge.

There is no way in which science can be used to make a prognosis on future international migration flows. Although migration flows between countries are regulated, rules change, and sometimes the streams cannot be controlled by rules. Many actors are responsible for the emergence of the new geopolitical map of Europe, and even with a deterministic approach — which we do not have — it would be impossible to specify a model of the complex dynamic system affecting international migration.

This chapter will therefore not try to estimate future migration streams within or out of Europe, discussing instead the potential streams that occur within certain scenarios of political and economic change. The main part of this chapter will, however, be descriptive and build on information from Soviet census data and from unpublished data on contemporary emigration. The discussion on future migration streams is to be seen as a first attempt to find reasonable figures based on sensible scenarios, not an effort to make a prognosis.

Background, definitions, sources

Three out of ten Europeans live in the European part[1] of the former USSR. These approximately 200 million inhabitants in what we call 'Eastern Europe' belong to a large number of ethnic groups having their own histories and languages. Although it is of course not easy to define a language, officially seventy languages are spoken in Eastern Europe. Newspapers are published in fifty languages! The religious split is less complex. While the Russian Orthodox Church dominates, there are also substantial minorities of Muslims, Roman Catholics and Protestants. Officially four different alphabets (Russian/Cyrillic, Latin, Georgian and Armenian) are used in this motley crowd of populations. Today there are seventeen 'nationalities' (ethnic groups with the official status of nationality) in Eastern Europe which have more than a million members.

As is well known, there have always been tensions and sometimes open wars between the different nationalities in Eastern Europe. Since the Middle Ages, the Russians have dominated both politically and culturally, and their influence has been spreading. Today around 15 million Russians live in non-Russian parts of Eastern Europe. Their 'historical rights' to live outside Russia are being questioned and will continue to be discussed during the coming years. When other large empires lost their power, such as the British in India or the Ottoman in the Balkans, a return migration of the ruling class to their homelands occurred. Will we see the same process now in Eastern Europe?

The Russians form the major ethnic group, about 115 million, in Eastern Europe. They are also the largest ethnic group in Europe as a whole. Other large groups are the 41 million Ukranians and the 10 million Belorussians. All three groups are Slavic. Some groups are classified as foreign because their historic origin is a territory which today is a sovereign nation. This makes them potential emigrants. The foreigners in Eastern Europe are, for example, Germans, Jews, Poles, Koreans, Turks, Hungarians, Greeks and Romanians. Ethnicity is officially registered in a passport. Every citizen over the age of 16 must have a passport where the 'nationality' (such as Russian, German, Jew or Tatar) is registered, irrespective of place of residence. If someone wants to migrate and work in another region, a document from the new employer and the passport must be presented to the police who will then register the move. When two persons with different ethnic backgrounds (e.g. a Russian and a Georgian) have a child, the child can then choose ethnic membership at the age of 16. As we will see later, these choices change over time depending on the relative status of different nationalities in different parts of Eastern Europe. It also means that a person belonging to the Russian ethnic group (according to the passport) could have 50 per cent Jewish 'blood'. The potential migrant stream to Israel is thus larger than the number of people registered as Jews. Also 25 per cent Jewish or German 'blood' will qualify for immigration visas to Israel or Germany. Later in the chapter, we will try to estimate the size of the 'foreign' ethnic population in Eastern Europe using different definitions.

Statistical information on ethnic groups in different parts of Eastern Europe can be found in censuses from 1897 (the first census in the Russian Empire), 1926, 1937, 1939, 1959, 1970, 1979 and 1989. We shall not use data for the countryside from the 1939 census because of their poor quality.[2] We have assumed that the quality of the other census data is adequate for our purposes. As demographers are aware, in large countries (like the USSR or the United States) there is always some uncertainty because people do not live where they are registered, some try to hide, and there are also practical problems in putting together the statistics correctly. In the censuses, nationality, native language, second language, and place of birth are registered. From 1926, 1937, 1959 and onwards it is possible to map 'mixed' individuals whose native language does not coincide with nationality.

Existing statistical sources do not allow a study of migration streams by nationality. Some indirect information on net migration can be obtained from a cohort enumeration in the censuses. The only source for contemporary ethnic flows is from the last census, 1989, where, as earlier, there was a question on moves during the previous year.

History

The short historical description in this section is based on common knowledge from historical books published outside Eastern Europe.[3] Modern Russian books, written before *perestroika*, give very inaccurate and biased historical overviews.

The histories of Western and Eastern Europe differ in many respects. Some people argue that differences in physical conditions helped to create specific habitats in the two parts of Europe. In Eastern Europe, endless plains, low population density and lack of easy communication with other cultures first created many ethnic groups and then made it possible for one of them to dominate the whole area. The rivalry between Christian and Muslim groups in border areas also made it easier for the dominating Russian group to gain support; otherwise, the alternative would have been domination by a power with a totally different religion. Others, on the other hand, would argue that deep cultural differences made the lifestyle very different in Eastern Europe compared with that of the rest of Europe. Irrespective of the causes behind history, we can describe some of the differences.

For more than half of this century the political ideologies have differed, with state capitalism in the East — often labelled as people democracies, and democracies in the West — often labelled as capitalistic societies. In the former USSR, state planning was an ideology, or, vice versa, the ideology was a complicated planning system, which first suppressed market behaviour during the Stalin era and later created corruption. In the West, the states built more physical and social infrastructure for their inhabitants, although this was never recognised in political language as state planning. The different political systems resulted in economic and human development in the West and in a stagnation of these aspects of life in the East. We shall come back to the differences in welfare and standard of living as a cause for potential outmigration from the former USSR. Now, we shall run quickly through the history of Eastern Europe, paying special attention to changes in the demographic composition of the population.

Building the Empire

Around the year 1000, the so-called Kiev-nation controlled an area from the Baltic almost to the Black Sea. Some hundred years later, the Mongols controlled large parts of this area. This Asian period lasted until 1480. The first Russian czar, Ivan IV, crowned in 1547, conquered the Tatar nations and expanded the territory to the Caspian Sea. He also began colonization in Siberia; parts of the Ukraine were incorporated into Russia in the middle of the seventeenth century; areas along the Baltic coast, such as Estonia, in 1721; large areas along the Black Sea later during the eighteenth century, including Crimea in 1783; large parts of Poland before 1800; Finland in 1809; and the remainder of Poland in 1830. All the time new areas were also included in Asia. A large powerful empire was thus created in which many ethnic groups were politically although not socially united.

The physical expansion of this empire came to a halt around a hundred years ago: in Southern Europe, in the Balkans, by the Berlin Congress in 1878; along the North American coast in 1867, when Alaska was sold to the United States; and in eastern Asia when Japan forced Russian troops to leave Manchuria in 1904 and 1905.

The Empire became weaker during the beginning of this century and was not successful during the First World War: the czar was overthrown in 1917 and Lenin became the new leader. Although several 'white' generals, with support from Western European countries and the United States, tried to fight the communists, they were defeated after some years of civil war. The USSR, the new empire, was formally created in 1922. The size of the new union was smaller in Europe than the old Russian Empire, and areas such as Finland and the Baltic states became independent and sovereign nations.

During its history Russia has taken several measures to encourage migration. Like other 'peripheral' countries, it needed technology and human skills to build its strength. In 1763 Katherine II wrote an edict, 'About permission for all foreigners to settle where they want to live'.

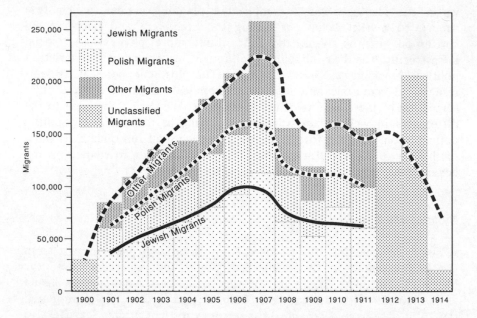

Figure 13.1   Ethnic composition of emigrants from Russia to the USA, 1900–14

Immigrants received privileges such as tax relief during the first ten years
and freedom of confession. They were also exempted from military
service. This migration policy led to large immigration flows. In total,
more than 4 million foreigners lived in Russia one and a half centuries
later. The largest group were the Germans, of whom there were more
than 2 million. The assimilation of foreigners was slow, partly because
they were prohibited from marrying a person from another ethnic group
with a different religion without converting.

During the last part of the nineteenth century, small groups of East
Europeans started to migrate to North America. In 1870 fewer than 1 per
cent of the immigrants to the United States were from Eastern Europe.
However, these immigrants were important because they transferred
information of a rich land with political freedom back to the motherland
and thus prepared the way for future large migration streams. After the
turn of the century every fifth immigrant to the United States was East
European. The large migration waves thus came in the beginning of the
century, the numbers of which are shown in Figure 13.1. The ethnic
composition of the emigrants from Eastern Europe is interesting: only
one out of twenty was Russian; nearly every second was a Jew (Figure
13.1). The estimated proportion of returning migrants was usually very
low, although there is one ethnic group where it was high: around 30–40
per cent of the Russians moved back to Eastern Europe.

Probably the main reason for the ethnic composition of the emigrants is that the Russian government changed its migration policy during the last years of the nineteenth century and encouraged outmigration from Russia of non-Russians. At the same time, Russians were encouraged to migrate within the Empire, preferably to border regions and Siberia. Non-Orthodox groups, such as the Poles or Jews, were not treated like the Russians. For example, only Orthodox Christians were given land for farming in Kazakhstan and Siberia.

A new emigration wave from Russia took place during the Civil War. Between 2 and 3 million left the country and moved to France, Germany, Czechoslovakia, Turkey and China. From 1926 emigration was not allowed.

In the Old Empire another interesting process also took place: temporary and seasonal migration across the border areas. For example, the population on both sides of the Russian–German border were Polish. There was a shortage of rural workers and high salaries on the German side of the border. Illegal border-crossing for work in Germany became more and more popular, and it was later accepted as legal if the workers moved back to Russia in the winter.

Within Russia too, people were often stimulated to move. Non-Orthodox Christians and unaccepted reformist-Orthodox often moved to border areas. Many conventional Orthodox Christians continued this process; in Kazakhstan and Siberia they received land and exemption from taxes if they contributed to the defence of the territory. One probable strategy was to achieve a Slavic majority in all parts of the Empire. This policy was successful except in the Baltic and Polish districts, where only around one-tenth of the population were Russian Orthodox according to the 1897 census. Also in the Caucasus, the proportion of Russians was low. Another resettlement wave occurred from crowded areas in Middle Russia to virgin land east of Moscow.

The Stalin era

Stalin, or Josef Vissarionovich Dsjugasjvili, born in Georgia in 1879, succeeded Lenin in the early 1920s. Some years later he became an absolute ruler with total control over life and death in the whole empire until his own death in 1953. He had a well-known interest in ethnic questions following his position in 1917 as a commissary for nationalities. Some of the ethnic structural changes during this regime are due to his personal will.

One of his early decisions was to transfer control over the Nagorno-Karabakh region, inhabited by Armenians, to Azerbaijan and also to create a buffer strip of land that would separate the region from the Armenian Republic. The historical background to this decision is complicated but the resulting conflicts have become very violent during the last few years. Most Armenians are Christians; most Azerbaijanis are Muslim and speak a Turkic language. Many Armenians see them as successors of the Turks who were responsible for genocidal attacks on Armenians in 1915.

Stalin expanded the physical borders of the Empire substantially during the Second World War, in both Asia and Europe. The borders of the old Russian Empire were restored. In Europe he occupied eastern Poland, Estonia, Latvia and Lithuania in 1939, keeping these areas after the war. He also conquered around 10 per cent of the Finnish territory. After the war Belorussia and Lithuania were expanded westward. The Ukraine was also expanded by incorporation of the Polish, Czechoslovak and Hungarian areas. Kaliningrad (former Königsberg) was taken from the Germans, and finally Moldavia, a part of Romania since the Russian Civil War, was again made part of the USSR. The new Soviet Union after the war was somewhat larger than the old Empire, consisting of ten republics in the European part of the union: three Baltic (Estonia, Latvia, Lithuania), three Slavic (Russia, Belorussia, Ukraine), Moldavia and three Caucasian republics (Georgia, Armenia and Azerbaijan). This is the main area we write about as 'Eastern Europe' in this chapter. Outside the Union he fashioned a border zone — Finland, Poland, the former GDR, Czechoslovakia, Hungary, Romania and Bulgaria — which we exclude from our definition of Eastern Europe for the purposes of this chapter.

During the Stalin era, the Union was industrialized and urbanized. Often urbanization is a local or intra-regional process, although in Eastern Europe it has, to some extent, also been inter-regional. Many rural groups during the Stalin era were sent out or moved to cities in Siberia. Urbanization during the Stalin era, however, was not as rapid as it became during the 1960s and 1970s. One reason for this was that the population living outside cities did not have passports and therefore could not move without prior permission. When Stalin came to power, two out of ten inhabitants in Eastern Europe lived in cities; when he died the figure was five out of ten. At present there are eighteen cities in the European part of the USSR with 1 million inhabitants or more, and twenty cities with 0.5–1.0 million inhabitants. The six biggest are Moscow (8.8 million), St Petersburg (5 million), Kiev (2.5 million), Baku (1.7 million), Kharkov (1.6 million) and Minsk (1.5 million).

The movement of ethnic groups in Europe at the end of the Second World War was substantial. The usual figure tells us that 25 million Europeans changed national location just after the war (Kosiński 1970). Half of them moved to non-communist countries, especially West Germany. All of these movements made it possible for Poles and others to occupy 'empty' territory. People from the Baltic states fled to Sweden and other Western countries. Many were moved because national borders changed, e.g., Poland gained some German territory in compensation for some of its eastern territory which became part of the USSR. During and after the war, Russians were moving into new territories in the Empire: Estonia, Latvia, Lithuania, Kaliningrad and Poland. Many former Jewish areas in eastern Poland and the Ukraine were empty since all the inhabitants had been killed by the Germans; they now became Russian. Several ethnic groups were moved from their home countries into Russia. Stalin wanted more people in Kazakhstan so he moved Germans from Volga and Tatars from Crimea to colonize new areas in the east. He also wanted more people in Siberia so he prolonged his earlier policy to have large concentration camps there for unwanted groups. The numbers involved in this sad part of Soviet history are discussed in the literature. A crude Russian estimate is 30 million totally resettled, including the 12 million who were killed or died in the camps. This figure could be low; figures twice as large are also mentioned (e.g. by Solzenitsyn). Of all Eastern Europeans born between 1880 and 1920, 5–10 per cent belonged to the group of forced migrants.

One could say that during the Stalin era, there were two categories of forced migrants. First were the non-conformists, e.g., people with the wrong attitude towards communist ideas, such as the farmers who did not like the collectivization of land in 1929 and people belonging to the wrong social class, groups or socialist party (1922 onwards). The same groups were later forced to move from the Baltic states, eastern Poland, western Ukraine and Moldavia (1939 onwards). Other groups that had to move to concentration camps were collected in areas that had been occupied by the Germans during the Second World War. Also some of the Soviet soldiers from German prison camps were transferred to Soviet labour camps, mainly in Siberia.

The second category of forced migrants had to move because of ethnicity. Non-Russians like Crimean Tatars and Greeks were moved from Crimea to Middle Asia. Around ten of the Caucasian nationalities were moved from Crimea to Middle Asia. As already mentioned, Germans from middle Volga had to settle in Middle Asia, Siberia and Kazakhstan.

Emigration during the Stalin era was regulated by edict: it was not allowed and there were only a few exceptions (Raeff 1990). Although immigration was allowed, very few people moved into the USSR during this period, and those who did were mainly intellectuals from other parts of Europe. However, Stalin did not trust them, and he usually had them killed.

From 'spring' to perestroika to sovereign nations

A few years after his death, Stalin was criticized as being inhuman, and a period of less repression started. The half of the population living in the countryside were given passports which increased their geographical mobility. There was no expansion of the Soviet territory, although

Table 13.1   Inhabitants, population density and share of non-nationals in Eastern Europe, 1989

	Population, 1989 (millions)	Population density (average distance in metres)	Share of non-nationals, 1989 (%)
Russia	147.0	232	19
Ukraine	51.5	119	27
Belorussia	10.2	157	22
Moldavia	4.3	97	36
Estonia	1.6	164	39
Latvia	2.7	138	48
Lithuania	3.7	137	20
Georgia	5.4	125	30
Armenia	3.3	105	7
Azerbaijan	7.0	122	17

Note: Average distance in metres (*ad*) is the preferred method of measuring demographic density: it represents the average distance between individuals if all people were distributed evenly over the area. For the whole of the USSR, *ad* is 300 metres; in the UK it is 70 metres, in Germany 73 and in France 107.

military efforts were made both to control border areas (Hungary 1956, Czechoslovakia 1968, and border fighting with China during 1969) and to support newly emerging allies (e.g., Cuba in 1962, and the invasion of Afghanistan in 1979).

We have access to three censuses from the 'spring period' of 1959, 1970 and 1979, and one census from the early *perestroika* period of 1989. Some basic data for the republics in 1989 are shown in Table 13.1. The restructuring forces during this period were substantial. One of the many well-known migration streams consisted of young Russians and Ukrainians moving to Kazakhstan. Instead of modernizing the countryside — including agriculture — in Russia and the Ukraine, the Communist Party invested large amounts of resources to develop new land in places like Kazakhstan. Today this has contributed to the well-known problem of the old countryside: poor living conditions and an ageing population.

A summary of how the balance between different ethnic groups has changed during 1959–89 is shown in Table 13.2. Although the data are for the whole USSR, including the Asian part, only nationalities with more than 100,000 members in Europe in 1959 are included. The groups are ranked according to their rate of change. Five groups have decreased — Jews by as much as 36 per cent. All of the other twenty-six groups have increased. Five of them have more or less doubled during the three decades — the Gypsies, the Kabardians, the Azerbaijanis, the Chechens and the Dagestanis.

While we were writing this chapter, several of the former republics of the USSR became nations in their own right. Estonia, Latvia and Lithuania were recognized as sovereign nations by both the USSR State

Table 13.2 Demographic change by nationality in Eastern Europe, 1959–89

Nationality	Population, 1989 ('000)	Population change 1959–89 (%)
Jews	1,449	−36
Finns	67	−28
Karelians	131	−22
Poles	1,126	−18
Mordvinians	1,154	−11
Estonians	1,027	+4
Latvians	1,459	+4
Hungarians	171	+10
Bulgarians	373	+15
Greeks	358	+16
Ukrainians	44,186	+19
Udmurts	748	+20
Chuvash	1,842	+25
Germans	2,039	+26
Belorussians	10,036	+27
Russians	145,155	+27
Lithuanians	3,067	+32
Tatars	6,489	+32
Romanians	146	+38
Koreans	439	+40
Ossetians	598	+46
Bashkirs	1,449	+47
Georgians	3,981	+48
Moldavians	3,352	+51
Gagauz	198	+60
Armenians	4,623	+66
Kabardians	391	+92
Gypsies	262	+99
Dagestanis	2,065	+118
Chechens	957	+128
Azerbaijanis	6,770	+130

Note: Some figures measure the number in the whole of the USSR, including the Asian part. The table includes all nationalities having more than 100,000 members in 1959. The 'new' larger groups not included in the table are the Turks (208,000 in 1989) and the Kurds (152,000 in 1989).

Council in Moscow and by the European Community in Brussels in September 1991. Three months later, eleven Soviet republics signed up as founders of the Commonwealth of Independent States. A new union was created. The old, the USSR, voted itself out of existence on 26 December 1991. The degree of independence among the independent states will take several years to sort out.

Restructuring forces and population change 1959–89

Within a given territory, three factors can change the ethnic composition of a population: natural increase in different ethnic groups (number of births minus number of deaths), net migration of members in the ethnic groups (number of immigrants minus number of emigrants), and assimilation between groups (reclassification of membership or biased classification of children in mixed marriages).

NATURAL INCREASE
This is usually the most important factor of change for large ethnic groups. Russians have fewer babies than most other ethnic groups, and, of course, any difference in fertility will, in the long run, change the power structure between ethnic groups. In some of the areas where large numbers of Russians have moved in and become the majority, the situation has now changed because of different reproduction rates. One example of a surviving minority that already has formed a majority is the Tatars in one of the regions in the Middle Volga.

A study of the level of reproduction in the ten republics, using cohort data for women born between 1935 and 1955, shows that, on average, women in Russia, the Ukraine, Estonia and Latvia have had fewer children (by 10–20 per cent) than the replacement rate (2.1 per woman). Close to replacement rate (though not above) are women born in Belorussia and Lithuania. Some natural population increase (2.2 to 2.6) was true for Moldavia and Georgia, and a little more for Armenia. Large increases took place in Azerbaijan, where Muslim women had many children. However, during this period of two decades, the average number decreased substantially in Azerbaijan from 4.4 to 2.6 children per woman (Boubnova 1989). The present and expected future population increases in Muslim areas are thus mainly due to the population structure. Many inhabitants are in age groups where they form families and have children.

MIGRATION STREAMS
These have changed radically during the last years of the old regime. Before 1988 there were no data on ethnic migration; however, by using indirect methods it is possible to make inferences from spatial distribution data. One such source is a data base on cohorts every tenth year. Here we shall use the census data from 1979 and 1989, including the information on migration during 1988, which is available in the 1989 census.

The first break in the old migration patterns shows that Russians return to Russia. Before, the Russians were moving to all parts of the USSR, although during the last decade the opposite occurred: they returned from the Central Asian republics and from Kazakhstan. This movement increased during the last years before 1989 when nationalism grew in strength. The clear tendency was: Russians go home. In the Caucasus their numbers were reduced between 1979 and 1989 by 9 per cent in Georgia, 27 per cent in Armenia and 18 per cent in Azerbaijan.

The second variation is that Slavic people in general seem to stop their geographic expansion. Earlier, Ukrainians and Belorussians were also moving to other republics. Some examples from the decade 1979–89 show that the number of Ukrainians increased by 34–39 per cent in the Baltic republics, by 22 per cent in Azerbaijan and by 35 per cent in Uzbekistan. For the USSR as a whole their numbers increased by only 4 per cent. While Belorussians increased by 6 per cent in the union, their numbers in Central Asia, Georgia and Azerbaijan increased by 50 per cent. However, during the last year of the period, in 1989, both Ukrainians and Belorussians were moving back to their 'homelands'.

The third deviation shows that the increasing strength of the Slavic population in the Baltic republics was coming to an end, even before they became sovereign states. Russians, Ukrainians and Belorussians were no longer welcome to settle there. The pull factor in the Baltic areas is evident: a higher standard of living. In spite of a long tradition, around two centuries, of Russian supremacy over the areas, only one out of five inhabitants was 'non-Baltic' when the USSR took control during the Second World War. After the war some Balts fled to the West, others were killed or moved eastward by Stalin, and a 'russification' process began, especially in the two northern Baltic states. The 1989 census shows that in one decade (Latvia) or two decades (Estonia) the native groups would probably have become minorities in their countries. This is one of many examples showing how geographical changes include both political change and consequences for the geography of population.

INTERNATIONAL MIGRATION

This is easier to control than internal migration. Outmigration from the USSR was nearly non-existent before *perestroika*.[4] Between 1987 and 1990 the flows to non-USSR countries from the European part of the union have more or less doubled every year (see Table 13.3). Other, short-term, flows of people working temporarily outside the union also started when this possibility was allowed in 1987.

The permanent outmigrants are usually Jews (Szulc 1992) or Germans (Wendt 1991). Statistics for the destination of USSR emigrants (not only from the European part) from 1976 to 1990 (see Table 13.4) show that nine out of ten emigrants were Jewish or German, or at least had a close family connection with one of these groups (some non-Jews obtained a Jewish registration in their passport by illegal methods).

ASSIMILATION

Over the generations, cohabiting ethnic groups mix biologically and culturally. Small and geographically-spread groups usually disappear if they do not work hard to maintain their cultural identity. Assimilation

Table 13.3   Migration flows from Eastern Europe to countries outside the USSR, 1987–90 (all data '000)

Republic of origin	1987	1988	1989	1990
Russia	9	21	48	104
Ukraine	7	18	50	95
Belorussia	1	3	15	34
Moldavia	2	2	7	21
Estonia	1	2	2	1
Latvia	1	1	3	5
Lithuania	1	1	3	6
Georgia	1	1	3	6
Armenia	6	16	12	5
Azerbaijan	0	1	3	12

Table 13.4   Destination of emigrants from USSR, 1976–90 (all data % except where stated)

Destination	1976–80	1981–5	1986	1987	1988	1989	1990
Israel	62	31	15	26	28	45	59
Germany	18	18	13	40	48	42	31
USA	7	3	6	16	17	6	2
Greece	1	2	6	3	5	6	5
Other	12	55	39	15	3	1	2
Total	216	46	7	40	109	236	454

Note: These data are for the whole USSR. Around one-third of the migrants, mainly Germans but some Armenians and Jews, are from Central Asia. These figures show more Jews migrating to Israel than in reality. This was a way to hide the fact that Jews were allowed to migrate to the USA. For the year 1990, the 59 per cent refers to **permissions** to emigrate. The actual percentage of emigrants to Israel that year was 46.

in Eastern Europe today takes place partly through intermarriage between groups. Statistics on this process are published for Jews, Germans and Poles.

The data show that in 1988 only 31 per cent of Jews married another Jew in Russia. The corresponding proportion in the Ukraine and Belorussia was around every second Jew (50 per cent and 56 per cent). In 'mixed' families it was common to give the children a non-Jewish nationality. The proportions of children in mixed Jewish families choosing a Russian, Ukrainian or Belorussian nationality in 1989 were 95, 94 and 93 per cent respectively. It is thus clear that large groups of Jews were assimilating into Soviet society before the opportunities to migrate to Israel opened up. This could be explained in many ways: some felt more like Russians, for example, than like Jews; others preferred to be registered as Russians in the hope of gaining privileges or to avoid being on probation.

Among German mixed marriages in Russia, a minority of the children (6 per cent) chose German nationality in their passports. In Kazakhstan, where there are more Germans than in Russia, 24 per cent of the children of mixed marriages chose German nationality. On average, Germans are much less assimilated than Jews, especially in the countryside. In the four republics or nations close to Poland, one out of five children born to Poles in mixed marriages chose Polish nationality.

Statistics on mother tongue also say something on how different groups have assimilated. They also show that large groups of people are classified in a way which has more to do with 'blood' and classification of earlier generations than the actual culture to which they belong. In 1989 the proportion of people with another native language than their own, according to nationality, were for some groups (percentages are in parentheses): Hungarians (6), Turks (9), Kurds (19), Romanians (39), Koreans (50), Germans (52), Poles (69) and Jews (87). Clearly a large majority of the Jews did not use Yiddish in their homes, and every second person classified as German no longer used the German language at home.

Character and form of present and future migration

Lately there has been a large interest in present and especially expected future migration within and out of the former USSR (Grečić, 1991). This section will first deal with potential ethnic migration within Eastern Europe to other parts of the world, and then discuss future economic migration within and especially out of Eastern Europe.

Eastern Europe today

As indicated earlier, in all parts of the former USSR there are now strong forces working for national or regional sovereignty. This could be the beginning of a more fundamental regionalization of the administrative power structure in Eastern Europe. In other parts of Europe, such as Spain, former Yugoslavia and the Czech and Slovak Republics, this tendency of ethnic control over 'homelands' is evident. In Eastern Europe there are enough Tatars, Chuvash, Chechens, Bashkirs and Moldavians to form small nations of their own as majority groups did in the new Baltic states. Also, smaller groups could form nations or autonomous regions within federal states. Figure 13.2 gives some idea of the ethnic mosaic in Eastern Europe.

In the Russian part of the northern Caucasus we find Slavic Russians and Ukrainians, Caucasus groups, Turks, Armenians and smaller groups of Greeks, Jews, Kurds and Assyrians. Just to give an insight into the ethnic problems that could emerge, we present a short overview of the

Figure 13.2   Ethnic composition of the European part of the ex-USSR

nationalities living in this particular area. In one autonomous republic, Dagestan, people of more than thirty nationalities, including Avarks (500,000), Dargins (400,000), Lesgians (300,000) and Kumuks (300,000), belong to the 1.8 million population. In another autonomous republic, South-Ossetia, we find Ossetins, who are mainly Orthodox, although there are also Muslims. Chechen-Ingushetia, another republic, is mainly inhabited by Sunni Muslims, Chechens and Ingush. There is serious ethnic tension in this republic. The Kabardino-Balkarskaya autonomous republic and the Karachaevo-Cherkesskaya autonomous region are formed by two nationalities, Karachayevtsy (140,000) and Balkartsy

(78,000), although they have the same language and are quite alike culturally speaking. The same is true for the Circassians (500,000) and the Kabardians (400,000), two groups living in separate settlements with different autonomies. Among other small groups are the Assyrians (26,000) who, like several other groups, have an interesting historical background: they are the descendants of the powerful ancient Assyrians. Among 'foreign' nationalities in the area we find Greeks, Kurds and Turks. Not surprisingly, given the ethnic hotchpotch, actual and potential ethnic conflicts are numerous here, as well as in many other areas in Eastern Europe. Even if there are no reliable statistics on ethnic social unrest, violence, civil war, etc., we know that a state close to civil war is evident in areas like the above-mentioned South-Ossetia in Georgia or Nagorno-Karabakh in Azerbaijan.

There is a new problem which is also an important indicator of ethnic conflicts in eastern Europe: the appearance of large numbers of refugees. The official number in 1988–90 was 600,000, as registered by the State Committee on Labour, Ministry of Internal Affairs, the KGB and the Defence Ministry. This figure comprises 420,000 refugees from Armenia and Azerbaijan, 70,000 refugees (mainly Turks) from Uzbekistan, 9,000 Caucasians from Kazakhstan, and 75,000 Russian-speakers (often military personnel with families), plus 25,000 other refugees from Baku. An unofficial estimate is 1 million refugees,[5] including more Turks from Uzbekistan, Russians returning from Tajikistan, Kirghizia and Tuva, and some Russian-speaking groups from Azerbaijan and the Baltic republics.

Potential ethnic migration within Eastern Europe

A rough estimate of potential ethnic problems could be based on the actual geographical distribution of minorities in Eastern Europe (see Table 13.5). An increase in Russian nationalism would make life harder for all minorities in Russia. Some of them, like the Baltic groups, have already net-migrated from Russia to their homelands. Others, like the Tatars, also have an autonomous republic where they dominate in numbers and therefore have some sort of homeland. Current ideas about creating an autonomous German republic within Russia will probably not stop the out-migration of ethnic Germans, which is already happening.

On the other hand, anti-Russian feeling in areas outside Russia could, depending on its strength, force Russians to 'return home'. A majority of the 3 million Russians in non-Slavic European nations, including 1.7 million in the Baltic and 0.8 million in the Caucasus, could move back to their motherland in the same manner as the Turks left the Balkans when the Ottoman Empire collapsed one hundred years ago. In addition, anti-Muslim feelings are present in Russia, Georgia and Armenia as well as in other parts of Europe, and future conflicts including civil wars with large numbers of refugees are always a threat.

Table 13.5 Minorities in the former European USSR in 1989 (all data '000, except Majority group)

Republics: Minorities	Rus 1	Ukr 2	Bel 3	Mol 4	Est 5	Lat 6	Lit 7	Geo 8	Arm 9	Aze 10
1 Russians	*	11,356	1,342	562	475	906	344	341	52	392
2 Ukrainians	4,363	*	291	600	48	92	45	52	8	32
3 Belorussians	1,206	440	*	20	28	120	63	9	1	8
4 Moldavians	173	325	5	*	1	3	1	3	1	2
5 Estonians	46	4	1	–	*	3	1	2	0	0
6 Latvians	47	7	3	–	3	*	4	1	0	0
7 Lithuanians	70	11	8	1	3	35	*	1	0	1
8 Georgians	131	24	3	1	1	1	1	*	1	14
9 Armenians	532	54	5	3	2	3	2	44	*	391
10 Azerbaijanis	336	37	5	3	1	2	1	301	85	*
Tatars	5,522	87	12	3	4	5	5	4	0	28
Chuvash	1,774	20	3	1	1	2	1	1	0	1
Bashkirs	1,345	7	1	1	0	1	0	0	0	1
Mordvinians	1,073	19	3	1	1	0	0	0	0	1
Germans	842	38	4	7	3	4	2	2	0	1
Jews	537	486	112	66	5	23	12	24	1	31
Poles	95	219	418	5	3	60	258	2	0	1
Majority group (in millions)	119	38	8	3	1	1	3	4	3	6

Potential ethnic migration from Eastern Europe

Ethnic tension will also affect outmigration from nations of the former USSR (Öberg and Springfeldt 1991). For example, the anti-Jewish feelings which exist in Eastern Europe cause the Jewish population to migrate to Israel or a Western country. There are 1.4 million Jews in Eastern Europe and still another 100,000 (in 1989) in the Asian part of the former USSR. And, discussed above, if a Jew marries a non-Jew (which is true for every second Jew), and if they have two children, then three more persons are allowed to emigrate, according to the present migration rules. The possible number of persons wanting to move to Israel in the future could be anything up to 2 or 3 million. By the end of 1992 probably half a million Soviet Jews will have poured into Israel, boosting that country's population by more than 10 per cent (Szulc 1991).

Other actual and potential emigration groups to other parts of Europe are the Germans, Poles and Greeks. While the Germans in Asia (1 million in Kazakhstan) have been less assimilated, the Germans in Russia (0.8 million) have had the same rate of assimilation with the Slavs as the Jews. A multiplier of two or three has to be applied to estimate the number of potential German immigrants.

Table 13.6 Number of 'relatives' of Eastern European nationalities living outside USSR, 1987

Russians	1,700,000
Ukrainians	1,300,000
Estonians	80,000
Latvians	70,000
Lithuanians	350,000
Georgians	120,000
Armenians	1,300,000
Azerbaijanis	7,700,000

Note: These statistics are based on census data from other countries, e.g., the USA. Belorussians are not registered as an ethnic group or a nationality outside the USSR and thus there are no figures. Approximately 1 per cent of the Belorussians live outside the USSR. Moldavians are registered as Romanians outside the USSR and hence there is no figure for them here.

Not only are groups with a 'mother nation' outside Eastern Europe probable ethnic migrants, but also groups with many relatives in other countries. Table 13.6 shows how many relatives the main nationalities have in other countries. Russians in other countries, e.g., France and the United States, emigrated so long ago that their relations to former relatives in Russia are probably weak. The Ukrainians and especially the Balts emigrated only one or two generations ago and thus they probably have stronger relations. Armenians are another group with large proportions in welfare states outside Eastern Europe: 10 per cent of all Armenians live in the United States and 4 per cent live in France. Azerbaijanis outside the former USSR are mainly neighbours living in Iraq.

Future economic migration within Eastern Europe

Urbanization would increase if existing restrictions on moving into the major cities were removed. To become a Muscovite in 1991 one had to:

1. be born in Moscow (the fertility level is low, 1.6 children per woman);
2. marry someone living in Moscow (30,000–50,000 in-migrants per year, often fictive marriages in spite of special rules to avoid this);
3. excel in certain professions (a small number of actors, engineers, scientists, etc., are allowed to move to Moscow every year); or
4. be a temporary worker in an industry with a shortage of workers or where Muscovites do not want to work. This last means has been the most common way of entering the capital (according to one source, around 150,000 succeed every year in acquiring the right of permanent residence after several years as a temporary worker).

Living conditions, including medical care, education, housing and the labour market, have generally been much better in the large cities, especially in Moscow. If free mobility were introduced, large flows of in-migrants to Moscow would probably be the result. Also St Petersburg (formerly Leningrad), capitals of other states and some other attractive cities have the same restrictions as Moscow on in-migration, and these cities could, with new rules, attract large numbers from rural areas and from smaller cities and towns.

Urbanization will undoubtedly continue, although at what pace remains to be seen. During recent decades, slightly fewer than 1 million (net) migrants per year in the whole union moved to cities. A little under 800,000 moved to European cities. However, during the transition from a command to a market economy, some of the living conditions, such as the availability of food, could be more complicated in large cities. This, together with present restrictions on immigration, could moderate the urbanization process. In fact, during 1989 the rate of urbanization slowed by 15–20 per cent. In the longer term, the proportion of the population living in large cities will probably increase, as happened earlier in the history of Western Europe.

East–West migration

The title of this chapter uses the word 'poverty' to indicate the difference in living standards between Eastern and Western Europe. From a global perspective, contemporary Eastern Europe is, of course, a rich part of the world with a comparatively well-educated population and great production potential of both human and natural resources (Alton 1984). However, if we make some simple calculations of how Eastern Europe can improve its present standard of living, it is easy to see that very little can happen during the coming decades, even if a heavy investment programme is implemented. Although we have experimented with various models based on common-sense ideas of economic growth,[6] all formulations produce the same message: even with large investments in social infrastructure (including education in accounting and marketing), in physical infrastructure and in technology, it will be impossible for the East to reach the Western standard of living during the coming decades.

Transfer of capital from Western to Eastern Europe will, of course, help to develop the latter's standard of living, although not to an extent that will be really noticeable 'during a short time such as one or two decades. If countries in Western and Northern Europe would send 1 per cent of their GNP per year to be added to the performance of the production system in Eastern Europe, then the standard of living, according to one of our models, would still be around 44 per cent higher in the West in 2010 instead of 49 per cent. Of course, capital streams are already existing. In late 1991, the Soviet Union owed Western creditors nearly 70 billion dollars, which is around $250 per capita.[7] If this money is invested in infrastructure etc. for future production, this will certainly help the economy in Eastern Europe; however, again it will take a long time before such progress is visible. This amount, incidentally, is less than the 1 per cent transferred yearly as a gift from Northern and Western Europe in our scenario above.

According to economic theory, the imbalance between capital and labour in the West compared with Eastern Europe could be corrected by a much larger transfer of capital eastward or a transfer of labour westward. If the difference in capital per labour ratio between East and West disappeared, the likely transfer of labour (with families) westward would be around five million persons per year during the coming two decades, ten times as high as the present figures. These figures are, of course, hypothetical. In reality these flows would not be accepted. For example, the amount of social engineering necessary to avoid conflicts between immigrants and others does not exist (see Brubaker 1989 and 1990; Bovenkerk *et al.* 1990 and 1991).

East–West commuting

For most citizens it is not possible to migrate permanently from Eastern Europe. It is not easy to obtain permission to leave or to be accepted in another country as an immigrant. There is, however, another possible way of leaving the country: by private invitation from a person outside the union. This method has been allowed since 1987 and practised since 1988. A new law allowing people to move without invitation is expected in 1993.

During such a visit to the West, it must be very tempting to work legally or illegally some hours, a week, a month or longer. The international value of the rouble is so low that any income in foreign currency is extremely valuable. If, for example, a Russian professor gave a two-hour lecture in Sweden in 1991, he or she could change this income (US$150) into as many roubles as a year's income in Moscow. If a visitor to Vienna works hard cleaning windows for one week, this will correspond to a year's income in Eastern Europe. The official exchange rate has been changing every third or fourth month on average during the last three years, and it will probably change many times in the coming years. However, the basic large difference in salaries will continue to exist for at least another generation.

The ratio between emigrants and short-term labour, including students and researchers with temporary grants, visiting other countries is estimated at one to five. This means that around 2.5 million visitors to the West every year are working on a short-term basis. This figure will probably increase in the future. When more people in the East receive information about the advantages of a short work period in a rich country, they will find a way to use these opportunities. Also many organizations such as households, firms, hospitals, research centres, etc., would like to employ cheap temporary labour. Each year more information is circulated on ways of overcoming the existing restrictions on mobility. Extensive East–West 'commuting' is thus a very probable alternative to large permanent migration from Eastern Europe.

Conclusion

The geopolitical changes in the former USSR are in a flux, and as we write this chapter the number of nations emerging from the former union is still unclear. Two things are, however, clear. First, there is a large economic gap between the former union, here labelled as Eastern Europe, and the rest of Europe. Under market conditions, there is a huge temptation for capital to move eastwards, where salaries are low, and for labour to go west, where the salaries are high. Second, ethnic tension among a large number of nationalities is now shown openly, and conditions close to civil war are apparent in several regions. Both of these conditions give rise to migratory flows, the potential strength of which is tremendous.

The ethnic migration of Jews, Germans, Greeks and Armenians will probably continue, partly for ethnic reasons but also for economic motives. The potential number of other migrants from Eastern Europe would be quite large — many millions per year — if economic conditions determined migration. In total the **economy** of Europe would be better off if around half the population of Eastern Europe were welcomed in other European countries. This figure is of course very superficial. However, a reasonable yearly flow of people westward and increased economic help going eastward will boost economic growth in Europe as a whole.

Notes

1. Here we shall not deal with the more than 90 million inhabitants living in the Asian part of the former USSR. We have included the Caucasus area in the European part of the union. Praxis differs on this point. Traditionally the Caucasus is geographically outside Europe, although ethnically parts of the Caucasus are typically European. Georgians and Armenians are Semitic Christians, and Azerbaijanis are Semitic Muslims. For practical reasons the whole area is sometimes, as in this chapter, included in Europe. Although our own definition of Eastern Europe as the European part of the former USSR is, we admit, unconventional, we prefer to include countries like Poland, Czechoslovakia, Hungary, Romania, etc. as part of Central Europe.
2. Stalin was not happy with the census in 1937, so he ordered a new census which was completed in 1939. However, the latter did not please him either, so very few results were published. From the 1937 data, which are now being published in Moscow, it was possible to see all the losses in the countryside due to famine after the collectivization efforts. Therefore he classified the data and sent most of the civil servants who had been working on the census to concentration camps (Tolz 1991).
3. For example, Nove 1982; Cohen 1985; Thompson 1990; and White 1990.
4. The exceptions were mainly Jews. On average, nearly 25,000 per year were allowed to leave the union between 1976 and 1986. This corresponds to one person among 100,000 inhabitants in Eastern Europe per year.
5. The figure also includes some 120,000–150,000 environmental refugees who has to leave the Chernobyl zone; they are not of direct interest in this chapter where we deal with ethnic and economic refugees.
6. Research carried out by the authors at the International Institute for Applied Systems Analysis, Laxenburg, Austria, in 1991. See also Denison and Poullier 1967.
7. According to Viktor Gerashchenko, President of the Soviet Central Bank, AP Reuters, 25 September 1991.

References

Alton, T.P., 1984, 'Economic growth in Eastern Europe, 1965, 1970 and 1975–83', LW International Financial Research, Occasional Paper 80, New York.

Boubnova, H., 1990, 'Demographic waves: causes, nature, forecasts', *Studia Demograficne*, 95: 45–8 (in Polish).

Bovenkerk, F., Miles, R. and Verbunt, G., 1990, 'Racism, migration and the state in Western Europe: a case for comparative analysis', *International Sociology*, 5(4): 475–90.

Bovenkerk, F., Miles, R. and Verbunt, G., 1991, 'Comparative studies of migration and exclusion on the grounds of race and ethnic background in Western Europe: a critical appraisal', *International Migration Review*, 25(2): 375–91.

Brubaker, W.R., 1989, *Immigration and the politics of citizenship in Europe and North America*, University Press of America, Washington.

Brubaker, W.R., 1990, 'Immigration, citizenship, and the nation-state in France and Germany: a comparative historical analysis', *International Sociology*, 5(4): 379–407.

Cohen, S.F., 1985, *Rethinking the Soviet experience: politics and history since 1917*, Oxford University Press, New York.

Denison, E.F. and Poullier, J.P., 1967, *Why growth rates differ: post war experience in nine Western countries*, The Brookings Institution, Washington.

Grečić, V., 1991, 'East–West migration and its possible influence on South–North migration', *International Migration*, 29(2): 241–52.

Kosiński, L., 1970, *The population of Europe*, Longman, London.

Nove, A., 1982, *An economic history of the USSR*, Penguin, Harmondsworth.

Öberg, S. and Springfeldt, P., 1991, *Swedish National Atlas: the population*, SNA, Stockholm.

Raeff, M., 1990, *Russia abroad: a cultural history of the Russian emigration, 1919–1939*, Oxford University Press, New York.

Szulc, T., 1992, 'The great Soviet exodus', *National Geographic*, 181(2): 40–65.

Thompson, J.M., 1990, *Russia and the Soviet Union: an historical introduction*, Westview, Boulder, 2nd edition.

Tolz, M., 1991, 'Repressed census in family and family policy', *Demography and Sociology*, 1: 161–78 (in Russian).

Wendt, H., 1991, 'Die deutsch-deutschen Wanderungen-Bilanz einer 40-jährigen Geschichte von Flucht und Ausreise', *Deutschland-Archiv*, 24(4): 386–95.

White, S., 1990, *Political and economic encyclopedia of the Soviet Union and Eastern Europe*, Longman, Harlow.

Chapter 14

New trends in mass migration in Germany

Franz-Josef Kemper

A new upswing of mass migrations

Since the late 1980s Germany has seen a marked rise in immigrants, the overwhelming proportion of whom have been coming to the western part of the unified country. Already in 1987 in West Germany, always officially denoted as a 'non-immigration' country, the inflow was larger than the combined counterparts in the traditional immigration states of Canada and Australia (Meier-Braun 1991, p. 21). In the extraordinary year of 1989 a new record was established with a net influx of 977,000 persons. This by far exceeds the number of approximately 600,000 immigrants to the United States in that year (cf. Heilig *et al*. 1990). After the unification of the two Germanys in October 1990, the amount of cross-border migration fell, simply because a certain proportion of international migrations were now redefined as internal relocations. Although official migration figures for the united Germany are not yet published, there can be no doubt that international mass migration flows continue to play a major role in the country.

Within the net inflow of nearly 1 million immigrants pouring into West Germany in 1989, three subgroups can be distinguished: first, 377,000 ethnic Germans from Eastern Europe (*Aussiedler*); second, 344,000 Germans from the GDR (*Übersiedler*); and third, about 250,000 foreigners who did not achieve the status of ethnic Germans, with 121,000 applicants for political asylum (Sommer and Fleischer 1991). Because migration motives and processes as well as likely future development are rather different for these subgroups, they are dealt with at first in separate sections of this chapter. The succeeding section on spatial patterns and regional effects then tries to compare the subgroups from a regional perspective, and in the final section estimates and scenarios for future migration flows are discussed.

Before a more detailed description of the migrant subgroups is given, two important aspects should be emphasized. The first is the close connection of recent mass migration flows with political changes and events. Of course the most striking example is the exodus of East Germans to the Federal Republic, first via Czechoslovakia and particularly Hungary and Austria, and after the opening of the Berlin Wall, directly to West Germany. In fact, it was because the migration wave grew so quickly, seriously threatening economic development in the GDR, that the unification of the two Germanys, unexpected by the vast majority of its inhabitants, could be accomplished so rapidly. Heilig *et al.* (1990, p. 30) rightly emphasized that 'while unification was born out of sheer economic nessecity, a demographic phenomenon, migration, triggered it'.

The second point to be stressed can also be related to dramatic political changes. The very high figures for recent immigration flows to Germany might suggest that they were unprecedented in the past. However, this is not so. Following the Second World War, huge population resettlements took place in Central Europe. Between 1945 and 1950 more than 10 million refugees and expellees came to West Germany, and in 1950 these groups made up nearly 20 per cent of the resident population in the FRG (Köllmann 1983). This influx has deeply influenced West German society, population and settlement, and the processes of the new immigration of Germans in the late 1980s and the 1990s can be compared with migration processes, spatial patterns and forms of social integration during the first decades after the war. Moreover, many facets of recent immigration policies in Germany, ranging from privileges for ethnic Germans to the treatment of asylum applications, can be understood only if one recognizes the historical situation of Germany after the Second World War.

Migrant groups

The inflow of ethnic Germans from Eastern Europe

As a consequence of the war and the crimes of the Nazi regime, the situation of ethnic Germans scattered over many parts of Eastern and South-Eastern Europe became very difficult during the early post-war years, and many had to cope with the pressure of expulsion. Therefore, in the 1949 constitution of the Federal Republic of Germany, an article (116) was included saying that ethnic Germans living under such pressure (as well as their offspring) were allowed to settle in the FRG and to obtain German nationality. Owing to this article it has been rather easy for an inhabitant of an East European country with a parent or grand-parent who had designated himself or herself as ethnic German to immigrate to the FRG, provided that the country of origin agreed to the resettlement. With the revolutionary changes in Eastern Europe during the last few years and the liberalization of migration policy, the possibilities for resettlement rose considerably; this explains the recent upsurge of 'resettlers' (*Aussiedler*) arriving in the FRG. So the number of 377,000 ethnic German immigrants in 1989 was surpassed in 1990 by 397,000.

Nowadays many of these immigrants can hardly speak the German language. Nevertheless, they can easily obtain German citizenship compared with the second or even third generation of the guestworker population in West Germany. Apart from the effects of Article 116, this different situation is rooted in the rules for acquiring nationality. In international law two such possibilities are provided for a new-born child. According to the first of these, the *ius soli*, the child automatically becomes a citizen of the state where she or he is born. In contrast, the *ius sanguinis* declares that the nationality of the parents devolves upon their offspring. In Germany only the *ius sanguinis* has traditionally been acknowledged by law. This is also true for most European countries (Kimminich 1990, p. 106), although it stands in contrast to immigration countries such as the United States, as well as France where after the French Revolution the *ius soli* was much more stressed (see Ogden's Chapter 6 in this book). It is well known that nation-building in Germany was much complicated and delayed in comparison with countries such as France and Britain. Whereas in France the nation-state was established upon a common language, in Germany during the late eighteenth and the early nineteenth century the construct of an ethnic nationalism evolved and was elaborated by philosophers such as Herder, Fichte and Schelling, although without being realized in practice. As Oberndörfer (1991) recently has shown, these traditional ideas of an ethnic nation and an ethnic character, which have also deeply influenced many countries in Northern, Eastern and South-Eastern Europe, even had some effects on the constitution of the Federal Republic of Germany, which otherwise stresses human rights of the population, not special rights for people of a specific ethnic origin. It seems that the rules for citizenship as well as the official declaration of being a 'non-immigration' country in today's Germany are some of the most important effects and relics of these ethnic traditions.

Figure 14.1 shows the time series of the influx of *Aussiedler* or ethnic Germans to the FRG from 1950 to 1990. After the Second World War many Germans from the eastern parts of the former Reich as well as from regions in other countries were forced to move westward and to resettle in the zones under control of the allies. By 1950 this process of steered relocation was more or less finished. Therefore, the number of *Aussiedler* was rather low in the 1950s and 1960s, with the exception of 1957 and 1958 when more than 200,000 migrants came to West Germany, 91 per cent of them from Poland. This exodus was the indirect effect of an outflow of 300,000 Poles from the Soviet Union to Poland, because the Soviets allowed all inhabitants of the former Polish eastern territories who held Polish nationality in 1939 to leave the country (Fleischer and Proebsting 1989, p. 583). Since 1976 the number of migrants have risen, because official agreements between the FRG and East European countries permitted the resettlement of fixed contingents of ethnic Germans. Altogether, between 1950 and 1987 nearly 60 per cent

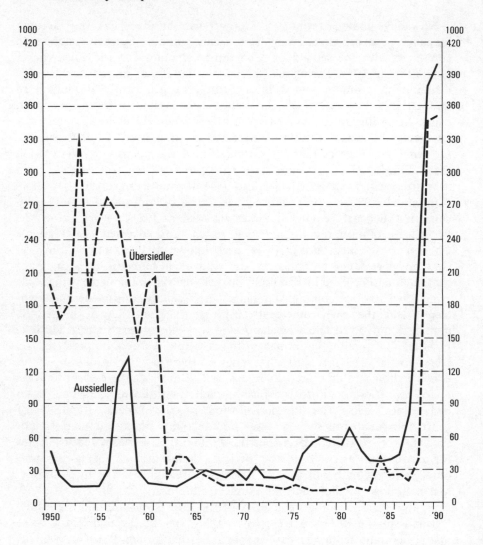

Figure 14.1   Immigrants from the GDR (*Übersiedler*) and from South-Eastern
Europe (*Aussiedler*), 1950–90

Source: Data from Statistical Yearbooks, FRG.

of the 1.42 million *Aussiedler* came from Poland, 14.5 per cent from
Romania, 7.7 per cent from the Soviet Union, 6.9 per cent from Czechoslovakia, 6.2 per cent from Yugoslavia and 1.1 per cent from Hungary
(Fleischer and Proebsting 1989, p. 584). While the resettlement from
Czechoslovakia, Hungary and Yugoslavia has come to an end, the recent
upswing of the flows is produced by migrants from the first three countries. These three groups show special characteristics and differ particularly
in their command of the German language and their cultural traditions.

For many centuries the ethnic Germans in Romania who had settled in some parts of that country could maintain their own culture and religion. Even today, an important part of the literature in the German language is represented by writers of Romanian origin, many of whom were forced to leave Romania under the Ceaucescu regime and now live in the FRG. Therefore, *Aussiedler* from Romania, 15 per cent of all ethnic German immigrants in 1988–90, speak German and generally have a fairly good chance of integration in the FRG (Heller and Koch 1987).

In the second group of immigrants from Poland (54 per cent of all *Aussiedler* in 1988–90), the younger generation, often coming from mixed marriages between Polish and German parents, hardly speak any German. Therefore special language instruction is necessary before they can apply for a position in the labour market. Such courses are offered to *Aussiedler* and are financed by the Federal Institute of Labour (Bundesanstalt für Arbeit).

Whilst a considerable number of ethnic Germans from Poland migrate as one-person households (in 1988, 25 per cent of all persons), *Aussiedler* from the Soviet Union arrive overwhelmingly with their families (94 per cent in 1988). In this group too many immigrants of the younger generation have only a poor command of the German language, although they have grown up in families with a special and very traditional cultural heritage. An example is the religious minorities such as Baptists and other Christian sects. In spite of the atheist propaganda put out by the Soviet state for so many years, only a small proportion of these immigrants have no denominational membership. The same is true for the *Aussiedler* from Poland, nearly all of whom are Catholic. In 1988–90, 30 per cent of all ethnic German immigrants to the FRG came from the Soviet Union, with increasing absolute numbers as well as a rising proportion (37 per cent in 1990).

A common characteristic of the *Aussiedler* groups is their age structure which differs considerably from that of the population in the FRG. Table 14.1 shows the percentages of age groups for ethnic German immigrants in 1989 in comparison with the total population of the FRG. The most striking differences are the high proportion of children, particularly those under the age of 6, for ethnic Germans, and the small proportion of elderly people. Among the population of working age, there are far more people in the 18 to 45 age-group than those between the ages of 45 and 65. This age structure of migrants in 1989 is quite typical of the immigration flows of ethnic Germans in the 1980s except that the proportion of young children was particularly high in 1989, and the average age was rather low. Overall, the migrants will have a delaying effect on the ageing of the resident population in Germany.

The occupational composition of *Aussiedler* also differs from that of the resident population (cf. Fleischer and Proebsting 1989; Franke 1989). In 1988, 49 per cent of the immigrant labour-force had occupations in manufacturing and handicrafts compared with 34 per cent for all

Table 14.1   Age structure of German immigrants in 1989 to the FRG (%)

Age group	Ethnic Germans	Immigrants from the GDR	Population of FRG
<6	13.1	8.6	6.3
6–18	18.4	16.6	11.9
18–25	13.2	22.1	11.1
25–45	36.2	42.2	29.4
45–60	11.6	7.8	20.4
60–65	3.7	1.1	5.5
>65	3.8	1.7	15.3

Source: Sommer and Fleischer 1991, p. 83.

Germans: unskilled workers and those employed in the mechanical trades were particularly over-represented. For skilled workers, engineers and many employees in the service sector, the immigrants' qualifications are often not adequate for the modern economy of West Germany, so that the unemployment rate of ethnic Germans is higher.

The exodus from East to West Germany

Although after the unification of the two Germanys the flow from East to West is now part of the internal migration system and can be compared to such streams as that from the North to the South in the 'old states' of the FRG, it has really been a type of 'mass migration'. From 1949 until 1 July 1990, when the special admission procedure for refugees and other migrants from the GDR was dissolved, East German migrants totalled 5.2 million (Wendt 1991). In Figure 14.1 several phases can be distinguished. The first, from 1950 to 1961, shows high annual numbers of *Übersiedler* who, mostly illegally, left their residences and jobs in East Germany. This exodus was suddenly stopped by the erection of the Berlin Wall in 1961. In the second phase, from 1961 to 1988, only some 10,000 persons annually were allowed to migrate from East to West, about 60 per cent with the permission of the East German government. Although the final stage lasted only one year, from mid-1989 to mid-1990, it effected the collapse of the German Democratic Republic. In that period 538,000 refugees and migrants arrived in West Germany.

The dominant flow from East to West Germany was always accompanied by a counterstream, particularly in the 1950s. During the forty-one years of the GDR's existence, this counterstream comprised fewer than 0.5 million people. Meanwhile, the country lost about 4.7 million inhabitants by migration to the West. The scale of this loss can be appreciated when it is remembered that the GDR had a population of 16.4 million at the end of 1989! Thus East Germany has always been an emigration country and has held an exceptional position in this regard over the post-war period (Dorbritz and Speigner 1990, p. 68).

Besides the volume of migration it is important to consider the selective effects of the flows. The age structure of the recent migration wave is shown in Table 14.1. Young adults dominate the migration stream, although children are also slightly over-represented. This structure is not typical of the former migratory phases, for in the 1960s and 1970s the elderly, who could obtain permission rather easily to leave the GDR, were the dominant group (Wendt 1991). Furthermore, a remarkable occupational selection could be observed. In 1989 East Germany lost about 3 per cent of its labour-force by emigration, in particular 8 to 9 per cent of employees in the building trade, and about 11 per cent of its physicians so that some hospitals were forced to close (Heilig *et al.* 1990, p. 31). In contrast to the occupational position of the ethnic Germans, the clear majority of the employed migrants from East Germany were in the service sector. However, similarly to their colleagues from Eastern Europe, unemployment seems to have been high after the emigration (Franke 1989).

The inflow of foreigners and asylum-seekers

The net inflow of foreigners to the FRG was considerably smaller in 1989 than that of the two groups of German immigrants. However, the numbers, particularly of asylum-seekers, are steadily rising and the problems connected with this upsurge are vehemently and controversially discussed in Germany. Whereas in 1989 121,000 people applied for asylum, the number increased to 193,000 in 1990, and probably more than 200,000 in 1991. If one looks at the period after the Second World War and restricts oneself to the industrialized countries, the migration streams of asylum applicants have been growing to a real mass migration phenomenon in the 1980s. Whilst by the mid-1970s only about 20,000 applicants were counted in Europe and North America, this figure rose to 600,000 in 1990 (Widgren 1990, p. 762). In the FRG the first peak of the annual numbers was reached in 1980 when 108,000 asylum-seekers arrived, followed by a decrease to only 20,000 in 1983. Then began the growth which has led to the recent high level. While such a development can be observed in most industrialized Western countries, the FRG has always been characterized by a very high level of asylum flows. From ten European countries with large numbers of asylum-seekers in 1984–6, 48 per cent were found in the FRG (Salt 1989, p. 451). In 1989 the FRG accounted for 39 per cent of the asylum flows in Europe, and in 1990 it took 46 per cent. What are the reasons for this special situation in West Germany?

For an explanation it is necessary to refer again to the distinct historical development of Germany. During the Third Reich many German refugees who were persecuted by the Nazis for their race, political affiliations, religion, etc., sought asylum, especially in Western countries. Therefore, in the constitution of the Federal Republic the right of asylum is particularly emphasized (Article 16). Anybody who claims asylum has the explicit right to have his or her application checked in an often lengthy procedure. Moreover, such asylum-seekers must not be rejected at the borders. Now it has been widely recognized that in recent years many refugees have come because of a bad economic situation, distress and hunger, not because of political persecution. Whilst other European countries reacted by numerically limiting the access of asylum applicants, in the FRG the conditions for the granting of an asylum claim were tightened up. Thus the proportion of successful claims diminished to 8.6 per cent in 1988 and 3.4 per cent in the first eight months of 1990. This cannot totally be put down to the enlargement of the volume of 'economic' migrants, but also to a more restrictive practice of acknowledgement. A comparison with France shows that in the first seven to eight months of 1990, 1 per cent of all claims by Romanians were accepted in the FRG, compared with 21 per cent in France; 24 per cent of Iranians in the FRG versus 73 per cent in France; 0.4 per cent of Yugoslavs compared with 16 per cent in France; while applicants from other countries such as Poland were unsuccessful in both states (Tribalat 1991; Weickhardt 1991).

In spite of this restrictive practice, the inflow of asylum applicants into the FRG has steadily grown. To understand this phenomenon, one must turn one's attention to the length of the procedure. During that period of often several years the applicants receive welfare benefits. Even if the asylum claim is not accepted, many can stay in the FRG. It has been estimated that in 1989, when the rate of acceptance was under 10 per cent, 60–65 per cent of the applicants were allowed to stay (although for an unknown period), 20–25 per cent disappeared, stayed as illegal immigrants or left the country, and only 8 per cent were deported (Flothow 1991).

Altogether, the practice of asylum procedures in the FRG is very unsatisfactory at present. Many applicants can come in, even if very few are finally accepted. For the others, the future remains completely uncertain. Until August 1991 asylum-seekers were not allowed to work during the period of processing their claim and often this remains so when they are accepted as *de facto* refugees (Frauendorf 1991). Therefore, they must rely on social welfare and that results in conflicts with the German population, a growing number of whom no longer maintain a liberal and tolerant attitude to foreigners.

The asylum-seekers' countries of origin have changed in the 1980s. Owing to political crises, civil wars, etc., there have been concentrations of applicants from countries such as Afghanistan, Sri Lanka, Iran and Lebanon in certain years. However, some general patterns can be observed which seem to be typical of Germany. During the 1980s the number of applicants from Africa was rather low in spite of wars and

Table 14.2 Countries of origin of asylum-seekers in the FRG and France, 1988–9

Country/region	FRG		France	
	No.	%	No.	%
Europe: total	144,803	64.5	29,529	30.9
Poland	55,115	24.6	2,245	2.3
Yugoslavia	40,235	17.9	705	0.7
Romania	5,755	2.6	1,856	1.9
Turkey	34,893	15.5	24,090	25.2
Africa: total	19,027	8.5	38,181	39.9
Asia: total	55,724	24.8	22,327	23.3
Iran	13,635	6.1	708	0.7
Pakistan	4,394	2.0	2,679	2.8
India	4,727	2.1	1,576	1.6
Sri Lanka	11,141	5.0	4,734	5.0
Total	224,394	100.0	95,625	100.0

Source: Statistical Yearbook FRG for 1990; Tribalat 1991.

revolutionary changes in that continent. By contrast, those from Eastern and South-Eastern Europe were of growing importance, even if the political systems in these countries were moving towards democratization and liberalization — the problem being that these processes were accompanied by economic crises. Whereas in 1980 people from Poland, Czechoslovakia, Hungary, Romania and Yugoslavia accounted for only about 6 per cent of all asylum-seekers in the FRG, this proportion rose to 44–54 per cent in the late 1980s. Although in 1990 the percentage decreased, the absolute numbers were still growing. Table 14.2 shows the countries of origin of the asylum-seekers in the FRG compared with those of the refugees in France, which has a long tradition of granting asylum. The figures indicate the predominance of Eastern Europe for the FRG, as well as the close relationship between Africa and France. This example clearly demonstrates that the destinations of asylum-seekers depend on factors such as spatial proximity, cultural connections, language, and former colonial relationships.

It should not be overlooked that besides an inflow of asylum applicants, there has also been a considerable immigration of other foreigners to the FRG in recent years. In 1989 a net migration could be observed of 48,000 Turks; 15,000 Greeks; and 118,000 Poles, many of whom were acknowledged as ethnic Germans. In spite of a high unemployment rate and the large immigration of Germans, the economy offers many jobs that hold no attraction for the German population. Thus in the first half of 1990 the Labour Offices have given 48,000 work permits to recently immigrated foreigners, because no German worker was available, particularly in restaurants, hotels, hospitals and nursing-homes (Meier-Braun 1991, p. 21). Further demand for (cheap) labour exists in subsectors of the building trade where firms in West Germany have made contracts with East European, particularly Polish, enterprises which send workers for a limited period (Oswald 1991, p. 424). Finally, an unknown number of illegal migrants have come to West Germany and have taken jobs as seasonal workers in agriculture, tourism and other sectors of the economy.

Regional patterns of mass migration

Migration streams are selective not only by demographic and socio-economic characteristics of the migrants but also by regions of origin and destination. In this part of the chapter some results concerning the regional effects of the migration subgroups within the united Germany are presented. Although such effects are rarely discussed in German mass media and social science literature (with the exception of the population decline in the former GDR), there are important regional differences. A first and most crucial point is that of the intensified East–West disparities in population density. It is well known that the former two Germanys showed considerable inequalities in the density of settlement and population. That of West Germany was about 250 persons per square kilometre in 1988, compared with 154 in East Germany. Because the overwhelming majority of ethnic Germans from Eastern Europe and foreigners from elsewhere migrated to West Germany, and because of the mass exodus from East to West Germany, these inequalities have been further intensified in recent years. Thus in 1989 and 1990 the population of West Germany increased by about 3 per cent, whereas East Germany lost about 3.5 per cent of its inhabitants (Sommer and Fleischer 1991).

The migration loss in the former GDR was by no means regionally homogeneous, showing instead striking spatial contrasts. In Figure 14.2 considerable north–south differences can be seen, with high values of net migration loss concentrated in southern districts of Saxony and Thur-ingia. Values above average also characterize East Berlin and the districts around Berlin. This spatial pattern is related to the degree of industrialization which is particularly high in Saxony, Thuringia and the Berlin agglomeration, and low in the northern territories. Furthermore, the urban cores often show higher values than the suburban and rural areas. This is clearly true not only of Dresden, Leipzig and Chemnitz in Saxony, and Erfurt, Weimar, Jena and Gera in Thuringia, but also of the larger cities in the north (e.g., Schwerin and Rostock). It should be noted that in the GDR suburbanization was rather low and blocks of new buildings were erected mainly in the larger cities and in those towns having administrative or specially planned functions. Overall, the exodus to West Germany has affected mostly the urbanized and industrialized

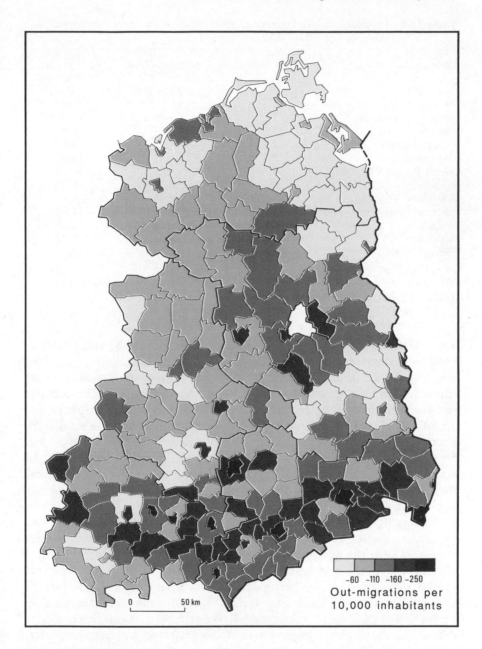

Figure 14.2 Population decrease as a result of net international migration in the GDR, 1989

Source: Schmidt and Tittel 1990.

Table 14.3   German immigrants from Eastern Europe and the GDR by federal states of the FRG, 1989

Federal state	Ethnic Germans	Immigrants from the GDR (per 1,000 population)	All German immigrants
Schleswig-Holstein	2.27	5.20	7.47
Hamburg	7.25	5.66	12.91
Lower Saxony	4.92	4.99	9.90
Bremen	7.57	6.03	13.60
North Rhine-Westphalia	7.64	3.75	11.42
Hesse	4.91	6.36	11.26
Rhineland-Palatinate	5.22	4.44	9.67
Baden-Württemberg	6.13	5.89	12.02
Bavaria	3.61	6.14	9.75
Saarland	5.35	4.54	9.89
West Berlin	5.53	18.37	23.90
FRG	5.62	5.57	11.19

Source: Computed after Statistical Yearbook FRG for 1990.

areas of the GDR. Interestingly, these areas had been the main destinations of the internal migration flows within the GDR because they were where new labour and particularly new housing opportunities were offered (Grundmann and Schmidt 1990a, b). So in 1989 East Berlin showed a net internal migration gain of 22,000 people, and a loss of 30–40,000 people who migrated to West Germany, including West Berlin. From this it can be surmised that the motives for internal migration and for migration to the West were different. The regional inequalities of emigration rates are also closely related to the selective nature of these migrations with high proportions of young adults and of people with a good education.

Concerning the regions of destination of migrants from East to West Germany, Table 14.3 shows the breakdown of numbers by state compared with the distribution of ethnic Germans from Eastern Europe. Several comments are worth noting. First and most important, the special situation of West Berlin has led to a very high proportion of migrants, particularly from East Berlin. Second, from the higher values of Hesse and Bavaria as well as Baden-Württemberg, it can be concluded that the economically prosperous south is preferred by many migrants, whereas states with the burden of old manufacturing industries like Saarland and North Rhine-Westphalia fall behind. Third, the urban states of Hamburg and Bremen show slightly higher values than the surrounding northern states.

The difference mentioned last is much more marked with the migrants from Eastern Europe. North Rhine-Westphalia holds the highest proportion of these, whilst Hesse and particularly Bavaria have low values. In contrast to the migrants from East Germany, the regional distribution of ethnic Germans is hardly related to economic prosperity, so other factors must be dominant. One very important factor seems to be rooted in the personal networks of the migrants who have come mostly as family groups, not as single migrants like many Germans from the GDR. Numerous ethnic Germans try to settle in the vicinity of relatives, neighbours or friends from their regions of origin. This is particularly true for members of religious groups such as Baptists and Mennonites from Russia, who have settled in Augustdorf in North Rhine-Westphalia, a rural community in which former army dwellings were at their disposal. Yet more typical as destinations of the majority of ethnic German immigrants are urban areas, e.g., the Ruhr area where especially immigrants from Poland have settled, taking up traditional connections with Silesia and other former German provinces in the East (during industrialization many miners and other workers migrated from these regions to the Ruhr area). In fact 94.5 per cent of ethnic German immigrants into the Essen region in 1989 were from Poland, whereas Polish immigrants as a whole accounted for fewer than two-thirds of the ethnic Germans entering the FRG in 1989.

Whereas the immigrants from Poland concentrate in the western parts of the FRG, ethnic Germans from Romania show another spatial pattern with high values in southern Germany (Figure 14.3). Also among this group particular localities are preferred which had often been settled by refugees after the Second World War. An example is the rural communities in southern North Rhine-Westphalia (Oberbergischer Kreis), analysed in detail by Koch (1991). These personal networks may facilitate a difficult integration, although this often also results in low mobility and lack of success in the labour market (Franke 1989).

As for the regional distribution of asylum applicants, very little information is available. Regional quotas have been officially defined for the states as well as for communities within a state to grant an equal burden for all regions. Such quotas also exist for German immigrants although they have little reference to the actual spatial patterns because Germans have the right to move freely within the country. This is not so for asylum applicants who are therefore represented in all parts of at least West Germany. In East Germany the numbers of asylum-seekers as well as of foreigners are rather low — only 1.5 per cent of the population are foreigners. Nevertheless, it is just there that hostility towards foreigners and 'social envy' are painfully high at present.

Future trends of migrations

After some years of a large influx of migrants to Germany, particularly to West Germany, it is now extremely difficult to predict future development, because such trends are heavily dependent on changes in migration

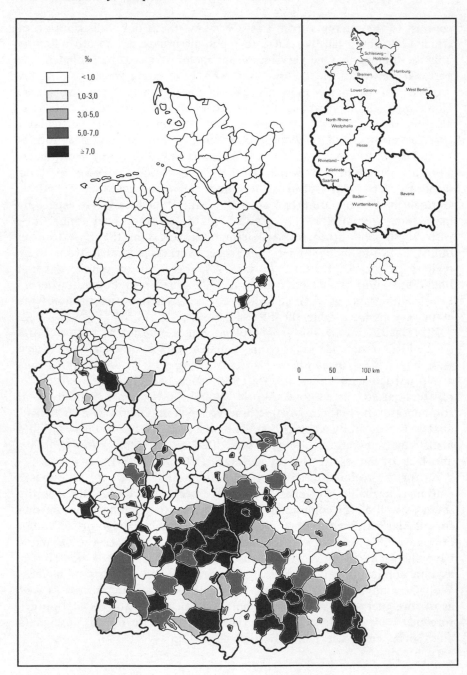

Figure 14.3   West Germany: ethnic Germans from Romania 1989 per 1,000
inhabitants

Source: Redrawn from Koch 1991.

policies which are to be expected in the near future, at the latest when the EC internal market is established. What can be done, however, is to explore the potential of migrants as well as to set up alternative scenarios with varying assumptions and to analyse their effects on future population growth and structure.

The potential of migrants should be divided into that of ethnic Germans from Eastern Europe and that of other foreigners. No exact data on the numbers of ethnic Germans exist because the figures depend on the definition of that group (cf. the problem of mixed marriages and their descendants). Recent information collected by Knabe (1992) has given the following results. The largest group of ethnic Germans live in the former Soviet Union. In the Soviet census of 1989 some 2 million people declared themselves to be German. This seems to be a minimum figure; taking account of mixed marriages etc. could enlarge it to 8 million. The uncertain destiny and the former persecution of these people are widely acknowledged and an autonomous region is planned for them in the near future. This, together with economic help from the German government, may relieve the pressure for emigration. Nevertheless, according to Knabe (1992), about 2 million ethnic Germans from the former Soviet Union can be expected to migrate to Germany between 1991 and 2000.

At the beginning of 1991, 200,000 ethnic Germans were living in Romania, and surveys have shown that most of them (80 per cent) are planning to leave the country. The situation in Poland is rather unclear because of a typical mixture of Polish and German origins for many inhabitants, particularly those from Silesia. Knabe (1992) estimates a migration potential of 500,000 ethnic Germans from Poland during the 1990s. Together with small groups from Hungary and Czechoslovakia, he calculates a total of 2.7 million ethnic Germans who can be expected to come to Germany in the period 1991–2000. Although this figure is rather high compared with other projections (Schulz 1990, has estimated a total sum of 1.3 million during the 1990s), it is by no means unrealistic.

Much more difficult is an estimate of the migrant potential of other foreigners. For Germany, the ongoing changes in Eastern Europe are of utmost importance. The liberalization tendencies as well as the burdensome transition from centrally planned to market economies could effect a considerable increase in emigration. A further factor leading to potential migration is the rapid growth of ethnic tensions and problems of nationality. Not least, minorities such as Jews and Gypsies have had to suffer from latent or overt persecution. Moreover, progress in information and communication as well as in transportation have considerably improved the possibilities for long-distance migration. An outflow to other countries is particularly probable in a country such as the former Yugoslavia with its tremendous ethnic and national conflicts. Because of strong migration connections between Germany and Yugoslavia established by guestworkers, a considerable immigration to Germany can be expected. For the period 1991–2000 Knabe (1992) estimates an influx of 1 million immigrants from Yugoslavia, half of them Gypsies. From Poland he expects 0.5 million foreign immigrants and from the former Soviet Union also 0.5 million; half of the latter would be Jews some of whom have unexpectedly settled in the last few years in Berlin, thereby reviving a tradition from the first decades of the century which also applied to other Russians (cf. Raeff 1990). Altogether, according to Knabe (1992), 2 to 3 million non-German immigrants from Eastern Europe could come to Germany in the 1990s.

These figures about migration potentials from Eastern Europe (ethnic Germans and foreigners) total roughly 500,000 immigrants annually until 2000, with no consideration of refugees, asylum-seekers, etc. from Third World countries. Such data can be implemented in population scenarios which show the effects of migration on population growth and age structure. In the last couple of years, some scenarios have been calculated, e.g. by the DIW (German Institute of Economic Research) in Berlin (Schulz 1990), by scholars affiliated to IIASA in Laxenburg (Heilig *et al.* 1990; Büttner and Prinz 1991), by Hof (1990) from the Institute of the German Economy in Cologne, by Steinmann (1991) and others. It is not possible here to compare the assumptions and results of these scenarios, yet all of them show that only with a huge immigration will the population of Germany not decline in the long run.

Büttner and Prinz (1991), for instance, developed three migration scenarios for West Germany. Even the 'extreme scenario' with 500,000 immigrants annually until 2000 only postpones a reduction in total population and the process of ageing. According to this scenario, the total population of the united Germany will decline from 78 million in 1990 to 67 million forty years later. From the 'benchmark scenario' with no immigration from 1991 onwards follows a population figure of 61 million in 2030 which is smaller than the population of West Germany before unification. Likewise, the simulations by Steinmann (1991) have shown that the median age in West Germany will rise from 38 years in the late 1980s to nearly 49 years in 2033 without immigration, and will only be relatively stable during the next century if 500,000 immigrants are admitted every year!

It must be expected, however, that the native population of Germany will not tolerate such high immigration figures for very long. Nevertheless, a limited annual influx of immigrants can be quite favourable for the economy and could help to relieve the burden of ageing to a certain extent, even if humanitarian aspects of protection for refugees are not considered. Therefore, it seems that a fixing of immigrant quotas, which allow an integration of foreigners and ethnic Germans without severe social conflicts, will be necessary in the next decade. This clearly requires that the fiction of Germany as a non-immigrant country should be abandoned and that the possibilities for foreigners to obtain German citizenship should be improved. Moreover, as Widgren (1990) has pointed out, national solutions urgently need to be embedded in comprehensive international policies for immigrants, asylum-seekers and refugees.

References

Büttner, T. and Prinz, C., 1991, 'Structure and impact of German East–West migration', in Lutz, W. (ed.), *Future demographic trends in Europe and North America*, Academic Press, London, 379–98.

Dorbritz, J. and Speigner, W., 1990, 'Die Deutsche Demokratische Republik, ein Ein- und Auswanderungsland?', *Zeitschrift für Bevölkerungswissenschaft*, 16(1): 67–85.

Fleischer, H. and Proebsting, H., 1989, 'Aussiedler und Übersiedler. Zahlenmäßige Entwicklung und Struktur', *Wirtschaft und Statistik*, 9: 582–89.

Flothow, J., 1991, 'Möglichkeiten und Grenzen der Integration von Flüchtlingen und Asylanten', *Zeitschrift für Kulturaustausch*, 41(1): 115–17.

Franke, H., 1989, 'Integration in Arbeit und Beruf: zentrale Aufgabe für die Arbeitsämter', *Der Landkreis*, 12: 550–2.

Frauendorf, L., 1991, 'Integration im rechtlichen Sinn nach der Reform des Ausländerrrechts', *Zeitschrift für Kulturaustausch*, 41(1): 101–14.

Grundmann, S. and Schmidt, I., 1990a, 'Zur Binnenwanderung in der DDR', *Zeitschrift für den Erdkundeunterricht*, 42(7): 235–41.

Grundmann, S. and Schmidt, I., 1990b, 'Außenwanderungen aus der DDR — Bilanz und Perspektiven', *Zeitschrift für den Erdkundeunterricht*, 42(8–9): 281–8.

Heilig, G., Büttner, T. and Lutz, W., 1990, 'Germany's population: turbulent past, uncertain future', *Population Bulletin*, 45(4), New York.

Heller, W. and Koch, F., 1987, 'Deutsche Aussiedler aus Rumänien — Landsleute oder eine Minorität? Zur räumlichen Mobilität einer Einwanderungsgruppe (eine Untersuchung aus geographischer Sicht)', *Jahrbuch für ostdeutsche Volkskunde*, 21–53.

Hof, B., 1990, *Gesamtdeutsche Perspektiven zur Entwicklung von Bevölkerung und Arbeitskräfteangebot 1990 bis 2010*, Deutscher Instituts-Verlag, Cologne.

Kimminich, O., 1990, 'Heimat, Zuflucht, Gastland. Menschliches Schicksal im Spiegel des Rechts', in Bocklet, P. (ed.), *Zu viele Fremde im Land?*, Patmos, Düsseldorf, 86–112.

Knabe, B., 1992, 'Hypothesen zu künftigen Wanderungsströmen zwischen der Bundesrepublik Deutschland und osteuropäischen Ländern (1991 bis 2000). Osteuropäische Faktoren des zu erwartenden Wanderungsverhaltens', *Informationen zur Raumentwicklung*: 11–12, in press.

Koch, F., 1991, *Deutsche Aussiedler aus Rumänien. Analyse ihres räumlichen Verhaltens*, Böhlau, Cologne and Vienna (Studia Transylvanica 20).

Köllmann, W., 1983, 'Die Bevölkerungsentwicklung der Bundesrepublik', in Conze, W. and Lepsius, M.R. (eds), *Sozialgeschichte der Bundesrepublik Deutschland*, Klett, Stuttgart, 66–114.

Meier-Braun, K.-H., 1991, 'Auf dem Weg zur multikulturellen Gesellschaft?', *Zeitschrift für Kulturaustausch*, 41(1): 9–26.

Oberndörfer, D., 1991, *Die offene Republik. Zur Zukunft Deutschlands und Europas*, Herder, Freiburg, Basle and Vienna.

Oswald, I., 1991, 'Die Öffnung der osteuropäischen Grenzen — Folgen für Osteuropa', *Die Neue Gesellschaft, Frankfurter Hefte*, 5: 423–8.

Raeff, M., 1990, *Russia abroad. A cultural history of the Russian emigration, 1919–1939*, Oxford University Press, New York and Oxford.

Salt, J., 1989, 'A comparative overview of international trends and types,

1950–80', *International Migration Review*, 23(3): 431–56.

Schmidt, E. and Tittel, G., 1990, 'Haupttendenzen der Migration in der DDR im Zeitraum 1981–1989', *Raumforschung und Raumordnung*, 4–5: 244–50.

Schulz, E., 1990, 'Veränderte Rahmenbedingungen für die Vorausberechnung der Bevölkerungsentwicklung in der Bundesrepublik Deutschland', *Vierteljahreshefte DIW*, 2–3: 169–83.

Sommer, B. and Fleischer, H., 1991, 'Bevölkerungsentwicklung 1989', *Wirtschaft und Statistik*, 2: 81–8.

Steinmann, G., 1991, 'Immigration as a remedy for birth dearth: the case of West Germany', in Lutz, W. (ed.), *Future demographic trends in Europe and North America*, Academic Press, London, 337–57.

Tribalat, M., 1991, 'Chronique de l'immigration', *Population*, 46(1): 113–43.

Weickhardt, W., 1991, 'Flüchtlinge und Asylsuchende — ein Überblick', *Zeitschrift für Kulturaustausch*, 41(1): 61–4.

Wendt, H., 1991, 'Die deutsch-deutschen Wanderungen — Bilanz einer 40 jährigen Geschichte von Flucht und Ausreise', *Deutschland-Archiv*, 24(4): 386–95.

Widgren, J., 1990, 'International migration and regional stability', *International Affairs*, 66(4): 749–66.

Chapter 15

Third World immigrants in Italy

Armando Montanari and Antonio Cortese[1]

Introduction

There has been a steady drop in migration from Italy towards Central and Northern Europe since the early 1970s. This slow-down in the rate of emigration, which has turned out to be definitive, can be attributed to the first oil crisis in 1973–4 and the resulting productive, economic and social transformations which led to a radical change in the migration scenarios throughout the whole of Southern Europe, for decades a reservoir of migrant labour. Although migration has not come to a complete halt, the number of migrants returning to Italy now more or less balances the lower rate of emigration. Actually, Italy first achieved a positive migration balance as early as 1972. This was due not only to the increasing importance (relative to emigration) of returning migrants, but also to the appearance on the Italian scene at about the same time of rising numbers of immigrants from Third World countries.

From the start it proved difficult to gauge the real dimensions of migration to Italy from Third World countries. The official statistics provided data only on migrants with regular residence permits and did not take into account so-called 'hidden' migration. Hidden migration refers to foreigners without regular permits, either because their permits have expired (*irregolari* or 'irregulars'), or because they never had one (*clandestini* or 'clandestines'). With the introduction of new laws in 1990, there has been a marked reduction of hidden migration and the October 1991 Census is expected to provide relatively precise qualitative and quantitative data.

The Recommendation of the United Nations (1980) on migration statistics and on the definition of what constitutes an immigrant has not been interpreted uniformly in all countries. This is partly owing to the need for the definition to evolve along with the phenomenon itself, according to its connotations in various countries and regions. In operational terms Italy has found it difficult to establish criteria for defining migratory flows as such, within the more general context of people entering the country (Natale 1989). Italy defines an immigrant as an individual who does not hold Italian citizenship, and who cannot be classed as a tourist, a business visitor, a person in transit, a member of the diplomatic service or of the armed forces of allied countries. However, following the sudden increase in the number of migrants from the Third World, Italy will have to find a way of defining more rigorously the characteristics and dimensions of migration.

In addition, the recent political and social upheavals under way in Europe have led many people to migrate to Italy from the former planned economy countries: Poland, Yugoslavia, Romania and now (1991) Albania. Although technically speaking these are not Third World countries, they pose Italy similar problems. Hence in this chapter we use the more general term 'less developed countries' (LDCs).

For the moment at least, other categories of migrants to Italy must also be included when calculating the number of LDC migrants, although this can reduce the significance of the data. These categories include former Italians (i.e., who have lost their nationality) returning to Italy, students, members of religious orders, foreign nomadic populations (gypsies, travelling people etc.) and political refugees.

In this chapter we shall try to define the characteristics of migration to Italy of people from East European countries, Africa, Asia and Central and South America. We shall take into consideration the possible reasons for these migratory flows and refer to some of the many studies that have been made in recent years to define — qualitatively and quantitatively — foreign migration to Italy. We shall consider how the situation can be expected to evolve over time, highlighting the particular problems that migration raises in terms of restructuring Italy's urban services and infrastructures (Todisco 1990).

Evolution and development of migration

Italy passed from being a country of emigration to one of immigration extremely rapidly. This might explain why the administrative structures of the country were not ready to cope with the phenomenon. Throughout the 1970s Italy had been mainly concerned with solving the problems of the many Italian migrants abroad: 5.5 million still holding Italian citizenship and tens of millions of Italian origin scattered all over the world. More than 5 million Italians had emigrated between 1876 and 1900, almost 10 million between 1900 and 1920, more than 3 million between 1920 and 1945 and almost 7 million between 1945 and 1970. In just one century a total of about 25 million Italians had emigrated, almost 12 million to countries outside Europe (Birindelli and Visco 1976). We should bear these figures in mind when considering migration to Italy of foreign citizens from countries with a large community of Italian origin.

From the 1950s, Italy's government agencies at both national and local level have also had to cope with strong migratory flows within the country itself, particularly from rural to urban areas and from southern to northern regions. Thus, migration into Italy of individuals mainly from

Third World countries further exacerbated some of the many problems that already existed and for which a satisfactory solution had yet to be found: for example, in the fields of housing, infrastructures and social services. Foreign immigration also posed problems that were more of a political nature, for example, the right to vote (an issue which has still not been satisfactorily resolved for Italians resident abroad). From the end of the 1970s the question was repeatedly posed concerning foreigners resident in Italy: should they be allowed to vote, at least in the administrative elections? In more general terms, the problem was a cultural one: the culture of a country which had traditionally been a country of emigration had to come to terms with the fact that it was now a country of immigration without confusing the problems of the former with those of the latter (Birindelli 1988). At first, the fact that Italy was a country with both an emigrant and an immigrant population posed some serious problems; in particular, Italy was reluctant to introduce restrictive immigrant measures. In the end, this resulted in the failure to formulate a satisfactory government policy to regulate migratory flows and at the same time guarantee and protect those who entered the country legally.

The phenomenon of foreign immigration into Italy is very heterogeneous in nationality and type of migrant, and it has impacted on the various Italian regions in different ways. Curiously, one of the first regions to be affected was Sicily, itself a poor region and one with a long emigration history of its own. However, already by the early 1970s foreign migrants registered a notable presence on the island. Proximity to a principal source area for the immigrants (North Africa) was one factor explaining this situation; another was the way in which the Sicilian labour market, dislocated by perhaps excessive out-migration and by the effects of the 1967 west Sicilian earthquake, created openings for low-grade migrant labour in agricultural work, fishing, construction and petty trading. The Sicilian example can be used to demonstrate the spatio-temporal process of penetration of flows of foreign migrants (see Figure 15.1). Until the mid-1970s there were about fifty municipalities with migrant communities. They were mainly coastal areas, along the Mazara del Vallo–Palermo axis in the west and the Marsala–Modica axis in the south (Cusumano 1976). It was only at the beginning of the 1980s that foreign migrants started to take up residence in the municipalities of inner Sicily between Catania and Enna (Guarrasi 1988).

Another way of documenting the development of foreign immigration in Italy is via the evolving political and academic interest in the topic: both the media and the scholarly community have become deeply interested in this changing aspect of the Italian demographic scene. As Figure 15.2 shows, many scientific publications on the presence of foreigners in Italy have been published since 1976, when migration into Italy started to increase to the level where it was regarded as a national 'problem'. Some 624 works had been published by 1990, covering the

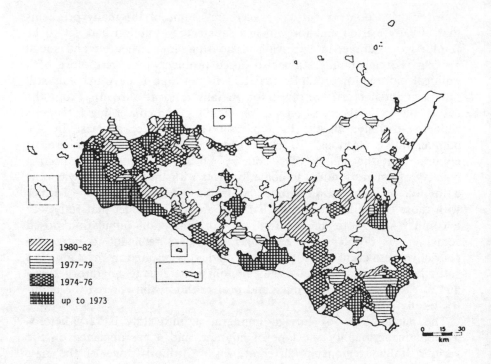

Figure 15.1   Foreign migrants in Sicilian municipalities by period of first
          settlement, 1973–82

Source: Guarrasi 1988.

following aspects: general studies; statistical sources (analyses and methods of recording); immigration and the labour market; living conditions of migrants; specific groups (refugees, students, domestics); individual ethnic communities, their situation and characteristics in particular cities, zones and regions of Italy (Cortese 1991a).

As far as the immigration itself was concerned, it was essential to define the process quantitatively and qualitatively. In the early years, only the legal aspects of the phenomenon were known, in so far as the only data available referred to those who had registered in the various municipalities or held a residence permit. However, even these data did not agree. The municipalities registered foreigners independently of whether or not they had a permit. It became compulsory to have a residence permit only in 1989 with the introduction of new registration regulations. Although the residence permits issued by the police contain much information, they are not suitable — unless reprocessed — for a statistical assessment for various reasons: they do not record information on minors under the age of 18, who are classified as dependants; they include in the final count permits that have not been renewed; and they

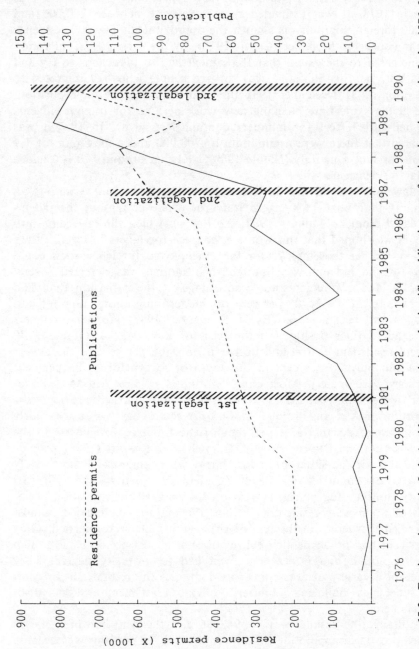

Figure 15.2 Foreign migrants in Italy (residence permits) and scientific publications on foreign immigrants in Italy, 1976–90

Source: Censis 1988; Cortese 1990; Istat 1990a and 1990b.

report aggregated data for territorial units under their own administrative jurisdiction.

The first fairly reliable, although very approximate, assessment was made in 1978. It was estimated that there were between 280,000 and 400,000 foreign migrants, as against the approximately 200,000 residence permits issued by the police (Censis 1979). By the early 1980s, migration had increased to the extent that Parliament had to take steps to try and regulate it. Its first initiative was to give people who had migrated to Italy prior to 31 December 1981 the chance to legalize their position, while at the same time blocking new work permits for foreign citizens. This had little effect for numbers continued to grow. In 1987 it was estimated that there were a minimum of 700,000 and a maximum of 1.1 million foreigners in Italy (Natale 1988), and that around 570,000 had a regular residence permit.

A law was passed on 30 December 1986 (No. 943) granting an indemnity to foreigners living in Italy for whatever reason; the indemnity dated from 28 January 1987, the day on which the law came into force. It was hoped that this would encourage foreigners to legalize their position.[2] Either the employer or the unemployed foreign worker could apply for the indemnity. Although the deadline was deferred several times, far fewer foreigners took advantage of the provision than had been expected. Only 20–25 per cent of 'hidden' migration came out into the open and became legal. By 30 September 1988, 118,706 foreigners had legalized their position on the basis of Law 943/86. Of these, 70 per cent resided in central and northern Italy (66 per cent of these were males) and only 30 per cent in the south or Mezzogiorno (85 per cent of whom were males). More than two-thirds of those in the Mezzogiorno were from Africa; in the central and northern regions the proportion of Africans dropped to 44.3 per cent. There was also a fairly large group of Asians (35.1 per cent of the legalized foreigners) in the centre-north (Istat 1991a, p. 66). Carvelli and Rossini (1988) provide more detail for the situation in Lombardy where migrants from literally hundreds of countries — Egypt, China, Philippines, Morocco, Sri Lanka, Tunisia, Yugoslavia, and so on — legalized their position. Two-thirds of them were resident in Milan, the majority unmarried (almost 70 per cent), whereas in the rest of the region most were married. Only 10 per cent had no academic qualifications at all; 23 per cent had a high school diploma; and 6 per cent even had a university degree. They worked in a variety of areas: most as domestics (more than 30 per cent) and others as builders' labourers, clerks, craftsmen, waiters, dishwashers, etc.

For many, the results of Law 943/86 and the way in which it was applied proved disappointing (Maccheroni 1989). In part this was because the 'indemnity' was not followed by the introduction of provisions governing the access of non-European citizens to Italy, preventing the entry and residence of 'false tourists'. Nor were steps taken to expel them from the country. The political debate on the issue was lively and even heated within the government itself (Costa 1989).

On 20 February 1990 another law was passed (Law 39), containing 'provisions for political asylum, the entry and residence of non-EC citizens, the legalization of the position of non-EC citizens and stateless persons already in State territory'. This law gave those who had entered the country illegally another chance to legalize their position. By 30 June 1990, 217,000 foreign citizens had taken advantage of this law.

As a result of the impact of these events and the ensuing political and cultural debate, the Italian Cabinet sponsored a National Conference on Emigration in Rome in June 1990. On that occasion, the National Statistical Institute (Istat) presented its estimate of the number of migrants resident in Italy in 1989 (Istat 1991a). During the Conference, forms of joint co-operation among the various bodies concerned were initiated, thereby contributing to the statistical analysis of the data available on residence permits.

On 31 December 1989, 490,388 foreigners had been granted a residence permit. Istat had estimated that in 1989 a total of 1,144,000 foreign migrants (963,000 from non-EC countries) were resident in the country. By 31 December 1990, 781,000 foreigners held permits, indicating a drastic drop in 'hidden' migration which up to that point had seemed to be rapidly becoming a pathological and irreducible phenomenon.

Geographical distribution of migrants

The year 1989 was the last for which two official data sets were available: that relating to residence permits issued by the police, and that provided by municipal registry offices. According to the new registration regulations introduced in 1989 and Law 39/90, foreign citizens were required to produce a residence permit in order to be able to register in the municipality. On 31 December 1989, as noted, 490,000 foreign citizens were registered as having a residence permit; the figures recorded at the municipal registry offices indicated 434,000 foreign presences, around 89 per cent of the former figure. However, the two data sets are not strictly comparable, first, because a certain percentage of migrants with a residence permit did not register at the municipal registry offices, and second, because a certain percentage of those registered in the municipal registry offices did not have a residence permit. Another important point to bear in mind is that the difference between the number of registrations in the two lists — 57,000 people — consisted almost entirely (99 per cent) of citizens from thirty-one LDCs, including three Eastern European countries: Yugoslavia, Poland and Romania (Istat 1991a, p. 62). As for citizens from Egypt and Vietnam, however, those with residence permits were even fewer than those registered at the municipal registry offices — respectively 10,200 versus 11,600 Egyptians, and 2,300 versus 2,600 Vietnamese.

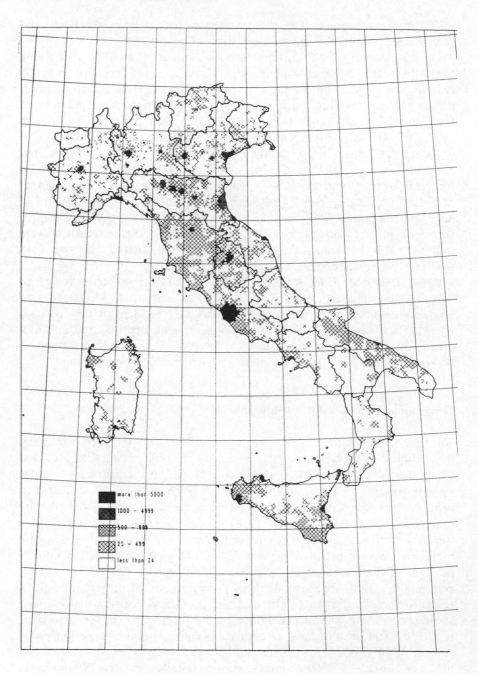

Figure 15.3   Foreign migrants present in Italy on 31 December 1989 by
municipality: absolute numbers

The data we have on the residence permits issued up to 31 December 1989 were drawn up by Istat at the municipal level of Italy's approximately 8,000 *comuni* and are the most recent figures we have at that detailed level of disaggregation. The Istat analysis of the presence of foreign migrants by municipality (Figure 15.3)[3] shows that 44 per cent of the migrant population are concentrated in the urban areas of six large regional capitals: Rome (30 per cent), Milan (9 per cent), Turin (2 per cent), Genoa (1.5 per cent), Florence (1.5 per cent) and Palermo (1 per cent).

We also find foreign communities of 1,000–5,000 migrants in some regional capitals of northern Italy (Bolzano and Trieste), in some provincial capitals of Lombardy (Varese, Brescia, Pavia), and within the urban network of Veneto (Verona, Padua, Venice) and Emilia-Romagna (Parma, Reggio, Modena, Bologna, Ravenna, Rimini). In central and southern Italy only some regional capitals have a large migrant community of more than 1,000 persons (Perugia, Ancona, Naples, Bari and Cagliari), and only one provincial capital (Messina). There is also an important fishing centre on the west coast of Sicily (Mazara del Vallo) with a large resident migrant population, mainly of Tunisians.

The map showing the spatial distribution of migrants as a ratio of the overall resident population (Figure 15.4) highlights a number of recurrent situations. In Trentino-Alto Adige, Friuli-Venezia Giulia, Valle d'Aosta, Emilia, Tuscany, Umbria and Latium, foreigners are distributed fairly evenly throughout the territory. In Piedmont, Lombardy, Veneto, Romagna, Marche and Abruzzi, the migrant distribution is uneven, foreigners being present only along certain particular axes: the Ligurian coast, the Adriatic coast, the Bergamo–Venice axis, and the area between Milan and the Swiss border. The smaller migrant community in Sicily is mainly concentrated in the area along the west coast of the island between Palermo and Agrigento, and down the east coast between Messina and Gela. In the rest of the Mezzogiorno there are, relatively speaking, fewer migrants and their distribution is confined to the following small areas: along the coast of Campania between Mondragone and Naples, and again south of Battipaglia; along the Adriatic coast of Apulia, in the Ostuni–Brindisi–Lecce axis; along the south-eastern coast of Calabria; along the north-western coast of Sardinia, between La Maddalena and Orosei; and along the southern Sardinian coast around Cagliari.

It was earlier noted that Istat had estimated that 1,144,000 migrants were resident in Italy in 1989 and 963,000 of these were from countries outside the EC (Istat 1991a). The estimate was made on the basis of both internal Istat sources (1981 population census, municipal registrations, national accounts, education statistics, prison statistics), and of external sources, including those of the Ministry of the Interior (residence permits, applications for legalization according to law 39/90, refugee lists), the Ministry of Labour and Social Security (unemployment and

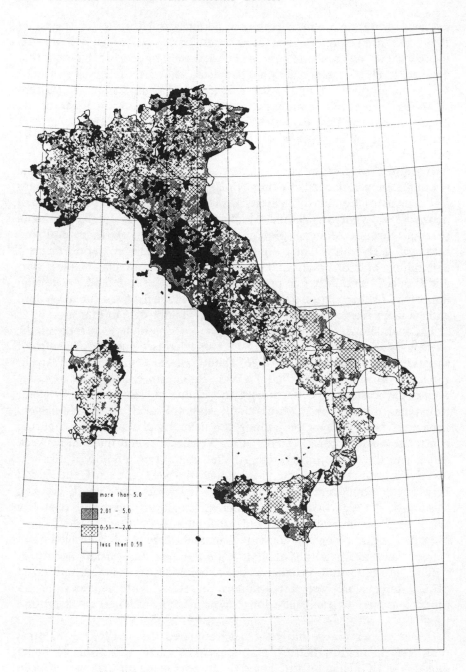

Figure 15.4   Foreign migrants present in Italy on 31 December 1989 by
municipality: ratio of foreigners to 100 residents

employment lists), the National Social Security Institute (insurance files), the Central Foreign Students Office (foreign students), and Caritas (social and welfare services provided by church-related organizations). The national data were then compared with the regional data processed by decentralized Istat offices. The figures were checked and also discussed with a select number of 'privileged' observers.

If we look at the ration of foreigners per 1,000 residents by region, we see that Umbria, where there is a very large foreign student community, has the highest ration (71.8 per 1,000). However, the data does not properly differentiate between migrants from Third World countries and other migrants. Migrants are simply divided into two classes: those from EC countries and those from non-EC countries. Hence migrants from developing countries (which obviously include members of religious communities, especially in Latium, and students, especially in Umbria) and those from the United States and Switzerland are all lumped into the one category. According to the Istat figures, 43 per cent of the migrants from non-EC countries reside in three regions: Latium, Sicily and Lombardy. Each of these regions has a migrant community of more than 100,000 people. Piedmont, Veneto, Emilia-Romagna, Tuscany and Campania each have a migrant community of 50,000–100,000 migrants, 34 per cent from non-EC countries (Istat 1991a, p. 30). It is instructive to compare these data with the figures calculated from the residence permits. On the basis of permits, it seems that 21 per cent of the foreigners from non-EC countries reside in the Mezzogiorno, whereas according to the Istat estimate the percentage is 31 per cent, not far short of the Mezzogiorno's share of the Italian population — 36 per cent.

Migrants in Italy after the passing of Law 39/90

We saw earlier that following the introduction of Law 39/90, more than 217,000 foreign citizens had legalized their position by 30 June 1990. More than 90 per cent were from LDCs: almost 40 per cent from Mediterranean Africa, with Morocco in the lead (23 per cent) and Tunisia next (12 per cent). The remaining 60 per cent were from other African countries (mainly Senegal, Egypt and Ghana), three Asian countries (Philippines, China and Sri Lanka) and two East European countries (Yugoslavia and Poland). More than half (53 per cent) resided in three regions: Latium, Lombardy and Sicily. In Sicily the number of migrants who legalized their position was even higher (102 per cent) than the number who were registered as having a regular permit on 31 December 1989. This ratio was also higher than the national average (38 per cent) in Sardinia (80 per cent) and Emilia-Romagna (58 per cent), although much lower in Umbria (6 per cent) with its large student community (Istat 1991b, p. 4).

Table 15.1　Regional distribution of foreigners in Italy with a residence permit on 31 December 1990 ('000)

Region	Eastern Europe	Africa	Asia	Latin America	Total
Piedmont	1.7	18.7	7.7	4.4	32.5
Valle d'Aosta	0.0	0.5	0.1	0.1	0.7
Lombardy	5.8	37.0	23.2	10.9	76.9
Trentino-Alto Adige	0.5	2.5	0.5	0.9	4.4
Veneto	1.9	11.5	5.5	3.2	22.1
Friuli-Venezia Giulia	1.5	1.1	1.1	1.2	4.9
Liguria	0.7	6.3	2.5	2.3	11.8
Emilia-Romagna	2.4	18.3	7.1	3.6	31.4
Tuscany	3.9	12.1	13.4	5.2	34.6
Umbria	1.9	4.5	10.8	2.2	19.4
Marche	0.9	3.0	1.6	1.9	7.4
Latium	16.6	49.9	54.9	19.3	140.7
Abruzzi	1.0	1.9	1.1	1.8	5.8
Molise	0.1	0.4	0.1	0.3	0.9
Campania	2.0	16.3	6.0	3.6	27.9
Apulia	0.5	7.3	1.3	0.9	10.0
Basilicata	0.1	1.0	0.2	0.3	1.6
Calabria	0.3	4.2	1.0	0.9	6.4
Sicily	1.3	37.0	7.2	2.1	47.6
Sardinia	0.3	4.6	0.5	0.3	5.7
Italy	43.4	238.1	145.8	65.4	492.7

Source: Istat 1991b, p. 5.

On 31 December 1990, more than 781,000 foreigners were recorded as having a regular residence permit. The fifteen largest foreign communities (making up 80 per cent of the total of foreigners) included migrants from six of the industrially more advanced countries (United States, Germany, United Kingdom, France, Greece and Switzerland), who represented almost one-quarter (24.5 per cent) of all migrants, and from nine other countries (Morocco, Tunisia, Philippines, Yugoslavia, Senegal, Egypt, China, Poland and Iran), who represented 35.7 per cent (Istat 1991b, p. 3). The following five regions had the highest concentration of foreign migrants (62 per cent of the total): Latium (197,000: 25.2 per cent), Lombardy (117,000: 15 per cent), Sicily (62,000: 7.9 per cent), Tuscany (61,000: 7.8 per cent) and Umbria (50,000: 6.4 per cent). The ratio to the resident population (the number of foreigners per 100 inhabitants) was highest in Umbria (6.1 per cent), Latium (3.8 per cent), Tuscany (1.7 per cent), Trentino-Alto Adige (1.5 per cent) and Friuli-Venezia Giulia (1.4 per cent). An attempt at gauging the number of LDC immigrants can be made by totalling the number of migrants from Africa, Asia, Latin America and Eastern Europe: 493,000, i.e., 63 per cent of all foreign migrants (Istat 1991b, p. 5).

Table 15.1 shows the data by continent of origin and region of residence in Italy. The 238,000 Africans accounted for 48 per cent of all LDC migrants. Most of the African migrants (61 per cent) are from the southern Mediterranean rim countries, with a high percentage of those resident in Sicily (18 per cent) coming from Tunisia (42 per cent). The number of Africans from non-Mediterranean countries was above the national average in Campania (54 per cent) and Latium (49 per cent). The 146,000 Asians accounted for 30 per cent of the migrants from LDCs. They were concentrated mainly in Latium (38 per cent), Lombardy (16 per cent), Tuscany (9 per cent) and Umbria (7 per cent). There were 65,000 migrants from Central and South America — 13 per cent of the total number of LDC migrants — distributed among many regions, including Latium (29 per cent), Lombardy (17 per cent), Tuscany (8 per cent), and Piedmont (7 per cent). The 43,000 migrants from East European countries accounted for 9 per cent of all migrants listed in Table 15.1 and were concentrated chiefly in Latium (40 per cent), Lombardy (14 per cent) and Tuscany (9 per cent).

Figure 15.5 shows the ratio between the Third World immigrant population (including Eastern Europe) and the resident population (on 31 December 1990) in the ninety-five Italian provinces. In the north, the ratio is particularly high in the urban areas of Turin–Vercelli, Milan–Bergamo, Verona–Vicenza, Genoa, and along the Parma–Reggio Emilia–Modena–Bologna and Ravenna axis. In central Italy, in the provinces located between Florence and Rome (a belt of territory characterized mainly by small and medium-sized urban settlements), the number of foreign residents is fairly homogeneous. The highest concentration is in the province of Perugia, which has a large foreign student community (Cortese 1982). In the Mezzogiorno, a high ratio is found only in the Sicilian provinces of Palermo, Trapani and Ragusa.

In 1990 the gender ratio of foreign migrants in Italy was 75 females for every 100 males. However, the ratio is lower for migrants from Africa (26) and Asia (67) and is particularly low for Mediterranean Africa (12). Campani (1989) provides more information on sex ratios based on earlier data sets. The 'old age' index, namely the ratio of those over 60 years of age to those under 26, was lower than the Italian national average (36.5) for all the developing countries and again was particularly low for Mediterranean Africa (3.5).

Residence permits were issued mainly for work-related reasons (49 per cent), with much higher values for Mediterranean Africa (71.5 per cent, although only 17 per cent for Libya), West Africa (71 per cent) and the Far East (70.5 per cent), Japan excluded. About 10 per cent of the permits were granted for reasons of study, with the highest values for migrants from Oceania (14 per cent), Europe (13 per cent), North America (11 per cent) and countries such as Japan (34 per cent) and Libya (19 per cent). Family reasons were higher than the national average (13 per cent) especially for migrants from countries with a large

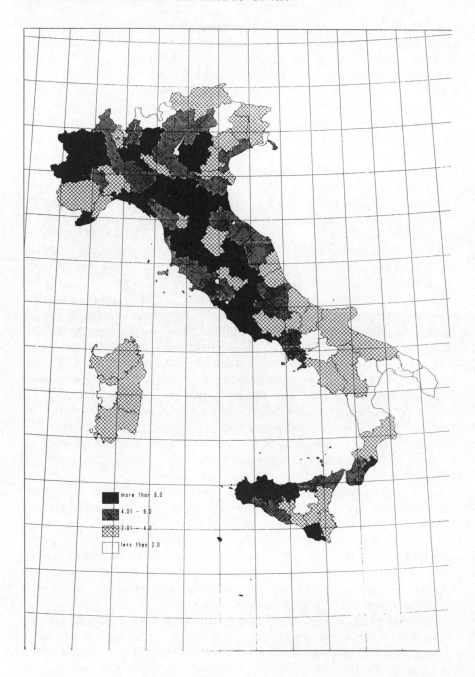

Figure 15.5   Migrants from Africa, Asia, Latin America and non-EC Europe
on 31 December 1990, by Italian province, per 100 residents

community of Italian origin: United States and Canada (40.5 per cent), Brazil (27 per cent), Argentina (24 per cent), Oceania (18 per cent) and EC countries (15 per cent). In considering the return to Italy of foreign citizens whose parents were Italian migrants or who had themselves migrated from Italy, a distinction is necessary: some return to Italy to enjoy the fruits of economic success acquired abroad, whereas others (in increasing numbers) decide to come back to Italy from countries such as Brazil or Argentina where recession has been increasing and jobs have become scarce.

If we look at residence permits in terms of their regional distribution, we see that in the northern regions they are issued mainly for work: Emilia-Romagna (62 per cent) and Lombardy (60.5 per cent) are in the lead. Umbria (4 per cent) is at the bottom of the list; here many applications are made for tourism (39 per cent) and study (52.5 per cent). Family reasons were the main reason for applying for permits in the south, with higher than average values in Molise (29 per cent), Apulia (25 per cent), Campania (22 per cent) and Calabria (20 per cent).

Current data do not permit a complete overview of the activities performed by LDC migrants. According to some unpublished Istat estimates, it is believed that around 9 per cent of migrants work in agriculture, 28 per cent in industry and the rest in the service sector. The estimate that more than 90 per cent of immigrants work in industry and services is confirmed by the fact that at least 80 per cent of all migrants from LDCs live in urban areas. If we knew exactly what activities were performed by these migrants, we should be able to judge whether their presence has an impact on the employment of local workers or whether the migrants are employed in areas that local workers reject. We should also be able to define more accurately the role of migrants in Italy's economic growth. It may be that, generally speaking, their role has been largely negligible (this could be true, for example, of street-hawking or washing windscreens at traffic lights) or even counterproductive (for example, prostitution, petty theft, drug-trafficking). Although there has been considerable discussion in Italy on the presence in the country of migrants from the LDCs, and numerous episodes of hostility and violence towards them, including even cases of murder of foreign workers, who are often involved in illegal activities,[4] so far no national political groups have assumed an explicitly xenophobic position or tried to canvass more votes by suggesting the closing of frontiers and the deportation of foreigners (see Chapter 8 in this book).

Although on the national level there are few reliable statistics on the economic activities of LDC migrants, it is possible to gain more information on the local level from various surveys that have been conducted. For example, according to a recent study in Campania (Calvanese 1991), 43 per cent of migrants from LDCs are employed in trade, 41.5 per cent in private services and almost 5 per cent in agriculture. All the migrants from Senegal, about 80 per cent of those from Morocco, and around 12 per cent of those from Tunisia are self-employed. For all other nationalities, self-employment is negligible and in all cases under 10 per cent. It is also noteworthy that migrants from certain countries work in one sector only. For example, workers from Cape Verde, the Philippines and Vietnam are all employed as domestics, or as restaurant and hotel workers in the private service sector; workers from Senegal are employed only in street-hawking; workers from Somalia, Ethiopia and Sri Lanka are employed mainly in the private service sector; and workers from Morocco only in trade. Migrant workers from other nations are more evenly distributed among various economic activities: workers from Ghana in trade, agriculture and building; those from Tunisia in trade and building; and those from Poland in trade, building, industry and agriculture. These generalizations are useful in creating a broad picture of the character of immigrant economic activities in Italy, although really accurate and insightful information can be acquired only through fieldwork — and this is a daunting task (Federici 1986).

Conclusion

The data on residence permits and estimates made in the 1989–90 period are useful for assessing the real size of the foreign migrant population in Italy and how this can be expected to grow in the future. This conclusion will first reconstruct the bare bones of the statistical picture, and second, review the present situation of immigrants in Italy in 1991 and likely trends in the near future.

In 1989, 190,000 migrants from EC countries and from other economically more advanced countries (United States, Switzerland, Austria, Japan, Canada, etc.) had a residence permit; and 300,000 from LDCs. In the same year Istat estimated that there were 963,000 immigrants from non-EC countries and 880,000 from LDCs, of whom 580,000 were illegal. By 1990, 288,000 migrants from EC and other advanced countries, and 493,000 from LDCs had residence permits. Our updating to the year 1990, on the basis of the 1989 Istat figures, yields estimates that in 1990 there were approximately 910,000 migrants from LDCs and Eastern Europe, of whom around 420,000 were illegal. Thus, in just one year — from the end of 1989 to the end of 1990 — the number of illegal migrants dropped by almost 30 per cent. Current indicators seem to point to a continuation of this trend

The year just ended, 1991, has been a particularly difficult one for migration. There has been a great deal of pressure from countries of Eastern Europe (Albania and Yugoslavia) geographically close to Italy in which the social, political and economic conditions have been deteriorating rapidly. In response to this and other pressures, the Italian government, along with other EC countries, has taken a more severe stance on illegal immigration during 1991.

Further insights into the entity and nature of the Italian immigration phenomenon will be gained when the full results of the thirteenth General Population Census of 20 October 1991 are known.[5] The census requires citizens to fill in specific forms recording data on the foreign population resident in the country. The form is composed of two parts. The first has to be filled in by all foreigners present and contains questions on sex, date of birth, civil status, citizenship, living conditions, co-residence, and length of stay in Italy. The second part is only for those foreigners who have been staying at hotels for less than a month and requests information on level of education, main reason for coming to Italy, and whether they have relatives and a job (Cortese 1991b). It remains to be seen how these data are used, although the availability of more information on migration and a stronger government stance on illegal migration could foster a national migration policy better able to protect those who have already migrated to Italy and lead to the definition of annual quotas of new migration.

Notes

1. Although this chapter is a joint effort, the Introduction and the section on the geographical distribution of migrants was written by Cortese, the rest by Montanari.
2. During the 1980s at least three other countries followed a similar procedure. In France 132,000 foreigners legalized their status during 1980–2, in Spain 44,000 during 1985–6, and in the United States 3 million during 1987–8. These figures are from a 1990 informational note of the OECD Secretariat.
3. Figures 15.3, 15.4 and 15.5 were prepared by A, Montanari with the computing assistance of C. Magnarapa within the framework of the CNR Strategic Project on Italian metropolitan areas, and are partly drawn from an atlas soon to be published. The equipment was provided by CNUCE/CNR.
4. In 1988, foreigners, who make up perhaps 2 per cent of the Italian population, contributed 11 per cent of those imprisoned in Italy. In some regions — Friuli, Tuscany, Umbria, Marche — they were between a quarter and a third of the prison population. Whilst these figures are highly suggestive, they are also potentially misleading. It is well known from other countries such as Britain and the United States that the police are more likely to suspect and arrest foreigners and blacks. For a revealing account of the over-reaction of the Italian authorities to the presence of immigrants see Andall 1990.
5. Provisional results of the 1991 census issued in March 1992 were disappointing on the immigrant issue. Only 502,000 immigrants were recorded and there was thought to be a marked underestimate of foreigners in the south of Italy.

References

Andall, J., 1990, 'New migrants, old conflicts: the recent immigration into Italy', *The Italianist*, 10: 151–74.

Birindelli, A.M., 1988, *Les étrangers en Italie: analogies et differences avec les Italiens à l'étranger*, Séminaire de Calabre (1986) on 'Les migrations internationales: problèmes de mesure, évolutions récentes et efficacité des politiques', Paper No. 3.

Birindelli, A.M. and Visco, G., 1976, 'L'emigrazione italiana con particolare riguardo all'emigrazione continentale nell'ultimo dopoguerra', in Istituto di Demografia (ed.), *L'emigrazione dal bacino mediterraneo verso l'Europa industrializzata*, Franco Angeli, Milan, 169–219.

Calvanese, F., 1991, 'Fattori di spinta e progetto migratorio', in Calvanese, F. and Pugliese, E. (eds), *La presenza straniera in Italia: il caso della Campania*, Franco Angeli, Milan, 86–121.

Campani, G., 1989, 'Du Tiers-Monde à l'Italie: une nouvelle immigration féminine', *Revue Européenne des Migrations Internationales*, 5(2): 29–47.

Carvelli, A. and Rossini, L., 1988, *La presenza straniera extracomunitaria in Lombardia*, Regione Lombardia, Milan.

Censis, 1979, *I lavoratori stranieri in Italia*, Istituto Poligrafico e Zecca dello Stato, Rome.

Censis, 1988, 'Speciale emigrazioni: oltre la residualità', *Quindicinale di note e commenti*, No. 5.

Cortese, A., 1982, 'Gli studenti stranieri in Italia', *Affari Sociali Internazionali*, 10(3): 37–51.

Cortese, A., 1991a, 'Bibliografia sulla presenza straniera in Italia', in *Gli immigrati presenti in Italia, una stima per l'anno 1989*, Istat, Rome, 73–96.

Cortese, A., 1991b, 'Proposte operative per il censimento degli stranieri', in *Gli immigrati presenti in Italia, una stima per l'anno 1989*, Istat, Rome, 39–48.

Costa, R., 1989, 'L'immigrazione verso l'Italia e l'Europa nelle previsioni per i prossimi venticinque anni', in Maccheroni, C. and Mauri, A. (eds), *Le migrazioni dall'Africa Mediterranea verso l'Italia*, Giuffrè, Milan, 15–26.

Cusumano, A., 1976, *Il ritorno infelice. I tunisini in Sicilia*, Sellerio, Palermo.

Federici, N., 1986, 'Difficoltà e problemi di ricerche sul campo relative alla presenza straniera in Italia', *Studi Emigrazione*, 82–83: 315–21.

Guarrasi, V., 1982, 'Donna, emigrazione e società mediterranee. Riflessioni sull'immigrazione familiare a Mazara del Vallo', *Donna e Società*, November: 489–509.

Guarrasi, V., 1988, *L'emigrazione straniera in Sicilia*, CRIS, Palermo.

Istat, 1991a, *Gli immigrati presenti in Italia, una stima per l'anno 1989*, Istat, Rome.

Istat, 1991b, 'La presenza straniera in Italia: analisi statistica dei dati sui permessi di soggiorno — anni 1989–90', *Notiziario Istat*, 12(5).

Maccheroni, C., 'Introduzione', in Maccheroni, C. and Mauri, A. (eds), *Le migrazioni dall'Africa mediterranea verso l'Italia*, Giuffrè, Milan, 9–14.

Natale, M., 1988, *La presenza straniera in Italia*, IRP/CNR, Rome.

Natale, M. (ed.), 1989, *Analisi delle fonti statistiche per la misura dell'immigrazione straniera in Italia: esame e proposte*, Istat, Rome.

Todisco, E., 1990, *Alunni stranieri nelle scuole italiane*, CSER, Rome.

Chapter 16

Skilled international migration in Europe: the shape of things to come?

John Salt and Reuben Ford

Introduction

Most of the recent upsurge of interest in international migration has concentrated on potential mass 'compass' migrations (East–West, South–North, etc); however, there has been a growing recognition of the importance of the much smaller volume of movement among the highly skilled. The main reason for this is not hard to find. Modern industries and services increasingly rely upon the acquisition, deployment and use of human expertise to add value to their operations. Where this expertise is not available locally, employers may search for it abroad, often within their own internal labour markets.

Recognition of the importance of migration of the highly skilled partly underlies recent policy decisions by the main settlement immigration countries. During the 1980s Australia, Canada and the Unites States have rethought their immigration policies, putting heavier emphasis on 'quality' aspects. They have developed programmes to increase the number and proportion of the highly skilled in their overall intake. These developments draw attention to the international immigration market among the highly skilled. This market is both a feature of and driving-force behind the development of a global economy characterized by the internationalization of companies and of human resources.

The opening up of Eastern Europe has led to speculation about a massive brain drain to the West. However, it is difficult to see Eastern Europe as a major source of high-level expertise. Some highly skilled may move, for example specialists in certain key sectors of science, technology and medicine, and in the 'caring' professions (especially those, such as nursing, where salary levels in the West are low and vacancies are endemic); nevertheless, generally the skills possessed in the East are unlikely to be high enough, at least initially, for vacancies in the West. For many, the trek West will result in deskilling, a consequence of familiarity with outdated technologies or inefficient bureaucracies.

Despite the obvious importance of migration by the highly skilled to the development and management of the international economy, knowledge of the patterns and processes of their movement is poor.

There are few accessible data on the scale and nature of their migrations. Partly this is because their small numbers easily render them statistically 'invisible', particularly in sample surveys such as the British Labour Force Survey (LFS). It is also because such people are not perceived to be a 'problem'. Many of them are EC nationals moving within the Community, so they may escape statistical accounting.

There are other gaps in our knowledge. A small, but closely connected literature has built up to explain migrations within the international labour markets (ILMs) of multinational organizations (see, for example, Salt and Findlay 1989). This has seen the close interdependence between skilled international migration and individual career motives and has forecast the persistence of corporate transfers for the foreseeable future. However, we know little about how those movements which entail a change of residence, albeit temporary in many cases, interact with other forms of business movements, including short-term trips and longer-term assignments. Nor are we at all well informed about how ILM allocation of expertise internationally interacts with other ways of acquiring skills, notably by the use of specialist business service firms, such as consultancies, or by new forms of business association, such as joint ventures.

It is impossible in this chapter to tackle all these issues. The aim here is to use largely unpublished empirical data relating to the United Kingdom to establish the main trends and characteristics of migration by the highly skilled. The chapter starts with a brief discussion of contemporary labour demand in Western Europe, with particular reference to the need for expertise, and attempts a definition of the highly skilled. It then moves on to analyse the international migration response so far as the United Kingdom is concerned. This section of the chapter begins with a review of the mass movement in skills accounted for by business travel. It then concentrates specifically on the patterns and characteristics of migration by professionals, employers, managers and technical specialists. The chapter concludes by suggesting how patterns are likely to evolve.

Europe's changing labour demand

Within Europe, large and permanent levels of unemployment exist which combine with frequently voiced shortages of some skills to create mismatches in the labour market (EC Commission 1991). These mismatches reflect structural changes in demand, with the growth of knowledge-based jobs at the expense of unskilled and semi-skilled ones. In addition to the new demands of technology, which have resulted in new processes and products, there has been a growing demand for administrative and managerial skills, together with professional expertise in a range of business services. Projections of occupational change in the United Kingdom, for example, show scientific and engineering professions increasing by 27 per cent between 1990 and 2000; teaching, health and other professions up by 26 per cent; corporate managers and administrators by 18 per cent. In contrast skilled manual trades are expected to decline by 8–10 per cent, semi-skilled operatives in industry and agriculture by 19 per cent (Institute for Employment Research 1991).

These changes suggest an increasing emphasis on the acquisition of expertise, adding to an already high level of demand. Projections of employment needs throughout the 1990s stress the demand for scientists, technicians and highly skilled workers in general. The German IAB Prognos study, for example, forecast a rise of 3.4 million highly skilled jobs during the period 1985–2010 (EC Commission 1991).

This skilling of demand foretells little opportunity for mass migrations of low-skilled guestworkers into the Western European labour market, at least not without a measure of labour market deregulation inconceivable in present circumstances. In contrast, demand for high-level skills will be much more buoyant.

Who are the highly skilled?

The highly skilled do not constitute a homogeneous group. In broad terms they may be described as professional, managerial and technical specialists, most of whom have a tertiary level qualification or its equivalent. However, this group as a whole consists of a series of largely self-contained and non-competing subgroups, among whom levels and duration of training are such as to lead to low elasticities of supply. Training represents an enormous investment by both employer and employee, often to develop very specific skills. Sometimes these skills relate to individual technologies, or even firms. To fill vacancies at these levels, companies have evolved complex recruitment and career development strategies, many of which entail migration, frequently internationally.

It is not possible here to discuss in any detail the various ways of defining and categorizing this heterogeneous group as a whole. One major subgroup consists of those who work for multinational organizations. Some of them are senior managers, exercising powerful control functions: a detached élite identified by their international mobility and high incomes (Standing 1991). Others occupy supporting roles, bringing to the company specific business and technological skills. Their international mobility often reflects individual product developments. More junior still are trainee managers, increasingly the recipients of carefully co-ordinated and controlled career development programmes, which often include international mobility experience (Meyer-Dohm 1991).

Not all the internationally mobile highly skilled personnel work for multinational companies. The growing world demand for business services and technical skills has created a group of quasi-independent professional and technical workers, many of them consultants, frequently very mobile internationally. Another group includes those who work for governments and supra-national bodies, into whose careers is built an internationalism that often entails long periods living away from their home country.

Other categorizations stress the importance of mobility *per se*. Gould (1988) developed a typology of skilled international migration based on the types of movement associated with levels of economic development. Another approach would be to classify the highly skilled working within international employing organizations according to the three predominant regimes of international mobility which typify their careers: permanent relocation, temporary secondment and business travel. In this scheme each form of mobility is a reflection of the interaction between the stage of corporate development reached by the employer, the nature of its business, and the career development phase of the individual.[1]

Movement of skills in the international economy

The principal flows of highly skilled workers have occurred under the influence of the global expansion of world trade, international expansion of companies or the auspices of recruitment agencies (Findlay and Garrick 1990). This has meant an evolution dependent not, as with other forms of migration, on the aspirations of individuals to move, but on the development of the organizational infrastructure under which the moves take place. Flows have occurred within a global division of labour which has arisen as a result of twentieth-century developments in travel technology. As the speed and reliability with which people and goods could be transported between regions has increased, so has the geographical distribution and complexity of industrial organizations able to exploit the newly accessible territories.

Migration of skilled people represents one element in this network of flows. In volume terms migration (a change of home) is heavily outweighed by various forms of shorter-term contact, most notably business travel. Migration studies have traditionally eschewed consideration of short-term visits within mobility regimes, although there are some grounds for thinking that to a limited extent at least, migration, secondment, short-term assignment and business visits are substitutable. For example, modern air travel means that it may no longer be necessary to have a permanent expatriate presence with a major overseas customer: if something goes wrong, a trouble-shooter can be sent out at a few hours' notice. Similarly, and particularly within Europe where distances are shorter, joint ventures may be serviced by frequent short-term trips rather than by secondment (see Salt 1990).

No cross-sectional or longitudinal data exist which enable length of stay of corporate relocations, secondments and business travel to be analysed. UK-born migrants as a whole have been found to spend increasingly less time overseas, the average duration falling from 3.8 years in the late 1970s to 2.9 years in the early 1980s (Devis 1985). Were this trend to hold across skilled international migration, it would indicate a declining reliance on skilled international migration for long-term projects, as observed by Findlay (1988). A recent survey of thirteen UK multinationals found short-term assignments becoming more widely used. One of the reasons given was to deliver a 'business objective flexibility' (Percom 1990).

International business travel: current patterns and trends

The significance of business travel

The role of business travel in modern economic development has been long recognized. One of the first researchers to isolate flows of information as being as vital to the development of societies with advanced division of labour and specialization as flows of goods and people was Törnqvist (1970). He speculated on the extent to which advances in telecommunications would diminish the relative advantages of face-to-face contacts. The frequency of direct personal contacts was hypothesized to decline as the new generations, familiar with technology, entered employment. Alternatively, communications advances could work the other way, enlarging the potential information flows, increasing the need for planning and decision-making — complex processes that can take place only through face-to-face encounters.

Events since these early prognostications have shown an increasing propensity for face-to-face contact. Visits are used to maintain links with established sites and with places where a permanent presence cannot be justified. Business travel is used for promotional and sales visits, trouble-shooting, servicing, attending conferences and meetings, for leave replacement, training, technical, supervisory and managerial functions. Thus the growth in business travel combined with the use of new transport links by the leisure industry in recent decades have produced an increase in short-term moves, on a scale which dwarfs other population moves (Romero 1989).

The temporary movement of skilled labour on a global scale is large and expanding. It has been estimated to account for 15 per cent of all world travel, and 42 per cent of hotel clientele — rising to 53 per cent if conferences are included (Senior 1982, p. 197). Since it may reasonably be assumed that the bulk of international business visits are made by those in the highly skilled category, the patterns and trends are a reflection of the way in which high-level expertise is deployed. Migration of highly skilled workers may not occur *en masse*, but business travel is one

Table 16.1   Trends in business visit flow to the UK, 1978–89

Country of origin	No. of business visits (thousands)		
	1978	1989	% change
Portugal	7	40	471.4
Gibraltar, Malta and Cyprus	8	24	200.0
Spain	49	140	185.7
Finland	19	54	184.2
Japan	42	116	176.2
Rest of the World	54	141	161.1
Eastern Europe	23	60	160.9
Rest of Western Europe	11	27	145.5
Austria	16	38	137.5
France	271	606	123.6
Australia	27	59	118.5
Italy	97	207	113.4
Western Germany	236	497	110.6
Sweden	79	166	110.1
Eire	189	373	97.4
Belgium and Luxemburg	124	239	92.7
Denmark	45	86	91.1
USA	316	562	77.8
Canada	41	68	65.9
Rest of Africa	56	89	58.9
Holland	233	360	54.5
Switzerland	80	123	53.8
Yugoslavia	10	15	50.0
Commonwealth Caribbean	9	13	44.4
Norway	67	80	19.4
New Zealand	9	10	11.1
South Africa	28	29	3.6
Greece	23	23	0.0
Latin America	26	24	− 7.7
Middle East	80	73	− 8.7
North Africa	22	20	− 9.1
Total	2,295	4,363	90.1

Note: Constitutent items may not add exactly to totals because of rounding.
Source: IPS data.

form of mass movement which allows international organizations and employers to function. In a very real sense, then, it is part of the ILM task allocation process.

Patterns of business travel

Data on business travel flows centred on the United Kingdom are derived from the International Passenger Survey (IPS). This allows estimates to be made of 'business visits' to the United Kingdom by foreign residents listed by country of permanent residence; it also enumerates UK residents' business visits overseas, by country of destination. Business travellers are those whose stated purpose of travel is 'business' and who intend to reside abroad or in the United Kingdom for less than a year.

There were 4,363,000 business visits to the United Kingdom by overseas residents in 1989 compared with 2,295,000 in 1978, a 90 per cent increase (Table 16.1). Whereas business visits represented 18 per cent of all visits to the United Kingdom in 1978, by 1989 this share had increased to 25 per cent. The greatest increase in numbers of overseas visitors was from the more distant parts of Europe: Portugal, Spain, Finland and Eastern Europe. Increases from the first two may be linked to their enrolment in the European Community, and from the last group to the disintegration of the Iron Curtain. As far as flows from the United Kingdom are concerned, the most prominent feature is the increase in business travel to nearly all parts of the world. Between 1978 and 1989 the number of business visits abroad by UK residents doubled. The biggest increases were in flows to the perimeters of Western Europe (including Portugal and Spain) and to distant developed countries such as Japan and the United States.

Examination of absolute flows, balance and trends reveals a business travel network centred on the United Kingdom, which broadly reflects the economic status of participating regions in accordance with established and newly-forming trade routes. In 1985, the latest year for which trade data are available, the correlation between gross business travel (to and from major world states and regions) and gross trade flows (in dollars) was 0.91.

Business visits vary in their duration. Short visits are likely to be made for meetings, conferences and fact-finding, whilst longer visits are required for sales ventures, trouble-shooting and training programmes. Trips of over six weeks in duration are likely to be for technical assignments, longer training courses and expatriate leave relief. Some 'visits' of just under one year in duration may represent secondments where projects have been completed ahead of schedule, or where premature return has occurred.

Unpublished data on the length of a business visit show the increasing importance of short-term travel over the period 1979–87, especially one to two-day trips which account for 40–45 per cent of all those made (Figure 16.1). Approximately half as many trips are made of three to ten days' duration as one to two-day visits. Half as many again 11 to 45-day trips are made. The number of trips of over 45 days in duration to the United Kingdom has remained small, at below 40,000 per annum (just over 1 per cent of all inbound trips). UK residents make a greater number of extended visits overseas, some 65,000 per annum (2 per cent of outward trips) — equivalent to the annual number of professional and managerial emigrants recorded in the IPS (see below) — however, this is quantitatively insignificant when compared with the number of short trips made. These trends in business travel by duration of visit seem to

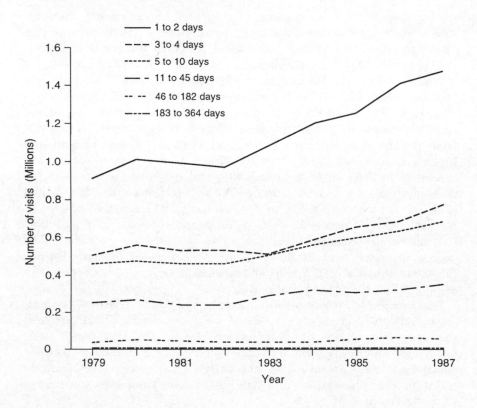

Figure 16.1 Business visits to the UK by length of stay, 1979–87
Source: IPS, unpublished data.

bear out the point made above: namely, that short-term trips are at least complements to, and may be substitutes for, longer-term relocation and migration.

International migration of highly skilled labour

Sources of data

Any attempt to forecast likely future migration trends by the highly skilled has first to cope with an inadequate knowledge of the present situation. The immediate problem is that of data availability. For the United Kingdom there are three statistical sources: The International Passenger Survey (IPS), the Labour Force Survey (LFS), and the issue of work permits by the Department of Employment. Only the first is available in a published form that allows international migration to be clearly differentiated. These sources measure different things in different ways. They all complement one another and illustrate the difficulties of painting a single picture.

The IPS is the only source to distinguish both immigration and emigration. It is a sample survey, unique to the United Kingdom of those entering and leaving via ports and airports. However, flows between the United Kingdom and Eire are not included, at a stroke removing from consideration the United Kingdom's principal overseas labour supplier. A migrant to the United Kingdom is identified in the IPS as an individual who has resided abroad for a year or more and who declares an intention to stay in the United Kingdom for a year or more. A migrant leaving the United Kingdom is a person who has resided in the country for a year or more and who declares an intention to reside abroad for a year or more. These definitions are problematic as far as assessing the true labour market impact of migration by the highly skilled is concerned, for there is no guarantee that individuals stay for the specified period. Reservations have been expressed about the validity of such data in the context of migration studies more generally (Coleman 1987). These reservations are based on the small sampling fraction — between 0.1 and 0.4 per cent of travellers — and the voluntary nature of response. In 1988, of some 174,000 interviews conducted for the IPS, the total of all incoming migrants detected was 1,299. The number leaving was 970. Estimates of immigrants and emigrants are obtained by grossing up interview responses by factors as high as 2,500. This produces substantial anomalies in large and small-scale flows alike (Coleman 1987). Likewise, the 15 per cent refusal and non-response rate reduces the reliability of estimates. Published labour flows from the IPS distinguish two groups only: 'professional and managerial' and 'manual and clerical'. Further breakdowns for single years, including regions of origin and destination, and foreign citizenship, are unwise owing to small cell size.

The LFS can be used to provide data on stocks of foreign nationals and inflows of migrants. It is a sample survey that produces transition data (a comparison of the situation one year ago with that at the time of the survey), rather than actual numbers of moves. An advantage it has over the IPS is its inclusion of those coming from Eire. The small sample size — 60–70,000 of those resident in private households (not necessarily migrants) — prevents all but a rough estimate of regions of origin. Cell sizes below 10,000 are likely to be based on interviews with forty or fewer people and are regarded as too prone to sampling error to be used. Given the rather low percentage of the total population accounted for by migrants or foreigners, detailed breakdowns are not possible. Because all EC member states carry out a LFS, with a core of questions that includes migration, comparable results ought to be available. Unfortunately, this does not happen owing to different sample sizes, methods and response rates.

Department of Employment data on work permit issue are the most

Table 16.2   UK socio-economic groups by nationality and gender, 1990

	Professionals Employers Managers	Other non-manual	Manual	Other	Total
(a) Numbers ('000s)					
Total					
All nationalities	5,792	8,840	11,833	193	26,658
UK	5,526	8,507	11,326	182	25,541
Foreign nationals	230	268	426	10	933
EC (excluding Eire)	36	43	72	4	150
Eire	64	96	158	4	322
Rest of the World	130	129	195	6	460
Men					
All nationalities	4,268	2,760	7,923	140	15,090
UK	4,076	2,650	7,609	131	14,466
Foreign nationals	165	87	262	7	520
EC (excluding Eire)	26	12	41	1	79
Eire	43	27	107	3	181
Rest of the World	96	48	114	1	259
Women					
All nationalities	1,524	6,080	3,910	54	11,568
UK	1,450	5,858	3,717	50	11,075
Foreign nationals	64	182	164	3	413
EC (excluding Eire)	11	31	31	0	73
Eire	20	69	52	0	142
Rest of the World	33	82	81	0	199
(b) Percentages					
Total					
All nationalities	21.7	33.2	44.4	0.7	100.0
UK	21.6	33.3	44.3	0.7	100.0
Foreign nationals	24.7	28.7	45.7	0.9	100.0
EC (excluding Eire)	23.8	28.5	47.7	0.0	100.0
Eire	19.9	29.8	49.1	0.2	100.0
Rest of the World	28.3	28.0	42.4	1.3	100.0
Men					
All nationalities	28.3	18.3	52.5	0.9	100.0
UK	28.2	18.3	52.6	0.9	100.0
Foreign nationals	31.7	16.7	50.4	1.2	100.0
EC (excluding Eire)	32.9	15.2	51.9	0.0	100.0
Eire	23.8	14.9	59.1	2.2	100.0
Rest of the World	37.1	18.5	44.0	0.4	100.0
Women					
All nationalities	13.2	52.6	33.8	0.4	100.0
UK	13.1	52.9	33.6	0.4	100.0
Foreign nationals	15.5	44.1	39.7	0.7	100.0
EC (excluding Eire)	15.1	42.5	42.5	0.0	100.0
Eire	14.1	48.6	36.6	0.7	100.0
Rest of the World	16.7	41.4	40.9	1.0	100.0

Source: LFS.

accurate for determining trends in labour flows into the United Kingdom, including professional and managerial workers. Data (unpublished) are available on a 100 per cent basis, so problems of small sample size do not exist. However, they do not include EC nationals, who do not require work permits because of the free movement provisions of the Treaty of Rome. Hence a major source of skills is missing, although this is a general problem for all EC countries.

Stocks of foreign highly skilled workers

In recent years the number of foreign nationals at work in the United Kingdom, recorded in the LFS, has been rising, from 744,000 in 1984 to 933,000 in 1990. About 230,000 foreign nationals in 1990 were professionals, employers and managers, 24.7 per cent of the total number of foreign nationals at work, compared with 21.6 per cent of UK workers in these occupations (Table 16.2). Workers from the rest of the European Community, excluding Eire, were also more likely to have such skills than UK nationals; those from the Rest of the World (non-EC) even more so (28.3 per cent). The last figure is high because of the operation of the work permit system; it is not higher because it includes some foreign nationals, mainly from Commonwealth countries, who have entry and settlement rights not dependent on their occupational status.

It seems that international migration by the highly skilled differentiates between the sexes (Table 16.2). Men of all nationalities are much more likely to be professionals and managers (and manual workers) than women, who are most likely to be in the 'other non-manual' category. Men from the Rest of the World are most likely of all to be in the professional, employer and managerial category, 37.1 per cent compared with 28.2 per cent of their UK counterparts.

Trends in flows

The trend in migration by the highly skilled is upward. Owing to the problems of accuracy of data sources outlined above, varying estimates can be made of the number of skilled international migrants entering and leaving the United Kingdom. Data from the IPS on flows by occupation indicate that some 76,000 professional and managerial workers entered the United Kingdom in 1989, balanced by an outward flow of 71,000. Flows in both directions have grown by around 20 per cent over the past ten years. Professional and managerial workers account for the majority of the gainfully employed among both immigrants and emigrants, about 60 per cent in recent years. Hence, not only are they the majority of those recorded, but it is also clear that a pattern of 'brain exchange' exists, with the United Kingdom more or less in balance. This balance can be explained to a substantial degree by highly qualified workers going abroad, either on corporate relocations or on fixed-term contracts. In most of these cases a return to the United Kingdom in two to three years can be expected.

However, this overall balance masks differences between nationalities. Analysis of occupation and citizenship shows that among those coming in, about equal numbers of professional and managerial workers were British and non-British (38,600 and 36,900 in 1989). Outflows were different. More of them were British (45,100) than non-British (25,600), suggesting some tendency for foreigners to settle in the United Kingdom while Britons did so abroad.

The LFS indicates a lower level of labour immigration, to be expected in view of the different methods adopted by the two surveys. For 1990 it recorded an inflow of 124,000 workers, of whom 59,000 were foreign nationals. Some 33,000 (27 per cent) of the total, and 15,000 of the foreigners (25 per cent) were in the professional and managerial category. Nevertheless, the data again point to substantial numbers of highly skilled workers entering the United Kingdom annually. There is every reason to believe that the same is true of other European states.[2]

Work permit issues: trends and characteristics

Most European countries issue work permits, though few details are published. The United Kingdom ceased publishing detailed tables in 1983. Work permit data for the United Kingdom differentiate between long-term (over one year) and short-term issues. It is the former that are discussed here. Work permits are issued selectively, generally only to highly skilled staff for whom suitable domestic (and other EC) supplies cannot be found (Salt and Kitching 1990). Not surprisingly, the overwhelming proportion of long-term issues go to professional and managerial workers — 15,356 in 1990, representing 81 per cent of the total and a 124 per cent increase since 1984. Despite this increase in magnitude, the proportion of professional and managerial to all work permits issued has changed little over the past five years. The United States (4,998 issues in 1990) and Japan (2,583) are the most important origins, with 40 per cent of the total between them. In broad terms, however, the occupational pattern is similar regardless of source (see Table 16.3). However, there are some differences in the make-up of the professional, employer and managerial category from different national origins. For example, a higher proportion of Japanese are in the general (senior) management group; Malays are more likely to be in managerial support, Nigerians in education, health and welfare. Such variations are hardly researched, yet could be of considerable importance, for example, in identifying particular sources of recruitment, or different ways of exercising control functions by expatriates according to national ownership of companies.

Table 16.3 UK long-term work permit issues, 1990

	USA No.	%	Japan No.	%	Australia No.	%	India No.	%	Malaysia No.	%	Nigeria No.	%	Total 1990 No.	%
General Management	895	17.9	604	23.4	82	8.1	43	5.3	9	1.3	7	1.7	2,249	11.8
Professional/Managerial Support	1,737	34.8	845	32.7	334	33.2	364	44.7	340	50.2	82	20.4	6,474	34.0
Professional/Managerial in Education, Health and Welfare	773	15.5	352	13.6	302	30.0	173	21.2	121	17.8	230	57.4	3,794	20.0
Professional/Managerial in Science and Technology	530	10.6	365	14.1	116	11.5	77	9.4	156	23.1	46	11.5	2,677	14.1
Other Managerial	37	0.7	44	1.7	5	0.5	6	0.7	1	0.1	2	0.5	162	0.9
ALL PROFESSIONAL/ MANAGERIAL	3,972	79.5	2,210	85.6	839	83.3	663	81.3	627	92.5	367	91.5	15,356	80.8
Literary, Art and Sport	572	11.4	33	1.4	71	7.1	46	5.6	3	0.4	9	2.3	1,359	7.1
Clerical and Related	1	0.0	2	0.1	1	0.1	0	0.0	0	0.0	1	0.2	15	0.1
Catering and Personal Services	80	1.6	89	3.4	23	2.3	41	5.0	35	5.2	4	1.0	810	4.7
Others	373	7.5	249	9.6	73	7.2	66	8.1	13	1.9	20	5.0	1,394	7.3
TOTAL	4,998	100	2,583	100	1,007	100	816	100	678	100	401	100	19,014	100

Source: Department of Employment.

The highly skilled nature of British labour immigration from non-EC sources is reflected further in the large numbers in Insurance, Banking and Finance, and Professional Services which had 3,568 (18.8 per cent of the total) and 5,149 (27.1 per cent) issues respectively, while both Miscellaneous Services and Metal Industries also had large numbers. Since 1984 the numbers of issues in the three major service categories (IBF, Professional, and Miscellaneous Services) have risen from 5,002 to 13,185, an increase of 264 per cent. These three service industries now account for 69 per cent of all long-term work permits (including the Training and Work Experience Scheme).

Inter-company transfers (ITCs)

One of the key factors identified in recent years in the migration of skilled workers, both within countries and internationally, is the practice of corporate relocation of staff. By this means, multi-site employers transfer skills within their ILMs according to the dictates of business and career development. Two official sources provide information on international moves within organizations. Both provide information only about flows into the United Kingdom. Those resident overseas a year ago, living and working in the United Kingdom for the same employer a year later, are estimated by the LFS at 156,000 for the six-year period 1986–90. Of these, 46 per cent were foreign nationals, a fifth were EC nationals. Forty-one per cent of all foreign nationals were corporate transferees.

Not surprisingly, in view of proximity factors and free movement provisions, EC workers are less likely to take part in corporate transfer than non-EC workers (25 per cent), though if the Irish are excluded the EC proportion rises to 32.9 per cent. Almost half of non-EC foreign nationals are corporate transferees.

Work permit data can also identify those (non-EC) nationals who are transferred into the United Kingdom from one of the employer's establishments abroad. In 1990 there were 8,596 such issues in the main scheme, and 1,012 in the Training and Work Experience Scheme. The number of ICTs has been rising steadily in recent years. The estimate of 57,000 non-EC national transfers to the United Kingdom over the period of 1985–90, recorded in the LFS, tallies reasonably well with ICT work permit issues over the same period of 47,500 for both main and training schemes. Thus, around a half of non-EC nationals moving to the United Kingdom from overseas stay with the same employer, as do about a quarter of EC nationals or a third if Eire is excluded (Salt and Kitching 1990).

An analysis of a sample of work permit issues for 1988 revealed a considerable contrast between those issued work permits as ICTs and those obtained for non-ICT moves (Salt and Kitching 1990). Transferees on the whole were older and substantially better paid than non-transferees. The mean duration of validity of their permits was also higher. Transferees were more likely to be male. Those of the sample in senior management and management support were mostly moved by their company while non-ICTs were mainly in professional and related activities. Of those issued a work permit for the training scheme, almost half were ICTs, this group receiving a mean salary almost 40 per cent higher than non-transferred trainees. These data illustrate the high status and increasing dominance of ICTs in labour flows to the United Kingdom. Moves within the ILM of companies form an increasingly important segment of skilled international moves, both quantitatively and qualitatively, especially as far as non-EC nationals are concerned.

Conclusions

The evidence presented and discussed in this chapter suggests that mobility by the highly skilled is on the increase. There are trends towards increased business travel, and of more professional and managerial migration, though at a slower rate. A substantial proportion of moves are corporate transfers, although volume trends in this group are less clear.

The principal feature of international moves by highly skilled labour is the presence of organizations which promote and support them: multinational companies and international recruitment agencies. These organizations are the prime forces behind patterns and trends in this mobility, especially in corporate transfers and in business travel. Employers have made use of individual career motivation to encourage mobility policies and place individuals overseas for longer and shorter periods of time. A highly sophisticated mobility system has built up within international organizations which is becoming increasingly dominant in flows centred on the United Kingdom and other developed world countries. This poses questions of explanation beyond the scope of this chapter, especially the need to move the search for explanation in migration beyond data collection about individuals and into the institutional sphere.

A more immediate issue is the future patterns and processes of movement by highly skilled labour in Europe. What has been described above owes much to the changing organization of production in modern economies. Both internal and external labour markets have become increasingly segmented in response to needs for specialist skills. Technological and communications changes have increased specialization and created a hierarchical system of function and control. Companies have had to become more organic in response, undergoing continual development and change. The largest have evolved into global organizations. The consequence of these developments is that multinational employers have restructured their allocation of labour in a highly segmented fashion, based on technical skills and qualifications, and on a geographical basis. A spatial relationship between parent branches and subsidiaries has evolved, with its own forms of migration of the highly skilled. The mobility of these workers is thus a consequence of how the market for specialist skills has metamorphosed.

This process is unlikely to halt in the near future, though there may be fluctuations in response to trading conditions. Migration of expertise should continue to rise as companies develop internationally in their business and organization, become more complex and increase in size. As the new economies in Eastern Europe become more market-oriented, new surges in high-level labour migration may be expected. Business travel, too, seems set on an upward path. By definition, however, these increases cannot continue for ever. There is growing evidence that some large companies are already introducing policies which reduce the mobility rate of their highly skilled staff. They are using a range of strategies which include joint ventures and greater use of specialist business services (Keeble *et al.* 1991). What we can envisage is a continuing trend towards a European economy characterized by exchanges of skills between countries. The volume of movement will stabilize, with a geographical pattern etched out in detail by technological change and business developments.

Notes

1. This research on migration amongst corporate employees is continuing at the Migration Research Unit, Department of Geography, University College London: further details upon request.
2. See recent SOPEMI Reports, OECD, Paris.

References

Coleman, D.A., 1987, 'UK statistics on immigration: development and limitations', *International Migration Review*, 21(4): 1138–69.
Devis, T., 1985, 'International migration: return migrant and re-migrant flows', *Population Trends*, 41: 13–20.
EC Commission, 1991, *Employment in Europe 1991*, EC, Brussels.
Findlay, A.M., 1988, 'From settlers to skilled transients: the changing structure of British international migration', *Geoforum*, 19(4): 401–10.
Findlay, A.M. and Garrick, L., 1990, 'Scottish emigration in the 1980s: a migration channels approach to the study of international migration', *Transactions, Institute of British Geographers*, 15(2): 177–92.
Gould, W.T.S., 1988, 'Skilled international migration: an introduction', *Geoforum*, 19(4): 381–5.
Institute for Employment Research, 1991, *Review of the economy and employment 1991*, Department of Employment, Sheffield.
Keeble, D., Bryson, J. and Wood, P.A., 1991, 'Small firms, business services

growth and regional development in the UK: some empirical findings', *Regional Studies*, 25(4): 439–58.

Meyer-Dohm, P., 1991, 'Human resources 2020: the structures of a learning company', *International Conference on Human Resources in Europe*, Eurostat, Luxemburg, 39–61.

Percom, 1990, *Managing internationally: Project Summary Report*, Percom Ltd, London.

Romero, F., 1989, 'The human dimension: cross-border population movements', in Wallace, W. (ed.), *The dynamics of integration in Western Europe*, Chatham House, London, 171–91.

Salt, J., 1990, *Foreign labour immigration and the UK labour market. Final Report to the Department of Employment*, Migration Research Unit, Department of Geography, University College London.

Salt, J. and Findlay, A.M., 1989, 'International migration of highly skilled manpower: theoretical and developmental issues', in Appleyard, R.T. (ed.), *The impact of migration on developing countries*, OECD, Paris, 159–80.

Salt, J. and Kitching, R.T., 1990, 'Labour migration and the work permit system in the United Kingdom', *International Migration*, 28(3): 267–94.

Senior, R., 1982, *The world travel market*, Euromonitor Publications, London.

Standing, G., 1991, 'Emerging modalities of work and labour: pursuit of occupation in flexible labour markets', *International Conference on Human Resources in Europe*, Eurostat, Luxemburg, 3–37.

Törnqvist, G., 1970, *Contact systems and regional development*, Lund Studies in Geography, Series B, 35, Lund.

Chapter 17

Irish graduate emigration: the mobility of qualified manpower in the context of peripherality

Ian Shuttleworth

Introduction and context

In the last decade the nature of international migration has changed: a decreasing number of countries accept settler immigration and there has been a drop in demand for low-skilled labour in the 'great honeypots of Western Europe and the Middle East' (Salt 1987, p. 241). Amongst other effects, these changes have served to direct new attention to the geographical mobility of highly skilled manpower (Salt and Findlay 1989). They form the background for this chapter which considers the migration of one particular type of qualified manpower — graduates — from one peripheral European country whose social and demographic history has been dominated by emigration. As Salt shows in his Chapter 16 in this book, the international migration of the highly skilled has grown and can be expected to increase further. One source of this growth is the awareness that the provision of qualified manpower (human capital) is a decisive factor in the performance of technology-driven economies (OECD 1990). This human capital can be created by investment in national education systems; it can also be imported, thus avoiding the costs of reproduction of highly skilled and highly educated labour. Second, the operation of the global economy necessitates international movements to transfer managerial and scientific expertise from one nation to another. On a smaller spatial scale these same trends towards the increased mobility of qualified manpower can be observed within Europe. Salt (1984), for example, draws attention to a 'brain exchange' between the countries of north-west Europe, while Findlay (1988) points out the changes in British international migration which have led to an increase in the numbers of skilled 'transients' at the expense of settler migration.

It has proved difficult to explain these flows of qualified manpower in terms of the existing classical models of migration. Instead explanations have been sought in the operation of the international labour market and the behaviour of transnational organizations. Whilst it is unnecessary to elaborate in detail the theoretical underpinnings of the approaches that population geographers have made to the mobility of qualified manpower, it is useful to summarize the general analytical context. The foundation of these explanations can be found in the new international division of labour (NIDL). This is a convenient shorthand way of summarizing world economic developments in the past twenty years, which have seen the restructuring of production along with a geographical relocation of productive activities from core economies to the global economic periphery. The salient features of the NIDL are the globalization of production and the growth of spatial inequalities in economic activities. A major agent in the creation of the NIDL, which acts directly in influencing the migration of qualified manpower, is the multinational corporation (MNC) which, by structuring production functions within its corporate framework, has provided an environment in which activities are both functionally and spatially separated. This organization of production demands the movement of manpower and by definition the internal labour markets of MNCs provide an international context within which migration can take place. This basic institutional framework has been elaborated by the concept of career development and the identification of the migration channels offered by international recruitment agencies and smaller companies with international contracts (Findlay 1990). Although the NIDL has been challenged as an interpretation of global economic developments, these approaches are a useful starting-point for the analysis of the migration of qualified manpower (Henderson 1991).

The above brief introduction summarizes the international context within which emigration from the Republic of Ireland (from now on known simply as Ireland) has developed during the past decade. The main purpose of this chapter is to assess the impact of these developments on Ireland using the mobility of Irish graduates during the 1980s as a case study. The analysis will be structured with reference to core–periphery approaches to the Irish economy based on the NIDL and dependency theory. Ireland is demographically and economically a member of the European periphery, and is comparable to other small labour-exporting countries such as those of the Southern European periphery (Greece and Portugal) and Finland on the northern periphery. Therefore a study of the Irish experience may be used to throw light on the migratory conditions of other parts of the European periphery. The chapter will be developed first of all by examining the demographic and social background to Irish graduate emigration during the 1980s. This material on Ireland will be briefly compared with that on other parts of the UK periphery such as Scotland. The discussion will then move on to analyse the causes of graduate emigration as a specifically peripheral phenomenon. As was seen in the first part of the introduction, the movement of qualified manpower within Europe, between the core economies, is seen as being highly structured by corporate agencies. One possible model to conceptualize graduate migration from periphery to core is suggested by Salt and Findlay (1989) who concentrate on the role of career development and promotion to those higher corporate functions located in the economic core as a motive force for graduate mobility. Graduate opportunities in the labour markets of the economic periphery are limited by the generally low-grade types of employment which are offered there by companies at the bottom of the corporate and spatial hierarchy. The question can therefore be posed: To what extent is Irish graduate migration structured in this way and how far is the generalized explanatory framework of the NIDL and core–periphery applicable? The claims of graduate migration as a novel phenomenon for Ireland will be balanced against evidence suggesting that it is a continuation of a traditional form of periphery-to-core migration which still sees the Irish cast in the role of a 'reserve army'. Reference here will be made to a major questionnaire survey carried out by myself in 1989–90 which collected employment and migration profile data on 383 respondents who had graduated from Irish universities in the mid-1980s, as well as to other surveys which I have made. Then, the policy implications of graduate emigration from Ireland will be examined in the light of the completion of the Single European Market. Finally, the value of core–periphery-based approaches to the migration of Irish graduates will be discussed.

The demographic background to Irish migration

Ireland has a unique population history amongst the nations of Western Europe (Coward 1986). From the foundation of the state in 1922 to the Census of Population of 1961 there was a steady fall in population. However, rates of natural increase have remained high; indeed a continuing high birth-rate and a fall in the death-rate led to a rate of natural increase that was twice as high in the 1970s as in the 1920s. The main factor influencing population change in Ireland is the rate of net migration. As Garvey (1985, p. 23) comments, 'emigration has been the most dominant and volatile component affecting demographic development in Ireland for the best part of 150 years.' This volatility has continued and is an even more appropriate description of the importance of Irish migration in the last twenty years. After a period of population decline and net emigration dating from the nineteenth century, the 1970s saw a 'decade of return' (Horner and Daultry 1980). For the first time in living memory the population of Ireland, boosted by the return of emigrants from the crisis-stricken economies of Britain and the United States, increased and this growth was expected to continue into the 1980s. However, the 1980s saw an equally dramatic resumption of net emigration from Ireland. This 'new wave of emigration' (King and Shuttleworth 1988) was marked by shifts in the occupational composition and origin of the flow. Sexton (1987) considered that it heralded a new type of Irish emigration. Moreover, because of the loss of qualified and educated

Table 17.1 Annual net migration balances for Ireland, Scotland and Northern
Ireland, 1980–90

Year	Ireland Net migr. ('000)	Rate	Scotland Net migr. ('000)	Rate	Northern Ireland Net migr. ('000)	Rate
1980–81	+ 2.0	+ 0.58	− 23.1	− 4.45	− 6.1	− 3.96
1981–82	− 1.0	− 0.28	− 14.9	− 2.88	− 9.9	− 6.44
1982–83	− 14.0	− 3.99	− 17.8	− 3.45	− 5.3	− 3.43
1983–84	− 9.0	− 2.55	− 9.1	− 1.76	− 4.0	− 2.57
1984–85	− 20.0	− 5.64	− 12.6	− 2.45	− 4.5	− 2.89
1985–86	− 31.0	− 8.76	− 16.1	− 3.14	− 3.6	− 2.29
1986–87	− 27.0	− 7.62	− 15.0	− 2.93	− 5.9	− 3.74
1987–88	− 32.0	− 9.04	− 24.7	− 4.84	− 7.9	− 5.00
1988–89	− 46.0	− 13.08	− 6.2	− 1.2	− 6.1	− 4.04
1989–90	− 31.0	− 8.84	+ 13.5	+ 2.6	n.d	n.d
1990–91	− 1.0	− 0.28	n.d	n.d	n.d	n.d

Sources: Census of Population in Ireland 1991, CSO, Dublin; *Register General's
annual report 1990*, HMSO, Edinburgh; *Annual abstract of statistics 1990*,
PPRU, Stormont.

manpower, this new emigration aroused atavistic fears of 'brain-drain'
and pushed population issues to the forefront of Irish economic and
social debate. This period of emigration, as the background to graduate
emigration, will now be examined more closely. First, Irish migration
trends will be compared briefly with those of adjacent peripheral areas.
Then attention will be turned to the structure of Irish migration flows.

In Table 17.1 annual net migration balances (both absolute and rates
per thousand population) for the period 1980–90 are set out for Ireland,
Scotland and Northern Ireland to see whether their migration trends are
comparable. Throughout most of the 1980s all three areas exhibit
outflows. The loss, when standardized as a rate per thousand population,
is similar between Northern Ireland and Scotland. For Ireland, not only
is the net loss much higher (especially after the middle of the decade),
but there is also a much greater volatility in the net migration balance
with net out-migration reaching a peak in 1988–9, and then suddenly
falling to nearly zero in 1990–1. This suggests that a migration
'turnaround' is again in progress, leading to net in-migration to
peripheral regions of the UK labour market. No data are available for
Northern Ireland. For Scotland the net migration balance changed from
− 6,200 in 1988–9 to + 13,500 in 1989–90, a reversal which is
unprecedented this century. With a year's lag, net emigration from
Ireland fell by 30,000. It is too early to state with authority the cause of
this phenomenon.[1] However, the main message of Table 17.1 is that
Ireland, as a country of emigration, shares some features with other
small labour-exporting peripheral areas, although there are marked inter-
periphery differentials in the timing and volatility of migration flows that

Table 17.2   The changing geography of Irish migration, 1981–91

Region	Net emigration per annum (per '000 pop.)		Gross emigration, 1988 (per '000 pop.)
	1981–86	1986–91	
East	− 4.7	− 6.6	− 16.8
South-east	− 4.0	− 8.0	− 14.5
North-east	− 4.5	− 9.1	− 14.8
South-west	− 3.7	− 7.2	− 12.1
Mid-west	− 4.4	− 9.2	− 16.3
Midlands	− 4.0	− 11.3	− 17.2
North-west	− 3.1	− 9.5	− 15.6
Donegal	− 1.2	− 8.4	− 15.6
State	− 4.1	− 7.7	− 15.9

Source: Census of population of Ireland, various years, CSO, Dublin; *Labour force survey* 1988, CSO, Dublin.

arise from different economic and cultural structures and relationships. These prompt a refinement of the way that the term 'periphery', as employed in world system analyses of migration, is used and suggest a move from an abstractly defined periphery to a more place-specific definition. This discussion will be picked up later.

The changing structure of Irish migration during the 1980s

Since the late 1950s Ireland has been subject to an accelerating pace of economic and social change. This change has influenced Ireland's external economic relations and its internal social and economic structures. Although it is difficult to articulate all the dimensions of these far-reaching and complex transformations, the rapid rate of industrialization since the 1960s (O'Malley 1989), increasing rates of participation in education, integration into the European Community (Kearney 1988) and the erosion of the ideal of Irish rural life have combined to create new social classes and new opportunities. This process, which may be termed loosely 'modernization', has altered the supply-side of the Irish labour market as the Irish populace has become more educated. For example, the last two decades, largely because of an interventionist manpower policy designed to foster the production of 'human capital', have seen an expansion of higher education in Ireland (Clancy 1986). Given the background of these developments, it is not surprising that the nature of Irish migration has changed.

On the basis of data from the 1981–6 inter-censal period, Sexton (1987) argued that the regional geography of Irish emigration had changed, with most population loss coming from the economically developed areas of Dublin and the East rather than the traditional areas of emigration in Munster and Connacht. Sexton went on to suggest that these spatial changes were a symptom of occupational and social developments that saw the more highly qualified and educated as forming a greater proportion of the flow. These hypotheses need to be qualified by recently released evidence from the 1991 census which shows traditional patterns of emigration reasserting themselves. Table 17.2 presents the regional data on net migration for the inter-censal periods 1981–6 and 1986–91. Whilst for 1981–6 the east (including Dublin) had the highest rate of net out-migration in the state, in 1986–91 this region had one of the lowest rates. This suggests that there was a reversion to out-migration from rural and remote areas as the net outflow from Ireland grew in the late 1980s. It should be noted that within the context of escalating emigration during the 1980s, the east's loss was still greater in 1986–91 than 1981–6. Table 17.2 also shows a 'snapshot' of 1987–8 gross outflow data from the Irish Labour Force Survey. This gross outflow data is a little more ambiguous for it shows that although the east is not the region with the highest outflow, it still has a higher emigration rate than the national average.

The evidence on the class and occupational structure of emigration is somewhat clearer. Sexton *et al.* (1990), using the results of a special Labour Force Survey tabulation covering the 'social group of the household head in which the emigrant previously resided', argue that migration outflows are now broadly representative of the social and occupational structures of Irish society, in contrast to an earlier period when it was made up largely of low-status, poorly educated emigrants from rural areas (see Jackson 1963). Those groups, which now have a higher emigration rate than the national average, include 'professionals, managers' and 'other non-manual', whereas those in the 'unskilled manual' group have a less than average propensity to emigrate.[2] Data cited by Breathnach and Jackson (1991) on the status of recent Irish immigrants to Britain found that over 20 per cent were graduates or in professional occupations. These are clear indications that Irish migratory flows have become more skilled and have a greater proportion of highly educated manpower than in the past. The rest of this chapter will concentrate on primary degree graduates (excluding those with higher degrees) as a subset of these skilled international Irish migrants.

Graduate emigration from Ireland

Figure 17.1 presents data on the rate of graduate emigration during the 1980s at 'first destination' nine months after graduation. This reached a peak of 26.1 per cent for 1988 graduates from a low point of 7.6 per cent for 1981 graduates. These data from the Higher Education Authority (HEA) give the most simple measure of graduate emigration

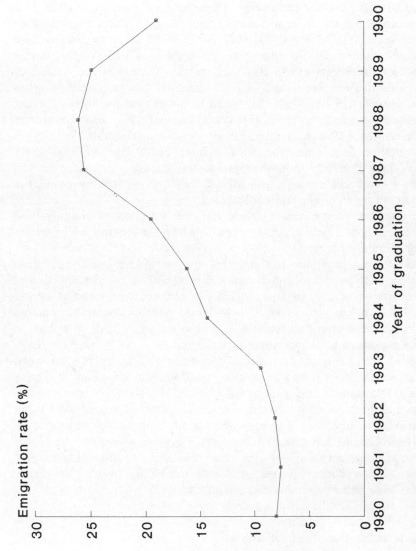

Figure 17.1 Graduate emigration rate from Ireland, 1980–90: movement at 'first destination'

Source: Higher Education Authority, Dublin.

and this is the headline figure that is most often cited. However, the information is limited to a snapshot of graduate careers and mobility at one point shortly after graduation. This type of survey does not allow sufficient time for career and migration patterns to become established and, high though the emigration rate seems, the extent of graduate emigration may be underestimated. More revealing of the true overseas experience of Irish graduates are the results of some surveys that have been undertaken in the last ten years. First of all, the results of a survey of graduates of the Dublin Institute of Technology who received their degrees between 1980 and 1987 showed that by 1988, 62 per cent had worked abroad or were still working abroad (Bolton Trust 1989). My own survey found that of graduates of five different Irish universities who graduated in 1983, 1984 and 1986, between 40 per cent and 50 per cent had been abroad or were abroad by 1 January 1990. The point that 'first destination' data, though a guide to trends, severely underestimates the extent of emigration is further made by two surveys (Scholefield 1980; Leonard 1983). The high rate of graduate emigration is also backed up by figures on the immigration of graduates. Some feeling for this is provided by data from the 1988 Labour Force Survey which estimates that 5,000 graduates entered Ireland in 1987–8 and that these formed some 30 per cent of the inflow, a proportion that outweighs their share of the Irish population.

Having established the existence of a large graduate outflow from (and inflow to) Ireland, we can now pose some important questions. Why do graduates leave Ireland, what are the mechanisms of their emigration and where do they go? To what extent does Irish graduate emigration conform to the ideas on the role of career development and the functioning of the internal labour markets of large firms outlined in the introduction? To what degree is Irish graduate emigration in the 1980s a truly novel experience, or does it, perhaps, have some features in common with more traditional Irish emigration? Finally, to what extent does Irish graduate emigration reflect the nature of the Irish economy and the development of the country's higher education system?

Let us first tackle the reasons why graduates emigrate from Ireland, using some of the results of the aforementioned questionnaire survey of graduates leaving Irish universities in the mid-1980s. It is important to collect such primary data on motives for leaving since there has been much sensationalism in the discussion of the reasons behind the 'haemorrhage' of Irish graduates abroad. Popular media opinion has it that Irish graduates are driven abroad by unemployment and high taxes in Ireland, or are 'head-hunted' by the predatory strategies of international firms (Bermingham 1987). Table 17.3, which presents the three most important reasons for emigration given by these graduates, shows that these popular conceptions are only partly true. The table groups reasons into three sections; employment, education and family and socio-cultural considerations. Such reasons, while possibly subject to *post-facto*

Table 17.3   Reasons for emigration for a sample of Irish graduates, 1983–86

	First reason	Second reason	Third reason
Employment/career reasons:			
High tax	9	16	21
Job offer abroad	35	25	5
Transfer abroad by firm	8	1	0
No work in Ireland	31	24	10
More money abroad	11	19	22
No challenging work in Ireland	18	20	13
Other	35	3	27
Educational reasons:			
Offer of post-graduate place	9	9	3
Broaden outlook	4	4	8
No funds for research in Ireland	4	2	1
No course in Ireland	4	4	8
Reputation of overseas institution	6	4	3
Other	5	2	5
Socio/cultural reasons:			
'Lifestyle'	49	13	5
Friends & relatives abroad	5	10	12
Spouse moved abroad	6	2	1
Other	12	14	8

Source: Author's survey data.

Note: N = 383; however, the number of responses totals to a higher figure because respondents can choose more than one option.

rationalization, are useful because they not only present some much needed hard data but also reveal some of the tensions that give rise to emigration and suggest some important mechanisms in directing the population flow. From this table it can plainly be seen in the employment/career group of reasons that 'job availability abroad' and 'low job quality in Ireland' are major issues. These findings bear out those of Murray and Wickham (1990), who also dismiss the contention that high taxation in Ireland is the key motive for graduate emigration. Noticeable too is the small numerical importance of 'job transfer overseas' as a cause of emigration. Educational reasons can also be largely dismissed as a reason for emigrating from Ireland. Instead some of the most important factors are found in the cultural/personal group of motives which offers factors other than those related to the labour market as a cause of graduate emigration. The leading factor here is 'lifestyle', which was taken by many respondents to mean a sense of adventure and a chance to escape the restrictions of life in Ireland. The explicit reasons for emigration are therefore mixed.

The importance of cultural and personal factors was also brought out in another survey carried out by myself, this time of the migration intentions of Irish, Scottish and English undergraduate students (Shuttle-worth 1991). A far higher proportion of Irish university students intended to emigrate compared with English respondents (the Scottish students were somewhere in between). Other questions in the survey revealed that the Irish respondents intending to emigrate were likely to be those who had high career expectations in terms of salary and promo-tion opportunities and low expectations of meeting their desires in Ireland. This finding is logical enough. However, of even greater impor-tance in the intention to emigrate were what may be termed social network and overseas contact variables. These showed that those under-graduates who had had a holiday job abroad, whose parents had been emigrants at some stage of their lives, whose siblings were or had been abroad and who had other overseas connections were likely to express an intention to emigrate. Moreover, the Irish students' scores were higher than those of the Scottish and the English (especially the latter): in other words a far higher proportion of Irish students had worked abroad or had a family history of emigration than British students, and were perhaps therefore more acculturized to emigration. The main survey of graduates introduced earlier found that the relationships with regard to migration intentions are borne out in practice: graduates who had been or were abroad were more likely to have been abroad as students or to have had a family history of migration.

It appears, then, that these facilitating cultural and personal factors are extremely important in determining graduate migration behaviour and planning. They show how Ireland's history of large-scale emigration creates the impetus for further emigration by the provision of inter-personal networks that may not only provide migration opportunities, enabling migrants to pass from 'known to known', but also act to influence expectations by processes of 'contagion' (Danziger 1984) and peer group pressure. Clearly Irish graduates view emigration in much the same way as mobility within Ireland; that is to say, as a commonplace of career planning especially because of the integration of the Irish labour market with that of the United Kingdom and increasingly with that of the European Community. This labour market context has clear implications for the destinations of graduates, the means by which they move and their overall patterns of socio-occupational and socio-spatial mobility. Not least among these considerations are their prospects for returning to Ireland.

The above findings mean that we can realistically speak of Ireland as possessing, perhaps more than any other country in Europe, a 'culture of emigration'. The reliance on existing Irish emigrant networks means that Irish graduate emigration can, in many respects, be regarded as a subset of Irish emigration in general rather than being differentiated from it in form and destination. Tabulation of destination data (see Table 17.4) shows that this is indeed true, with the exception of the European Community (excluding Britain) which receives, proportionately, more than

Table 17.4   Ireland: destinations of all emigrants and graduate emigrants (first
destination), 1988 (% data)

Destination	Graduate emigrants	All emigrants
Britain	68.4	68.6
Other EC	11.9	5.3
United States	10.2	13.8
Other countries	9.5	12.8

Source: Labour force survey, CSO, Dublin, 1988; *First destinations of award
recipients in higher education 1988*, HEA, Dublin.

twice as many graduates as non-graduates. The increasing orientation of
graduates to continental Europe is an interesting trend which has yet to
be fully documented or analysed. Work by MacEinri (1991) on the Irish
community in Paris shows that the rapid formation of the community
(estimated by MacEinri at around 6,000) has been pioneered by
graduates, and we may hypothesize that the Irish communities that exist
in other European capitals such as Brussels and Rome are also graduate-
led. Although the establishment of these new European Irish
communities by professionals, bureaucrats and wandering students is a
departure from the history of working-class Irish communities in Britain
and North America, the Irish mechanisms of social networking function
to maintain them and foster their growth.

This 'networking' approach to graduate emigration challenges the
mechanism of high-skill migration proposed by Salt and Findlay (1989),
who suggest that MNCs may be important agents in directing periphery-
to-core migration flows. Whilst foreign-based companies do recruit
graduates to work abroad on their milkround visits to Ireland,[3] this
mechanism does not seem to be generally applicable to Ireland. From my
own survey work this channel appears to account for less than 10 per
cent of graduate emigration at first destination. The evidence of a lack
of a formal corporate structure for Irish graduate emigration is compelling when other information is taken into account. Interviews carried out
by myself amongst a group of University College Galway graduates in
London in 1989 found that half did not seek a job in London before
departure from Ireland, waiting instead until they arrived and then
finding employment either through the standard channels of press advertisements and employment agencies, or through informal contacts in the
Irish community. Returning for the moment to the main survey of Irish
graduates which I carried out, it was found that the two most
numerically important means by which a first job abroad, after graduation, was obtained were press advertisements and the careers office. A
second job abroad, after a first job in Ireland, was most often found by
means of press advertisements or information supplied by friends or
relatives.

Table 17.5 Migration moves of the 1986 Irish graduate cohort

Time of move	Within Ireland	From Ireland	Outside Ireland	To Ireland	Total moves	Net Irish migration balance
June 1986–June 1987	42	17	2	0	61	−17
June 1987–June 1988	41	25	7	1	74	−24
June 1988–June 1989	24	20	12	5	61	−15
June 1989–Jan. 1990	13	12	5	2	32	−10

Source: Author's survey data.

Finally, the mobility patterns of Irish graduates can be examined to give a broad overview of their movements. The salient feature to remark on is the porosity of Ireland to international migration. Some 35 per cent of all movements of graduates are estimated to be international in the sense that they are to or from Ireland. Though graduates do return to Ireland, the net pattern of migration between successive places of residence or employment is away from Ireland. For example, an examination of the 1986 cohort of graduates in my main survey shows that the net movement away from Ireland each calendar year until 1990 was some 10 per cent of the size of the cohort in Ireland in 1986. Table 17.5 gives further details of the annual migration behaviour of this cohort of 1986 graduates. This simplifies the general patterns of graduate migration, although it may give a depressing impression of the scene. Perhaps it is more accurate to use the word 'transience' to describe the types of mobility that we observe (cf. Findlay 1988). Many graduates were found to travel to different parts of the world, often returning to Ireland before moving on again. Moreover these graduates spend only fairly short periods abroad, an average of 20 months.

Prospects for Irish graduate migration in the 1990s: policy implications

The history of population loss from Ireland, combined with the recent impact of emigration in the 1980s, has made Irish attitudes to population different from those evident in other European countries. With the completion of the Single European Market looming, a comparison of hopes and fears in Ireland with those in other European countries is instructive. In many EC nations it is assumed that net inflows of population will increase, leading to a danger of overcrowding and declining standards in the labour-force (see, for example, Molle and van Mourik

(1990) on The Netherlands). In Ireland, the view from the periphery sees any migration problem as being the complete reverse to this caution about uncontrolled inflows. In the 1979 'All-Saints Day Manifesto for European Union' it was recognized that monetary union would lead to a flow of labour and capital from the periphery to the core. It is this realization that leads many Irish observers to suggest that the completion of the Single European Market will create the conditions in which emigration, particularly of qualified manpower, will accelerate. Sexton (1990) articulates these fears clearly and forecasts a long-term growth in graduate emigration as economic activity becomes concentrated in core economies of the Community.

There are, however, other arguments for being more cautious about Sexton's predictions for a further growth in the already high level of graduate emigration. First, even before '1992', the Irish labour market has always been open and closely linked with the United Kingdom. The United Kingdom is the main destination for all classes of Irish emigrants, and it is hard to imagine, at least in the short term, that this relationship will be changed by '1992' when language barriers will still be important. Second, the fact that many European-based companies such as Philips have already taken a close interest in the Irish graduate labour market in the 1980s suggests that the labour market barriers, which will be removed in the 1990s, are not deterrents to companies who wish to be actors in the Irish graduate labour market. Finally, the agenda of '1992' is primarily economic. Social and cultural barriers will remain much as in the same ways that borders remained between England and Wales after the Union of 1536 and between England and Scotland after the Union of 1707. These cultural barriers may remain important for some migrants.

Despite these arguments for believing that policies to influence graduate mobility are beyond the power of government, there has been an increasingly heated debate in Ireland about the loss of qualified manpower. This debate has ranged from labour market measures to encourage return (for example, the Irish Productivity Centre's 'Reverse Mobility' scheme) to more general recommendations based on the concept of qualified manpower as 'human capital' which is a product of state investment. The main theme of this latter interpretation is that the funding of higher education should be altered on the basis that state investment in higher education is lost when graduates emigrate. Accordingly it is suggested that graduates should either be charged the full price for their courses or a system of student loans for education could be adopted (see Walsh 1989; Sexton *et al.* 1990). Such schemes have several shortcomings. Higher education is already more expensive in Ireland than in other European countries because of high fees and the poor grants system. The suggested schemes are likely to be inoperable because of the mobility of Irish graduates which, if anyone was minded not to pay, would make any repayment schemes easy to avoid. They also ignore the arena of education policy and funding where the European Community is likely to make some difference. Higher education is now a Community-wide activity and Ireland takes part in many flows of students (King and Shuttleworth 1989) which make a national interpretation of the costs and benefits of higher education anachronistic. A more realistic policy would be an enhanced transfer of resources to Irish higher education from the European Social Fund and other sources.

Conclusion: peripherality and the migration of qualified manpower

One of the main aims of this chapter, left until now, has been to use Irish graduate migration as a case study of the emigration of qualified manpower from the periphery of Europe. How is Irish graduate migration 'peripheral' and what concept of 'periphery' is useful in this instance? The concept of peripherality, as used implicitly up to now, has been very abstract. Three dimensions of the term may be recognized. Most obviously Ireland is part of the geographical periphery of Europe, remote from the 'Golden Triangle' of the Rhineland and having rather tenuous links to continental Europe. In this spatial sense it is difficult to argue that Ireland is not a member of the periphery or that movements from Ireland to centrally located countries of the European Community are not in some sense a periphery-to-core migration.

Moving beyond the strictly geographical expression of peripherality, we can also acknowledge the relevance of structural and historical features of the Irish economy. This economic-historical dimension of peripherality has in turn a number of key aspects. First there is Ireland's role in the British colonial system which blocked any initiatives for industrial developments and which created a dual role for Ireland as a supplier of primary products and labour to Britain (Breathnach 1988). Following on directly from this is Ireland's position as a 'late-comer' to industrialization (O'Malley 1989). Especially in the 1960s and 1970s, this industrialization took the form of a branch-plant colonization by foreign-owned factories. Finally, taking the logic of the argument a step further, there is the nature of the Irish labour market which, because of its small scale and the concentration of decision-making structures in the foreign headquarters of MNCs, is shorn of the top layers which would normally be attractive to graduates. In short, Ireland has a 'truncated' labour market, in which the shortage of graduate-level employment forces highly educated people to go abroad to find suitable jobs (Hayter 1982). This is the essential economic character of the Irish periphery which differentiates it from other peripheries of Europe such as the rural Mediterranean or the depressed industrial areas of lowland Scotland and northern England.

However, geography, history and economics are only part of the story. This case study of Irish graduate emigration has shown the relevance of socio-cultural and even psychological variables in illuminating the specificity of the character of the Irish periphery. Emigration, even of graduates, is part of the collective psyche of Ireland, born of localities with long traditions as 'emigrant nurseries'. Beneath the guise of the 'Young Europeans' — the slogan used by the Industrial Development Authority (IDA) to attract firms to Ireland to take advantage of the highly educated labour force — the young qualified manpower of Ireland is still being cast as a permanent reserve army of labour. Meanwhile the Young Europeans have lived up to their name in a way not envisaged by the IDA by migrating to Europe. Thus, the *Irish Times* headline of Ireland as the 'human resource warehouse of Europe'[4] is unconsciously apt for a nation that, through the impetus of past migrations, still accepts migration as a collective inevitability, or on the individual level, as part of a strategy of career development and personal survival. If the warehouse has fallen into disuse in the past couple of years as the economies of Britain and Europe slide into recession, it is very likely that emigration will resume as economic conditions change.

Notes

1. Anecdotal information from population statisticians suggests that return migration from the south-east of England, fuelled by the downturn of the UK economy, is the main motive for the return. This impression is borne out by data from the National Online Manpower Information Service (NOMIS) which shows that Scotland has a positive net migration balance of 4,111 with the south-east of England in 1990.
2. Sexton *et al.* (1990) demonstrate that education is a key determinant of emigration. Analysing data from the cohort study of 1982 school-leavers, they find that there is an increasing propensity to migrate with higher levels of education. Thus, it is those with third-level educational qualifications who have been most mobile, both internally and outside Ireland.
3. The most remarkable instance of this was the recruitment by Phillips of the majority of a graduating class of engineers from Trinity College Dublin.
4. See the *Irish Times*, 3 March 1989.

References

Bermingham, J., 1987, 'Headhunting the top students', *Business and Finance*, 28 May: 13–19.
Bolton Trust, 1989, *Graduates of the eighties*, Dublin Institute of Technology, Dublin.
Breathnach, P., 1988, 'Uneven development and capitalist peripheralisation: the case of Ireland', *Antipode*, 20(2): 122-41.
Breathnach, P. and Jackson, J., 1991, 'Ireland, emigration and the new international division of labour', in King, R. (ed.), *Contemporary Irish migration*, Geographical Society of Ireland, Special Publication 6, Dublin, 1–10.
Clancy, P., 1986, *Who goes to college? a second national survey of participation in higher education*, Higher Education Authority, Dublin.

Coward, J., 1986, 'Eire', in Findlay, A. and White, P. (eds), *Western European population change*, Croom Helm, London, 102–18.

Danziger, N., 1984, 'The contagion effect: an additional aspect of the dynamics of emigration: the case of Israel', *International Migration*, 22(1): 33–44.

Findlay, A., 1988, 'From settlers to skilled transients: the changing structure of British international migration', *Geoforum*, 19(4): 401–10.

Findlay, A., 1990, 'A migration channels approach to the study of high-level manpower movements: a theoretical perspective', *International Migration*, 28(1): 15–24.

Garvey, D., 1985, 'The history of migration flows in the Republic of Ireland', *Population Trends*, 39: 22–30.

Garvey, D. and McGuire, M., 1989, *Structure of gross migration flows, 1988 Labour Force Survey Estimates*, CSO, Dublin.

Hayter, R., 1982, 'Truncation, the international firm and regional policy', *Area*, 14(4): 277–82.

Henderson, J., 1991, *The globalisation of high technology production*, Routledge, London.

Horner, A. and Daultry, S., 1980, 'Recent population changes in the Republic of Ireland, *Area*, 12(2): 129–35.

Jackson, J., 1963, *The Irish in Britain*, Routledge, London.

Kearney, R., 1988, *Across the frontiers: Ireland in the 1990s*, Wolfhound, Dublin.

King, R. and Shuttleworth, I., 1988, 'Ireland's new wave of emigration in the 1980s', *Irish Geography*, 21(2): 104–8.

King, R. and Shuttleworth, I., 1989, 'The movement of Irish school-leavers into British higher education: a potential brain-drain', *Geographical Viewpoint*, 17: 75–85.

Leonard, N., 1983, *Career patterns of biological science graduates of University College Cork 1970–1980*, Higher Education Authority, Dublin.

MacEinri, P., 1991, 'The Irish in Paris: an aberrant community?', in King, R. (ed.), *Contemporary Irish migration*, Geographical Society of Ireland Special Publication 6, Dublin, 32–41.

Molle, W. and van Mourik, A., 1990, 'Labour mobility', in Wolters, M. and Coffey, P. (eds), *The Netherlands and EC membership evaluated*, Pinter, London, 160–7.

Murray, P. and Wickham, J., 1990, 'Irish graduate migration and the Single European Market', *Studies*, 79: 56–62.

OECD, 1990, *Labour market policies for the 1990s*, OECD, Paris.

O'Malley, E., 1989, *Industry and economic development: the challenge of the latecomer*, Gill and Macmillan, Dublin.

Salt, J., 1984, 'High-level manpower movement in North-West Europe and the role of careers', *International Migration Review*, 17(4): 633–51.

Salt, J., 1987, 'Contemporary trends in international migration study', *International Migration*, 25(3): 241–51.

Salt, J. and Findlay, A., 1989, 'International migration of highly skilled manpower: theoretical and developmental issues', in Appleyard, R. (ed.), *The impact of migration on developing countries*, OECD, Paris, 159–80.

Scholefield, D., 1980, *Arts graduates five years on: career development and satisfaction*, Higher Education Authority, Dublin.

Sexton, J., 1987, 'Recent changes in the Irish population and in the pattern of emigration', *Irish Banking Review*, Autumn: 31–44.

Sexton, J., 1990, 'The labour market implications of the completion of the internal labour market', in Foley, N. and Mulreany, A. (eds), *The Single European Market and the Irish economy*, Institute of Public Administration, Dublin, 335–50.

Sexton, J. *et al.*, 1990, *The economic and social implications of emigration*, NESC Report 90, Dublin.

Shuttleworth, I., 1991, 'Graduate emigration from Ireland: a symptom of peripherality?', in King, R. (ed.), *Contemporary Irish migration*, Geographical Society of Ireland Special Publication 6, Dublin, 83–95.

Taylor, J., 1986, 'The employability of graduates: differences between universities', *Studies in Higher Education*, 11(1): 17–27.

Walsh, B., 1989, 'Emigration: some policy issues', *Irish Banking Review*, Summer: 3–14.

Index